SOAS Studies on South Asia
Understandings and Perspectives Series

Institutions and Economic Change in South Asia

SOAS Studies on South Asia

Terence J. Byres, ed., *The State and Planning in India*
Nigel Crook, *India's Industrial Cities. Essays in Economy and Demography*
Dagmar Engels, *Beyond Purdah? Women in Bengal, 1890–1939*
Sudipta Kaviraj, *The Unhappy Consciousness. Bankimchandra Chattopadhyay and the Formation of National Discourse in India*
Peter Robb, ed., *Rural India, Land, Power and Society under British Rule*
Peter Robb, ed., *Society and Ideology. Essays in South Asian History presented to Professor K.A. Ballhatchet*
Peter Robb, ed., *Dalit Movements and the Meanings of Labour in India*

South Asia: Understandings and Perspectives

Nigel Crook, ed., *The Transmission of Knowledge in South Asia. Essays on Education, Religion, History, and Politics*
C.J. Fuller, ed., *Caste Today*
Peter Robb, ed., *The Concept of Race in South Asia*
Peter Robb, ed., *Meanings of Agriculture. Essays in South Asian History and Economics*

SOAS Studies on South Asia
Understandings and Perspectives Series

Institutions and Economic Change in South Asia

edited by

BURTON STEIN
SANJAY SUBRAHMANYAM

DELHI
OXFORD UNIVERSITY PRESS
BOMBAY CALCUTTA MADRAS
1996

Oxford University Press, Walton Street, Oxford OX2 6DP

Oxford New York
Athens Auckland Bangkok Bombay
Calcutta Cape Town Dar es Salaam Delhi
Florence Hong Kong Istanbul Karachi
Kuala Lumpur Madras Madrid Melbourne
Mexico City Nairobi Paris Singapore
Taipei Tokyo Toronto
and associates in
Berlin Ibadan

ISBN 0 19 563857 3

Camera-ready copy prepared in the Centre of South Asian Studies,
School of Oriental and African Studies, University of London
Printed in India at Print Perfect, New Delhi 110064
and published by Manzar Khan, Oxford University Press
YMCA Library Building, Jai Singh Road, New Delhi 110001

CONTENTS

SOUTH ASIA: UNDERSTANDINGS AND PERSPECTIVES
GENERAL EDITOR'S INTRODUCTION

The present volume continues a project sponsored by the School of Oriental and African Studies, University of London, and initiated during my tenure as chairman of the SOAS Centre of South Asian Studies. It involves many members and associates of the Centre. The intention is to take a number of important terms or concepts, and to discuss each one's different meanings. The subject of this volume is economic institutions. Others consider agriculture, race, gender and religion, caste, history, information and education, aesthetics, popular culture, and human rights. Each volume comprises a critical introduction (here chapters 1 and 2) to sum up and reflect upon the state of our knowledge, plus a number of illustrative essays containing their own analysis, which may or may not agree with that of the introduction. The essays are also intended to be fairly detailed and empirical in emphasis, so as to stand in regard to the introduction in something of the relationship of evidence to interpretation. The project is directed both at specific problems and at a number of fundamental debates on the nature of discourse; and yet it is not intended primarily to generate new theory but rather to make its contribution by approaching questions from a new direction.

Part of the dissatisfaction which lies behind the project is with Eurocentric terminology. This is not because we deny the possibility of there being any universal terms, nor because we think all knowledge produced by Europeans essentially the same and equally corrupted by power. It is because we are impressed by the need to avoid all essentialism, and by the importance, both intellectually and in practical situations, of an appreciation of difference. It is because we are uncertain how larger categories may properly be constructed. Similar concerns are expressed in various ways in many disciplines, and constitute a crisis of interpretation.

We want to start with detailed and concrete studies. Part of our question is: what is it that constitutes 'South Asian' perceptions? We do not think there is—that is, that anyone can provide—an adequate answer to this question as a whole. Moreover we do not intend our work to be merely comparative, especially not between South Asia and Europe, as if the latter were a yardstick. Though we investigate the question, we are not at all sure that there *are* peculiarly South Asian perceptions, as a type, and we are interested in differences within the region and over time. It will be seen that the present volume attempts a balanced position on these questions, stressing the agency of South Asian actors, but at the same time denying both that economic practices were everywhere essentially similar, *and* that South Asian practices were wholly distinctive. In this respect, and by approaching its questions through specific details, this book represents the methods and conclusions of the project as a whole.

The present volume includes specially-commissioned papers, but mainly comprises revised versions of selected papers from a conference which was held in SOAS, in July 1992, concurrently with others on the 'Meanings and Purposes of Agriculture' and on Japanese and comparative insights into Indian local economies. It thus shares common features with the publications which have arisen from those workshops; one considers agriculture in the present series, and the other is Peter Robb, Kaoru Sugihara and Haruka Yanagisawa, eds., *Local Agrarian Societies in Colonial India. Japanese Perspectives* (Collected Papers on South Asia No.11; London 1996).

Generous financial assistance was given to this work by the School of Oriental and African Studies, University of London. This included a short fellowship in SOAS for Sanjay Subrahmanyam. Very warm thanks are due, as ever, to Janet Marks for the preparation of the camera-ready copy, and to the support and efficiency of Rukun Advani and the Oxford University Press in New Delhi.

Tragically, Burton Stein fell ill and died as this book was in a late stage of preparation. This is a very great loss to SOAS and to scholarship and to all Burt's many friends and colleagues; an appreciation by Sanjay Subrahmanyam will be found below. As with a previous volume in this series, edited by Nigel Crook, an untimely death thus meant that I took over the task of correcting the final version as printed, in this case with help from Sanjay Subrahmanyam and, once again, Janet Marks. If printing errors still remain, they are my responsibility.

Peter Robb
Department of History, SOAS

CONTRIBUTORS

Amiya Kumar Bagchi, who heads the Centre for the Study of Social Sciences, Calcutta, is author of very many works on Indian economic history (particularly industrialisation and banking) and development.

G. Balachandran, Reader at the Delhi School of Economics, is author of a monograph and a number of papers on inter-war monetary history. His current research focuses on Indian maritime labour in the colonial period, and the history of the Reserve Bank of India.

Jan Brouwer, an anthropologist from Leiden University, has written a monograph on the artisan communities of Karnataka in recent times. He is currently working as part of the Indo-Dutch programme on development in Karnataka.

Sumit Guha, currently a Fellow of the Nehru Memorial Museum and Library, and affiliated to St Stephen's College, Delhi, is the author of a monograph on the rural economy of colonial Deccan, and editor of a number of collected volumes. His current research concerns the social and economic history of western India in the early modern period.

Barbara Harriss-White is the author of a number of works concerning agricultural development and rural change in modern India. She is currently affiliated to Queen Elizabeth House, University of Oxford.

Douglas Haynes teaches history at Dartmouth College; he is the author of a monograph on colonial Surat, as well as co-editor of a volume on everyday forms of resistance in India. His recent research focuses on the role of textiles in colonial India.

David Ludden is Associate Professor of History at the University of Pennsylvania. He has written a number of articles, and a monograph, on peasant history in southern India. He is currently completing a volume on agriculture for the *New Cambridge History of India*.

Claude Markovits, Directeur de recherche at the Centre Nationale de Recherche Scientifique, Paris, has written a monograph on Indian businessmen and national politics, has edited a history of modern India, and is researching the diaspora of Sindhi businessmen in the colonial world.

Prasannan Parthasarathi is the author of a thesis on the textile industry of eighteenth-century southern India from Harvard University, forthcoming as a monograph from Cambridge University Press.

Peter Robb is Professor of the History of India in the University of London at the School of Oriental and African Studies.

Sanjay Subrahmanyam is Professor at the Delhi School of Economics, and Directeur d'études at the Ecole des Hautes Etudes en Sciences Sociales, Paris. He is the author and editor of a number of works on early modern South Asian and Iberian history and economic history.

Burton Stein (1926-96)

Burton Stein was Professorial Research Associate in the Department of History and the Centre of South Asian Studies, at the School of Oriental and African Studies, University of London. Author of a large number of works on the history of pre-colonial and early colonial southern India, before his death in April 1996 he had completed a history of India for Basil Blackwell.

Burton was trained at the University of Chicago, where he wrote his thesis on the Tirupati temple in the fifteenth and sixteenth centuries. He went on to teach at the University of Minneapolis, and the University of Hawaii, before taking early retirement and settling in London. In the 1960s and 1970s, he produced a series of important papers on medieval state formation in southern India, challenging the orthodoxy of those times by bringing in fresh anthropological perspectives to a reading of inscriptional materials. His major work on this theme, *Peasant State and Society in Medieval South India* (1980), continues to be amongst the most widely-cited works of its generation. He then went on to inaugurate a series of projects on the early colonial polity and economy, of which the most well-known is his monograph on Thomas Munro (1989).

Burton Stein will be remembered by his friends and colleagues for his warmth, and scholarly generosity; and by a far larger readership for bringing South India to the centre of wider comparative debates, both within South Asia, and on the Eurasian stage.

Sanjay Subrahmanyam

Chapter 1: Introduction

INSTITUTIONS AND ECONOMIC CHANGE IN SOUTH ASIA

Burton Stein & Sanjay Subrahmanyam

In an era when economic history has apparently become increasingly unfashionable, the present volume brings together a set of eleven essays that attempt to reconfigure the issues raised by the economic history of the Indian subcontinent in the long term, that is, over a period of roughly four centuries. Between the 1960s and 1970s, and the mid-1990s, the overwhelming importance given to studies of agrarian conditions in different regions, or to craft and industrial production, has been displaced in scholarly circles preoccupied with South Asia, by an emphasis on the constituents of the colonial and post-colonial 'discourse' on such subjects, as historians and social scientists have become increasingly self-conscious in their usage of categories and materials. Abandoning the veritable object of their research, to a great extent, many of our scholarly colleagues have exclusively plunged into epistemological and even ontological questions, debating the nature of the knowledge with which they work, and the conditions of its production. The results of this self-regard, while initially heady, have subsequently turned out to be somewhat mixed, even destructive of certain types of research.

The strategy chosen here is to return to the older Indian economic history; it was applied in a workshop convened at the School of Oriental and African Studies, University of London, in July 1992. The announced focus of the workshop was units of work and their contexts in India, and the purpose was to stimulate a debate among historians, economists, and others, on the forms of institutional mediation between the loci of production and larger environments. The latter, or 'macro-structural' level, was deemed to include not only the 'economic', narrowly defined, but also the political and cultural contexts of production.

Among the earliest to attempt to bridge gaps such as these in the scholarship on South Asia, and more generally to demystify its history, were Marxists, best represented by the polymath D.D. Kosambi—Sanskritist, mathematician, natural scientist, numismatist and historian. His generalisations on the broad sweep of Indian history may seem hasty and occasionally unacceptable today, but his works had the merit of posing bold and frequently fecund hypotheses for investigation, and his errors have certainly been more useful than the conventional certainties of many others. From scholars beyond South Asia, in the post-World War II period, have come frequently stimulating heuristic models, derived from a variety of disciplines (especially anthropology), allied to a more or less strong empiricist bent. Even if latterly the shadow cast by the alliance of an ahistorical Orientalism and a form of post-modernism has somewhat marred this record, there have also been corrective moves by scholarly sceptics.

It is probably true that the discipline of economics has been the least sceptical and self-reflexive of the social sciences in respect to India (as indeed more generally). Despite genuflections in the direction of linking the theoretical bases of micro- and macro-economics in the 1970s and thereafter, the traffic between the two has been largely unidirectional: more a search for the 'micro-foundations' of the macro-economy than a reflection on how macro-contexts affected the decisions of actors in a micro environment. Despite the 'Keynesian revolution' which, *inter alia*, swung the weight of the discipline towards giving a relatively higher degree of autonomy to macro-economic developments, the marginalist heritage of neo-classical economics, and its rootedness in the notion of rational, maximising individuals as the primitive actors on whose backs the system was built, proved hard to shake off. Conceptions of property, the money and banking systems, and forms of production whose structures were formed and re-formed constantly by the dynamics of capitalistic development, were hardly given the attention due to them, once the feeble remnants of the Veblenesque institutionalism had died away. Partly, this was a matter of the technological constraints within which the discipline of economics was built, which left little space for dialectical processes of interaction between different levels. It was thus either a matter of deriving the institutions as a result of the interactions of rational (or strategically rational) individuals, or of posing the institutions as exogenous constraints, within the bounds of which micro-actors carried out their functions. Both these lines of development are represented within what has been called Chicago-school economics, whose votaries range from Milton Friedman and George Stigler, to Douglass North and Gary Becker.

The participants in the workshop were, however, not asked to reflect on abstract propositions of economic theory such as that 'macro-economic policy cannot target real activity' (a formulaic phrase favoured by recent editorialists in London's *Financial Times*, for example).

Rather, they were invited to return to a consideration of some concrete site of research and to consider both the micro- and the macro-structural elements in their analyses, to the extent possible. Now, the household unit of production has been typical for South Asian farmers and artisans since at least late pre-colonial times, when households of farmers and craft-producers were also already often deeply involved in markets for their survival. In a certain sense, we may assert that such households very often could not reproduce themselves except in relation to commodity, labour and credit markets, a seeming paradox if one approaches peasant production from a strictly Chayanovian viewpoint. This naturally calls into question what the meaning of the term 'peasant production' might be, and whether it is useful to present it as a category distinct from that of 'commercial agriculture'.

This reflection logically impinges in part on the prolonged 'mode of production' debate carried on in the pages of the *Economic and Political Weekly* during the late 1970s and 1980s. We may thus ask ourselves whether the terms of that debate were, historically speaking, not misconceived, and whether this does not go a long way towards explaining its inconclusive character. Indeed, recent research findings continue to confirm not only a high level of market penetration into eighteenth-century agriculture, but the sensitivity of producers to changing political, social and cultural configurations as well. In recent times, several historians have emphasised the extent to which the Bengal and Bihar grain markets in the latter half of the eighteenth century were worked by merchants using a system of advances, to bring a very large part of the crop under the logic (and 'discipline', as it has become fashionable to say) of the market-place.[1] In Bengal a least, one of the consequences of this merchant involvement seems to have been that the balance of economic power between grain-traders and producers increasingly shifted in favour of the former group. Farmers no longer ate the grain they produced; often they did not even own it, as the crops had been extensively hypothecated, and cultivators lived off, and through, advances. Amidst cycles of debt and within a web constructed by a complex interaction of micro- and macro-circumstances, farmers in eastern India endured what they could not alter, but also (by voting with their feet, or even espousing other forms of market-mediated resistance) at times

[1] Kum Kum Banerjee, 'Grain traders and the East India Company: Patna and its hinterland in the late eighteenth and early nineteenth centuries', and Rajat Datta, 'Merchants and peasants: a study of the structure of local trade in grain in late eighteenth-century Bengal', both in Sanjay Subrahmanyam (ed.), *Merchants, Markets and the State in Early Modern India* (Delhi, 1990).

altered what they could not endure.[2]

Again, in parts of peninsular India, investments in irrigation during the eighteenth century (as well as before), came from rural entrepreneurs—a stratum of political and economic magnates—who also often held offices in the mercantilist states that emerged in that period.[3] Some of these were members of communities which had long resided in these regions; others were latecomers, accompanying the expansive waves of Mughals, Marathas and Afghans into interior Andhra, Karnataka and Tamil Nadu. As a gentry class that worked as a hinge between historical communities that had often enjoyed significant amounts of autonomy over long historical periods, and the newly centralising state regimes of the epoch, these magnate-entrepreneurs ('portfolio capitalists', to return to an earlier usage) could appropriate a significant portion of expanding production either directly (as commodities), or indirectly, in the form of privileged access to land and labour.

Their activities impinged on not just agriculture but on craft production as well. Those artisans who were resident in urban centres were obviously enmeshed in the politics of mercantilist regimes, but even in rural south India, relations between merchants and producers appear to have changed in the course of the eighteenth century. This is pretty much well-established for the period after about 1740, but recent research using the records of the English East India Company has also claimed as much for the first quarter of the eighteenth century.[4] Thus, even if the artisanal household survived (and survive it certainly did into the late nineteenth and twentieth centuries), the question does remain of whether its relationship with the market (and more generally with its social and economic environment) had not altered in fundamental ways despite the seeming air of continuity.

At the same time, it is clear that the role of groups, which it had been imagined were immutably fixed at the lowest end of the social hierarchy, itself must have undergone some twists and turns. It is no longer possible for us to assume that the position of dependent or attached

[2] Rajat Datta, 'Agricultural production, social participation, and domination in late eighteenth-century Bengal', *Journal of Peasant Studies*. XVII (1989).

[3] Cf. the useful study on the subject by Tsukasa Muzushima, *Nattar and the Socio-economic Change in 18th –19th-century Tamil Nadu* (Tokyo, 1986).

[4] Prasannan Parthasarathi, 'Relations between weavers and merchants in South India, 1680-1740' (mimeo. 1990); see also the forthcoming book by the same author, and his essay in this volume. For the latter half of the eighteenth century, see S. Arasaratnam, 'Weavers, merchants and company: the handloom industry in South-eastern India, 1750-1790', in S. Subrahmanyam (ed.), *Merchants, Markets and the State*, pp.190-214.

labourers (or agrestic serfs) had been fixed from time immemorial by something like the jajmani system. Indeed, whether the village 'community' itself was marked by the dominance of 'custom' has been called into question by some recent critics of the idea of jajmani; Simon Commander, for example, has argued from records of early colonial northern India that the payments received by labourers often followed a market logic, with differential payments being allocated 'rationally' to tasks with differential labour requirements.[5] By the late eighteenth century, in south India too, market relations directly affected labour relations. Even if labourers were frequently paid in 'customary' shares of the crops that they helped to produce, these were often not consumed by the labourers' households but were instead sold or bartered to acquire food. Further, since labour was the significant scarce resource still, efforts were made in a variety of ways to fix farm-workers, and reduce their spatial mobility. This often proved a daunting task, though one strategy was indeed successful: eighteenth-century *zamindars* and tax-farmers found that the mobility of cultivators and artisans could be limited and, at the same time, made to yield a larger surplus by investments in irrigation, roads and bazaars, which both fixed and increased the efficiency of labour. When these methods of fixing labour failed, resort was at times had to coercion, such as the forced movement of labour and battle from the realms of rivals into his own, practised by Tipu Sultan after his eighteenth-century conquests in the Tamil country; later, the East India Company regularised the use of certain forms of torture and other compulsions, as part of its 'normal' usage under *raiyatwari*.[6]

In 1804, a class-sensitive survey of households was conducted by one of the makers of raiyatwari (or 'ryotwar', as it was called in the period), Thomas Munro, in the dry, drought-prone Deccan tracts of the so-called Ceded Districts of Madras Presidency. It was recorded in the course of this survey that poor agricultural labourers, who constituted about a third of the agriculturally dependent population there, were as heavily involved in market transactions as their wealthy employers,

[5] Simon Commander, 'The jajmani system in North India: an examination of its logic and status across two centuries', *Modern Asian Studies*, XVII (1983), pp.283-311; also the valuable survey in C.J. Fuller, 'British India or traditional India?', *Ethnos*, 1977.

[6] On peasant mobility in southern India, see David Ludden, *Peasant History in South India* (Princeton, 1985); also earlier, Brian J. Murton, 'Some propositions on the spread of village settlement in interior Tamil Nadu before 1750 A.D.' *Indian Geographical Journal*, XLVIII (1973), pp.56-72.

who comprised about one-fifth of the agricultural population. Those with little or no land in this region, as in Bengal, were thus drawn, or forced for their survival, into the wage-labour market.[7] The largest class of producers in the region, about 45 per cent of cultivating households in the Ceded Districts in 1805, were middle cultivating households; they neither hired labour in nor out, and met most of their food and cloth requirements through self-production or barter. Nevertheless, they did enter the market with a part of their output, especially of sugarcane and cotton. However, the major commodity producers in the dry Ceded Districts were not these middle farmers, but rich ones, with draught cattle, reserves of seed and food carried over into drought years, cash that was available for loans to other cultivators, and also in a position to employ outside labour. Notwithstanding these substantial resources, however, rich farmers still entered into crop-sharing contracts with traders in agricultural commodities, who were prepared to offer manure, seeds, and even additional draught animals for opening up cotton lands in return for a share of the output. Merchants from Karnataka, like the Vartakas, for example, found it necessary to invest in commodity production in order to obtain stocks for trading.

Lateral contracts of this sort, between persons of nearly equal wealth and resources, may partially be explained in relation to state policy. It is true that East India Company revenue and commercial policies created pressures for an increased output of commodities like cotton and sugar; however, despite these compulsions, wealthy farmers on their own were unwilling to bear the risk of cash-cropping beyond certain rather cautious limits. One of the constraints seems to have been set by their desire to maintain grain production on their 'home farms', for most were traders in grain as well as major employers who used food as a partial wage; foodgrains still vied with money as a medium of exchange. The dry Deccan region at the turn of the nineteenth century thus presented not only a situation of considerable commerce and petty commodity production, but also a high degree of defensiveness by rich farmers as well as trading households, who pooled risks with local usurers.

Here and elsewhere, rural creditors, on gaining access to state office, could insist on certain kinds and qualities of goods, thus interfering in the production process; this was recorded in the East India Company's long struggle to take control of cloth production, but it affected matters

[7] Burton Stein, *Thomas Munro: the origins of the colonial state and his vision of empire* (Delhi, 1989), p.82. At that time, Munro was Collector of the Ceded Districts.

in other states too. Thus, according to his revenue regulations of the 1790s, Tipu Sultan envisaged a partially state-managed textile industry; the same regulations also stipulated that agricultural advances (*taqawi*) be generously provided by state officials to stimulate the production of other cash crops: opium, sugar, indigo and betel.[8] The same approach to cash-crop production, with the state intervening in a major way as an agent to provide credit in the form of taqawi loans, may be seen with the Bhonsle Rajas of Tanjavur in the eighteenth century, with the crop in question there being rice.[9] The demands for high-value cash crops, and irrigation investments, could have a significant impact at a micro-level, within the producing household: wet-rice production (involving the transplantation of seedlings) made huge demands on female labour, and cotton did the same on both female and child labour. Certain forms of 'wet' agriculture also required both intensive capital investment and extensive 'gang-labour', and thus deepened already stratified relations within agrarian society, emphasising the cleavage between landowners, their supervisory agents, and field-labourers. Thus if, from some angles, the pre- and early colonial worlds of South Asian agricultural and artisanal production appear eternal and unchanging, from others they certainly do not.

The various questions that have been raised in this discussion can be organised under a few general rubrics. Of special significance regarding the 'farm', and the ambient economic and political context within which it operated, were the changing purposes of, and measures taken by states regarding credit and capital mobilisation involved in commodity production. By setting and manipulating the pitch of revenue demand among various tax-paying groups, for example, certain outcomes were favoured. The East India Company's 'investment' policy, which provided for the state's procurement of commodities using land revenue receipts, was put in place by Cornwallis at the same time as the Permanent Settlement, or *zamindari* fiscal regime. This last measure was but one of the mercantilist features to be discarded in the 1820s, with the new commitment of the Company to what is often, and erroneously, called 'laissez-faire', but which was really an early form of imperial preference for the European capital of managing agencies, as against the interests and established positions of Indian capitalists, both

[8] Burton Stein, 'State formation and economy reconsidered', *Modern Asian Studies*, XIX(3), 1985, pp.387-413.

[9] Sanjay Subrahmanyam, 'The politics of fiscal decline: a reconsideration of Maratha Tanjavur 1676-1799', *Indian Economic and Social History Review*, XXXII(2), 1995, pp.177-217.

bankers and big traders. In contrast to this policy, currency and tariff measures were resorted to more frequently in the later nineteenth century.

Labour control was another form of intervention by the state, such as when the authorities instituted vagrancy laws in Madras (after the domestic British example), though ironically to drive rural labourers seeking improved employment in towns back to the land, in support of the low wage rates paid out by landlords. Attempts to influence labour migration patterns were, however, not always successful, and were sometimes even found to be a dangerous mode of control, given unstable climatic and untamed ecological conditions, not to mention the consequences of an excessive dependence on the part of even common migrant labourers on market-based exchange, in a situation where prices oscillated wildly. In effect, capitalism was not a spontaneous phenomenon which appeared miraculously 'from below'; it was strongly sustained by the interventions of increasingly centralised states, and made its advance most clear by the threats it posed to the older mechanisms of reproducing labour power. This was manifested in the famines that beset Bengal in the 1770s, and Andhra in about 1790, when the fragile market seriously failed, and was once more emphasised in the late nineteenth century, when famines were probably aggravated by the movement of food away from poverty-stricken zones that lacked the purchasing power to retain their own produce let alone attract that of other richer regions, not to speak of the external market.

By the 1820s, the social history of capitalism in South Asia can be thought to have entered a distinctly 'colonial' phase, or so it is argued by a number of scholars in recent times. A century later, after the creation of the railway system and the opening of major irrigation works in northern India had helped transform the conditions of commodity production, the 1920s and 1930s once more saw a major restructuring of the macro-context, which eventually augured the beginning of the 'national' phase in the economies of South Asia. Two important features in these long transformations, that begin in the eighteenth century, need to be emphasised. The first is the continuing relative importance in the class balance in South Asia of what may be termed the 'petty bourgeoisie', partly as a result of the persistence of the household as centre of much production as well as exchange. The second is the complex interaction between the locality and its co-ordinates (in terms of a secular and sacred geography, sense of identity and rootedness), and the larger processes of class formation. True, the initial processes of capitalistic development in India focused on 'fixing' the household in space, so that its production could be better controlled; but it is a remarkable fact that four-and-a-half decades of 'intermediate regimes' in post-Independence South Asia have been unable to alter this hybrid, compromised, character of affairs, in favour of a more 'pure' type, less dependent on established anchorages in locality and community. It remains to be seen whether the triumphal march of 'globalisation' will have a major effect on these processes.[10]

It may appear from the remarks above, that what we proposed here (to return to the phrase made famous by Theda Skocpol), was to 'bring the State back in' to the narrative of South Asian economic history with a vengeance; if that were the case, objections would immediately (and rightly) be raised to such a state-centred view. In fact, it was not the purpose of the workshop to gloss the macro-context simply as 'state policy', and different authors have engaged the problems posed by our two 'levels' of analysis rather differently. Yet we believe that there is a unifying thread that runs through these papers, namely a determination to see South Asian actors in processes of economic change in relation to a changing gamut of institutions. If these actors were forced at times to accommodate to the institutional structure, they were also influential in shaping them; thus neither the one nor the other can be given a prior status in the discussion that follows.

The papers themselves range from broad-sweep surveys to detailed analyses of particular economic activities. Thus, the first essay by Sanjay Subrahmanyam examines a very wide range of secondary literature to produce a double critique: against those who argue that there are no significant differences between historical (and more specifically economic) processes in India and the West, and those who construct false and absurdly exaggerated differences. The first refers to a tradition in development economics and economic history, the latter to much anthropological work on India. An examination of a body of writings, extending from the neo-classical to the post-Weberian, reveals certain promising avenues for comparative analysis. It is heartening in this context to note that even those anthropologists who continue to approach economic activity in South Asia as a phenomenon to be explained in terms of a single category, caste, have in recent times

[10] The concept of the intermediate regime is of course owed to Michal Kalecki, *Selected Essays on the Economic Growth of Socialist and Mixed Economics* (Cambridge, 1972); see also K.N. Raj, 'The politics and economics of intermediate regimes', *Economic and Political Weekly*, 7 July 1973, pp.1189-98, and Burton Stein, 'Towards an Indian petty bourgeoisie: outline of an approach', *Economic and Political Weekly*, 26 January 1991, PE9-PE20.

adopted a more nuanced, historicised, view of what a 'caste' might be.[11] In a similar mode, neo-classical economic analysis and its notion of 'market failure' is subjected to a searching analysis by Amiya Kumar Bagchi who explores the utility of this concept for an understanding of the colonial Indian economy. Bagchi observes that such market failures, rather than the exception to some golden rule, were an integral part of the functioning of the colonial Indian economy, where extractive fiscal demands (from the time of the Permanent and Ryotwari Settlements) took precedence over the theoretical notions of Adam Smith. Indeed, it is ironical that colonial policies often frustrated the efficient working of markets that might have led to a more rapid economic growth in the colonial period.

Two papers deal with commerce and the state, focusing largely on the eighteenth century. Sumit Guha provides another empirical challenge to the notion that, from Mughal times, pre-colonial urban centres parasitically drained their hinterlands of resources, thereby creating disincentives for commerce, unless it were imposed by force. Maratha sources from the Deccan in the eighteenth century seem instead to suggest that there were strong symbiotic relations between countryside and town, hinging on the dynamic engagement of local gentry groups, which were actively involved in production and trade in both spheres (rural and urban). Guha thus provides reinforcement to the arguments put forward by V.D. Divekar, G.T. Kulkarni and Frank Perlin (for Maharashtra), and Muzaffar Alam and C.A. Bayly (for northern India) on the pivotal role played by petty urban centres.[12] Through such activities, small-town trade and production were equally linked to larger circuits of money and banking. In his paper, Prasannan Parthasarathi outlines the convergence of politics and commerce in eighteenth-century India, drawing on examples from south-eastern India. He argues that the interests of the emerging colonial regime of the East India Company in that region drew closest to that of a part of the Indian mercantile community, but that there were nevertheless some conflicts between the two as the mercantilist structure of Company authority took shape. He argues that in the long term, a capitalism with partly indigenous

[11] We refer here, for example, to David West Rudner, *Caste and Capitalism in Colonial India: the Nattukottai Chettiars* (Berkeley, 1994).

[12] Indeed, earlier than all these authors, this issue was addressed in B.R. Grover, 'An integrated pattern of commercial life in the rural society of North India during the seventeenth and eighteenth centuries', reprinted in Sanjay Subrahmanyam (ed.), *Money and the Market in India, 1100-1700* (Delhi, 1994), pp.219-55.

origins was built by squeezing surplus from producers, a process in which both Indian and British capital participated. He further argues that the transition to colonialism should be posted in relation to shifts in the nature of the labour process, and not merely in terms of intra-elite transformations.

Only two of the contributions in the volume address the vexed issue of 'caste' in a significant way; one of them is David Ludden's essay on the socio-economic niches through which commercial development proceeded in Tirunelveli in the late eighteenth and nineteenth centuries. He argues that the role of caste (that is, *jati*) must be seen in the form of localised clusters that crystallised in the process of the opening up of new regions, often with the active encouragement of the state. These alliances, or caste clusters, may appear from Ludden's analysis to be smoothly-working coalitions, following a pattern of challenge and response; but it is implicit that the formation of alliances equally necessitated the exclusion of some groups. Hence, conflict was an inherent part of the process, as the indigenous literature (*jati kaifiyats*, and caste-*puranas*) of the epoch, makes clear.

Still in the far south of the peninsula, Sanjay Subrahmanyam's second contribution brings a touch of ecological history to the volume, and analyses the successive regimes under which the pearl-fishery of the Gulf of Mannar was organised between about 1500 and 1925. Rescuing the fishing from its purely exotic place in the literature, he shows that it was a major and shifting economic activity, which (despite its uncertainty) was consistently able to draw upon a complex web of labour and capital. Tens of thousands of men were involved as divers, mariners and traders, and capital flowed in first from southern India and Sri Lanka, and later from even as far as Bombay and London. It is further argued that the fishery effectively mirrors the vicissitudes of European involvement in the control of natural resources in India between the sixteenth and twentieth centuries.

The next two papers were not presented in the original workshop, but are later invited contributions, in view of the rich additional perspectives they bring to the subject under discussion. Thus, Douglas Haynes explores the complex processes involved in the production of textiles in western India, in effect revisiting some of the classic debates on 'deindustrialisation' under colonial rule with a fresh eye. He notes the coexistence of systems of dispersed household production by weavers under merchant domination, with the emergent form of *karkhanas* controlled by master weavers; each system had its own logic and consequences, and neither simply 'triumphed' over the other. Haynes's argument is located in the larger debate on the nature of the labour process in colonial India, an issue that is equally addressed (albeit from a different perspective, and using very different materials) by G. Balachandran. His paper opens up a neglected area in Indian labour history, the place of Indian seamen (or lascars) in the formation of British maritime dominance in the nineteenth and early twentieth centuries. Balachandran argues that colonial officials mistakenly insisted on casting the nature of recruitment and workplace authority on board ships in the image of the familiar *sardari* system, examined, for example, by Dipesh Chakrabarty in a study of Calcutta jute mills. He criticises Chakrabarty's notion that such institutions as sardari simply reflected a cultural failure on the part of workers to free themselves from pre-capitalist consciousness; instead, he proposes a far more complex (and active) history of the engagement of maritime labour with both shipowners and government

The notion of the niche, implicitly explored by Ludden in the context of the role of jati in the formation of the agrarian landscape of Tirunelveli, is the explicit heuristic device used by Claude Markovits in his effort to understand the role played by the Tatas in the industrialisation of colonial India. In a succinct presentation, he argues that the successes and failures of large industrial firms can be seen in relation to their niche in a larger politico-economic context, and that the niche found by the Tatas left them ideally placed to exploit the late colonial situation. However, later, in a changed post-independence context, they had to cede place to the Birlas, and more recently to a number of other firms, each of which has been able to exploit a particular macro-conjuncture, as much social and political as economic.

The final two papers bring us still closer to current times, and involve a dialogue between disciplines. Thus, Barbara Harriss-White's essay, written primarily from the point of view of a sociologically sensitive development economist, attempts to address the different types of regulatory regimes imposed on agricultural producer co-operatives in Tamil Nadu, Andhra Pradesh, Karnataka and West Bengal, with particular attention to the ways in which both restrictions and opportunities are negotiated by various producer groups. In contrast, Jan Brouwer uses materials derived from years of anthropological fieldwork in Karnataka to address the successes and failures of artisan castes (carpenters and goldsmiths) in the face of government programmes that were designed to improve their economic performance. He associates the differing adaptation of different caste groups to the ideational implications of their putative *varna* status, with some being inclined to cooperation and collective activity, and others to individual advancement (often by shifting from artisanal to salaried employment).

A collection of this type cannot pretend to a completeness that has eluded even those works on the economic history of South Asia which were explicitly conceived to provide a view of the 'state of the art'. In any event, that was never the intention here, nor do the essays in this volume reflect a complete agreement between their authors. To cite but one example, the essay by Parthasarathi is located in an ongoing debate on the place of merchants in the eighteenth century, in which both editors of this volume have participated (with somewhat different positions). Nevertheless, it is hoped that the present collection will serve as a significant sign of life in a field that many consider moribund, in the face of the dominance of culturalist history and textual studies.

If this objective is attained, it will be due in part to participants in the workshop who have not contributed papers to the volume. Papers were initially presented not by their authors but by commentators, who both introduced and critically discussed them. This format helped the process of revision, and the editors are grateful to all commentators for their contribution: Michael Anderson, Devdas Moodley, B.R. Tomlinson and David Washbrook. Peter Robb played a stellar role in launching the series of workshops of which this was a part, and a number of others at the School of Oriental and African Studies, in particular Janet Marks, helped to bring it to fruition. As said above, three of the collected papers were not presented to the workshop: these were the first paper by Subrahmanyam, and the contributions of Haynes and Balachandran. Lastly, as mentioned in the General Editor's introduction, we may note that complementary perspectives on a number of issues relating specifically to agriculture in colonial and post-colonial India are to be found in another volume, from a companion workshop also organised at the School of Oriental and African Studies by Peter Robb and Utsa Patnaik.[13]

[13] Peter Robb (ed.), *Meanings of Agriculture. Essays in South Asian history and economics* (Delhi, 1996).

Chapter 2

INSTITUTIONS, AGENCY AND ECONOMIC CHANGE IN SOUTH ASIA: A SURVEY AND SOME SUGGESTIONS[1]

Sanjay Subrahmanyam

> What I am saying is that for the economic historian, there seem to be no analytically significant differences between Indian *civilization* and any other.[2]

Introduction

Between the small and the large in the economic domain, the 'micro' and the 'macro', the apparently tangible phenomena that the observer directly sees and those that are constructed in the abstract sphere, there lies a no-man's land. Most Indians today deal with money, coinage, banknotes, and some even with bank accounts, but few have any sense of what 'the money supply' means. Even students of economics in India and elsewhere routinely confuse wealth, which they can grasp, with income, which eludes them conceptually. The South Asia-based economic anthropologist has over the years effortlessly used a notion of microcosm to deal with this: to him or her, the unit that he or she can observe is morphologically equivalent to society itself. Similarly, for a certain brand of economist or economic historian, the 'firm' becomes the same as 'industry', the 'farm' the same as 'agriculture'.

At one level, this is a problem of scale. But at another, there is also a rather basic question of the relationship between the parts and the whole. It is more than a little illusory to believe that for every abstract concept, there exists a tangible field of observation where its concrete equivalent can be found. To advance one's understanding of Christianity, one needs to do more than look at the Bible, its concrete textual 'source', or examine an individual whom one designates the 'typical Christian'. Indeed, the very process of identification of such an individual requires some prior knowledge of the abstract system that he or

[1] This essay has grown out of lectures and discussions at the Delhi School of Economics since 1989-90. I am grateful to several of my colleagues and past students there for provoking me into this attempt at synthesis, and particularly to G. Balachandran and Kaushik Basu.

[2] Morris D. Morris, 'Values as an obstacle to economic growth in South Asia: an historical survey', *Journal of Economic History*, XXVII, 4 (1967).

she allegedly typifies. Thus, the no-man's land between these levels is an iterative field: the 'micro' is defined in dialogue with the 'macro' and vice versa. The problem assumes alarming dimensions in any study of institutions.

The challenge of the new institutional economics

One of the compelling reasons for the relative absence of a meaningful dialogue between economists and historians in the present century has allegedly been the lack of concern of the former for 'institutions'. The division of labour that took root in the social sciences with the professionalisation of economics under the influence of Alfred Marshall and the neoclassicals was such that the concrete analysis of institutions was (somewhat disdainfully) left to sociologists and anthropologists, and to those who inhabited the very pale of the social sciences themselves, the historians.[3] The institutional economics proposed as a reaction to the Marshallian revolution by Thorstein Veblen and his followers seems largely to have ground to a halt in the inter-war period, for lack of credibility and fire-power. Still, over the years, institutions kept creeping back, in one or the other guise. Economists were only too happy, in the post-World War II period, for example, to take on board a functionalist theory of institutions from the Parsonian sociologists, and this found its way into W.W. Rostow's 'stage theory' of economic growth, which while claiming to be a 'non-communist manifesto', nevertheless shared certain preoccupations with Marxist economists. Most important amongst these was the idea of a laundry list of preconditions for successful take-off into sustained industrialisation, whether under the aegis of capitalism or socialism. While some of these preconditions (indeed those on which Rostow laid great stress) were clearly quantitative in character, such as a certain threshold for the rate of investment, and the average and marginal rate of aggregate savings (analogous, it turns out, to ideas of primitive accumulation), others were institutional in nature.[4]

[3] Cf. John Maloney, *Marshall, Orthodoxy and the Professionalisation of Economics* (Cambridge, 1985).

[4] W.W. Rostow, *The Stages of Economic Growth: a non-Communist Manifesto* (Cambridge, 1960), and various subsequent editions; for an extensive set of early discussions around this work at the International Economic Association, see W.W. Rostow (ed.), *The Economics of Take-off into Sustained Growth* (New York, 1965). For a kind retrospective look, see Barry Supple, 'Revisiting Rostow', *Economic History Review*, XXXVII, 3 (1984), pp.107-14. Finally, for Rostow's views on India (whose take-off he locates in 1952), see Rostow, *The World Economy: history and prospect* (Austin, 1978), pp.509-21.

It thus became possible to trace success/failure dichotomies on the basis of whether some societies crossed certain dividing lines, while othere remained mired in 'traditional' quicksands. These dividing lines or thresholds could be linked (although it is not clear that this exercise was ever rigorously conducted) to ideas of growth trajectories as poised delicately on a knife-edge, or to notions of dual equilibria given a set of parametric conditions and functional relationships—one of the equilibria assuring growth, and the other guaranteeing stagnation. A particular spin-off of these theories was a set of ancillary exercises which sought to establish why the societies that had 'failed' to catch the industrialisation wave of the period 1750 to 1850 had fallen by the wayside. This literature can broadly be summed up under the head of the 'potentialities of capitalistic development' literature: two sub-branches developed, one claiming that institutional factors within the 'failed' societies themselves were responsible, the other claiming that the very success of the successful industrialisers guaranteed the failure of the others. The latter route led to dependency theorising with its causal dichotomy of development/underdevelopment, and in its most extreme form stated that the presence of colonies or a periphery that could be exploited was a *sine qua non* for any successful industrialising nation (be it Britain or Japan). The former route, favoured by writers such as Irfan Habib for India, and Ahmad Ashraf for Iran, asserted that these latter societies were themselves caught in an equilibrium trap, perhaps for reasons of class structure, or perhaps for more profound reasons of 'cultural failure'.[5]

A modification which was proposed to the general formulation, albeit still largely within the challenge/response framework of institutional theory, enjoyed a certain influence in the 1960s and early 1970s; this was Alexander Gerschenkron's refinement of the standard Rostowian framework through the theory of 'substitute factors' in his *Economic Backwardness in Historical Perspective.*[6] What Gerschenkron

[5] Irfan Habib, 'Potentialities of capitalistic development in the economy of Mughal India', *Journal of Economic History*, XXIX, 1 (1969), pp.32-78; Ahmad Ashraf, 'Historical obstacles to the development of a bourgeoisie in Iran', in M.A. Cook (ed.), *Studies in the Economic History of the Middle East* (Oxford, 1970), pp.308-32. The 'cultural failure' hypothesis is set out by Irfan Habib's *alter ego* M. Athar Ali, 'The passing of empire: the Mughal case', *Modern Asian Studies*, IX, 3 (1975), pp.385-96.

[6] Alexander Gerschenkron, *Economic Backwardness in Historical Perspective: a book of essays* (Cambridge, Mass., 1962, reprinted 1966). The key first essay of this volume had already appeared in 'Economic backwardness in historical perspective', in Bert F. Hoselitz (ed.), *The Progress of Underdeveloped*

argued was that there was no fixed list of institutional requirements or preconditions that had to be met in order for an Industrial Revolution ('Modern Economic Growth' in the Kuznetsian terminology of the 1950s and 1960s) to begin. Rather, each society evolved its own institutions to facilitate industrialisation, bearing in mind its 'relative backwardness' in relation to the leader of the pack, and also (implicitly rather than explicitly) its own historically-given institutional baggage. Gerschenkron made three further assumptions of crucial importance: first, that even if in each concrete instance the institutional complex was different, there was nevertheless a sort of *Ur*-list of pre-conditions that had to be substituted for; second, that the principal agents of change would be an élite which would be affected largely by an international demonstration effect, which is to say a desire to keep up with the Joneses; and third that, whatever the precise combinations of factors in the short-term, in the long-term, institutional trajectories would tend to converge.

As can be seen even from the above brief discussion, these 'theories' remained rather *ad hoc*, and indeed were less rigorous theories than the stylised presentation of the observation of empirical regularities and irregularities: the relatively comprehensive and agnostic 'serial economics' pioneered by statistically-minded economists like Simon Kuznets, largely came to fruition after both Rostow and Gerschenkron. Indeed, after these two economists, the search for a more rigorous theory of institutions within economics led in several directions.[7] Of these, two are of relevance to economic history: on the one hand, the path to quantification and hypothesis-testing through the elaboration of counterfactuals (and thus to cliometrics); and on the other hand, the road to a New Institutional Economic History. The central figures of these two streams, respectively Robert W. Fogel and Douglass C. North were, as it happens, the joint recipients of the 1993 Nobel prize for economics.

Cliometrics was much discussed in the late 1960s and 1970s, but as

---

Countries (Chicago, 1952). But its publication with the other essays lent it a greater weight and influence. For a set of essays around related themes, see Henry Rosovsky (ed.), *Industrialization in Two Systems: essays in honor of Alexander Gerschenkron* (New York, 1966). The entire debate is summed up and critically commented on by Patrick O'Brien, 'Do we have a typology for the study of European industrialisation in the XIXth century?', *Journal of European Economic History*, XV, 3 (1986), pp.291-333, with Gerschenkron's work being analysed closely on pp.304-23.

[7] Simon Kuznets, *Modern Economic Growth: rate, structure and spread* (New Haven, 1966); Kuznets, *Economic Growth and Structure* (New York, 1965). The latter work contains comments critical of Rostow, from an empiricist viewpoint.

a wave it appears to have lost its impetus in the course of the 1980s. The same is not true of the other stream that we have identified. What indeed did the new Institutional Economic History have to offer that was 'new' in relation to its predecessors? It proposed, quite simply, to *endogenise* institutions, to treat them as phenomena to be explained within economic history rather than as parameters which defined a field of action within which economic actors arrived at outcomes through transactions. This shift from parameter to endogenous variable can be considered, for example, in the context of a specific institution, say, bonded labour. Whereas the old-style economic historian might analyse the agrarian economy of a nineteenth-century Indian region in terms of the alternative labour systems that obtained in it—including bonded labour—the New Institutionalist would seek to *explain* bonded labour as an arrangement that itself arose from the actions of optimising agents. Similarly, the abolition of bonded labour through legal enactments would be seen not as a parameter shift but as the substitution of one institution by another—thus, as a phenomenon to be explained.

An example of this form of reasoning may be found in a work by Douglass C. North and Robert P. Thomas, entitled *The Rise of the Western World*, that enjoyed a certain ephemeral celebrity and which seeks among other things to explain the decline of manorial feudalism in Western Europe.[8] The North-Thomas model here is partly derived from an earlier exercise by Evsey Domar, intended to explain the causes of the rise and decline of slavery and/or serfdom.[9] Domar had argued that such forms of unfreedom arise because labour is scarce relative to the complementary factor, usually land. Landholders thus find it in their interest to tie down labour as this enhances their profits relative to a situation of a free labour-market. Imagine, however, that population increases: this is the crucial parameter shift, since all models need at least *some* exogenous variables. As the labour pool increases, it eventually ceases to be of any interest to the landlord to enforce the earlier institution since he can obtain the same labour through the free market without incurring any supervision or enforcement costs. It is thus possible to bring about a change in institutional arrangements where an agent (labour) can be made better-off without making another

[8] Douglass C. North and Robert Paul Thomas, *The Rise of the Western World* (Cambridge, 1973); earlier, North and Thomas, 'The rise and fall of the manorial system: a theoretical model', *Journal of Economic History*, XXXI (1971), pp.777-803. North's methodological position is set out at length in his *Structure and Change in Economic History* (New York, 1981).

[9] Evsey D. Domar, 'The causes of slavery or serfdom: a hypothesis', *Journal of Economic History*, XXX, 1 (1970), pp.18-32.

(the landowner) worse off—that is, a Pareto-improvement. Nevertheless, during an interim epoch, the older institution persists, until the 'transactions costs' have been overcome and the shift is deemed worthwhile.

This is a highly stylised, simple model, indeed simplistic might be a better word. Empirically, it has been successfully challenged in the case of the Western European transition of the late Middle Ages, most notably by Robert Brenner in a series of celebrated articles.[10] Note that it carries over into it certain functionalist baggage: institutions exist because they perform certain functions, and when they cease to do so, they are eventually replaced. There is also a certain institutional Darwinism that exists in the model: since the institutions that survive seem to be the 'fittest' under the circumstances. Underlying it, moreover, is the idea that the appropriate primitive, or starting point of analysis, is the optimising individual, in whom agency is thus unequivocally vested.

The new Institutional Economic History has been the centre of a limited, and at times esoteric, debate in learned journals devoted to economic history. A critic of North, Alexander Field, first argued that the former's methods led ineluctably to a set of optimal institutional outcomes which were patently unrealistic, and which were, moreover, the result of his methodological individualism.[11] Thus, Field implied in effect that North committed the error of Candide's preceptor, Dr. Pangloss, in stating that, by definition, 'there is no effect without a cause and that...this [is] the best of all possible worlds'.[12] For Field, this was a cardinal error, since the methods of neoclassical economics could not be used to judge or evaluate institutions; rather, they could only work once institutional constraints were given. One of his essays thus concluded:

[10] Cf. Robert Brenner, 'Agrarian class structure and economic development in pre-industrial Europe', *Past and Present*, 70 (1976), pp.30-75. For the debate that ensued, see T.H. Aston and C.H.E. Philpin (eds.), *The Brenner Debate: agrarian class structure and economic development in pre-industrial Europe* (Cambridge, 1985). A part of Brenner's argument had been anticipated, albeit from a neoclassical methodological standpoint, by Stefano Fenoaltea, 'The rise and fall of a theoretical model: the manorial system', *Journal of Economic History*, XXXV, 2 (1975), pp.386-409.

[11] Alexander J. Field, 'The problem with neoclassical institutional economics: a critique with special reference to the North/Thomas model of pre-1500 Europe', *Explorations in Economic History*, XVIII, 2 (1981), pp.174-98.

[12] Voltaire, 'Candide' in Ben Ray Redman (ed.), *The Portable Voltaire* (New York, 1968), p.230. The figure of Pangloss is often thought to be a caricature of the German philosopher Wilhelm Gottfried Leibniz (1646-1716).

> Utilitarianism and the methodological individualism frequently associated with it have historically performed yeoman service in calling into question various established institutions and procedures. But its weakness had been the problem of order...[I]n order to maintain analytically an arena of human choice in which means-end type calculations can legitimately be assumed to prevail, one must assume a complementary range of options that are ruled out of consideration by individuals, in spite of the fact that means-end calculations would suggest to them opportunities for individual gain from doing otherwise. For any historical situation, the delineation of that arena is a tricky but essential business and it cannot be done on the basis of first principles.[13]

Field's point here can be interpreted as an intervention in the domain, for example, of peasant studies, where James C. Scott's model of the 'moral economy of the peasant' was attacked by Samuel Popkin on the grounds that individual peasants (or peasant households) would have an incentive to 'free-ride' on the moral norms, that is, to violate them for individual advantage;[14] furthermore, that this free-riding would eventually destroy the system of norms, just as price-undercutting would destroy a cartel. Field suggests here that there should be a clearly demarcated domain over which, axiomatically, individuals do *not* maximise their returns ruthlessly, and that this extra-economic domain is that of exogenous institutions.[15]

Interestingly, this point was partly conceded by North himself in an essay written soon after, on the notion of 'transactions costs'. After developing a theory rather similar to that set out by him earlier, North concluded with a plea to include exogenous elements of 'ideology' in theories of institutions. Thus, he wrote:

> No theory of institutions can be complete that does not include ideology as a constraint of maximizing at certain margins, because measurement and enforcement are costly and the actions of individuals can be affected by their perceptions of the fairness or justness of contracts. Ideology can be measured by the premium individuals are willing to incur rather than to free-ride; in its

[13] Alexander J. Field, 'Microeconomics, norms and rationality', *Economic Development and Cultural Change*, XXXII, 4 (1984), p.705.

[14] Samuel L. Popkin, *The Rational Peasant: the political economy of rural society in Vietnam* (Berkeley, 1979), especially pp.1-31; in response to James C. Scott, *The Moral Economy of the Peasant* (New Haven, 1976). Popkin's model of 'peasant behaviour' derives directly from a canonical text, namely Milton Friedman and L.G. Savage, 'The utility analysis of choices involving risk', *Journal of Political Economy*, LVI (1948), pp.279-304, which he characteristically isolates from its context (and its critics) in the economics literature.

[15] A relevant discussion in this context is that by Amartya K. Sen, 'Rational fools: a critique of the behavioural foundations of economic theory', *Philosophy and Public Affairs*, VI (1977), pp.371-44, reproduced in Sen, *Choice, Welfare and Measurement* (Oxford, 1982), pp.84-102.

absence—in a world of universal maximizing by individuals—the costs of contracting would be so great that economic activity would be limited and institutional stability impossible. It is ideological conviction that underlies the stability of institutions, and ideological alienation that both raises costs of contracting and induces individuals to engage in large-group action to change institutions.[16]

This in itself is a rather curious formulation, implying that ideologies exist prior to and independent of institutions. Ideology is thus a sort of 'deadweight loss' of utility forgone, to be measured in a comparative static analysis in which one compares the situation where the individual holds an 'ideology' to one where he does not. The Panglossian content of the theory remained largely untarnished, since even this act of giving up utility in order to be ideologically charged is based on voluntarism; the existence of some sort of meta-utility function is implied. However, later participants in the debate argued, quite convincingly too, that within the methodological framework based on the idea of the optimising individual as the primitive agent, one could still consistently arrive at collective equilibria that were sub-optimal even in a Paretian framework. The extensive literature from welfare economics and choice theory on individual and collective rationality, and the difficulty of arriving at the latter from the former, were cited. Further, more recent theoretical formulations on the strategic interaction (whether within a game-theoretic framework or not) of optimising agents was equally cited, to show that this methodology did not automatically lead to the functionalist fallacy. Institutional arrangements (or collective equilibria) which were highly sub-optimal (or dysfunctional) coud be shown to persist even if one espoused such a methodology, as demonstrated in the simple case of the so-called 'Prisoners' Dilemma', and even more so with triadic interaction.[17] Every individual in a society might be aware that there existed an alternative way of organising his relations with other members of that society which was manifestly superior to the present one, but there might be no means within the 'logic of collective action' (to borrow Mancur Olson's phrase) to escape the existing arrangement. Seeking illustrations of such arrangements, economists naturally turned to such phenomena as the 'caste system' in

[16] Douglass C. North, 'Transactions costs in history', *Journal of European Economic History*, XIV, 3 (1985), pp.557-76, quotation on pp.571-2.

[17] Kaushik Basu, Eric Jones and Ekkehart Schlicht, 'The growth and decay of custom: the role of the new institutional economics in economic history', *Explorations in Economic History*, XXIV, 1 (1987), pp.1-21. For triadic interaction, also see Kaushik Basu, 'One kind of power', *Oxford Economic Papers*, XXXVIII (1986), pp.259-82.

India. The New Institutional Economic History thus seemingly had its applications to 'development economics'.

The Weberian edifice

But once in the Indian context, economists found themselves rather out of their depth, having long since handed India over to social and cultural anthropologists as their playground. India could provide the New Institutional Economists with no more than a few stylised facts, which were culled from the tips of the icebergs of other disciplines.[18] The implicit geographical counterpart of the post-Marshallian division of labour in the social sciences had been, after all, to locate *homo economicus* in the West, and *homo anthropologicus* (as well as his special case, *homo hierarchicus*) in Melanesia, Java, South Asia, Brazil, Africa and other parts of the *tristes tropiques.*

The most significant line of argument for a long view of the development of the economy thus turned out to be the Weberian one, which, we are now repeatedly reminded by scholars of intellectual history, was one where India was actually treated rather incidentally and off-handedly, and as part of a comparative exercise to determine what made India, China and other civilisations different from the West.[19] The major conclusions of this analysis are with us even today, and may be summed up as follows.[20] First of all, the notion of other-worldliness, and of a civilisation which had from fairly early in its history evolved a philosophical basis that was largely different from that of the West and which cared little or not at all for material gain. A civilisation, thus, where the contemplation of the abstract was seen as the highest ideal, and where it was clear that the one who renounced the material world was the ideal figure. Weber was, of course, too intelligent not to realise the empirical limits of this generalisation, seeing groups such as the Gujarati *banias* as exceptions to this rule, perhaps. It was as exceptions

[18] A favourite example was, of course, the 'caste system'; cf. George Akerlof, 'The economics of caste and of the rat race and other woeful tales', *Quarterly Journal of Economics*, XC, 4 (1976), pp.599-617, especially pp.606-18. Akerlof's understanding of 'caste' draws almost entirely on J.H. Hutton, *Caste in India* (4th edn., 1961).

[19] Henri Stern, 'Religion et société en Inde selon Max Weber: analyse critique de *Hindouisme et Bouddhisme*', in *Informations en sciences sociales* (Paris), X, 6 (1971).

[20] Cf. Max Weber, *The Religion of India*, ed. and trans. H.H. Gerth and D. Martindale (Glencoe, Ill., 1958), preceded in its English translation by Weber, *The Hindu Social System*, ed. and trans. H.H. Gerth and D. Martindale (Minneapolis, 1950).

that they remained in his system, and this brings us to the second aspect of the system which allowed such exceptions to remain sealed off without contaminating other groups.

This is vexed question of caste, as the characteristic of not only Indian society but of the economy which was embedded therein. From Weber onwards, a series of grand theorists, culminating (though not quite) in Louis Dumont, argued forcefully for caste as *the* essential Indian institution, that which made India different, and that which meant that the historical trajectory of India would remain circumscribed within certain limits.[21] Caste here was more than the vulgar phenomenon of *jati* itself; rather, it represented the idea of a society which was fundamentally embedded in notions of hierarchy and thus of the specificity of groups of agents, and which would hence remain at odds with universalist notions of agency that characterised post-Enlightenment Western society. As the Indologist J.C. Heesterman has rather disarmingly put it, matters had gone so far by the mid-twentieth century that it could be declared: 'Who says India says caste, or so it seems'.[22]

The centrality of caste went much beyond discussions of marriage, rank, commensuality, village morphology and so on; caste impregnated all possible discussions on India, and not least the discussion of economic change. The 1950s and the 1960s were undoubtedly the decades when this caste-economy nexus was developed to its height in academic writings; a fair representative of the genre is Gunnar Myrdal's *Asian Drama* (1968), published at a crucial time when the post-independence Indian planning process had entered into a crisis with the Fourth Five-Year Plan.[23] According to Myrdal, the failure of India to escape the quicksands of tradition and endemic poverty could be large-

[21] Louis Dumont, *Homo Hierarchicus: the caste system and its implications*, trans. Mark Sainsbury (London, 1970); Dumont, *La Civilisation indienne et nous* (Paris, 1975). For a partial listing of such literature, see Jean-Luc Chambard and Catherine Clémentin-Ojha, *Bibliographie de l'Hindouisme et de l'anthropologie Religieuse en Inde*, fasc.1 (Paris, 1994), pp.11-17 and 41-50.

[22] J.C. Heesterman, 'Caste, village and Indian society', in *The Inner Conflict of Tradition: essays in Indian ritual, kingship and society* (Chicago, 1985), p.180; also see Heesterman, 'Is Indian wisdom at loggerheads with development? Is there an Indian wisdom?', in C.A.O. van Nieuwenhuijze (ed.), *Development Regardless of Culture?* (Leiden, 1984).

[23] Gunnar Myrdal, *Asian Drama: an inquiry into the poverty of nations* (3 vols., New York, 1968); Paul Streeten and Michael Lipton (eds.), *The Crisis of Indian Planning: economic planning in the 1960s* (London, 1968); a curious paper in this collection is that of David Pocock, 'Social anthropology and its contribution to planning', pp.271-89.

ly attributed to two factors: on the one hand, social institutions, notably caste, which ensured that change and social mobility were kept in check;[24] on the other, the fact that the Indian state lacked the degree of autonomy and agency required to impose change on society. This latter part of the formulation led to the well-known slogan of the 'soft state', with its ambiguous political overtones.

Myrdal's view, while criticised by participants in the planning process itself, such as P.C. Mahalanobis, was quick to gain very wide currency both inside and outside India, since it represented a formal statement of a cliché that already had a long history.[25] It came to be inscribed in general works on comparative economic history that argued that certain long-term institutional factors of the sort listed by Myrdal had inhibited and continued to inhibit both growth and change more generally in India. Writers such as Eric Jones, while seeking to explain what they saw as Europe's unique trajectory (the 'European miracle') focused largely on caste and the ineffective character of the Indian state (both in the pre-colonial and post-colonial periods) as the fundamental reasons for why the Indian economy remained stubbornly unchanged.[26] Other analysts, of the so-called 'World-Systems' school, while ostensibly less optimistic about the historical trajectory of Western capitalist development, nevertheless argued for a traditional and largely stagnant economy in India from 1500 onwards, in views that echoed the simple essence of the Weberian formulation. This traditional and stagnant economy was to Immanuel Wallerstein and his followers merely an exotic stage on which the inevitable triumph of the European capitalist core was played out once more, as South Asia was 'incorporated' into the capitalist world-system.[27]

Most recently, the same formulation was restated in a language closer to that of the New Institutional Economics by Deepak Lal, who argued that while caste had in its origins been functional and efficient

[24] In this Myrdal effectively echoed the formulation of P.T. Bauer, *Indian Economic Policy and Development* (London, 1961), pp.19-25, who, like Akerof cited above, also draws heavily on J.H. Hutton.

[25] P.C. Mahalanobis, '"The Asian Drama": an Indian view', *Sankhya: the Indian Journal of Statistics*, series B, XXXI, 3-4 (1969), pp.435-58; Sukhamoy Chakravarty, 'Gunnar Myrdal', in Chakravarty, *Selected Economic Writings* (Delhi, 1993), pp.505-8.

[26] Eric L. Jones, *The European Miracle: environments, economies and geopolitics in the history of Europe and Asia* (Cambridge, 1981), pp.192-201.

[27] For the debate around Wallerstein's interpretation of South Asian history, see Sugata Bose (ed.), *South Asia and World Capitalism* (Delhi, 1990). Also see S. Subrahmanyam, 'World economies and South Asia, 1600-1750: a skeptical note', *Review* (Fernand Braudel Center), XII, 1 (1989), pp.141-8 .

as an institution, it had over time become encrusted in society to the point that it constituted the single most important barrier to economic change in India. Caught in a 'Hindu equilibrium' which was largely the result of a Brahmanical value-system wherein the profit motive was despised, even state planning in India could not escape the bind. The plea was thus made for a thoroughgoing liberalisation which would free the mercantile and profit-making ethos from the shackles illegitimately imposed on it, whether by earlier Brahmanical priesthood or by latter-day Brahmanical Fabians such as Jawaharlal Nehru.[28]

Most of these arguments are clearly located in certain ideas concerning a structural shift between the 'traditional' and the 'modern'. We may note that the statistical underpinnings to theories such as those of Rostow and Gerschenkron were first set out by Kuznets in his celebrated work called *Modern Economic Growth*, which sought to argue that economic growth (and indeed economic change more generally) was not only quantitatively but qualitatively different after the British industrial revolution than before it. This 'modern' character now attributed to economic processes stemmed from their links with an unremitting form of technological progress, which had direct implications for the process of production. Of crucial significance were the facts that, once modern economic growth had been set in motion, standards of living and the quality of life improved uniformly, and that the social co-ordinates of economic processes—demography, urbanisation, and so on—were altered dramatically once and for all. Both explicit and implicit was therefore an idea of a 'before' and an 'after', and a Great Transformation, to use Karl Polanyi's classic phrase, that marked them off.

We may see in this the tendency inherent in the Western European discourse on modernity to claim that there was only *one* historical event of any significance, namely the birth of modernity itself. Associated by some in its political dimensions, oddly enough, with the fall of Constantinople in 1453 to the Ottomans, and by others with the French Revolution in 1789, the birth of economic modernity obviously varied from country to country in Kuznets' view. The literature of the 1950s and the 1960s, which we have briefly noted above, was thus also concerned with how Indian 'tradition' would 'modernise'.

As might be expected, those who argued that caste represented an

[28] Deepak Lal, *The Hindu Equilibrium*, vol.I, *Cultural Stability and Economic Stagnation, c.1500BC-AD 1980* (Oxford, 1988); see also the review of that work by the present author in the *Journal of Development Economics*, XXXIII (1990), pp.399-403.

alternative, and total, system of a 'traditional' type, as opposed to 'modernity' (which was a Western export, in this view), argued that the transformation would either be a wrenching one or fail altogether. Structuralist anthropology of that period also veered towards this view by forcing binary divisions on societal classifications. On the other hand, there was an attempt made fairly early on to argue that elements of Indian 'tradition' could be carried over quite easily into 'modernity', and that the transition—the reality and inevitability of which was not in itself contested—would not be quite so wrenching as had been thought.

The most thoroughgoing formulation of this type was provided by the labour and industrial historian Morris D. Morris, though elements of the same may be found in the writings of some other political scientists and empirically-oriented development economists and anthropologists, even from Chicago.[29] Morris argued in 1967, in an explicit attack on Weber's *The Religion of India*, that the existing literature had tended to overestimate vastly the significance of 'values' as an obstacle to economic change in South Asia, particularly in the colonial period. He argued that Indian entrepreneurs seized opportunities when they were presented with them, and that even labour in India did not exhibit the sort of archaic features that were often attributed to it wholesale. Basing himself on his study of cotton-mill workers in early twentieth-century Bombay, he argued that workers too responded 'rationally' to incentives in terms of salaries, and that many of the seemingly eccentric features of their behaviour could be explained as rational responses to a work environment characterised by a shortage of capital, a high rate of labour turnover, and a low level of skill required on the job.[30]

There seems little doubt that Morris's arguments, even if out of step with the times in which they were written, were of far greater significance than they have been credited with. It is certainly true that Morris was dismissive of 'cultural' explanations in general, preferring to see his economic agents as 'rational actors' maximising pecuniary benefits in a classic textbook sense. Indeed, his approach reflects the common distaste shared by many neoclassical economists for cultural (or, to them, 'irrational') explanations for phenomena which can be explained

[29] Morris D. Morris, 'Values', pp.588-607. Also see Milton B. Singer, *When a Great Tradition Modernizes: an anthropological approach to Indan civilization* (New York, 1972). For a gentle, but unconvincing, Weberian riposte, partly directed at Morris, see R. Stephen Warner, 'The role of religious ideas and the use of models in Max Weber's comparative studies of non-capitalist societies', *Journal of Economic History*, XXX, 1 (1970), pp.74-99.

[30] Morris D. Morris, *The Emergence of an Industrial Labor Force in India: a study of the Bombay cotton-mills, 1854-1947* (Bombay, 1965).

through the framework of the interaction of rational, and atomistic, agents with well-behaved utility functions. Further, Morris in this paper as elsewhere, worked within a rather curious teleological framework: for him, India was not peculiar, it was merely Western Europe with a lag of four to five hundred years! This is nicely summed up in the following passage:

> [T]here is no precise definition of a 'Hindu value system' that can be identified as a significant obstacle to economic growth or change. Nor does the value system working through the caste system exhibit any decisive impact on the process of change. While *jati* seems to be the operative unit, it behaves historically as extended kin groups have done elsewhere. For example, the descriptions of entrepreneurial behaviour in nineteenth- and early twentieth-century India resemble similar activities in Renaissance Europe and seem to reflect primarily the limited scope of economic opportunities rather than any specific form of social structure.[31]

India in the twentieth century is thus to be equated to the Europe of the Medicis and da Vinci. Of still greater significance for our purposes is that Morris threw down a gauntlet to those Weberians who argued that capitalism in India would have a 'pariah' character, recruiting its labour from untouchable communities and its capital from marginal social groups like the Parsis or the Memons, because rigidities in the traditional structure (for which we may largely read caste) would ensure that no other possibilities were left open.[32]

The gauntlet was not picked up, and studies have instead proliferated on the peculiar characteristics of different entrepreneurial groups that allowed them to be exceptions to the rule that was defined by caste-based rigidity. Indeed, if some recent literature is to be credited, extreme Weberian explanations of economic change in India are still the most acceptable ones in many circles. We may take the case of a recent study by Pierre Lachaier published in the French journal *Annales ESC*, which, while studiously ignoring Morris's work, proposes the model of

[31] Morris, 'Values as an obstacle', p.607. Also see Morris, 'The growth of large-scale industry', in Dharma Kumar (ed.), *The Cambridge Economic History of India*, vol.II (Cambridge, 1983) for a development of the same point.

[32] Cf. for example, Richard G. Fox, 'Pariah capitalism and traditional Indian merchants past and present', in Milton Singer (ed.), *Entrepreneurship and the Modernization of Occupational Cultures in South Asia* (Durham, 1973), pp.16-34; also earlier, Fox, 'Family, caste and commerce in a North Indian market town', *Economic Development and Cultural Change*, XV, 3 (1967), pp.297-314. For a study of Tamil Muslim merchants from the same time, which is critical of this approach, aligning itself rather with Morris and Singer, see Mattison Mines, *Muslim Merchants: the economic behaviour of an Indian Muslim community* (New Delhi, 1972).

'assignated lineage capitalism' as native to traditional India, wherein 'lineage-based merchant firms' represent a peculiar sort of *bonsai* development.[33] According to the author of this study, whose empirical materials are drawn from rather limited contemporary field-work with Kacchi Lohana gunny-sack merchants in western India, there exists a perfect form of dualism in India between such firms as those of the Lohana, whose roots can be traced back directly and without further ado to the 'civilisation of classical India' and other 'capitalists of the "bourgeois" type, promoted by the [British] colonisers' in nineteenth- and twentieth-century India, by which one presumes entrepreneurs like the Parsis. The 'traditional' firm, it would appear, partakes of the 'social values prevalent in the whole of Indian society', which must of course be traced back to such Sanskrit concepts as *artha*, 'which have no equivalents in French, English, or German'. Indeed, the ahistoricity and acontextuality of approach that permits Lachaier to freely associate the pattern of residence of his merchants with the architecture of Auroville in Pondicherry, and thence with the concept of *moksha*, is of a piece with his easy acceptance of the reductionist Dumontian *mantra* that 'in a holistic society like India, relations between men are more valorised than relations between men and things'.

It is of some interest that the sole historical work referred to by Lachaier to buttress his argument is the well-known monograph of C.A. Bayly on north Indian society in the late eighteenth and nineteenth centuries. Bayly's positon, which is as a matter of fact rather complex, is in this instance in need of defence not from his detractors, but from his admirers like Lachaier. Indeed, Bayly begins his discussion of the Weberian legacy early in his work by regretting the greater importance given to Weber relative to Werner Sombart, whose investigation of the origins of demand was at least as important, in his view, as Weber's focus on entrepreneurs. He notes:

> There is indeed a body of opinion which might concede the political importance of individual capitalists in pre-colonial Indian politics but argues that the culture and political ideas of India made it virtually impossible for merchants and townsmen to achieve any significant degree of autonomy or corporate identity in the face of ruling landed elites. Ultimately, these ideas derive from

[33] Pierre Lachaier, 'Le capitalisme lignager assigné aujourd-hui: les marchands Kutchi Lohanna du Maharashtra (Inde)', *Annales ESC*, XLVIII, 4-5 (1992), pp.865-88. It is interesting to note the contradiction between the approach of this paper and the attack by Pierre-François Souyri in his 'Introduction', pp.785-7, of the same number, on the glib assumptions of old-fashioned Orientalism, to the effect that 'India had no history, and that of China repeated itself'.

Max Weber's brilliant generalisations on the religion and institutions of India. According to Weber, occupational specialisation based on caste fragmented Indian artisan, merchant and service populations, so inhibiting the development of mercantile trust, let alone political action. Caste restrictions made impossible the civic fraternisation out of which emerged Western corporate institutions, while the 'passivity' of Hinduism denied rising groups an ideology which could validate their political independence. Thus, urban centres and states remained dominated by the 'patrimonial' regimes of warrior bureaucrats, and for Weber as for Marx, true social change awaited the impact of colonial rule.[34]

Reading Weber is instructive here; for he had after all asserted that India was barely held together by the glue of colonialism. To Weber then,

> [T]he removal of the thin conquering strata of Europeans and the Pax Britannica enforced by them would open wide the life and death struggle of inimical castes, confessions, and tribes; the old feudal robber romanticism of the Indian Middle Ages would again break forth.[35]

Bayly, for his part, notes that the ideas of Weber and the Weberians are 'almost circular' given the nature of the sources, and that in late pre-colonial north India, 'changes were not frustrated by caste fragmentation or the passivity of Hinduism: on the contrary, caste and religion provided building blocks out of which mercantile and urban solidarities were perceptibly emerging'. Further, he argues, there is no reason to imagine that those means for building corporate solidarities that Weber argued were used in the medieval and early modern West—namely corporate dining relations and marriage ties—should work precisely in north Indian society; these were after all not the only means available for the purpose.

It is puzzling in the light of this discussion that Bayly exerts himself later in the same work to effect a compromise with the Weberian position. He argues, for example, in his concluding chapter that the Indian context was not 'in any way as favourable as that provided by Roman and feudal law in Europe' to gentry and merchant groups, ignoring the fact that the historical trajectories of those societies which had at some time been under Roman and feudal law have themselves been vastly different. Again, he argues that while structural change did take place in pre-colonial India, 'by comparison with developments in the west, these were weak forces for social change'. At these moments, Bayly's

[34] C.A. Bayly, *Rulers, Townsmen and Bazaars: North Indian society in the age of British expansion, 1770-1870* (Cambridge, 1983), p.174; also see the discussion of Weber and Sombart on pp.58-9.

[35] Weber, *The Religion of India*, p.325.

work comes closest to being a variant of the Marxian-Weberian model of 'potentialities of capitalistic development' in the non-Western world.[36]

Nevertheless, the broad thrust of Bayly's work is—it appears to me—a denial of the *determining and all-encompassing nature* of a holistic and pan-Indian concept of caste (or for that matter 'untranslatable terms' like *artha*) for an understanding of economic activity in late pre-colonial northern India. He argues that

> an account which ignores the social dimension of Hindu and Jain business life (or Islamic gentry life) is ultimately unsatisfactory, simply because it is unable to explain much of what merchants did and even more of what they appear to have thought.

But this must be balanced against his view that the Indian business class of the period had 'something in common with those found in other Asian or Islamic agrarian monarchies'. Apparently, there were features that were unique, deriving from 'caste, marriage and religion', but others that lend themselves to generalisation across broader zones than simply South Asia. Indeed, a little reflection shows that some of these 'unique' features were not civilisational properties of India, from the Brahmaputra valley to Sind, and Kashmir to Tirunelveli, but far more locale- and region-specific. The particular strategies of the merchants of early nineteenth-century Banaras, and the manner in which they were embedded in marriage, piety and credit, cannot be extended without further ado to the behaviour of fourteenth-century merchants in Karnataka.

Labour and economic change

If the 'middle classes' and mercantile and entrepreneurial institutions have received their fair share of attention in recent writings that seek to take a long view of economic change in India, the place of labour in the same processes remains curiously occult. Any consideration of labour itself must begin with a look at the activity that provided the greatest employment to South Asians, be it in the sixteenth or the nineteenth century, namely agriculture. Agrarian studies did make a transition in

[36] Bayly, *Rulers, Townsmen and Bazaars*, pp.470-2; also the earlier, and extremely ambiguous, discussion on pp.424-6. Here, it is stated for example that 'external agencies...initiated industrialisation' in India, but is this not analogous to the statement (which Bayly criticises) that factionalism, communalism and the fragmented nature of modern Indian politics should be attributed 'solely to structure and aims of the colonial government'?

the 1970s from a consideration of primarily fiscal systems to studies of agrarian regions (in an *Annales*-inflected style), with the basic questions of peasant studies being reflected in both Marxist and neo-Chayanovian literature. The closest equivalent to a full-blown Chayanovian model of a peasant household for India was presented in Kessinger's study of a village in the Jalandhar *doab* region of Punjab, which in fact anticipates, in a morphological sense, many features of Bayly's discussion of the merchant family.[37] It was argued here that the peasant 'family farm' provided the atomistic primitive from which the rural economy was constructed, and that the family worked within the constraints provided not only by wealth, but by clan and status.

Chayanov's own model of the peasant farm, while it has been universalised by his followers, does of course contain a large number of juridical and institutional features derived from the Russian experience of the post-1861 period.[38] While the most abstract elements of the 'model', namely the relationship between the dependency ratio in the family and labour availability, do not closely reflect any particular historical context, other assumptions (such as that land is freely available without a steep increase in its cost) obviously do not fit the historical experience of a number of societies. Indeed, the key insight of Chayanov lies in the notion of household as primitive agent; under such an assumption, the usual logic of labour deployment in the text-book neoclassical sense may break down, as marginal returns to labour are no longer equated to individual leisure forgone. The behavioural assumptions are different, and to use the terminology of Alexander Field, here we must assume that individualistic means-end type calculations are not allowed to prevail for members of the family, 'in spite of the fact that means-end calcuations would suggest to them opportunities for individual gain from doing otherwise'. It is another matter that Chayanovian models may thus suppress real tensions and problems that exist within the peasant family (over the distribution of nutrition, for example), by claiming the existence of a relatively consensual moral economy.

Questions naturally arise concerning the domain within which this 'family farm' of peasants operates. One position would have been to

[37] Tom G. Kessinger, *Vilayatpur, 1848-1968: social and economic change in a North Indian village* (Berkeley, 1974).

[38] A.V. Chayanov, in D. Thorner, B. Kerblay and R.E.F. Smith (eds.), *On the Theory of the Peasant Economy* (Illinois, 1966); for a historical exposition, see Teodor Shanin, *The Awkward Class: political sociology of peasantry in a developing society—Russia, 1910-1925* (London, 1972).

link it with an older literature on the notion of the unitary village, which was possibly self-sufficient, and thence to a notion of a pan-village network of relations. The village could here become a metaphor for India itself, and the organising principle of the village could be exalted to the level of a fundamental relational concept. This was the role long played by the notion of *jajmani*, which seems to appear in the English-language literature in its fully-developed form in the 1930s. *Jajmani*, by the late 1950s, was being described as a system that existed within all Indian villages, and which encompassed both ritual and non-ritual relations between landowning families and their clients. Embedded in a barter economy, with the payments for goods and services often described as 'customary', *jajmani* became shorthand for an entire 'moral economy' which fitted both the anthropologist's notion of unchanging, traditional India, and post-independence claims for a self-regulatory and non-conflictual *Ramarajya* based on enduring village institutions.[39]

This view has been thoroughly exposed, first in an empirical mode by Marxist-oriented historians of pre-colonial northern and western India such as Irfan Habib and Hiroshi Fukazawa (who wished to emphasise that village society in that epoch was a class society), and now more recently and systematically by historians of colonial India and anthropologists.[40] In a trenchant critique based on a careful examination of recent secondary literature, C.J. Fuller has shown, for example, that the so-called *jajmani* system 'is largely a figment of the anthropological imagination', though historians and economists too are implicated in its invention.[41] He notes that there exists a plentiful (and

[39] For an early nationalist articulation of this conception, which does not however use the term *jajmani*, see S. Radhakrishnan, *The Hindu View of Life* (London, 1927; reprint New Delhi, 1993), pp.67-92.

[40] Cf. Hiroshi Fukazawa, *The Medieval Deccan: peasants, social systems and states (sixteenth to eighteenth centuries)* (Delhi, 1991), pp.91-113 and 199-244, reprinting earlier papers by this scholar. A purely empirical exposition, but a significant one, is that of B.R. Grover, 'An integrated pattern of commercial life in the rural society of North India during the seventeenth and eighteenth centuries', in Sanjay Subrahmanyam (ed.), *Money and the Market in India, 1100-1700* (Delhi, 1994), pp.219-53; the paper was first published in 1966.

[41] C.J. Fuller, 'Misconceiving the grain heap: a critique of the concept of the Indian *jajmani* system', in J. Parry and M. Bloch (ed.), *Money and the Morality of Exchange* (Cambridge, 1989), pp.33-63; also important is an earlier paper by Simon Commander, 'The *jajmani* system in North India: an examination of its logic and status over two centuries', *Modern Asian Studies*, XVII (1983), pp.283-311. Fuller's conclusions are confirmed by Peter Mayer, 'Inventing village tradition: the late-nineteenth-century origins of the North Indian

even standard) literature by economic historians to show that by the seventeenth century, monetised transactions could be found in a large number of rural areas, whether on account of the state's revenue-demand in cash, or for other reasons. Further, Fuller notes the conflation of the idea of *jajmani* with the analytically distinct notion of *baluta* (village servants), which obtained in Maharashtra. And finally, it is noted that land rights could be and were in fact transacted in the pre-colonial period, suggesting that even patron-client relations were not stable within a particular rural society.

One of the larger implications of this critique of *jajmani* is to locate the peasant family within a larger domain than the village, and to argue for the critical interplay of horizontal and vertical mobility in determining the status and resources available to groups of households over a long time-span. The ambitious if somewhat schematic work of David Ludden on the Tirunelveli region of the far south of Tamil Nadu attempts this, arguing for a shifting equilibrium of peasant communities based on successive strata of migration into the region, the expansion of agriculture on the extensive margin, and the development of new markets and external linkages.[42] While the major focus is on middle and rich peasant groups, it is possible to attempt a historicisation of the trajectory of even the poorest and most marginal rural households over the long-term. Seen from this perspective, the movement of members of peasant families to metropolitan towns, or even overseas as indentured labour in the nineteenth and twentieth centuries, is not a wholly radical break with a tradition of rural mobility that had existed 'from time immemorial'. Naturally the modalities and imperatives that lay behind such migration had changed considerably, as had the larger implications of such moves. The point, however, is that such labour mobility was born of an earlier fluidity, rather than a once-and-for-all prising out of the household from a deep encrustation in a local environment.

Correspondingly, arguments can be made for long-term mobility for other labouring groups as well, be they artisans or 'service' labour. Of these artisanal groups, by far the best represented in the literature are weavers, for whom both detailed cross-sectional works and long-term schematic studies may be found. The importance of weaving in the historiography is related both to the relative abundance of materials available on weavers, and to the real importance of weaving as an economic activity, which in turn is reflected in the choice of weaving as a test

"*jajmani* system"', *Modern Asian Studies*, XXVII, 2 (1993), pp.357-95: it is surprising, however, that Mayer does not cite Fuller.

[42] David Ludden, *Peasant History in South India* (Princeton, 1985).

case for the 'deindustrialisation' hypothesis for colonial South Asia.

By the seventeenth century, it is evident that in a number of regions of South Asia, such as parts of the Coromandel coast, Bengal, Gujarat and the mid-Gangetic valley, large clusters of weavers could be found dominating regional economic activity, with other groups whose activities were ancillary to weaving located in their vicinity. Here, as in the case of Ludden's portrayal of peasant economies, it seems to be of some importance to pay greater attention to spatial elements than has conventially been the case in South Asian historiography.[43] Some debate exists as to whether these weavers were in fact part-time agriculturists (or even warriors); on balance, the evidence seems to suggest that while some households may have had mixed profiles, individuals probably did not mix weaving and agriculture save in moments of great economic distress, when they may have reverted from weaving to subsistence agriculture. By the late-seventeenth century, clear evidence exists for parts of the Coromandel coast, showing how weaving households had become considerably differentiated in terms of access to wealth and status, although it seems simplistic to assimilate such differentiation to a model of the emergence of the 'master weaver', signalling the rise of an indigenous capitalism from below or even a process of proto-industrialisation.[44]

Since one part of weaving was tied up with overseas trade, weavers were among the first labouring groups to feel the impact of the growing political power of the English East India Company in the eighteenth century. In the case of the Coromandel coast of south-eastern India, S. Arasaratnam has argued that these relations began to change from about 1740, with the growing political hegemony exercised by the Company in the long transition from the Nạvayat to the Walajahi dynasty at Arcot.[45] Where Bengal was concerned, the work of Ham-

[43] Cf. Sanjay Subrahmanyam, 'Rural industry and commercial agriculture in late seventh-century southeastern India', *Past and Present*, 126 (Feb. 1990), pp.76-114.

[44] For a general consideration on a pan-Indian scale, see Frank Perlin, 'Proto-industrialisation and pre-colonial South Asia', *Past and Present*, 98 (1983), pp.30-95. For the 'master weaver' hypothesis, see Vijaya Ramaswamy, *Textiles and Weavers in Medieval South India* (Delhi, 1985). For one particular weaver community, the Kaikkolars, see the inappropriately-titled work by Mattison Mines, *The Warrior Merchants: textiles, trade and territory in South India* (Cambridge, 1984).

[45] S. Arasaratnam, 'Weavers, merchants and company: the handloom industry in south-eastern India, 1750-1790', reprinted in Sanjay Subrahmanyam (ed.), *Merchants, Markets and the State in early Modern India* (Delhi, 1990), pp.190-214.

eeda Hossain follows the well-known study of N.K. Sinha in documenting a similar shift, as the Company and Company servants acting in a private capacity after the 1750s sought to squeeze the returns to both artisanal labour and intermediate merchant groups.[46] Debates continue on how precisely the gains and losses were distributed in this shift, with some historians such as Sinha, Arasaratnam and Hossain arguing that indigenous weavers and producers both were squeezed out by the Company and its servants, and with others—notably David Washbrook—insisting that the transition represents the triumph of capital in general over labour in general.[47]

Whatever be the outcome of this debate, it remains incontestable that the years after 1780 saw a shrinking in the market for Indian textiles, and a corresponding decline in weaving as an activity. The extensive and at times tedious debate on Indian 'deindustrialisation' seems to have produced a consensus on at least some questions.[48] It is now generally admitted that the coastal regions, and some inland regions, which had been relatively export-oriented saw a decline in output as cheap English cloth undercut them in the European market, and then in Asian markets, both in West Asia and Southeast Asia. Then, over the nineteenth century, a shrinking in domestic demand too became evident, first on account of the fall in consumption by inland courts, and second because imported textiles gradually penetrated even interior markets, albeit with considerable regional variation in terms of timing.[49]

Nevertheless, handloom weaving as an activity remained surprisingly important in absolute terms into the twentieth century.[50] This seem-

[46] N.K. Sinha, *The Economic History of Bengal, from Plassey to the Permanent Settlement* (3 vols., Calcutta, 1965-70); Hameeda Hossain, *The Company Weavers of Bengal: the East India Company and the organization of textile production in Bengal, 1750-1813* (Delhi, 1988).

[47] David A. Washbrook, 'Progress and problems: South Asian economic and social history, c.1720-1860', *Modern Asian Studies*, XXII, 1 (1988), pp.57-96, an essay whose sweeping generalisations are rarely rooted, however, in well-defined empirical materials. For a recent and partially valid critique of Washbrook, see Partha Chatterjee, *The Nation and its Fragments: colonial and post-colonial histories* (Delhi, 1994), pp.27-33.

[48] Michael J. Twomey, 'Employment in nineteenth-century Indian textiles', *Explorations in Economic History*, XX, 1 (1983), pp.37-57.

[49] Cf. Peter Harnetty, '"Deindustrialization" revisited: the handloom weavers of the central provinces of India, c.1800-1947', *Modern Asian Studies*, XXV, 3 (1991), pp.445-510; Sumit Guha, 'The handloom industry of central India: 1825-1950', *Indian Economic and Social History Review*, XXVI, 3 (1989), pp.297-318.

[50] This is the central thesis of Tirthankar Roy, *Artisans and Industrialisation: Indian weaving in the twentieth century* (Delhi, 1993), already set out in Roy,

ing paradox requires investigation, at the level of institutional history. Three solutions suggest themselves in this context. The first would be to argue that while superior and more efficient forms of production triumphed in general, handloom weavers found specific niches—notably at the lower and upper ends of the market, producing very coarse and very fine textiles—where their skills or products could not be replicated. Thus, a dual-product market emerged to parallel the dual-production structure. The second solution would be to seek parallels with agriculture, in order to argue that weaver households worked on a different calculus from factories: like the Chayanovian peasant, they thus engaged in 'self-exploitation' to ensure the viability of the enterprise. This form of explanation has of course been used to explain the persistence of small farms in agriculture in the face of seemingly more efficient large-scale production.

A third line of explanation would be to explore the extent of the real contrast between the 'traditional' and the 'modern' sectors in Indian textile production after the advent of the factory. It is a cliché that European factory inspectors in the early twentieth century decried the survival of what they saw as 'archaic' forms of labour organisation even in the jute-mill industry in Calcutta or the cotton-mills of Bombay. Indeed, as noted briefly above, one of the purposes of Morris D. Morris's analysis of Bombay cotton-mills was to argue that such features as high labour turnover, the presence of 'slack' labour on the shop-floor, and the continued attachment of urban labour to its rural origins were 'rational' in view of the structure of comparative costs in western India, both from the viewpoint of employer and employee. In contrast, and more recently, Dipesh Chakrabarty has argued in the context of the jute-mills of the Calcutta region that the very features that Morris saw as rational must be seen as peculiar results of the colonial character of Indian capitalism in the epoch.[51] Drawing, somewhat ironically, on elements from C.A. Bayly's monograph discussed above, Chakrabarty argues that the jute-mill worker's world reproduced in a fossilised form the structure of pre-capitalist hierarchical relations typical of the rural setting in northern India.[52] No equivalent of a Thompsonian English working-class consciousness could thus emerge, but—in a twist to the standard argument—the blame for this is laid at the

'Size and structure of the handloom weaving industry in the mid-thirties', *Indian Economic and Social History Review*, XXV, 1 (1988), pp.1-24.

[51] Dipesh Chakrabarty, *Rethinking Working-class History: Bengal, 1890-1940* (Delhi, 1989).

[52] Ibid., pp.112-13, citing Bayly, *Rulers, Townsmen and Bazaars*, pp.316-17.

door of colonial capital, which failed to provide the objective correlates for such a transformation in mentalities. In other words, since the 'modern' sector itself remained curiously 'traditional', how could it triumph over the 'traditional' sector?

The structure of Chakrabarty's argument shows how at times the language of post-modernism can conceal a reworking of an ethnocentric position, so that matters come full circle, as it were, from the reports of the factory inspectors. To Morris, from a resolutely modernist and universalist viewpoint, the behaviour of Indian workers had to be explained as a rational response to stimuli provided by a conjuncture (that of relative factor availabilities and costs); to Chakrabarty, they represent cultural differences between the workers of the received Thompsonian wisdom and those of colonial Calcutta, differences which cannot be bridged. The factory inspectors, or more recently the economic historian Gregory Clark, would argue that these differences were intrinsic, perhaps racial, certainly cultural.[53] Chakrabarty for his part would argue that the differences (which he too feels must be *explained*) between the behaviour of Indian factory labour and its counterpart in Lancashire or Sheffield is cultural, and that this culture is a pre-colonial residue. Lacking an adequate sense of change in pre-colonial India, and dependent still on the framework in which the only real change is that between 'tradition' and 'modernity', Chakrabarty thus has no option other than to fall back on a notion of intrinsic differences, wherein the nature of authority in the Calcutta jute-mill can be assumed very vaguely (and without real investigation) to derive from 'the relationships of community, kinship, religion, and so on, and in the ideas and norms associated with them'. Ironically enough, the discourse of radical post-modernism here fuses almost effortlessly into the discourse of Orientalism.[54]

[53] Gregory Clark, 'Why isn't the whole world developed? Lessons from the cotton-mills', *Journal of Economic History*, XLVII, 1 (1987), pp.585-624; in response, John R. Hanson II, 'Why isn't the whole world developed? A traditional view', *Journal of Economic History*, XLVIII, 3 (1988), pp.668-75. As Hanson points out, Clark's views are almost exactly those of D.H. Buchanan, *The Development of Capitalist Enterprise in India* (New York, 1934).

[54] It is my impression that this inability to distance themselves from an ahistorical vision of India's pre-colonial past is the most fundamental weakness of the Subaltern Studies school in general. This makes them particularly susceptible to binary structuralist dichotomies and reductionist Orientalist constructs for that period, of a type which they would criticise if applied to the colonial period; cf. Ranajit Guha, *Elementary Aspects of Peasant Insurgency in Colonial India* (Delhi, 1983).

For a comparative cultural economy

This partial circularity of evolution in analysis may appear to leave us at something of an impasse. If, as Rajnarayan Chandavarkar has argued, neo-classical stage theories, functionalist analyses and Marxist writings on the subject of economic transformations subsumed under the head of 'industrialisation' all share significant common traits, are we in a position to provide an alternative to them?[55] As is well-known in India, the small peasant farm shows no signs yet of giving way to the large farm, employing wage-labour, as the dominant form of agricultural organisation.[56] In the case of manufacturing, the most significant feature in certain sectors such as cotton textiles since the 1970s has been the development not of larger factories, but of a powerloom sector, which has been able to circumvent the limits set to wages by unionisation, and to obtain inputs (often only semi-legally) at rates lower than those of larger operations.[57]

A widening of comparative horizons may be instructive here. The standard literature, we have seen, has tended to focus repeatedly and obsessively on the contrast between the Indian evidence and a particular construct of Western European economic history. The Weberian project was a clear expression of this way of posing issues, and we have noted its survival into very recent times. The Marxists, for their part, have veered between two extremes: on the one hand a teleological vision (primitive communism in the Vedic Age, slavery in ancient India, feudalism after the Guptas, and capitalism after 1757) that runs parallel to that of the Weberians, and on the other the eminently Orientalist construction of the Asiatic Mode of Production, which suggests

[55] Rajnarayan Chandavarkar, 'Industrialisation in India before 1947: conventional approaches and alternative perspectives', *Modern Asian Studies*, XIX, 3 (1985), pp.623-68. For the general debate in which this paper may be located, see Stephen A. Marglin, 'What do bosses do?', in André Gorz (ed.), *The Division of Labour: the labour process and class struggle in modern capitalism* (London, 1976), pp.13-54; and David S. Landes, 'What do bosses really do?', *Journal of Economic History*, XLVI, 3 (1986), pp.585-624.

[56] Cf. Alan Heston and Dharma Kumar, 'The persistence of land fragmentation in peasant agriculture: an analysis of South Asian cases', *Explorations in Economic History*, XX, 1 (1983), pp.199-220; also see, for a contrasting mode of explanation of a similar phenomenon, Çaglar Keyder, 'Small peasant ownership in Turkey: historical formation and present structure', *Review*, VII, 1 (1983), pp.52-108.

[57] Cf. Omkar Goswami, 'Indian textile industry, 1970-1984: an analysis of demand and supply', *Economic and Political Weekly*, XX (21 Sept.1985), pp.1603-14.

that India had no real history until its encounter with and subjugation by the West. When attempts have been made to seek comparisons elsewhere, there have been occasional borrowings of structural models (from African history, notably), and the odd comparison with the post-Meiji Restoration Japanese experience.

Comparing India with Japan may on the face of it appear incongruous, but it is probably less so than comparing India with Britain (which is the implicit purpose of many of the analyses mentioned above). However, the Japanese comparison has been used rather fitfully and opportunistically by economic historians dealing with India, first to demonstrate how India could have developed had it been independent (as Japan was), and more recently by B.R. Tomlinson to show how the uniqueness of Japan renders such an exercise largely invalid.[58] Still more recently, development economists have turned their attention to the contrast between India and South Korea, or India and Taiwan, to see what lessons can be drawn from these East Asian 'tigers'. The India-China comparison, has also been a favoured exercise since the 1960s, particularly for those who wish to see a trade-off between democratic institutions and industrial and agricultural growth, in the spirit of Myrdal's 'soft state' hypothesis.[59]

These exercises often have a purely technocratic flavour about them, reduced as they are to comparisons of the Effective Rate of Protection, or the extent of state subsidy to this or that industry. However, if we look at the larger historiographical context within which it is necessary to embed each exercise in comparison, certain curious conclusions emerge. This is best exemplified by the case of Japan, where the historiography on the period after 1500 is particularly copious.

Writings of the immediate post-World War II period had tended to emphasise how the 're-opening' of Japan, after its 'closure' to the West in the Tokugawa era, was the catalyst that set off change. The Meiji Restoration of 1868 was given a role here of a decisive break from an earlier feudal past, and the Japanese state was credited with following innovative policies in order to 'catch up' with the West. Japan was hence seen as a latecomer to Modern Economic Growth which made use of 'substitute factors' (in the Gerschenkronian sense) to accelerate

[58] B.R. Tomlinson, 'Writing history sideways: lessons for Indian economic historians from Meiji Japan', *Modern Asian Studies*, XIX, 3 (1985), pp.669-8.

[59] See Jagdish Bhagwati, *India in Transition: freeing the economy* (Oxford, 1993), pp.10-17, for a sceptical view of India-China comparisons, and Sukhamoy Chakravarty, 'Marxist economics and contemporary developing economies, in Chakravarty, *Selected Economic Writings*, pp.140-68, for the India-South Korea comparison.

change. Now Gerschenkron himself is not known to have espoused this formulation, though it was certainly favoured by some of his disciplies like Henry Rosovsky.[60] The writings of the 1970s tended to cast even further doubt on its validity.

In the first place, the myth of *sakoku*, or the 'closed country' of the epoch before Commodore Perry was called into question.[61] Second, a reformulation began to emerge in which continuities between the Tokugawa period and later developments were stressed. This had long been recognised at the level of entrepreneurship, and David Landes and Reinhard Bendix had even proposed models comparing the Japanese Samurai-entrepreneurs of the late nineteenth century with the German Junker-entrepreneurs of the same epoch.[62] Analysts of the agrarian economy and of rural manufacturing joined their voices to these; and in a final blow, Susan Hanley and Kozo Yamamura argued that even the Japanese demographic experience showed greater continuity between the seventeenth and nineteenth centuries than had been suspected.[63]

These shifts in the Japanese historiography called into question the received European model of modernisation for a number of reasons. For one, Japan by the 1970s had been given honorary European status in the economic history literature, to the extent of being admitted into *The Cambridge Economic History of Europe*![64] The insistence of histo-

[60] Henry Rosovsky, *Capital Formation in Japan, 1868-1940* (Glencoe, 1961), is cited with guarded approval in Gerschenkron, *Economic Backwardness*, p.7. For a later attempt at applying Gerschenkron to Japan, see Rosovsky, 'Japan's transition to modern economic growth, 1868-1885', in Rosovsky (ed.), *Industrialization in Two Systems.*

[61] Ronald P. Toby, *State and Diplomacy in Early Modern Japan: Asia in the development of the Tokugawa Bakufu* (Princeton, 1984), and also Toby, 'Reopening the question of "Sakoku": diplomacy in the legitimation of the Tokugawa Bakufu', *Journal of Japan Studies*, III, 2 (1977), pp.323-63.

[62] David S. Landes, 'Japan and Europe: contrasts in industrialisation', in W.W. Lockwood (ed.), *The State and Economic Enterprise in Japan: essays in the political economy of growth* (Princeton, 1965), pp.93-182; Reinhard Bendix, 'Preconditions of development: a comparison of Japan and Germany', in R.P. Dore (ed.), *Aspects of Social Change in Modern Japan* (Princeton, 1967), pp.27-68.

[63] Susan B. Hanley and Kozo Yamamura, *Economic and Demographic Change in Pre-industrial Japan, 1600-1868* (Princeton, 1977).

[64] Koji Taira, 'Factory labour and the industrial revolution in Japan', and Kozo Yamamura, 'Entrepreneurship, ownership and management in Japan', in P.J. Mathias and M.M. Postan (eds.), *The Cambridge Economic History of Europe*, VII, 2 (The Industrial Economies: capital, labour and enterprise; the United States, Japan and Russia) (Cambridge, 1978), pp.166-214 and 215-64, respectively.

rians of Japan that the trajectory of that country was different, and worse still that the differences had persisted, was cause for disquiet. Management theorists had meanwhile invented the category of 'Japanese-style management', to account for the Japanese version of a modern economy, which was nevertheless constituted (in the cliché, at least) by firms characterised by paternalism, overwhelming male domination, and a 'moral economy' of the factory that stressed consensus, collectivism and participation.[65] The Weberian master discourse was turned on its head, as revisionist theorists came to the conclusion that the Confucian ethic was in fact eminently suited to a 'modern' cultural context.[66] It was even claimed that while the Japanese economy was a modern one, the mentalities of entrepreneurs and workers worked through concepts that were untranslatable in Western languages. One recent work actually begins with the following rather bewildering formulation, wherein one finds a happily unconscious redefinition of the notions of 'tradition' and 'modernity':

> As the first non-Western nation to reach an advanced state of modernization, Japan illustrates the myriad ways in which traditional patterns of meaning persist and are made vital in the present. The vexing question is assessing the degree of influence these patterns, developed over a long, rich, and quite distinct history, have in shaping economic behaviour.[67]

Some hard-headed attempts at 'de-mystification' have proposed a common East Asian model of industrialisation in which the state had a far greater role to play than had hitherto been recognised. The South Korean experience with the particular type of large firm termed *chaebol* (similar to the Japanese *zaibatsu*) has been noted, and it has been argued that the state in post-war Korea too had played a role of stra-

[65] For a pointed denial that neoclassical models of the firm apply to Japan, see Masahiko Aoki, 'The Japanese firm in transition', in Kozo Yamamura and Yasukichi Yasuba (ed.), *The Political Economy of Japan*, vol.I: *The Domestic Transformation* (Stanford, 1987), pp.263-88.

[66] Michio Morishima, *Why has Japan Succeeded?* (Cambridge, 1982). For an even more extreme formulation, W.T. O'Malley, 'Culture and industrialisation', in Helen Hughes (ed.), *Achieving Industrialisation in Asia* (Cambridge, 1988). Also see the polemical monograph of Ronald Dore, *Taking Japan Seriously: A Confucian perspective on leading economic issues* (London, 1987). Finally, for a comparative sociological perspective, see T.N. Madan, 'Asia and the modern West: Indian and Japanese responses to Westernization', in Madan, *Pathways: approaches to the study of society in India* (Delhi, 1994), pp.226-45.

[67] Daniel I. Okinoto and Thomas P. Rohlen (eds.), *Inside the Japanese System: readings on contemporary society and political economy* (Stanford, 1988), p.1.

tregic intervention similar to the Japanese MITI.[68] While these revelations may have given scant comfort to proponents of 'free-market' industrialisation and economic development, they did not resolve the issue of the meaning of modernisation in these different contexts. Indeed, casting one's net further to consider the Latin-American experience only further confused the issue; if a common economic trajectory was difficult to isolate, the convergence of cultures and mentalities seemed even more elusive.

It is instructive in this context to consider one of the more interesting recent critiques of the tradition-modernity dichotomy, that of C.J. Fuller. Fuller argues that the line of thought in anthropology stemming from Karl Polanyi's work has constructed an axiomatic dichotomy between these two categories, but that the two are not symmetrically located. Rather, the 'modern' is proposed as the thesis, the 'traditional' as the antithesis, 'generated as the negative of the modern by defining the traits which are *not* characteristic of modern economies, or rather those which are not susceptible to interpretation by Western economic theory'.[69]

One suspects here that Fuller's notion of 'Western economic theory' corresponds to standard text-book neoclassical micro-economic theory of the 1960s: consumers maximising well-behaved utility functions subject to a budget constraint, producers maximising a profit function in a world of perfect information, a Pareto-efficient general equilibrium outcome. This, at any rate, is what most social scientists who are not economists believe contemporary economics to be about. Industrial organisation theory has however departed from this to a major extent over time, particularly to take account of the strategic interaction of agents.[70] On the other hand, theorists of the firm had already begun several decades ago to question the assumption of simple profit maximisation, arguing for notions such as sales maximisation in corpora-

[68] On South Korea, see, for example, Dennis L. McNamara, *The Colonial Origins of Korean Enterprise, 1910-1945* (Cambridge, 1990), as well as Toshio Watanaba, 'Economic development in Korea: lessons and challenge', in Toshio Shishido and Ryuzo Sato (eds.), *Economic Policy and Development: new perspectives* (London, 1985), pp.95-111. In contrast, L.J. Cho and Y.H. Kim (eds.), *Economic Development in the Republic of Korea: a policy perspective* (Honolulu, 1991), present a more culturalist explanation, stressing Confucian values, and concepts like *chung kyo* (loyalty to the state, filial piety and harmony).

[69] Fuller, 'Misconceiving the grain heap', pp.55-6.

[70] For a recent survey, see Kaushik Basu, *Lectures in Industrial Organisation Theory* (Oxford, 1993).

tions, or—to follow Herbert Simon—of 'satisficing' in a world of bounded rationality for decision-makers.[71] These paths have not been pursued, however, with as much vigour as the interplay of game theory and industrial organisation theory. It remains true thus that economic theory is more often than not culturally insensitive, though there is no formal constraint to defining the objective functions of agents to account for a certain range of behavioural variations.

Does this really matter? Fuller's object, we see, is to argue that the category of the 'traditional' is too sweeping; he writes that 'there is no *a priori* reason to believe that different traditional economies have positive common features'. Further, and as a result, 'there is no place in the scheme for genuine change within the traditional category, since no such change could replicate the great transformation, by definition the sole begetter of significant structural development in the economic domain'.[72]

On the other hand, it is curious and significant that the category of the 'modern' appears to him wholly unproblematic; if Fuller is certain that there is no historical unity between the Indian and African traditional economic systems, he is equally sure that these can be contrasted 'with *the genuine unity that does exist amongst modern economies*, all products of an interconnected transformation into an international, industrial market system' (emphasis added). If such a 'genuine unity' does indeed exist, neoclassical economics is right to be culturally insensitive to possible variations in the economies of the modern world. It is no good appealing to the idea that there are 'traditional' elements and mentalities in the 'modern' world in the face of this genuine unity, and little point in stating that two firms that operate in the same market, say, Lever Brothers and the Birlas, may have quite different objectives and conceptions of how to operate. If modernity is indeed such a powerful dissolving solution, there should logically no longer be a problem of vairations in institutions and mentalities.

I would argue that such an approach would be a fundamental error, roughly equivalent to the German philosophers' slogan of the early

[71] Herbert Simon, *Models of Bounded Rationality*, vol.II: *Behavioural Economics and Business Organization* (London, 1982). Also William J. Baumol, *Business Behavior, Value and Growth* (rev. edn., New York, 1967), and Baumol in Elizabeth E. Baily (ed.), *Selected Economic Writings* (New York, 1976), pp.475-86 and 559-66; in the latter set of essays, Baumol—unusually for a theorist of his generation—admits the influence on him of Thorstein Veblen.

[72] Fuller, 'Misconceiving the grain heap', pp.56-7; it is instructive in this context to read Eric L. Jones, *Growth Recurring: economic change in world history* (Oxford, 1988).

twentieth century that modernity meant 'the Europeanisation of all foreign parts of mankind'.[73] It would appear to me that we should be prepared to investigate the hypothesis that 'modernity' is as complex and nuanced a phenomenon as 'tradition', with a history, but also with the possibility of significant cross-cultural variation. The Weberian comparative sociologist S.N. Eisenstadt was surely mistaken when he wrote three decades ago that 'historically, modernization is the process of change towards those types of social, economic and political systems that have developed in Western Europe and North America from the seventeenth century to the nineteenth'.[74] Early theorists of modernisation had expected a convergence at all levels: the convergence of demographic experiences through the Theory of Demographic Transition, the emergence of a single rationality embodied in a unitary notion of scientific progress, the convergence of societal structures and mentaities through the formation of a 'global village', as the formulaic cliché went. They were mistaken.

Conclusion

Recent formulations by political scientists concerning 'civilisational faultlines' separating 'Islam' from 'Europe', and both of these from 'Hinduism' and the 'Confucian East', while profoundly erroneous and ahistorical, nevertheless capture the disquiet that has emerged both among comparative sociologists, and journalists and politicians, as the idea of 'difference' in the contemporary world does not melt away. The simplest solution that has been offered is that of 'imperfect modernisation', that is, the view that a number of societies which have remained 'underdeveloped' have retained large elements of their 'traditional' institutions. Golden Age theorists from these countries have been complicit in such a formulation, arguing that such 'traditional' institutions are in fact superior ways of dealing with ecological and human relations, and—in their most extreme view—even seeking to find common cause between Gandhi, Mao and Khomeni, all three heroic opponents of modernity, which is here glossed to mean 'the

[73] Wilhelm Halbfass, *India and Europe: an essay in understanding* (Albany, 1988), pp.440-1.

[74] S.N. Eisenstadt, *Modernization, Protest and Change* (Englewood Cliffs, 1966), p.1. For a quite contrary view from a Sinologist, see Pierre-Etienne Will, 'Chine moderne et sinologie', *Annales HSS*, XLIX, 1 (1994), pp.7-26, as also the important case study of Java, in Denys Lombard, *Le Carrefour Javanais: essai d'histoire globale* vol.I (*Les limites de l'occidentalisation*) (Paris, 1990). Note that the volume is *not* called 'les limites de la modernisation'!

West'. What else, after all, is one to make of radical critics of received theory who write such words as these, echoing the most banal constructions of Orientalism?

Throughout their history the Chinese divided thre world into two spheres, one inhabited by barbarians and the other by civilized folk. The Son of Heaven, his court, Chinese society, constituted civilized society, the true measure of significance. People, ideas, technical inventions and commodities from outside the realm were of little consequence or import. In India too, up to about 1800, the society retained similar notions of self-containment and sufficiency, and though there might have been migration abroad, by and large the collective mind did not feel the need to replace its ideas and values with alien ones.[75]

A comparative analysis which looks not merely at an imagined Western Model (for it is a moot point to what extent 'the West' itself is perfectly unitary), but at the complex and diverse experiences of other societies within Asia and outside it, may thus free us from the burden of both fruitless counterfactuals for the past, and improbable visions for the future (based on either a return to the past, or the transposition of the two-car modal family to India).[76] It may also help us come to terms with the analytically significant differences between the institutional trajectories of South Asia and other societies in the world, without necessarly reducing these to simple differences in the immanent natures of civilisations.

This essay represents a foray into an unusual mode for its author. But there is a reason to abandon the careful analysis of concrete historical materials and situations for a broad historiographical canvas—even if only temporarily. This is, that the general has too often remained the monopoly of the 'generalist', who blithely and often irresponsibly uses the work of the 'specialist' as grist to his own mill. We may take, by way of a last example, the work of a well-known group of comparativists, published as late as 1988, seeking to explain the 'European miracle'. Herein, we encounter from the pen of Jean Baechler, an essay on the 'origins of modernity', which seeks to compare Japan and India

[75] Claude Alvares, *Science, Development and Violence: the revolt against modernity* (Delhi, 1992), pp.91-2, but also see pp.142-63. For less extreme formulations of a similar genre, Frédérique A. Marglin and Stephen Marglin (eds.), *Dominating Knowledge: development, culture and resistance* (Oxford, 1990), and Ashis Nandy, *Traditions, Tyranny and Utopias: essays in the politics of awareness* (Delhi, 1987).

[76] A rather profound doubt on the unitary nature of the West European experience is raised, for example, in Çaglar Keyder and Patrick O'Brien, *Economic Growth in Britain and France, 1780-1914: two paths to the twentieth century* (London, 1978).

with Europe.[77] Baechler distances himself from Weber, calling his attempts 'admirable but vain', and claims moreover that he himself does not evoke 'ideological factors' to explain the contrast between the Indian trajectory of economic change and that of the West. Is this then a new and innovative departure?

Alas, most definitely no. To begin with, Baechler has only the vaguest conception of history, conflating the Mauryas and the Mughals with happy abandon. The eighteenth-century structure described by Bernard Cohn for the Banaras region appears to him no different from what one finds in the *Mahabharata*: 'The Mogul structure is certainly very ancient'! Further discoveries are in store: 'India did not possess another indispensable mainstay of civil society: a peasantry'; in India, 'Towns...are only nerve centres of political authority, the markets and the merchants are exclusively in the service of the class enjoying power and leisure'; there is 'a permanent lethargy as regards the economic activity of exchange'; finally, 'There are no aristocrats in India, unless they are local, such as the Mahrattas, who represent tribal revival'![78] We note that an unfamiliarity with even the elementary works with which the undergraduate student of Indian history is supposed to be familiar, is an indispensable aid to such bold analysis.

This brings us to Baechler's grand conclusion: the problem with India is not its other-worldiness but its lack of political stability.[79] This absence of political stability leads to the invention of nothing less than the caste system, in its incarnation as 'the regime of *jati* castes'. Combined with *jajmani*, which for Baechler is, incidentally, a totally unproblematic concept, *jati* 'ensures economic, cultural and demographic self-sufficiency, independent of any political framework'.[80] Unchang-

[77] Jean Baechler, 'The origins of modernity: caste and feudality (India, Europe and Japan)', in Jean Baechler, John A. Hall and Michael Mann (eds.), *Europe and the Rise of Capitalism* (Oxford, 1988), pp.39-65.

[78] As regards at least two of these points, see the papers collected in Sanjay Subrahmanyam (ed.), *Money and the Market in India*, especially the editor's 'Introduction', pp.1-56. I should note that when this text was presented at a seminar at the Centre d'Etudes de l'Inde et de l'Asie du Sud, Paris, in November 1992, some Dumontian anthropologists accused the present writer—in a curious reversal of roles—of being unfamiliar with 'Indian reality', which was apparently their exclusive possession!

[79] Baechler's conclusions are echoed by John A. Hall, 'States and societies: the miracle in comparative perspective', in Baechler, Hall and Mann (eds.), *Europe and the Rise of Capitalism*, pp.24-8.

[80] Cf. in this context, Nicholas B. Dirks, *The Hollow Crown: ethnohistory of an Indian kingdom* (Cambridge, 1987). While I must express reservations concerning certain parts of Dirks's approach (including his backward reading of

ing India, self-sufficient villages, a tradeless economy and unstable polity, and above all the all-encompassing idea of 'caste', these then are spectres that are far from disappearing in Western social science discourse.

It may thus be true, as has been argued recently, that 'true universalism, that which constitutes the horizon necessary for a comparative exercise, does not consist of superficially denying differences, but in attempting to comprehend them as particular cultural forms of access to the universal'.[81] We may read this, for example, as an unintended critique of Morris D. Morris's proposition which served us as a point of departure. It remains to be seen with what success such differences can be analysed as historically constituted, rather than as timeless constructs that separate Them from Us. If Morris's vision appears to us simplistic and unsatisfactory, it is equally certain that the paths variously taken by Weber, Dumont and Baechler are dead-ends. To ignore this is to ignore an entire generation of historiography concerning India between 1500 and the present day.

---

the pre-colonial history of Pudukkottai from largely colonial sources, and his exclusively political conception of caste), the work is as much an important antidote to such writers as Baechler, as it is to Dumont.

[81] Jacques Pouchepadass, 'L'Etat et la structuration de l'espace politique dans l'Inde coloniale', in J. Pouchepadass and H. Stern (eds.), *De la Royauté à l'Etat dans le monde indien* (Paris, 1991), p.48, n.6; the remark is in fact directed at Ronald B. Inden, 'Orientalist constructions of India', *Modern Asian Studies*, XX, 3 (1986).

Chapter 3

MARKETS, MARKET FAILURES, AND THE TRANSFORMATION OF AUTHORITY, PROPERTY AND BONDAGE IN COLONIAL INDIA[1]

Amiya Kumar Bagchi

Pure competition and market failures

Economists working in the tradition of Leon Walras and Vilfredo Pareto have derived a theorem about the dual correspondence between a purely competitive equilibrium and a Pareto-optimal state. This means roughly that every such equilibrium displays the zero-sum properties of Pareto optimality (that is, nobody can be made better off through a reallocation of activities without making somebody else worse off) and that every Pareto-efficient state can be supported by a set of prices such that every economic agent seeking to maximise utility or profits (which in equilibrium must be zero) with the prices as given ends up with the trades prescribed by the purely competitive equilibrium. Once the stringent conditions of such correspondence became clear,[2] some of the more perceptive economists began to worry about the numerous ways in which markets failed. Market failure may mean at least two different kinds of outcome. The first is that the given market may fail to produce an equilibrium in positive prices and quantities, as when a large supply of fish suddenly arrives in a market, and there are no takers even at zero prices, so that the sellers (or more often, public authorities) have to dispose of the surplus at a positive cost. The second is that there is an equilibrium but that equilibrium is sustainable only if either the seller or the buyer (and sometimes both parties) has a determinate influence on the price at which the commodity or service is traded. The rise of Keynesian macro-economics has been seen by many

[1] I am indebted to the participants in the international workshop on 'Meanings of Agriculture' and 'Production Units in Micro- and Macro-structural Perspective', held under the auspices of the Centre of South Asian Studies, School of Oriental and African Studies, University of London, in July 1992, for their comments on an earlier version. I alone, however, remain responsible for any errors in the paper.

[2] G. Debreu, *Theory of Value* (New York, 1959).

economists as the emergence of the study of market failure on a grand scale. The endemic unemployment in rural areas of Third World countries and the failure of even subsistence wages to bring about full employment is another example of market failure. The second type of market failure was long recognised in the literature as the case of industries with decreasing costs at the point of equilibrium.

Traditional neo-classical theory dealt with situations in which all features of the commodities were fully known to everybody. This theory was extended to situations in which states of nature were uncertain, but all the agents had full information about the possible states of nature and the probability of each of them occurring.[3] But Radner showed that when the agents had incomplete information about states of nature and about each other's behaviour, problems arose about the existence of competitive equilibrium; when the equilibria existed they could not be proved to be Pareto-efficient either.[4] Radner further demonstrated that if agents did not have unlimited computational ability (and unlimited time for carrying out the computations), the nicely behaved competitive equilibria would vanish. In the case of both uncertainty about agents' behaviour and limited computational ability, money would be needed to tide over the uncertainty and the limits of computational ability; thus the existence of competitive equilibria in any economy using money becomes a hazardous affair.

While neo-classical economics has something to say about the local conditions of market success (to coin a phrase) or even the varieties of market failure, it has virtually no light to shed on the conditions for sustainability of market success, or the reasons for persistent market failure. For the former, we have to turn to the followers of Keynes and Kalecki, and, of course, to the followers of classical political economy from Adam Smith to Karl Marx. For the latter we have to turn to discourses going far beyond the boundaries of traditional economics or traditional political economy as taught in academic institutions. The core of classical political economy has been claimed to be the investigation of the conditions for promoting the wealth of nations primarily through the instrumentality of capital accumulation, and of the determi-

[3] K.J. Arrow, 'Le rôle valeurs boursières pour la repartition la meillure des risques', *Econometrie* (Paris, 1953); translated as 'The role of securities in the optimal allocation of risk bearing', *Review of Economic Studies*, 31 (1964), pp.91-6; Debreu, *Theory of Value*, ch.7.

[4] R. Radner, 'Competitive equilibrium under uncertainty', *Econometrica* 36,1 (1968), pp.31-58; reprinted in P. Diamond and M. Rothschild (eds.), *Uncertainty in Economics: Readings and Exercises* (New York, 1978).

nants of income distribution between landlords, capitalists and workers.[5] The latter in its turn was thought greatly to influence the speed of accumulation and its quality through its influence on the distribution of workforce between productive and unproductive labour. In pre-Marxian classical political economy, very roughly speaking, the shifting of the income distribution from landlords to capitalists was supposed to promote economic growth by promoting accumulation and helping to shift labour from unproductive to productive uses (since landlords' consumption was regarded as the source of employment of unproductive labour).

I have argued elsewhere that Malthus overestimated the significance of effective demand failures in the British economy of his time and came to decidedly wrong conclusions regarding the remedial measures needed.[6] I would now argue, *pace* Eltis, that Malthus confused issues of short-run demand failure with those of long-term sluggishness of investment, and failed to see that abolition of landlordism was necessary in order finally to release the long-run propensity to invest from the shackles of pre-capitalist, non-market power and pre-capitalist incentives.[7] That the British, with the advantage of the first start and global dominance in manufactures, were able to make landlordism wither away rather than abolish it formally, is another matter.

Political economy as the rhetoric of British imperialism in India

It is this corpus of political economy that the more theoretically-minded British policy-makers in India turned to when trying to rationalise their policies. That the justification was couched in terms of political economy has been eloquently argued by Ranajit Guha and Eric Stokes.[8] But that the justification was often no more than a cloak for expediency in many contexts has been argued by Rabitoy and Stokes in his later work.[9] On balance of the evidence, my sympathies lie more with the

[5] K. Bharadwaj, *Themes in Value and Distribution: Classical Theory Reappraised* (London, 1989), chs.1-5.

[6] A.K. Bagchi, 'Problems of effective demand and contradictions of planning in India', in Bagchi (ed.), *Economy, Society and Polity: Essays in the Political Economy of Indian Planning* (Calcutta, 1988), pp.227-66.

[7] W. Eltis, *The Classical Theory of Economic Growth* (London, 1984).

[8] R. Guha, *A Rule of Property for Bengal* (Paris, 1963; new edn., Calcutta, 1981); E. Stokes, *English Utilitarians and India* (London, 1959).

[9] N. Rabitoy, 'System vs. expediency: the reality of land revenue administration in the Bombay Presidency, 1812-1820', *Modern Asian Studies* 9, 4 (1975), pp.529-46; E. Stokes, 'The land tenure system of the North-Western Provinces and Bombay Deccan 1830-1880: ideology and the official mind', in

latter view than with the former.[10] I have argued this in some more detail in a recent paper.[11]

I find the view that land tenure arrangements in India were modelled either on the experience in Britain or on the tenets of Ricardian political economy untenable for the following reasons. First, the British never created a set of landlords with freehold rights in India except in the region of tea plantations where they gave most of the land away to European planters on a nominal payment. Correspondingly, they never created a set of capitalist tenant farmers with a secure tenure or long leaseholds. Secondly, for most of the period of British rule in India there were severe constraints on mobility of labour and capital. So this idea of an economic rent to be calculated on the basis of a given market wage and a uniform rate of profit was mostly a fantasy. Both these reasons for the non-applicability of the British model and of the Ricardo-Malthus theory of rent were known to Richard Jones (1831), but their significance for conducting any discourse on land markets, commodity markets, or peasant rights has not been grasped by most analysts in the field.

Economic theorists love to indulge in fantasies of the first weaver meeting the first agriculturist to exchange each other's products in a completely spontaneous manner. But anthropologists and historians have long known that the actual functioning of markets has generally required them to be connected with social networks, political authority, and organisation of merchants and financiers transcending the borders of states.[12] In pre-British India one of the ways in which the rulers sought to establish their legitimacy and extend their authority was by licensing markets, augmenting the facilities for merchants to bring their wares to their realms, and making tax concessions to attract trade from neighbouring kingdoms or chiefdoms.[13] Of course, rapacious rulers sought also to treat merchants and bankers as lambs to be fleeced, but unless this was only a short-term expedient, the rule of such chiefs and

---

C.H. Philips and M.D. Wainwright (eds.), *Indian Society and the Beginnings of Modernization* (London, 1976; reprinted in E., Stokes, *The Peasant and the Raj*, Cambridge 1978, pp.90-119).

[10] A.K. Bagchi, 'Ideas, ideologies and the other side of the moon', *Frontier* 15, 10-12, 1982, pp.15-20.

[11] A.K. Bagchi, 'Land tax, property rights and peasant insecurity' (mimeo.), Occasional Paper, Centre for Studies in Social Sciences, Calcutta, 1992.

[12] F. Braudel, *Civilisation and Capitalism, 15th-18th Centuries*, vol.2, *The Wheels of Commerce* (tr. S. Reynolds; London, 1982).

[13] Hamida Khatoon Naqvi, *Urbanisation and Urban Centres under the Great Mughals, 1556-1707* (Simla, 1972).

princes did not generally endure. British rule greatly disrupted this network of markets, most of which were oriented towards domestic exchange, and the extension of overseas trade failed often to compensate for this disruption. Secondly, in pre-British India the successor states of the Mughals had to nurse their core domains in order to survive or gather the resources for further aggression. In proto-capitalist Europe poor laws, guild regulations and state patronage of the economy were designed to ward off the shocks of famines, wars and foreign competition. The British never treated such policies as part of their agenda of rule over India. Naturally, the incursion of unregulated international influences often led to uncompensated income losses and to the spread of monopolistic power of local controllers of money and authority over markets for goods, credit, labour and land—to the point at which it became meaningless to talk about the working of a self-regulating market.

Market-places and long-distance trade: creation and destruction

At the time of the British conquest of Bengal and other major provinces, there were commodity markets for most consumer goods, there was long-distance trade in many staples, and there were money and credit markets linking the major centres of trade and government. The direction of trade and the location of markets were greatly influenced by the pre-British structures of regional power and the pre-British style of governance. As we have mentioned already, the market-places were themselves often created through the specific political act of a local ruler, a regional power or the supraregional authorities.[14] Colebrooke commented in 1795 on the decline of market-places in Bengal after the customs and other commercial duties (*sa'ars*) levied by the zamindars or the local rulers on the traders were abolished. The abolition of these tolls was part of the Cornwallis reforms turning the decennial settlement into the Permanent Settlement, and clipping the power of the big revenue farmers.[15] On the other hand, the British effort to 'rationalise'

[14] B.S. Cohn, 'The initial British impact on India: a case study of the Benares region', *Journal of Asian Studies* XIX, 4 (1960), pp.320-42; reprinted in B.S. Cohn, *An Anthropologist among the Historians and Other Essays* (Delhi, 1987).

[15] H.T. Colebrooke and Lambert, *Remarks on the Husbandry and Internal Commerce of Bengal* (Calcutta, 1795), pp.47-8. Colebrooke commented: 'Wanting the regulation, and protection received from officers of the sayer, markets have declined; and many have been totally disused, since the abolition of the sayers. This is undoubtedly an evil.... Numerous markets by promoting intercourse, contributed to general prosperity. The discontinuance of many markets in the short space of four years, and the decline of the existing marts is

the internal tolls of the country made them much more burdensome than before, and especially damaged those manufactures which depended on long-distance supply of raw materials such as cotton, since the reforms had a cascading effect on costs.[16] Moreover, imported goods came to enjoy a tariff preference in the Indian market over the produce of Indian industry, varying between 2.5 and 10 per cent *ad valorem*,[17] as the British conquest of the country opened up the whole of the conquered territory to the influences of transoceanic trade. Of course, these influences had to negotiate all the real transport barriers, and other physical barriers to easy communication posed by the land mass of India, breached by the flow of the great rivers and their tributaries and deltaic offshoots. Then there was the fragmentation of the territory with internal tolls and custom duties which were survivals of pre-British times, though transformed by British diktat and practices. Finally, the rapid expansion of India's import and export trade was checked repeatedly by the recessionary force generated by the British conquest. This story of the survival and transformation of pre-British structures melding with market failures as an accompaniment of the impact of British rule, or even of institutional changes effected through international economic pressures, would repeat itself in different regions and different phases of the two centuries of British rule.

The recessionary impact of British rule was felt in the late 1760s in Bengal. This was the immediate occasion for the East India Company's appeal to the British parliament for financial help and led to the first Act passed by the parliament to regulate the Company's rule in India. This was also the occasion for the Company's decision to commission Sir James Steuart to examine the scarcity of money in Bengal and suggest possible remedies, which resulted in the introduction of a Scottish system of banking and note-issue in the Company's territories.[18]. In many cases of British conquest, unrequited transfers and consequent

---

an alarming circumstance' (ibid., p.48). This passage was omitted when Colebrooke published a revised version of his part of the book in 1804. (Lambert, who wrote the part on the external commerce of Bengal, had died in the meantime.)

[16] C.E. Trevelyan, *Report upon the Inland Customs and Town Duties of the Bengal Presidency* (second edn., Calcutta, 1835; reprinted with an introdution by T. Banerjee, Calcutta, 1976), pp.92-3.

[17] Ibid., p.96.

[18] J. Steuart, *The Principles of Money Applied to the Present State of the Coin in Bengal* (London, 1772); W.J. Barber, *British Economic Thought and India 1600-1858: a study in the history of development economics* (Oxford, 1975), ch.4.

impoverishment of the territory occurred long before the formal assumption of power by the British. Such was, for example, the case of the territory of the Nawabs of Arcot, or of the territory of the Nawab of Awadh. However, a more dramatic displacement of authority could be followed, as in the case of Bengal, by a noticeable recession and widespread failures of markets, such that producers of crops were unable to sell them except at ruinously low prices. This monetary stringency led to widespread shortfalls in revenue, which is how the phenomenon came to the attention of the authorities, just as it was the failure to finance the Company's 'investment' with its normal territorial revenues that had provoked the enquiry into the problems of shortage of specie in Bengal. The fall in demand as a result of the fall in money incomes ensuing from the dismissal of the Peshwa's soldiers and effective dissolution of his court at Poona was cited as a major reason for the disastrous fall in prices of grain in the erstwhile Peshwa territories.[19] This recession also was one of the causes of the decline of handicrafts in the Bombay Deccan.[20] The latter in turn fed the forces of recession and merged with the general phenomenon of depression in prices and economic activity in most parts of northern, western and southern India from the middle of the 1820s down to the beginning of the 1850s.[21] Almost certainly this led, in many cases, to a contraction of the sphere of circulation of money. Symptomatic of the stagnation in demand for credit was the fact that although directors of the Bank of Bengal proposed to raise its capital from Rs.5 million to Rs.20 million, these limits of capital and note-issue were not reached until the abolition of the banks' right of note-issue from 1861.[22]

Land tenures and market failures in bundles and fractions of claims

The most contentious area in the historiography of the British Indian

[19]*Gazetteer of the Bombay Presidency*, vol.XVII, *Ahmadnagar* (Bombay, 1884), p.433; *Gazetteer of the Bombay Presidency*, vol.XVIII, *Poona*, pt.II (Bombay 1885), p.373.

[20] S. Guha, *The Agrarian Economy of the Bombay Deccan 1818-1941* (Delhi, 1985), ch.2.

[21] S. Sreenivasa Raghavaiyangar, *Memorandum on the Progress of the Madras Presidency during the last Forty Years of British Administration* (Madras 1893); P.J. Thomas and B.N. Pillai, *Economic Depression in the Madras Presidency 1820-1854* (Madras, 1933); A. Siddiqi, *Agrarian Change in a Northern Indian State: Uttar Pradesh 1819-1833* (Oxford, 1973).

[22] A.K. Bagchi, *The Evolution of the State Bank of India. The roots 1806-1876*, pt. I, *The Early Years 1806-1860* , ch.10, and pt. II, *Diversity and Regrouping 1860-1876* (Bombay, 1987), ch.23.

economy has been the subject of land tenures. It is not only the intentions or the ideologies of the policy-makers which have been under debate, but also the nature of land rights. One of the hardiest perennials in colonial India's historiography has been the contention that British colonial administrators introduced, or intended to introduce, capitalist farming of the type they were familiar with in Britain. The foundation of the prosperity of the agrarian bourgeoisie which ruled England from the Commonwealth period down to the eighteenth century was an absolute property in land, which was considered to be more or less inviolate.[23] The land tax which this bourgeoisie imposed upon itself was light, and was neither the first charge nor the essential condition for the landlords to retain their land. In India, both in the Permanent Settlement and in the raiyatwari areas, the payment of the tax to the treasury became the first charge and the essential condition for the landlord's (zamindar's) or the smallholder's (raiyat's) right to the fruits of the land, a share of the rent in one case, and a share of the value of the produce in the other. What was sought to be commoditised was not the full present value of the land as a productive asset, but only certain shares or bundles of claims to the produce or the rent of the land—these claims being threatened with extinction every time the revenue payment (*kist*) became due. Such commoditisation itself was confronted repeatedly with problems of market failure—during the first thirty years or so, in the case of the Permanent Settlement in Bengal, and during an even longer period in the case of the raiyatwari settlements in the Bombay Deccan and in Tamil Nadu.[24] Zamindars often failed to meet the undertaking for rent payment they had entered into with the government, and when their claims (their so-called 'estates') were disposed of, they often had to be sold at no more than the value of two or three years' revenue demand. Even then, often there were no purchasers at all at these auction sales. Some of the purchasers withheld their bids fraudulently, but 'fraud' was the counterpart of extortion by agents who

[23] See, for example, J.V. Beckett, *The Aristocracy in England 1660-1914* (Oxford, 1986); W.D. Rubinstein, *Elites and the Wealthy in Modern British History* (Brighton, 1987); L. Stone and J.C. Fautier Stone, *An Open Elite? England 1540-1880* (Oxford, 1984); F.M.L. Thompson, *English Landed Society in the Nineteenth Centyry* (London, 1963); E.P. Thompson, 'The patricians and the plebs', in E.P. Thompson, *Customs in Common* (London, 1991), pp.16-96.

[24] C.J. Baker, *An Indian Rural Economy 1880-1955: the Tamiland countryside* (Oxford, 1984), ch.3; S. Guha, *The Agrarian Economy of the Bombay Deccan,* and 'The land market in upland Maharashtra c.1820-1920', pt.I, *Indian Economic and Social History Review* 24, 2 (1987), pp.117-44.

had very little information about ground-level reality. Even then, a very large fraction of the zamindari rights changed hands between the institution of the Bengal Settlement of 1793 and the close of the second decade of the nineteenth century.[25]

Market failures in the zamindari areas might have occurred on an even more extensive scale, but for two reasons. In some cases, at the time of the settlement itself, the British administrators recognised the structures of local power in which the prospective revenue-payers could be expected to realise that rent out of which they would pay the government's demand. Additionally, the British either legalised, or deliberately averted their eyes from, that exercise of power without responsibility which became the style of rural governance by the local magnates recognised by the British. The explicit recognition of the local structures of lineage and local political structures, while settling land revenues, comes out clearest in the case of Banaras when Jonathan Duncan as British Resident at the court of the Raja of Banaras introduced Permanent Settlement there.[26] Duncan recognised that 'corporate groups as well as individuals had landed rights' in these territories.[27] According to Cohn:

> Duncan wanted to collect the revenue from and to grant zamindari rights to what he termed the 'village zamindars' by which he meant those men in lineage territories or taluks who stood forward as leaders of the corporate body, or those individuals who could establish their rights to parts of villages or whole villages, either as grants from previous government or through tradition.[28]

Viewed from the standpoint of individual and exclusive property rights, a great deal of confusion resulted. Claims to shares were often based not on the rights alleged to be enjoyed by immediate ancestors but on the bases of those enjoyed by the ancestors of ancestors.[29] There were claims and counter-claims which had to be arbitrated by the British officers in charge or by a recognised leader of the locality, often on the basis of oral tradition only. These modes of settlement built into

[25] S. Islam, *The Permanent Settlement in Bengal: a study of its operation 1790-1819* (Dacca, 1979), chs. 5 and 6.

[26] B.S. Cohn, 'The initial British impact on India: a case study of the Benares region', *Journal of Asian Studies* XIX, 4 (1960) and 'Structural change in Indian rural society 1596-1885', in R.E. Frykenberg (ed.), *Land Control and Social Structure in Indian History* (Madison, 1969), pp.343-421 (both reprinted in Cohn, *Anthropologist among the Historians*).

[27] B.S. Cohn, 'Structural change', p.355.

[28] Ibid., p.356.

[29] See, for example, the case of the Raghubansi Rajputs of Dobhi taluk in ibid., p.357.

the power structure of superior land right-holders a bias towards traditional, pre-commercial and rather arbitrary modes of decision-making. They also led to the effective abrogation of the rights of inferior right-holders:

> No record of rights of subordinate members of proprietary groups was recorded. Internal division of the revenue obligation was left to be recorded by members themselves. No record of rights of permanent tenants and other tenants was kept, so that subordinate cultivators had no legal protection.[30]

Cohn has shown how some new groups acquired zamindari rights in the Banaras division—groups which were connected with Banaras rajas, or other influential Indian chiefs of the region, with some of the early British Residents and other British officers and, increasingly, with the British apparatus of revenue collection. In the process, one caste, namely the Rajputs, declined decisively as landholders. However, after the initial upheavals caused by British take-over, it is remarkable how stable the structure of landownership became and how effective banking, trade and subordinate offices under the British still remained as routes to acquisition of zamindaris and power until the beginning of the twentieth century.[31]

In the case of Bengal, the Regulation of 1790 was the real beginning of the Permanent Settlement and it required the revenue farmers to issue written undertakings (*pattah*) to tenants. However, in many cases, tenants, following earlier usage, claimed hereditary rights of occupancy, which the pattahs would deny to them. The pattahs also restricted their rights in other ways by increasing even their legal dues to extortionate levels. Intermediaries below the revenue-payers to the government used pattahs fraudulently to deprive the hereditary occupiers of their rights by entering their own or their family members' names in the pattahs. For all these reasons, probably the vast majority of the hereditary occupiers and cultivators failed to secure true records of rights and became mere tenants-at-will.[32] Under the new legal process instituted by the British, a single written document could overturn the information and judgment of a whole community, and these tenants-at-will had to fight for more than a century-and-a-half to get even a modicum of

[30] Ibid., pp.358-9.

[31] See in this connection H.R. Nevill, *Benares, a Gazetteer* (*District Gazetteers of the United Province of Agra and Oudh*, vol.xxvi; Allahabad, 1909), pp.113-23.

[32] B.B. Chowdhury, 'Agrarian Relationships in Bengal after the Permanent Settlement 1793-1819', unpublished D.Phil. thesis, Calcutta University, 1958, ch.3.

security of tenure.

The Permanent Settlement story of failure of markets and institutions that act as operative vehicles of markets did not end there. By Regulation VII of 1799, the government armed the zamindars with powers that bypassed that legal process, and allowed them to realise whatever they considered to be their dues from cultivators. As the Collector of Midnapore wrote in 1801, the demand for Regulation VII came from the zamindars who could now transmit the coercion exercised by the Company's officers down to the lowest level—that is to the cultivator or the actual occupier of the land.[33] The Bengal zamindars had already started creating various subordinate intermediate rights in order to facilitate the collection of the revenue. After the passing of Regulation VII, this process, and naturally the exploitative pressure on the tenant, were accentuated. Soon Bengal ended up with the score of layers of intermediaries and the hundreds of sharers in both the originally recognised zamindari rights, and the intermediary rights of later creation with which we are familiar.[34]

Thus the state in this case, in order to take care of a market failure, privatised part of the coercive powers that it claimed to monopolise. Such private coercive rights were also usurped by the European planters. In the districts dominated by the planters it was not always clear whether the district collector or the big planters were the real rulers of a particular district. All this did nothing to unshackle the market in the countryside. In the meantime, the deindustrialisation process, the failure of private accumulation and the decay of pre-British irrigation works in the Permanent Settlement areas enormously increased the pressure of a burgeoning population on the land.[35] But these same forces created a thriving market in various intermediary rights in land. That did not mean that 'land' became a free asset, because what was sold was bundles and fractions of claims to the produce of the land. Moreover, land remained the sole productive asset in many villages and the major anchor of social and political power, and in some cases, the sole instrument against the threat of pauperisation, bondage or exile. All kinds of non-market methods were used to obstruct transactions in claims to the rent or the produce of the land. Extremely unequal relations between creditors and debtors, and between the big buyers of produce and the peasant sellers prevailed. Thus pervasive dominance by a

[33] Ibid., pp.125-7.

[34] A.K. Bagchi, 'Relation of agriculture to industry in the context of South Asia', *Frontier* (Calcutta), 8, 22-24 (1975), pp.12-24.

[35] Ibid.

few big players allowed them to force the peasants to make their transactions in labour, produce, credit and land-rights in an interlinked manner.[36] Not surprisingly, the Permanent Settlement areas were characterised by endemic market failure. Although there were some respects in which the raiyatwari areas differed from the zamindari or taluqdari areas, market failure was as characteristic of the former as of the latter.[37]

Uncertainty, market failure and interlinkages of the credit, land and labour markets

In a society in which the majority of the people derive their livelihood from agriculture, the uncertainty faced by peasants plays a very important role in determining their relations with the rest of the society and the state, and in determining the form which market success or market failure takes. Conversely, the relations of peasants to landlords, to traders and moneylenders and to the state greatly influence the nature and degree of uncertainty faced by the peasant.

Except under highly unusual conditions, all cultivators face uncertainty in production—an uncertainty created by nature in the form of uncertain distribution of rainfall, uncertain levels and timing of inundation of rivers, uncertain incidence of floods and of pests. In the market for agricultural produce, peasants face uncertainty in prices: this uncertainty can in turn take the form of seasonal variations or annual changes. For poor peasants, the distinction between seasonal and longer-term changes often becomes meaningless, but for more substantial cultivators and landlords this distinction makes sense. In addition to price and production uncertainty, there is the influence of the land tenure system in determining the shape of things for the peasant. Does the peasant pay his tax in kind or in money? Does the payment depend on the state of the harvest or is it a fixed payment? If it is fixed, is it fixed in terms of produce or in terms of money? Does the payment become due at fixed times of the year? If it does, then the peasant may face a liquidity crisis even if he may be judged solvent in the long run. Are there other claims on the peasant's produce than those of the state? Are they themselves fixed or variable?

A typical Indian peasant would face this complex of uncertainties

[36] K. Bharadwaj, *Production Conditions in Indian Agriculture: a study based on Farm Management Surveys* (Cambridge, 1974), ch.1.

[37] For a more detailed discussion of one particular raiyatwari area from the point of view of peasant insecurity, peasant dependence and peasant resistance, see A.K. Bagchi, 'Land tax, property rights and peasant insecurity'.

under either a landlord system (zamindari or taluqdari) or a smallholder (raiyatwari) regime. But under the first perhaps the number of claimants to his produce other than the state would be larger. To simplify slightly, we will concentrate our attention entirely on the problems of a peasant ruled by a raiyatwari tenure.

The introduction of raiyatwari tenure in the Bombay Deccan, or in most parts of the Madras Presidency, did nothing to mitigate the risks faced by the peasant in respect of production. But by converting variable assessments into payments fixed in terms of money, the British regime enormously increased the variance of returns expected by the peasant.[38] When this was combined also with an increase in the mean share of produce claimed by the state, it led to a severe increase in the downside risk. In many areas the government had earlier granted production loans or advances (*taqavi*) to cultivators. The cessation or severe retrenchment of such advances under British rule led to a decline in supply of credit to the peasants exactly when the need for it increased.[39]

Borrowers and lenders in the market for credit to the peasantry, faced with such uncertain prospects, were caught up in problems of incomplete and asymmetric information, adverse selection and unequal bargaining power. Because of the risk of bankruptcy, a higher rate of interest offered by a prospective debtor is not necessarily an indicator of his/her better credit-worthiness. Since the principal and the interest rate cannot be the only variables characterising a loan, the quality and value of collateral acquire special significance in equilibrating the credit market.[40] Moreover, since the information about and assessment of risks faced by the debtor is bound to be different as between the debtor and the creditor, the equilibrium inevitably is characterised by credit rationing, the lender almost always extending a smaller loan than the debtor wants.[41] The creditor seeks to guard against loss through lack of information by extending his monitoring mechanism. This is one of the motivating factors behind the debt bondage so often observed in an extreme or a mild form in virtually all rural areas under

[38] Bagchi, 'Land tax, property rghts and peasant insecurity'.

[39] E. Whitcombe, *Agrarian Conditions in Northern India*, vol.I, *The United Provinces under British Rule 1860-1900* (California, 1972), p.161.

[40] C.F. Azzi and J.C. Cox, 'A theory and test of credit rationing: comment', *American Economic Review* 66, 5 (1976), pp.911-17; D.W. Jaffee and T. Russell, 'Imperfect information, uncertainty and credit rationing', *Quarterly Journal of Economics* 90, 4 (1976), pp.651-66.

[41] J.E. Stiglitz and A. Weiss, 'Credit rationing in markets with imperfect information', *American Economic Review* 71, 3 (1981), pp.393-410.

British rule. This monitoring may extend to surveillance over all the activities of the debtor—including his operations in the labour, produce and land markets. It is one of the structural bases of the interlinkages of markets we have already noted above. But the interlinkage of markets within these structural constraints is also an indication of the extreme inequality of economic and political power if, by political power, we denote all the relations of dominance in society which may have non-market coercion as their ultimate sanction.

Although this way of posing the problem has acquired academic currency only in recent years, the basic causes were known to many British administrators. Edward O'Brien, as Settlement Officer of Muzaffargarh in Punjab in 1878-79, came to the conclusion that the moneylenders had stepped into the position of pre-British (Sikh) governments, which had minutely superintended agriculture in the area, whereas the British government had failed to remedy the deficiency of landowners as farmers and managers.[42] Market failure and institutional failure were the joint progenitors of interlinked markets.

In the raiyatwari areas of Bombay Deccan, the British revenue officials realised the importance of moneylenders, both for tiding the raiyats over from one season to another, and for enabling government officials to collect the land revenue demands. In fact, for some years, the moneylenders had been recognised as sureties for realisation of the revenue from the peasants. During the years of depressed prices, with high assessment rates, the value of land as collateral was so low that the moneylenders had little incentive to sell up the raiyats for unrealised dues. The local moneylenders, or sowcars, initially depended more on their personal relationship with the peasants than on courts of law to realise their dues. Even then, out of a desire to protect the rights of peasants, some officials in the 1840s suggested revision of civil court procedure and the restriction of the right to transfer land through sale or mortgage.

With a rise in prices and a decline in the proportion of produce realised as land tax, the value of the land increased, and local moneylenders were increasingly replaced by outsiders. Hence the problem of alienation of land in settlement of debt assumed major proportions and received increasing official attention. In fact, the peasant tended to be subject to the moneylender's will in respect of the allocation of his own and his family's resources long before the land became formally alienated. In many cases a combination of usufructuary mortgage and share-

42 P.H.M. van den Dungen, *The Punjab Tradition: influence and authority in nineteenth-century India* (London, 1972), pp.126-7.

cropping yielded a better return to the creditor than the outright acquisition of the land would have done. As is well known, ultimately the dissatisfaction of the majority of peasants in Bombay exploded in the Deccan riots of 1875-76, and forced the government to pass the Deccan Agriculturists' Relief Act in 1879. The Act, *inter alia*, provided that the immovable property of the agriculturists

> should not be attached or sold in execution of a decree unless it had been specifically mortgaged and that even in such cases the court might direct the lands to be cultivated by the debtor for a number of years on behalf of the creditor, after which the debt was discharged.[43]

Many British administrators were dismayed alternately by the 'success' of markets, when the occupancy rights in land passed from less enterprising to more enterprising proprietors, and by market failures when the increased value of land as collateral merely strengthened the hold of the moneylender on the peasants without leading to agricultural improvement or peasant prosperity. This alternation led to interventions in the market process from the very beginning of conquest in at least one extensive territory, that is to say, the British Punjab (which comprised modern Punjab, Haryana and Himachal Pradesh in India, and most of Punjab and the North-West Province in Pakistan today). In that larger Punjab, as in other regions, just after British conquest, prices fell drastically.[44] Partly in response to this fall, and partly because of a protective attitude towards village communities (whether they really existed on the ground or not), the Board of Administration in Punjab prescribed a rule of pre-emption in 1892. The Board pointed out that 'the land... did not belong to the proprietor in an absolute sense, it was subject to land tax, and the Government had an undoubted right to prevent the deterioration of the revenue capacity of the village'.[45] The Board had already prohibited the practice of subletting villages for the purpose of discharging the revenue demand. In 1852, it was laid down that if, for any reason, land was alienated, it had first to be offered to a member of the village community at an equitable price according to a procedure outlined by the Board.[46] These protective rules were crystallised in the Punjab Civil Code of 1854. It empowered the courts to 'set aside unreasonable alienations (that is, alienations to spite heirs or

[43] R.C. Dutt, *The Economic History of India*, vol.2, *In the Victorian Age 1837-1890* (London, 1906; reprinted Delhi, 1963), p.241.

[44] B. Narain, *Indian Economic Life* (Lahore, 1929; reprint, Delhi, 1984), ch.6.

[45] Van den Dungen, *The Punjab Tradition*, p.43.

[46] Ibid., p.44.

relatives), if challenged by the aggrieved parties within the legal period';[47] it 'reiterated the rule of pre-emption in regard to permanent transfers of land'; and made it applicable to 'the sale of land for debt in execution of decrees'.

The Punjab case illustrates that the introduction of transferable property rights in land (however fragmented and conditional they might be) by the British had been from the very beginning hedged about with restrictions introduced for the sake of long-term stability of revenue demand and of social structure. Village communities were virtually invented, especially in the trans-Indus districts; restrictions on transferability were transferred from Hindu law into Muslim law which had not recognised such restrictions earlier.

After 1866, when the general Code of Civil Procedure was introduced into Punjab and the post of the Judicial Commissioner was replaced by the institution of the Chief Court, difficulties arose about the interpretation of the rule of pre-emption and the procedures to be followed in reviewing compulsory sales in satisfaction of land revenue demand or in execution of decrees for settlement debt. But these problems and the resulting debates did not overturn the rules of pre-emption.[48] There was a pause in government intervention in the land market between the 1870s and the 1890s. But during the pause opinion grew stronger, with the opponents of such opinion losing ground, for further restrictions on transfer of land rights. In particular, it came to be a matter of policy severely to constrain voluntary transfers of land. In the debates that sprawled across the reports of Settlement Officers, Deputy Commissioners, Revenue and Financial Commissioners and Lieutenant-Governors, particular conceptions of the characteristics of castes and communities figure prominently. The fates of the 'improvident' Meo caste and the 'proud and unproductive' Rajputs (who could be either Hindus or Muslims), the sturdy Jats, 'the crafty' but enterprising Khatris were all sought to be weighed by a new all-embracing piece of legislation. Thus was born the Punjab Alienation of Land Act, which came into force in June 1901.

As Bhattacharya, Fox and others have pointed out,[49] there were

[47] Ibid., p.47.

[48] Ibid., chs. 2 and 3.

[49] N. Bhattacharya, 'The logic of tenancy cultivation: central and south-east Punjab', *Indian Economic and Social History Review* 20, 2 (1983), pp.121-50, and 'Agricultural labour and production: central and south-east Punjab 1870-1940', in K.N. Raj *et al.*. (eds.), *Essays on the Commercialization of Indian Agriculture* (Delhi, 1985); R.G. Fox, 'British colonialism and Punjabi labour', in C. Bergquist (ed.), *Labour in the Capitalist World Economy* (New Delhi,

regional as well as local differences among the peasants and landowners in Punjab. Different communities had different attitudes to manual work in the fields, and average members of particular communities enjoyed different statuses: some were almost fated to be agricultural labourers, and some could not earn their living through honest sweat even if they were pauperised. However, members of 'respectable' peasant castes often joined the ranks of 'peasant proletarians',[50] that is, small peasants in the Lenin-Mao characterisation of rural classes.[51] Some Khatri moneylenders or traders had become landlords even before the British advent, and many Muslim landlords themselves became moneylenders to their share-croppers and to other landowners. The British imposed a set of administrative imperfections of their own or market failures that had been caused by the multiple sources of uncertainty faced by peasants, by pre-capitalist status rankings, and by the inequality of bargaining power caused by inequality of asset distribution. This administratively engineered interference in an imperfect market mechanism may or may not have arrested depeasantisation. But arresting depeasantisation was only a means to an end—that of finding a local political constituency among landowners and their dependent peasantry. It is possible that in soliciting a greater degree of loyalty among the landowners, the British might have exacerbated their brewing conflict with urban traders and bankers.[52] The political stance of the administrators of the British Punjab at the end of the nineteenth century showed that British officials had very largely shifted their expectation of a natural support base among the traders and bankers to that among the landlords and the dependent peasants. As the functioning of markets changed, so did the social basis of authority exercised by the British, although, of course, the shift was not uniform in all parts of the country.

In Punjab, the British went further than merely to bolster a landowning gentry and the upper stratum of peasant proprietors. In the canal colonies they effectively created a new class of landlords. That operation went hand in hand with the extraction of an ever larger revenue from the land, especially that which had the benefit of irrigation from

---

1984), pp.107-34.

[50] N. Bhattacharya, 'Agricultural labour and production', pp.120-4.

[51] A.K. Bagchi, *The Political Economy of Underdevelopment* (Cambridge, 1982), ch.6.

[52] Cf. the critique of the Punjab Land Alienation Act by Hubert John Maynard, a high-ranking British official, before and soon after the Act was passed, as summarised by van den Dungen, *The Punjab Tradition*, pp.287-95.

government irrigation works[53] It is difficult to maintain that unfettered operation of competitive market forces took precedence over either the extraction of a remittable surplus, or over the maintenance of a support base for imperium even in the high noon of empire in India, long after the phase of mercantile control had passed in the metropolis.

British rule as awesome theatre, and the price of distancing, discrimination and landlord consolidation

All rule involves theatre, including democratic rule, as anybody who watched the performance of Ronald Reagan as President of the United States can vouchsafe. But some theatre is more awesome than others, and some theatre involves more pomp and circumstance than others. The theatre of rule also involves careful management of the distance between the watchers and the actors. The British administrators who came to India, habituated as they were to the ways of 'gentlemanly capitalism',[54] and as agents of a mercantile organisation owing its birth to that same compromise that legitimised the landlord oligarchy of the eighteenth century, were well used to the nuances of the theatricality of public rule.[55] If Richard Wellesley, the 'glorious little man' inspired awe among his subordinates and naturally among the Indian subjects of the East India Company by his pomp, aggressiveness and the hauteur of the local court he created (he was the builder of the first government palace in Calcutta), he was creature enough of his society to mind terribly when he was fobbed off with a mere Irish marquisate. (Of course he would be even more galled when his younger brother rose to the dignity of a ducal seat.)

We have fortunately a very clear account of the strategies used by the more far-seeing British conquerors and rulers for creating distance but also instilling a sense of the British superiority in character (and hence in claims to the right to rule over Indians) in the instructions issued by John Malcolm to officers serving under him in 1821.[56] Mal-

[53] Imran Ali, *The Punjab under Imperialism, 1885-1947* (Delhi, 1989), ch.5.

[54] P.J. Cain and A.G. Hopkins, 'Gentlemanly capitalism and British expansion overseas. I. The old colonial system 1688-1850', *Economic History Review*, XXXIX, 4 (1986), pp.501-25.

[55] For an analysis of oligarchic governance in eigthteenth-century England as theatre, see E.F. Thompson, 'The patricians and the plebs', pp.43-7.

[56] J. Malcolm, 'Sir John Malcom's Instruction and Orders to Officers: Instruction by Major-general Sir John Malcolm, G.C.B., K.L.S., to Officers acting under his Orders in Central India, in 1821', Appendix VIII, in J. Malcolm, *The Political History of India (1784-1823)* Vol.2 (London, 1826; reprinted in edition edited by K.N. Panikkar, New Delhi, 1970, pp.307-407).

colm appreciated that want of union among the Indians was 'one of the strongest foundations' of British power. He also foresaw that the reduction of Indians to the common yoke of British rule was likely to make them 'more accessible to common motives of action'.[57] According to him, while British power had so far 'owed much to a contrast with misrule and oppression', this strength was daily diminishing. Moreover, 'we have also been indebted to an indefinite impression of our resources, originating in ignorance of their real extent; knowledge will bring his feeling to a reduced standard'.[58] Malcolm wanted due respect to be paid to Indian perceptions of rank and authority:

Though it is essential, in our intercourse with natives who are attached to and give value to ceremonies, to understand such perfectly, and to claim from all what is due to our station, that we may not sink the rank of the European superior in the estimation of those subject to his control; it is now the duty of the former to be much more attentive to the respect which he gives them than what he receives, particularly in his intercourse with men of high rank. The princes and chiefs of India may, in different degrees, be said to be all dependent on the British government; many have little more than the name of that power they have enjoyed; but they seem, as they lose the substance, to cling to the forms of station. The pride of reason may smile at such a feeling; but it exists, and it would be alike opposite to the principles of humanity and policy to deny it gratification.[59]

The elements of oriental pomp and the style of the British landlord oligarchy were being mixed and remixed in different proportions throughout the period of British rule long before Lytton's apotheosis of Queen Victoria as the Empress of India, and long after the world had been treated to the spectacle of a 'naked fakir' sitting down at the same table as gentlemen who knew the proper attire for every hour of the day. But the maintenance of British power was not simply a matter of theatre. Might had to be demonstrated occasionally by blowing a score of Indian sepoys off the mouth of a cannon, by spectacularly finishing off the last mansion (*haveli*) of a recalcitrant chief, or publicly hanging the adult males of a whole hamlet when the need arose. There were other ways of demonstrating British might, as King Thibaw knew to his cost, and as Sayaji Rao II was made to realise through his humiliating treatment after an imagined slight to the 'durbared' Emperor of India.

The distancing, of course, had its material aspects: the high and mighty had to be maintained at a far higher cost than their servitors. This was emphasised as a principle during the Cornwallis reforms, and

57 Ibid., p.378.
58 Ibid., p.377.
59 Ibid., p.389.

this became ingrained in every cell of the structure of British authority in all spheres of life. For instance, around 1795, whereas the 77 Indian employees in the Banaras district court together earned Rs.1,020 per month, the salary of the sole British judge presiding over the court was Rs.2,200 per month.[60] Again, when the Bank of Bengal started functioning in 1809, the salary of the British secretary and treasurer was Rs.800 per month, that of the highest paid Indian employee, the cash-keeper (*khazanchee*) (no less a person than Raja Ramachandra Roy, great-grandson of Clive's financier, Naku Dhar) was Rs.300, and the aggregate pay of the rest of the Indian staff together was Rs.500 per month.[61] The disparity in the salaries of Europeans and Indians did not change before the First World War. For example, in 1878, whereas the three principal European officers of the Bank of Bengal drew an aggregate salary of Rs.5,833 per month, the total wages of the Indian staff of the cash-keeper's department were Rs.4,224-8 per month. The secretary and treasurer alone drew Rs.2,600 per month; and if we exclude the salary of Rs.1,200 drawn by the khazanchee, the total of 112 employees in his department drew Rs.3,024-8 per month.[62] Keeping the Europeans in their noble positions had its economic costs. For example, down to 1878 (and I suspect, in many cases, even afterwards) European brokers were paid twice the fee paid to Indian brokers for government securities bought and sold. The 'taste for discrimination' exacted its toll by keeping technically and businesswise better-qualified people out of many occupations. Eventually, as Indian businessmen penetrated European preserves, the taste could no longer be so freely indulged in. The wonder is not that European dominance of Indian large-scale business crumbled in many sectors after the First World War; the surprising part is that it did not crumble much earlier.

The explanation for this delay would have to be sought in the enormous importance of government patronage, the interlocking nature of British domination of higher administration and large-scale business, the ideological hegemony imposed on Indian educated opinion by British imperium, and the sluggishness of accumulation produced by the haemorrhage of colonial remittance overseas. The last two factors had a major impact in shaping Indian society and technology, and hence their influence can be still traced in post-colonial India.

60 B.S. Cohn, 'The initial British impact on India', p.330.

61 A.K. Bagchi, *The Evolution of the State Bank of India*, pt.I. The modal salary of an Indian employee was around Rs.10 per month.

62 A.K. Bagchi, *The Presidency Banks and the Indian Economy 1876-1914* (Calcutta, 1989), p.23, and internal records of the Bank of Bengal.

I have argued elsewhere that the imposition of the imperial view that Britain led the world in every sphere on educated Indian opinion and, of course, on British businessmen and technologists working in India, had harmful consequences for Indian technological development.[63] In the cotton textile industry, not only did the policy of 'one-way free trade' and the discriminatory treatment of Indian spinning and weaving mills hamper accumulation; by persuading mill managers to install obsolete and technologically inappropriate mule spindles in Indian mills long after they had been discarded in Japan, the USA and most countries of continental Europe, the ideology of 'British is best' hobbled the Indian cotton mills more or less permanently in their competition with their new rivals from the early 1900s, namely the Japanese cotton textile industry.

The distancing and discrimination practised by members of the expatriate British community had discernible real costs for the economy as a whole. The virtual monopolisation of the management of all joint-stock banking by Europeans for most of the nineteenth century meant that most Indian business was denied credit on terms which were granted to large-scale European business, unless the particular Indian group had powerful European collaborators. For example, Nursey, Kessowjee & Co. was supported in their loan applications to the (New) Bank of Bombay by the direction of W. Nicol & Co. long after both the groups had become bankrupt.[64]

There was a double gap in the information flows between European-controlled banks and their Indian customers: the ordinary Indians, or even Indian businessmen, were badly informed about the business affairs of the powerful European constituents of, say, the Bank of Bengal, the Bank of Bombay, or Arbuthnot & Co., especially if the major part of the Europeans' business happened to be located abroad. Correspondingly, the bank managements were badly informed about the business affairs of Indians. The managements could generally pass on their losses to the Indian guarantors or collaborators of bankrupt firms. The Indians had no such remedy, and suffered very badly through the failures of the major agency houses in Bengal in the 1830s, the failures of the mushroom banks of the North-Western Provinces in the 1840s and 1850s, the failures of W. Nicol & Co. and Finlay Scott & Co. in 1878-79, and Arbuthnot & Co. in 1906. Only perhaps in the case of the fail-

63 A.K. Bagchi, 'Colonialism and the nature of "capitalist" enterprise in India', in G. Shah (ed.), *Capitalist Development: Critical Essays* (Bombay, 1990), pp.45-76.

64 Bagchi, *The Presidency Banks and the Indian Economy*, p.190.

ure of the Bank of Bombay in 1867 were the responsibilities and the losses of the Europeans and the Indians evenly distributed.

There is yet another area in which racially-based discrimination probably had real effects on the economy. Practically all Indians were excluded from technical and supervisory positions in British firms and most public technical organisations. In modern parlance, no amount of signalling by Indians acquiring superior education could get them past the barriers manned by uninformed British management. All Indians were pushed below a threshold level, and a pooling equilibrium ruled with all higher levels of technical and supervisory work being entrusted to less-qualified Europeans.[65]

Market failures of this kind were perhaps inevitable given the prevailing structure of unequal economic interdependence of the world economy and the structure of power implicit in colonial rule. But the colonial authorities adopted other measures directed at social and economic engineering even in the period since the 1870s, and these measures freshly clogged up the market mechanism in distinct ways, even as they created new channels for the market forces to flow into. One major illustration of this development is the social engineering practised by the British authorities in the canal colonies. The network of canals constructed by the British in Punjab and Sind from the 1880s added largely to the land revenue of the region (thus belying the claim that land revenue declined very significantly as a source of tribute for the empire). Moreover, the irrigation works were themselves, with the sole exception of Upper Jhelum Canal, enormously profitable, especially from the 1920s.[66] Instead, however, of settling the colonies with working peasants (on the pattern, say, of the settlements under the U.S. Homestead Act of 1862), the British deliberately created a layer of landlords in the canal colonies, and these landlords were distinguished both by caste and by class from others. Whereas the peasant grantees belonged to such castes as Jat, Arain, Kamboh, Saini, the larger grantees (those with grants of 50 acres or above) were Rajputs, Qureshis, Sayyids and Gujars.[67] Inevitably, this spawned a whole congeries of intermediary formations familiar in older, landlord-dominated regions —such as managers or lessees of absentee landlords, revenue farmers

[65] For a discussion of pooling equilibrium in markets characterised by asymmetric information, see D.M. Kreps, 'Out-of-equilibrium beliefs and out-of-equilibrium behaviour', in F. Hahn (ed.), *The Economics of Missing Markets, Information, and Games* (Oxford), pp.7-45.

[66] Imran Ali, *The Punjab under Imperialism, 1885-1947*, pp.162-3.

[67] Ibid., p.73.

acting as agents of landlords—and, of course, all types of dependent peasantry and workforce.[68] Thus, through all the changes in structures of authority during the two centuries of British rule, certain social formations continued to be reproduced through the very working of the colonial system—depressing accumulation and generating flows of distorted information—and through deliberate policy measures.

Capitalist colonialism works by introducing and exploiting markets. But the structure of colonial power is essentially political and not just a passive reflection of imperatives dictated by an impersonal market. Hence, market failures—deliberately engineered or systematically generated—are as much a component of the working of the system as market successes. Contradictions of capitalist colonialism expressed as market failures have been too little studied so far; hence I have concentrated on the failures rather than on the successes. A fuller account will have to deal with their interaction as a dynamic or dialectical process unfolding through history.

[68] Ibid., chs.2, 5 and 6.

Chapter 4

POTENTATES, TRADERS AND PEASANTS: WESTERN INDIA, c.1700-1870

Sumit Guha

Introduction

The controversy around eighteenth-century Indian history initiated by the publication of Bayly and intensified after the appearance of Wink's work, bears, among other things, on the nature and fate of towns and trade in the eighteenth and early nineteenth centuries.[1] Nevertheless, Irfan Habib has reiterated his understanding that the extensive urbanisation and lively commerce of the Mughal empire depended essentially on the circulation of the economic surplus that the state extracted from the natural economy of the village by coercive means—and the rise of zamindar-led agrarian resistance was inevitably followed by the decline of towns and trade.

> The towns and their commerce were then entirely dependent on the system of state-enforced agrarian exploitation.... When the breakdown occurred, and the centralised despotism collapsed, towns and trade inevitably suffered.[2]

This implies that the relation between village and city was a purely tributary one—there was no reciprocal exchange of goods and services between the two. Specialisation of function and exchange occurred within the urban economy, but the villages had no part in this—they grew impoverished but remained self-sufficient, receiving little or nothing from the urban economy sustained by their surpluses.

As against this, David Ludden takes the view that the commercial economy had independent origins, though

> States played active roles in India's pre-colonial agrarian economies, but development generated by workers and investors at key places in the countryside produced the commercial economy that states tapped for revenue and which

[1] C.A. Bayly, *Rulers, Townsmen and Bazaars: North Indian society in the age of British expansion* (Cambridge, 1983); A. Wink, *Land and Sovereignty in India: agrarian society and politics under the eighteenth-century Maratha Svarajya* (Indian edn. Hyderabad, 1986).

[2] Irfan Habib, 'Classifying pre-colonial India', in H. Mukhia and T.J. Byres (eds.), *Feudalism and non-European Societies* (London, 1985), esp. pp.48-9.

they portrayed in scattered and fragmentary but consistent bodies of evidence.[3]

The Marathas and the British were obviously the most important of the successors to the Mughals, and this paper addresses the issue of the relations between state and market as well as town and country in western India over the eighteenth and nineteenth centuries. It discusses attitudes and policies towards commerce, long-run trends in the commercial economy, functional relations between town and village, and the pattern of settlement resulting from these.

Maratha markets

Satish Chandra has recently suggested that the Marathas retarded urbanisation, and their territory was characterised by a low level of urbanisation and a poorly-developed artisanal base.[4] Marathi documents, however, do not support this view. The *Ajnapatra*, the celebrated treatise on statecraft attributed to the minister Ramachandra Pant, and dated to the beginning of the eighteenth century, devotes a whole chapter to a eulogy of the importance of traders and bankers to the state.

> Sahukars are ornaments of the realm. By them the kingdom is made prosperous and populous. Goods otherwise unavailable are brought by them. The kingdom becomes rich. They advance money during crises and the crises are overcome. Extending protection to sahukars brings great advantages (to the king). Therefore they should be honoured, and on no account must they be oppressed or insulted.... Foreign sahukars should be induced to come and settle. If it is not convenient for them to come, tempt them to at least send their agents and give them shops in suitable places.[5]

By itself, this evidence is not sufficient: the gap between prescription and practice existed in eighteenth-century as in twentieth-century India. But there is substantial documentary evidence that both rulers and gentry shared Ramachandra Pant's perception of the profitability of encouraging trade and protecting *sahukars*. Thus Chandrarao More of the famous Javli family assured the *shete-mahajans* and merchants of Shirale *kasba* in his *jagir* that if they lost even a piece of hemp, he would replace it with a chain of gold.[6]

[3] David Ludden, 'Agrarian commercialism in eighteenth-century South India', *Indian Economic and Social History Review*, XXV (4) 1988, p.495.

[4] Satish Chandra, 'Some aspects of Urbanisation in medieval India', in I. Banga (ed.), *The City in Indian History* (Delhi, 1991).

[5] S.N. Banhatti (ed.), *Ajnapatra Arthat Shivajirajanchi Rajniti* (Nagpur and Pune, 1961), pp.33-4.

[6] Cited in A.R. Kulkarni, 'Business under the Marathas (seventeenth cen-

Rhetorical flourishes apart, the establishment of new *peths*, or market towns, and the expansion of existing ones was actively pursued by petty gentry and great nobles alike in the eighteenth century. As early as 1706, when the Maratha regime had but a tenuous hold on west Maharashtra, Pilaji, son of Changoji Jadhav, purchased a half-share of the *patilki* right to an undistinguished village, Nanded, near Khadakvasla in the western part of Pune district, for the not inconsiderable sum of Rs.500. Four years later, he had the transaction verified by an assembly of the notables of the regions, and secured a declaratory testament (*mahzar*) in his favour, and then secured a royal order of confirmation from Shahu Chatrapati, spending no less than Rs.770 for the latter. Sambaji, brother of Pilaji, then decided to improve the family property by establishing a new peth there, and in 1714 secured a royal order exempting it from taxes for four years in order to encourage the settlers. Three years later, another royal order bestowed on Sambaji the traditional hereditary *shetki* and *mahajanki* property (*watans*) in the new peth, on payment of Rs.150. Substantial additional expenditure must have been incurred in gathering the notables and hereditary officials of Pune, Saswad and other places to witness and confirm this award. Finally, since the tax exemption was due to lapse, the *shet*'s dues now had to be fixed, and the notables (*gotsabha*) decided that they should be the same as in the oldest peth of Pune, or Kasba Pune, and an attested list of these was brought from that town.[7] The Jadhavs thus went to no small trouble and expense over their new peth, and they clearly expected substantial gains from this enterprise.

The Purandare family provides another instance of local gentry interest in the establishment and management of peths. Dhondo Malhar Purandare held half the patilki watan of Vadule, a village in Shevgaon subdivision. In 1769 he issued an assurance to all the Marvadis and traders frequenting the place that a low, fixed transit duty would be levied there. By 1784, the village (*mauza*) Vadule Kurd had gained in prosperity, and was described as a new peth. The question of the dues of the *patil*, *kulkarni*, shete and mahajan now arose. Possibly in order to avoid alienating the new settlers, a letter was written to the officials of a nearby, older peth, Arapur, to ask them to send a detailed, itemised

---

tury', p.9, of paper presented at a seminar on 'State and Business in India: an historical perspective', I.I.M., Ahmadabad, 1984.

[7] Based on the following documents: Appasaheb Pawar (ed.), *Tarabaikalin Kagadpatre—Khand Pahila* (Kolhapur, 1969), docs.175, 224-7, and 293; G.S. Sardesai (ed.), *Selections from the Peshwa Daftar* (Bombay, 1933), vol.31, no.187.

account of dues collected in their market, describing both the rate and manner of collection.

Lesser claimants were not permitted to disturb a Purandare-established mart. Dhondo Pant had issued a *kaul* (deed) granting certain exemptions to settlers in Murti, where he intended to establish a new peth. A *watandar* claiming certain dues by virtue of holding the office of *gauda*, was told that such claims had been suspended for the period of the kaul, and he also had to wait till it expired.

The settlers of Vadule enjoyed their exemptions for a remarkable period: in 1832 we find them being informed that they had been exempt from the tax called *motarfa* since its founding, but they would now have to pay Rs.25.[8]

The *Ajnapatra* had advised the ruler to levy ransom on merchants in the enemy country, but also to treat them well, and entertain them upon release, the object being to induce them to settle in the kingdom.[9] The numerous local chiefs who contended for power in north Karnatak in the beginning of the nineteenth century may never have seen this text, but conformed to its suggestions. Marshall remarked that petty Desais set up as 'Master Robbers', but were also much given to establishing market-towns. The Desai of Jamboti had founded two; and the formidable Kittur chief set up Nandgarh in around 1813. The last was the only place in Khanapur *taluka* where moneylending sahukars were to be found. The Kitturkar levied heavy fines and tributes from merchants and artisans outside his territory to induce them to settle there; if they came, they were exempt from taxes for nine years. Unchecked and violent competition could, of course, have very destructive effects: thus in Hungunda *pargana* of 106 villages, three new markets had been founded in the past since 1785, but six had been utterly deserted.[10]

Agricultural investment

But did all this merely signify that the surplus squeezed out of the self-sufficient village was flowing briskly in Maharashtra? Did the village and its production have no connection with the fairs held in its vicinity, or with the pack bullocks and carts playing across its lands, as Habib's

[8] This paragraph is based on R.V. Oturkar (ed.), *Peshvekalin Samajik va Arthik Patravyavahar* (Pune, 1950), docs.103, 106, 109 and 121.

[9] Banhatti (ed.), *Ajnapatra*, p.35.

[10] Thomas Marshall, *Statistical Reports on the Pergunnahs of Padshapoor, Belgaum, Kalaniddee and Chandgurh, Khanapur, Balgakot and Badamy and Hoongoond in the Southern Maratha Country* (Bombay, 1822), pp.56, 71 and 96-7.

argument would imply? Was the *Ajnapatra's* reference to the kingdom being populated by the sahukar mere mercantilist rhetoric?

There are indications that this was not so. When the Peshwa Madhavrao I wished to restore the prosperity of the country around Pune—recently ravaged by the Nizam's armies—one of the measures taken was the waiver of customs dues in Pune till Dasahra 1764. Rice, salt and provisions coming from the Konkan which had escaped the ravages of war were not to be taxed, because the peasants had been stripped of their stocks during the recent disturbances and would come to Pune to purchase these articles. No dues were to be taken from them; but professional traders should still be made to pay. Furthermore, many peasants had lost their cattle, and would buy new animals in Pune, and they were not to be pressed to pay the sales tax on these (*shingoti*). We may also speculate on where the peasants, who are described as having been plundered and stripped (*kunbi lutle*, *nagavle*), got the money for these purchases—it is difficult to believe that the sahukars and mahajans did not advance at least some of it.

Nor was the flow of urban resources into land necessarily confined to periods of crisis: in 1770/1, a *shiledar* cavalryman purchased farm bullocks worth Rs.130 in Pune, and was sufficiently influential to get them exempted from transit dues en route to his village, which is why a record of this survives.[11] Linkages of this type were far from uncommon, particularly among the Chitpavan Brahmans who supplied much of the administrative manpower of the Peshwa's regime. We may take the modestly prosperous, second-ranking Pendse lineage as an example. They were Konkanasth Brahmans who diversified into soldiering (one died at Panipat), clerkship, priestcraft, medicine and *savakari*, while one branch became hereditary mahajans of Murudi in the Konkan. They owned fields and house-plots in various villages, and we find one Abaji Ballal Pendse investing some Rs.800 to reclaim eight bighas from the sea in 1789, and receiving a kaul promising a reduced rate of taxation for a certain period, as well as hereditary right to the land reclaimed.[12]

Nor does it seem that the rural elite were the only participants in the market system: the lists of commodities to be taxed in even the modest rural mart of Nanded suggest fairly wide access to the market. The document specifies the dues payable by greengrocers, sellers of bananas, lemons and grapes, by sellers of *pan* (*tambolis*), by butchers and

[11] G.C. Vad *et al.* (eds.), *Selections from the Satara Rajas' and Peshwas' Diaries: Madhavrao I*, pt.2 (Pune, 1911), p.68.

[12] This is based on the narrative and documents in K.V. Pendse, *Pendse Kula-Vrittanta* (Pune, 1938), pp.19-69.

grocers (*bakal*), by sellers of sugarcane, by weavers, bangle-makers, oil-pressers, tailors and shoemakers, among others.[13] Some of this may have been anticipation rather than reality, but tailors in some number were certainly present in Nanded by 1730, when a dispute arose about the allocation of stalls during an annual fair held at the nearby town of Saswad. The order settling the quarrel allotted five stalls in one row to the tailors (*simpi*) from Nanded: as many as those allotted to Pune men.[14]

Certain commodities seem certainly to have entered popular consumption. When the Peshwa hired five carpenters (skilled men, paid Rs.17 to 20 a month), they were given provisions by the state. Interestingly, apart from the ordinary necessities such as rice, wheat, dal and salt, they received a *ser* of ghee, a quarter-ser of supari, and a quarter-ser of tobacco per month, as well as 280 pan leaves of the cheaper green variety.[15] Pan certainly seems to have become a widely consumed commodity, so much so that the office of pan-seller (tamboli) had been established as hereditary watan in many villages. So, for example, we find one Kasim, son of Baji, being assured of the uninterrupted enjoyment of his tamboli watan along with its house-plot in the village (mauza) of Garade, near Pune, subject to the payment of Rs.2 a year, and the free supply of 50 pan daily to the local authorities.[16]

Tobacco had entered popular consumption by 1748/9, when we find the wholesale monopoly of it in the two parganas of Sashti (Salsette) and Atganv being farmed to Ramji Shivaji Prabhu for Rs.8,501 a year. He was not permitted to monopolise the retail trade, being peremptorily forbidden from selling to the raiyats, and enjoined to sell solely to sahukars and traders at the fixed price of Rs.5.5 a man. If a village had no shop, then he might sell to its raiyats in bulk—upwards of half a man at a time.[17]

But the best evidence of the entry of exotic commodities into village consumption is to be found in the list of goods available in the shops of Loni village in 1819, compiled by the British surgeon, Thomas Coats.[18]

Loni was no entrepôt, being merely a village of 557 inhabitants, twelve miles distant from Pune, and it is likely that its five shops

13 G.S. Sardesai (ed.), *Selections*, vol.31, no.187.
14 R.V. Oturkar (ed.), *Patravyavahara*, no.97.
15 G.C. Vad *et al.* (eds.), *Diaries: Madhavrao I*, pt.2, pp.66-7.
16 R.V. Oturkar (ed.), *Patravyavahara*, no.63.
17 G.C. Vad *et al.* (eds.), *Diaries: Balaji Baji Rao*, pt.I, pp.324-5.
18 Thomas Coats, 'Account of the present state of the Township of Lony', in *Transactions of the Literary Society of Bombay*, vol.III (1823), esp. p.222.

catered chiefly to its own inhabitants. Coats writes:

The following is a list of some of the many articles that are sold in the shops: All the kinds of grain and common cloths worn by the inhabitants, clarified butter, sugar fine and coarse, turmeric, almonds, dates dry and moist, gum arabic, asafoetida, cummin-seed, ginger, cherita a fine bitter, cocoa-nut, mustard, coriander seed, soap, poppy seed, blue vitriol, arsenic, alkaline salts, catechu, honey, camphor, cloves, cardamom-seeds, nutmeg, mace, saffron. musk, salt, bhang, opium, wax, castor-oil and seeds, cowitch, quicksilver, brimstone, saltpetre, paper and ink, sal-ammoniac, senna-leaves a species of, a salt of mercury like corrosive sublimate.

These were not newly-introduced commodities in west Maharashtra: many of them were sufficiently widely traded to be carefully listed in a document specifying the rates of customs duty in the later seventeenth century; among the items included were various drugs and poisons, and the more familiar nutmeg, a special mango-flavoured turmeric, asafoetida, opium, black pepper, sugar, gur and molasses, dried green dates, tamarind, areca nut, turmeric, the homely onion, garlic and dried coconut, as well as truly exotic luxuries such as musk and the scent gland of the civet cat![19]

Commercial trends

This paper has so far looked essentially at qualitative evidence. It seems clear that an active commercial economy generating considerable profits and taxes existed in the Western Deccan in the early eighteenth century, and the opportunities were sufficient to attract immigrant merchant groups—such as the Gujarati and Marwadi—into the area. The seigneurial dues generated from commerce and manufacture were sufficiently large to attract the attention of petty village magnates, intermediate chiefs and zamindars, and rulers such as the Bhonslas, Gaikwads and successive Peshwas themselves. Finally, we have evidence that the commercial economy was not exclusively a supra-village phenomenon: men, goods and funds moved in both directions in response to opportunities for profit and chances of investment.

But purely qualitative information cannot easily tell us of trends within the system over time. Was the resource base expanding or shrinking? The furious scramble for the dues and profits of trade might in fact destroy or erode the base from which they were generated, especially as central authority, that might set bounds on the methods

[19] *Bhatara Itihasa Samshodhaka Mandala Quarterly*, XX, 4 (1940), pp.157-8.

employed, was weakened in the early nineteenth century. Perhaps what we observe are not successful political entrepreneurs and portfolio capitalists, but the throws of desperate players trapped in a succession of negative-sum games, where the aggregate losses exceed the aggregate gains in each round and the pool shrinks as the players become more desperate and violent in their play.

This is not a scenario that can be ruled out *a priori*, and the leading historian of Mughal India, Irfan Habib, has presented a somewhat similar picture of the agrarian crisis that ended the Mughal empire, a downward spiral of decline initiated by excessive demands on the rural economy. Nor are acid comments on the misrule, rapine and ruin consequent on Maratha rule lacking—especially in the English sources. However, issues such as commercial expansion or decline are essentially quantitative in nature, and need to be addressed by quantitative sources; these are both scanty and unreliable—but the issue is important enough to warrant the attempt.

Collections from octroi and transit dues (*zakat*) afford some indication of the state of trade. In 1774/5, the zakat of Pune and Junner was farmed for Rs.35,000 annually to Dhanshet Karje.[20] Twenty years later, the Peshwa Madhavrao I renewed the zakat farm at a concessional rate, since the farmer claimed to have suffered losses during the Nizam's invasion. So he now received a four-year contract, with the amount payable increasing each year to reach one *lakh* in the fourth year, or 1768/9. Despite containing the capital, Pune-Junner was not the most active trading area in the Peshwa's dominions: the five-year contract for Kalyan-Bhivandi (modern Thana), stipulated a total payment of 15 lakhs over the whole period, to be collected at 85 specified *nakas* (checkpoints).[21] The last Peshwa, Bajirao II was bedevilled by internal resistance and external interference, but, by Elphinstone's estimate, still received some 5 lakhs yearly from the transit dues around 1816,[22] despite the exemption given to British goods. The British administration withdrew this exemption and tightened administrative control, though they periodically exempted items such as grain and firewood from zakat.[23] In 1827/8, their collections from Bajirao's former territory amounted to about 10 lakhs, despite a 30 to 40 per cent fall in prices. The British Pune collectorate—approximately the same area as

[20] G.C. Vad *et al.* (eds.), *Diaries: Balaji Baji Rao*, pt.I, pp.310-12.

[21] G.C. Vad *et al.* (eds.), *Diaries: Madhavrao I*, pt.2, pp.74-5 and 84-5.

[22] M. Elphinstone, *Report on the Territories Conquered from the Paishwa* (Bombay, 1872), p.29.

[23] See R.D. Choksey (ed.), *The Period of Transition* (Pune, 1945), p.59.

former Pune and Junner—paid Rs.241,000, while transit dues, wood-cutting fees, liquor licences and ferry fees in Thana yielded three to four lakhs.[24] The evidence certainly does not support the notion of a breakdown in commerce during the 'time of troubles' at the beginning of the nineteenth century, or even of stagnation in trade under Maratha rule.

But even if the level of commercial activity increased under Maratha rule, had it shrunk since the heyday of the Mughals, as Habib's argument would suggest? Comparisons of absolute levels are fraught with many difficulties, but we may perhaps compare the relative importance of land and other revenues at different points in time. Shireen Moosvi estimates that 15.7 per cent of the revenue of sarkar Agra at the end of the sixteenth century was from non-agricultural sources;[25] while in 1827/8, in Pune collectorate *sahyer* plus zakat accounted for 23.7 per cent of the revenues, even after the Peshwa had left for Bithur, and Pune city lost from a fifth to a tenth of its inhabitants; in the four collectorates of the Deccan as a whole, non-agricultural taxes came to 17.2 per cent of the total.[26] The comparison is tentative, but clearly does not support the view that the fall of the Mughals led to an agrarianisation of the economy and the relative decline of towns and trade.

Key places in the countryside

The pattern of peth-founding and commercial activity that we have outlined would obviously affect the human geography of Maharashtra. The numerous peths—established and potential together—would constitute so many places in the countryside, and be favoured as the residences of the great, the resort of merchants, centres of manufacture, and be the foci of the activities of the small traders and pedlars of the vicinity, like those described by an official in 1821:

> Grain is usually consumed within a few coss of the spot where it is produced, except in a scarcity, when it is worth while to transport it to a distance. A dealer in grain, it is calculated, who has his own carriage, nets about one seer per rupee, or about one anna to three-quarters of an anna, as the market may be.... Greengrocers' dealings are confined within the limits of a few coss; their gains

[24] For the Collectorates above the Ghats, all data taken from W.H. Sykes, 'Special Report on the Statistics of the Four Collectorates of the Dukhun', in *Report of the Seventh Meeting of the British Association for the Advancement of Science 1837*, esp.pp.296-99; for Thana, *Gazetteer of the Bombay Presidency*, vol.XIII—*Thana*, pt.2, p.575.

[25] S. Moosvi, *The Economy of the Mughal Empire* (Delhi, 1987), p.315.

[26] W.H. Sykes, 'Special Report', p.295.

vary from fifty to a hundred and fifty per cent, but the perishableness of their goods...renders this apparently inordinate profit less usurious: in fact, they generally make four or five trips during the month, at each of which they bring about one rupee's worth of vegetables.[27]

Nor surprisingly, the eighteenth-century documents almost always specify the dues payable per head-load, ass-load, bullock-load and cart-load of goods coming to a market.

These little towns often became the bases of important local families (if they had not been founded by them), and the interests of these great households extended into landholding and agriculture in the vicinity, often buttressed by the acquisition of tax-free lands close by. Some, at least, of the tax-farming village landlords (*khot*) of the Konkan originated in this way,[28] and we may see the beginnings of such a process at work in Kasba Jayakade, Prant Baglan, Khandesh, where in 1770/1, Ragho Narayan Kulkarni was to advance the Rs.8,000 to Rs.10,000 needed to rebuild two dams washed away by floods, and receive a tenth of the land thus irrigated, or 40 *bighas*, as *inam*. The kasba was already a substantial place, paying Rs.5,000 in revenue, and this was to increase to Rs.8,500 over the next 14 years.[29]

Sixty years later, in 1834, another official, the head accountant, Govindrao Aya, made a similar investment. He secured the farm of two villages at a concessional rate, and spent Rs.30,000 on a tank to irrigate their lands. He recovered his capital over 23 years from profits calculated at Rs.30,917, or a compound rate of hardly three per cent per annum.[30] The social and spatial structure resulting from the pattern of activity discussed above, is most fully described by the perceptive Thomas Marshall, writing on the small peths and kasbas of north Karnatak:

The Brahmans are found only in the large and more comfortable villages, but in them they are in considerable numbers. With the exception of the Poojaries at the various temples who are altogether a different class of men, they consist almost entirely of the relations, connections and dependants of the Zumeendars (hereditary officials) whose families having been always in better circumstances, and better able to resist or evade the various vexations that have borne so hard on the mass of the people, are the only ones that have increased and spread themselves. They cultivate much land, either that which they hold in

[27] *Selection from the Papers at the East India House...under the Company's Governments in India* (London, 1820-26), vol.IV, p.803.

[28] André Wink, *Land and Sovereignty in India*, pp.359-65.

[29] G.C. Vad *et al.* (eds.), *Diaries: Madhavrao I*, pt.2, pp.26-7.

[30] India Office Records, vol.379/32, no.5072, Rev.Commissioner N.D. to Govt. 25 May 1857, and enclosures.

their own right, government land as common ryots, or still more extensively the surplus of the Zumeendars' lands that they cannot till themselves....

The 74 government villages comprising the little pargana of Khanapur had a total of 8,181 inhabitants; each village was dwarfed by the kasba of Khanapur with its population of 2,648. Its social structure illustrates the importance of such places as centres of elite residence and consumption.

A very few Brahmuns are scattered over the villages; in the town of Khanapur is a considerable body, about 120 families of them, part attached to the religious establishments, the remainder the Deshpandees and their connections.... The town lands are almost entirely Inam or Joodee; the former held either by the members of the religious establishments, or by the Jumeendars and their connections; the latter by the Municipal officers, all these may be considered as possessing some property, decently lodged, and in circumstances that are at least sufficiently distinct from poverty; the same may be said of the trading orders. The poor are chiefly the servants and dependants of the classes just enumerated, and the very poor those whom the wants of such a town furnish with less constant and regular occupation, but who, as gleaners in the great field of labour, are able to pick up a scanty subsistence.

Marshall noted that the Deshpandes tended to hold many if not all of the kulkarni watans in their parganas.[31]

Detailed occupational censuses taken during settlement operations in some parts of Khandesh during the 1850s and 1860s afford us a glimpse of the livelihood structure of these towns. Data are available for 941 settlements: of these I have selected 16 as being market and administrative centres of importance on the basis of a list of Khandesh *kasbas* prepared in 1835/6; as a consequence, a few small towns have been lumped in with the villages, even though their occupational structure is closer to that of the *kasbas*. The two sets of settlements are compared in Table 1.

The data presented in Table 1 need to be used very cautiously: in particular, agriculture and agricultural labour are severely underestimated by the classifications adopted, but the figures nonetheless bring out the noticeable structural differences between the little towns and the surrounding villages. The figures in Table 1 exhibit a relatively high degree of concentration, with over a quarter of the population living in the 16 kasbas; but that these settlements were more than large villages is indicated by their occupational structure. Agriculture is still important, but there is also a concentration of craftsmen and traders. The large number classified as 'hired servants' in the source (and distin-

[31] Thomas Marshall, *Statistical Reports*, pp.16 and 93-5.

Table 1. *Numbers and percentages of persons supported by various occupations*

Occupation	Kasbas	Villages	Percentage of total in: Kasbas	Villages
Agriculture	13,829	118,723	14.8	50.2
Writing	6,644	3,667	7.1	1.5
Weaving	6,817	4,793	7.3	2.0
Shopkeeper & sahukar	8,712	7,631	9.3	3.2
Goldsmith	2,707	3,420	2.9	1.4
Blacksmith	750	1,277	0.8	0.5
Tailor	2,175	2,419	2.3	1.0
Hired servant	10,281	8,054	11.0	3.4
All occupations	93,725	236,607	100.0	100.0

Source: Compiled from data in *Selections from the Records of the Government of Bombay* (new series), nos.72, 93 and 97.

guished from field labourers and crop-watchers) suggests that the towns were also places of elite residence. That the villagers resorted to these centres for their needs is mentioned in the Settlement Reports, and also suggested by the fact that a number of villages did not have resident shop-keepers (*wanis*). Taking Dhulia taluka as an example, we find that 'Wanis and Sowcars' (moneylenders) are present in 35 out of 114 villages; their number (including families) exceeds 50 in nine of them, and 88 per cent of them live in these nine towns. Nearly 70 per cent of craftsmen and tradesmen such as barbers or washermen are also to be found here, but only 37 per cent of 'agriculturists' and 19 per cent of crop-watchers and labourers. Thus the taluka structures replicate those of the district as a whole.

Trade figures for this period are unfortunately not available, but we have data on the import and export trade in goods and grain of the 41 'Principal Towns' of Khandesh for the single year 1835/6. Not surprisingly, the towns are large net importers of grain, to the assessed value of Rs.232,105 in that year; they offset this to an extent by the export of other goods, whose net value is Rs.78,312.[32] The incomes of officials, landowners and sahukars resident in these towns, with dealings in the countryside, may have balanced the account.

Finally, we should also note the presence of social and political ties

[32] Compiled from data in the 'Langford Records', vol.II, Bombay Archives.

linking these little towns and their rural hinterland which was vividly illustrated in the brief insurrection known as the Khandesh Survey riots of 1852. The leaders, as indicated from the signatories of a petition that heralded the outbreak, lived in the petty towns we have been discussing—Savda, Yaval, Raver, Nasirabad, Adawad—but were able to mobilise peasants from all over the subdivision, and even from other talukas, such as Erandole. This was explained by the fact that the Kunbis (members of the peasant caste) were led by 'the chief men of their own caste and occupation....' The report continues that,

> This may be accounted for without reference to caste, by the fact that many and indeed most of the wealthy and influential men in these districts who are connected with agriculture, are Coonbees. Some of them hold extensive farms and pay revenue to the Government to the amount of 500 rupees and upwards.

These men were sufficiently influential to summon the Kunbis to gather at Faizpur, and threaten the recalcitrant with defilement and outcasting.[33]

Nor, perhaps, was this the last protest mediated by these links. In 1873 the Poona Sarvajanik Sabha, one of the earliest nationalist organisations in Maharashtra, formed a subcommittee to collect evidence for a protest against British land revenue policy, and particularly against the revision settlements then under way. Almost all the witnesses whose evidence was recorded were landowners, sometimes farming through hired labour but often leasing out on a share or cash basis. Witness no.6, for instance, owned 25 acres in Bharatgaum village, Haveli taluka, Poona, which he had cultivated by a family of resident servants; no.15 owned 45 acres in Bhimthadi taluka, leased out on half-share basis, with the owner supplying half the seed. A village Kulkarni had land assessed at Rs.400, on which he employed 12 servants and 32 bullocks 'besides he and his two brothers personally work with the servants'. A Deshpande (hereditary official) of Barsi had both *inam* and *miras* lands, and employed two permanent servants to cultivate 45 bighas; another Despande from Amalner, Khandesh district, owned land assessed at Rs.225 and employed eight permanent servants to till it, as well as 32 bullocks. He also traded in cotton. A Konkan *khot* (village landlord) is also among the witnesses.[34] It is tempting to see

[33] Based on the following sources: India Office, Board's Collection 1853/4, no.146775, vol.2534, especially pp.185-6, and S. Mansfield, Collector, and G. Wingate, Survey Commissioner, joint letter to Secretary to Government, R.D., 8 January 1853, ibid., pp.298-302.

[34] *Report from a Sub-Committee of the Poona Sarvajanik Sabha on Matters Relating to India* (Poona, 1873), all citations from ch.I.

these men as the social if not the lineal descendants of Abaji Ballal Pendse or Raghu Narayan Kulkarni whom we encountered earlier, striving to maintain their social position in adverse circumstances.

Conclusion

Our hasty survey of fragmentary evidence suggests that the Maratha potentates, both great and small, who emerged as successors to the Deccani sultans and the Mughal emperor, were aware of the potential value of commerce for their regimes, and eager to realise that potential. Competition for merchants and craftsmen was keen, and sometimes violent, and trade seems to have grown—at least over the period from the 1740s to the 1820s covered by our data. Nor was growth confined to the supra-village level: commodity circulation and credit flows significantly affected village production and consumption. Men and resources moved into and out of the villages to shape the ties that linked them to the larger world of commerce and politics. And finally, we see that political economy came to shape the landscape of human settlement into an integrated social and political network, one more complex than anything the polar opposition of parasitic imperial capital and exploited monadic village could ever generate.

Chapter 5

MERCHANTS AND THE RISE OF COLONIALISM[1]

Prasannan Parthasarathi

Introduction

A growing body of scholarship argues that the rise of new, regional states in the eighteenth century gave merchants greater political influence. Some have referred to this as a South Asian form of mercantilism. My research suggests quite the opposite. Rather than benefiting merchants, state mercantilist policies threatened fundamental merchant interests and led to a deeper division between the state and merchants. In this essay I will present a new, albeit provisional, interpretation of merchants in the social and political order of late eighteenth-century South Asia.

This new interpretation of relations between merchants and the state sheds light on the origins of colonial rule in South Asia and the nature of the colonial economy itself. The English East India Company state incorporated merchants—who were excluded from political power within the indigenous order—and gave them political voice. In turn, merchants became crucial supporters of the Company state. Colonialism in South Asia had very important indigenous origins.

From portfolio capitalists to mercantilism

The interpenetration of merchant and state power in late pre-colonial South Asia has been conceptualised in several ways. The weakest, or most limited interpenetration of merchant and state power, is contained in the concept of 'portfolio capitalists', which has been explicated in an essay by Sanjay Subrahmanyam and Christopher Bayly. The purpose of the essay, according to the authors, is to question 'certain long-cherished notions concerning the separation of mercantile activity and military and political power in "traditional" India' and 'to argue that at least some [merchants] were able to straddle the worlds of commerce and

[1] The following abbreviations are used in the footnotes: APSA, Andhra Pradesh State Archives, Hyderabad; IOL, India Office Library and Record Office, London; MPP, Madras Public Proceedings; TNA, Tamil Nadu Archives, Madras.

political participation'.[2] To these figures they have attached the label portfolio capitalists.

The authors are the first to admit that portfolio capitalists were not an enduring feature of late pre-colonial South Asia. They acknowledge that 'these figures demonstrate a certain fragility'; that they were 'volatile, more dependent on political favours; in so far as they persisted, it was through buying or fighting their way into land rights'. In addition, in their usage the term is not restricted to merchants. In fact, in eighteenth-century north India, according to the authors, most portfolio capitalists were of military or administrative origin. It should also be noted that the term portfolio capitalists is used only to refer to major actors. That is, those men who were able to command sizeable resources.[3]

To sum up, the portfolio capitalist view does not seek to establish that merchants as a whole penetrated the state. Rather, its primary purpose is to point out that there was not an absolute separation of political and commercial spheres in late pre-colonial South Asia. This is a laudable goal, but the time has come to go beyond it. Perhaps the more important and central question is: did merchant penetration lead to enduring changes in the nature of the state? Furthermore, as an analytical category, the term portfolio capitalists obscures important distinctions between categories of merchants.

Stronger claims have been made about the interpenetration of merchants and indigenous states in the writings that describe a South Asian mercantilism.[4] According to these writers, the goal of mercantilism in South Asia was explicitly to increase the control of the state over resources. However, in the process, states became increasingly dependent upon merchants, who were necessary to implement the mercantilist policies. The key elements of mercantilist practice in South Asia were state commercial systems and revenue-farming. Both of these required the services of merchant capital, which led to a thoroughgoing penetration of the state by merchant interests, according to these writers. And, according to Burton Stein and David Washbrook, merchant access to state power at the end of the eighteenth century is also reflected in the greater ability of merchant capital to subordinate labour.

[2] 'Portfolio capitalists and the political economy of early modern India', *Indian Economic and Social History Review*, XXV (1988), p.401.

[3] Ibid., pp.401, 416 and 417.

[4] See C.R., Bayly, *Rulers, Townsmen and Bazaars* (Cambridge, 1983) and *Imperial Meridian: the British Empire and the world, 1780-1830* (London, 1989); B. Stein and D.A. Washbrook, 'States and societies: configuring state and capitalism in early modern India', paper presented at the Ottoman-Mughal-Safavid Workshop, Harvard University, March 1991.

I will now examine the propositions for a South Asian mercantilism, with particular reference to south India, in some detail.

Merchants and state commercial systems

The late-eighteenth century was a very turbulent time in south India. Social conflict and warfare widened and escalated. There was intensified competition between and among states, merchants, and producers for resources and shares of the social product. Merchants often found themselves at the centre of the conflicts of the period. Their position as intermediaries between the state and producers made them vulnerable to the claims of both and, as a group, merchants found it difficult to compete against the claims of either.

It is well known that the English East India Company played a major role in these conflicts. Its attempts to command a larger share of south India's wealth brought the Company into conflict with indigenous states and many groups in south Indian society. It would be a mistake, however, to attribute the growing turmoil at this time simply to the process of colonial expansion. The Company's attempts at political and economic consolidation were only one source of conflict. Many indigenous states were following policies similar to the Company state and generating much the same opposition from within south Indian society.

Many of these policies emerged in response to the fiscal crisis many states in south India faced at the end of the eighteenth century. This crisis had its origins largely in changes in methods of warfare—most notably the rise of standing armies—as well as the widening of military conflict. To compete militarily against their rivals, states were forced to expand their powers of taxation as well as conceive other methods by which to command wealth and income. This led to the development of new, more centralised state formations that had greater control over resources within their territories. Burton Stein has compared these changes in eighteenth-century South Asian states to military fiscalism in early-modern France.[5]

One method by which states could increase their incomes was by raising land revenues. This was no easy task as it often met with fierce resistance from entrenched agrarian groups. The power of these groups was often formidable. Recent writings indicate that the resistance of dominant agrarian classes to higher revenue exactions was a major fac-

[5] Burton Stein, 'State formation and economy reconsidered', *Modern Asian Studies*, 19 (1985), pp.387-413.

tor in the decline of the Mughal state.[6] There is also evidence for similar resistance in south India. The Lingayat peasantry in Mysore, for example, rebelled against attempts by Chikkadevaraja Wodeyar to raise the land revenue.[7] A second source of income for states was commerce. There is evidence that from as early as the seventeenth century customs collections were essential for the fiscal viability of south Indian states. It is likely that in the eighteenth century tax collections from trade became an even more vital component of state revenues.[8] Rulers, however, did not confine themselves only to taxing trade.

From at least the seventeenth century, states and rulers attempted to increase their incomes from trade by entering directly into commerce themselves.[9] The fiscal pressures of the late eighteenth century made state commerce more widespread and many states and rulers in south India —both large and small—entered trade. The commercial activities of Mysore and Travancore are the best known, but state commerce, in a wide variety of commodities, spanned the whole spectrum of state forms.

Not only was there an increase in state commerce in the late eighteenth century, but the form also changed dramatically. States sought to increase their profits from commerce by creating state monopolies. By monopolising trade, states increased their incomes by capturing the profits that had previously gone to merchants and other intermediaries that stood between the state and producers. Monopolies further added to state coffers by giving the state greater power in price setting. Monopoly power enabled the state to drive down procurement prices to producers and simultaneously push up selling prices. Thus these monopolies came into direct conflict with the interests of both merchants and producers.

This was precisely the impact of the English East India Company cloth monopoly, which I have described elsewhere.[10] First, the mono-

[6] Muzaffar Alam, 'Aspects of agrarian uprisings in north India in the early eighteenth century' in S. Bhattacharya and R. Thapar (eds.), *Situating Indian History, for Sarvepalli Gopal* (New Delhi, 1986).

[7] Burton Stein, 'State formation', pp.400-1.

[8] Burton Stein has speculated that for some eighteenth-century regimes' customs collections exceeded the land revenue. See his 'Class and pre-colonial Indian mercantilism', paper presented to the workshop on Early-Modern Empires and Economies, Harvard University, March 1990.

[9] Sanjay Subrahmanyam, *The Political Economy of Commerce* (Cambridge, 1990), ch.6.

[10] See my Harvard Ph.D. thesis, 'Weavers, Merchants and States: the south Indian textile industry 1680-1800', ch.4. See also S. Arasaratnam, 'Weavers, merchants and company: the handloom industry in southeastern India, 1750-

poly enabled the English to drive out merchants and appropriate their profits. Second, the cloth monopoly gave the Company the market power to drive down the procurement prices to weavers—in the process creating a crisis of subsistence for weavers. And by limiting the purchases of Dutch, French, and other European competitors, the Company was able to increase cloth auction prices in Europe. However, it is worth noting that in the late eighteenth century the Company's monopolies were not unique. They are merely the best known and the most often cited monopolies, being used especially as an example of the consequences of colonial rule. The English Company looms large in accounts of eighteenth-century innovations, but many indigenous states were following similar policy lines.

Monopolies were formed in a large number of goods and by a wide variety of south Indian states and rulers. There is evidence that the Nawab of Arcot attempted to create a monopoly in the cloth trade and one of his *amildars* tried to corner the grain market.[11] A Company servant reported that the Rajah of Ramnad was also active in monopolising many goods—grain being the most prominent.[12] The frequent incidence of *gudem* (forced grain sales by the state) at the end of the eighteenth century suggests that a number of state officials were becoming involved in the grain trade.

Mysore under Tipu Sultan and Travancore under Martanda Varma are the best known south Indian examples of state monopolies and systematic commercial policy.[13] The policies of the Mysore state were perhaps the most ambitious and successful. It created a far-reaching system of monopolies in a number of its most valuable export goods such as sandalwood, areca nuts, pepper, and cardamom. Travancore also created a very large commercial system in which monopolies played a central role. The jewel in Travancore's crown was its monopoly of pepper. Due to the paucity of records from these eighteenth-century states, our understanding of the operation of these monopolies

---

1790', *Indian Economic and Social History Review*, XVII (1980), pp.257-81.

[11] South Arcot Collectorate Records, Cuddalore Consultations, 1788, vol. 94, pp.3-5, TNA; MPP, 1794, vol. P/241/46, pp. 1152-4, IOL.

[12] Tanjore Collectorate Records, Nagore Factory Records, 1793, vol. 3323, pp. 5-10, TNA.

[13] For Mysore see Asok Sen, 'A pre-British economic formation in India of the late eighteenth century: Tipu Sultan's Mysore', in Barun De (ed.), *Perspectives in Social Sciences* I (Calcutta, 1977), pp.46-119; Nikhiles Guha, *Pre-British State System in South India* (Calcutta, 1985), ch.2; and Burton Stein, 'State Formation'. For Travancore see Ashin Das Gupta, *Malabar in Asian Trade* (Cambridge, 1967), ch.2.

is limited. Ashin Das Gupta's study of the Travancore pepper monopoly is the most detailed examination of any monopoly in south India and it contains a great deal of information on the impact of the monopoly on agriculturalists and merchants.

Travancore's pepper monopoly was one of the earliest monopolies in south India . It was formed in the first half of the eighteenth century by Martanda Varma. Merchants were gradually pushed out of the trade and replaced by a state commercial department which was specifically established to operate the pepper trade. The transformation took place slowly but the outcome is unmistakable. As Ashin Das Gupta describes the changes:

> The merchants became suddenly of little significance. It was 'the Government's contract' that now supplied the English at Anjengo. It was the king with whom they were now to haggle from year to year about the quantity that could be procured. The king's officials had to be bribed. The new order was there to stay. Merchants within the kingdom of Travancore would never be permitted the freedom they had known before.[14]

The English East India Company's cloth monopoly drove out merchants in much the same fashion and it is likely that state monopolies in other states had a similar impact on merchants. Such a conclusion about the relationship between merchants and the state in the late pre-colonial period runs counter to much of the recent literature on merchants in eighteenth-century South Asia.

The general import of this literature is that the development of the state in the eighteenth century, especially the expansion of its commercial interests, gave merchants greater access to state power. The interpretation given here, however, is that the development of the state in eighteenth-century South Asia, which others have called mercantilism, did not benefit merchants. Rather, the development of the state *excluded* merchants. Merchants were driven from some of the most profitable lines of trade and economic activity. The aim of South Asian mercantilism and state commercial activities was to increase the power of the state and in no way enhanced the position of merchants. Rather it was accomplished at the expense of merchants. In the language of Christopher Bayly, the 'commercialisation of royalty' may have prevented the 'royalisation of commercialism'.[15]

A second way in which merchants were gaining access to state power, according to recent work, was by entering the state revenue collection machinery. Merchants are thought to have increasingly gained

[14] Ibid., p.39.
[15] Bayly, *Rulers, Townsmen and Bazaars*, p.460.

leverage over states by extending loans to states and rulers. And by becoming revenue farmers, merchants are thought to have achieved direct access to state power. These propositions will now be examined.

Merchants and revenue systems

A number of scholars have noted that the military changes of the eighteenth century increased the cash needs of states. Merchants met these needs, either directly in the form of loans to states, or indirectly by becoming tax farmers. The merchants who could bid on and become revenue farmers became prominent figures in the political economy of late eighteenth-century South Asia. Bayly has gone so far as to assert that 'the men who could mobilise capital on a scale large enough to speculate on farms of revenue or state commercial duties were the century s most obvious entrepreneurs'. He goes on to argue that their entry into the revenue collection system, as tax farmers, gave merchants greater political power and, at times, leverage over states.[16]

Burton Stein and David Washbrook find strong corroboration for these arguments in south India . However, Stein and Washbrook are more precise than Bayly about the nature of the political power merchants derived as tax farmers and, consequently, have moved the discussion of the eighteenth century in very important and fruitful directions. They argue that by gaining access to revenue systems, merchants were able to use state power to subordinate and control labour. As a result, they conclude, the position of labour deteriorated considerably by the end of the eighteenth century: 'however much larger the aggregate of its production may have been, peasant and artisanal labour entitlements to a share of it became smaller. That was guaranteed by intensified and conjoined demands of investment capitalists, tax-collectors and the new centralised states'.[17] As I shall show shortly, I believe this statement misconstrues the events and changes of the late eighteenth century.

Bayly, Stein, and Washbrook have generalised about merchants, but have treated merchants as a homogeneous and undifferentiated category. In fact, existing descriptions of merchants, such as portfolio capitalists, blur the profound differences between merchants and have led to misinterpretations of the position of merchants in the political order.

[16] Ibid., pp.165 and 170-4.

[17] Stein and Washbrook, 'States and Societies', p.28. In more recent writings Washbrook appears to have modified his position. See his 'Land and Labour in late eighteenth-century South India: the golden age of the pariah?', in P. Robb, (ed.), *Dalit Movements and the Meanings of Labour in India* (Delhi, 1993).

Once the differences among types of merchants are taken into account, the relationship between merchants and the state appears quite different. Merchants in eighteenth-century South Asia were involved in three types of activities: banking, trade in goods, and advancing capital for production. The lines between trading and the other two activities were not rigid. Traders were often forced to finance production in order to get a lien on commodities. Thus they established direct relations with producers. Similarly, bankers often received loan repayments in kind, which forced them to enter the world of trade. For our purposes here, the crucial distinction is between merchants who were primarily bankers and those who were directly involved in advancing credit for production—what I will call, for want of a better term, the financiers of production.

All available evidence suggests that banking and the financing of production were separate merchant spheres and were carried out by distinct groups of merchants. Each of these activities required specialised knowledge and status. No research has been done on bankers in pre-colonial south India. However, evidence from North India indicates that there were several conditions that had to be met to enter the world of finance and banking.[18] For instance, to act as a banker a merchant had to have a credit standing in the market for financial assets. Only then would his *hundis* (credit notes) be accepted.

The financing of production also required extensive and specific knowledge, in this case, of producing areas, the producers, and the nature of the production process. I have shown this in the case of cloth traders who possessed detailed knowledge of weavers and weaving centres.[19] Cloth traders also commanded a large network of brokers and supervisors who distributed advances to the weavers and received and sorted the completed cloth. Bayly himself has recognised that this merchant role as financiers of production was important in eighteenth-century South Asia. He has noted that merchant capital was applied directly to agricultural production to a 'small but significant' extent.[20] But he does not explore the dynamics of conflict between merchants and producers and the role of the state in this conflict.

Once this distinction between types of merchants is made, it is apparent that Bayly's arguments about the increasing political influence of mechant capital apply to only one section of merchants: namely, bank-

[18] Some of these conditions may be gathered from Irfan Habib, 'Banking in Mughal India', *Contributions to Indian Economic History*, 1 (1960), pp.1-20.
[19] See my 'Weavers, Merchants and States', ch.3.
[20] Bayly, *Rulers, Townsmen and Bazaars*, p.107.

ing capital. In fact, much of Bayly's discussion itself pertains to bankers in north India, particularly large banking houses. These merchants operated at the apex of the revenue collection machinery and supported the state via loans directly to the state as well as to large revenue farmers. Merchants rarely took up tax farms at this level themselves. Thus the political power of *banking interests*—not that of all merchants—was increased in the eighteenth-century successor regimes. However, greater political power for bankers did not translate into greater power for merchants as a whole, and more critically, for financiers of production.

Little is known about the social origins of the tax farmers who operated below the apex of the revenue system. A reading of Wink for western India and Mizushima for south India suggests that the tax farmers at the lower tiers of the revenue system were drawn from the ranks of local notables and traditional power holders.[21] However, in south India merchants occasionally purchased farms, especially farms of commercial taxes. Among these were merchants whose livelihood came from financing production. There is extensive evidence from throughout the eighteenth century that merchants who supplied cloth to the English East India Company rented such farms in Company territories. However, the political benefits that merchants derived from this role, especially when it came to conflicts with weavers, appear to have been minimal. There is no evidence at all that cloth merchants who were tax farmers more easily commanded the labour of weavers. In fact, evidence from the late-eighteenth century makes questionable the proposition that holding tax farms was a method by which merchants subordinated labour.

At the end of the eighteenth century, cloth merchants held a number of tax farms for zamindars in the Northern Circars. Noting this, a Company servant observed that weavers received the best treatment precisely in those places where the tax collector was also a cloth merchant.[22] This suggests that these merchants were not using their access to state power (which they gained by their position as tax farmers) to drive down the incomes of weavers and thereby increase their own profits. Rather, exactly the opposite appears to have occurred. Weavers were attracted to these areas because the cloth merchants who held tax farms were able to provide them with revenue benefits, such as reduced

[21] André Wink, *Land and Sovereignty in India* (Cambridge, 1986); Mizushima Tsukasa, *Nattar and Socio-economic Change in South India* (Tokyo, 1986).

[22] MPP, 1789, vol. P/241/15, p. 3137, IOL.

taxes, which increased their incomes. Thus, these merchants sacrificed their revenue interests to promote commercial aims, all to the benefit of weavers.

In conclusion, the merchants who may have increased their political power in the late-eighteenth century were large banking houses and were few in number. The segment of merchant capital which depended on production for its livelihood was not a beneficiary of state power. The next sections will show that with the rise of the Company, and later the colonial state, relations between this category of merchants and the state were transformed. The Company state was able to incorporate financiers of production, which attracted these merchants to the Company. In turn, these merchants became important backers of the Company and its emerging state in south India .

The indigenous origins of colonialism

Scholars are still very far from understanding how a small group of English traders came to achieve political supremacy over the whole of the Indian subcontinent. Traditional explanations have pointed to external factors, such as European economic or technological prowess, as decisive in the rise of English power. However, recent research has focused on internal factors and explored the dynamics of the eighteenth-century South Asian political economy to explain the rise of colonialism. This work has emphasised that colonialism in South Asia had indigenous origins. Nevertheless, these origins still remain obscure and the term 'indigenous origins' has been used loosely to refer to a number of phenomena. And despite the insistence on indigenous origins, the agency for the making of colonialism continues to rest with Europeans: the focus of much of this writing continues to be Europeans and their actions.

In his path-breaking work, *Rulers, Townsmen and Bazaars,* Christopher Bayly has used the concept of indigenous origins in two senses. The first sense is to indicate that the pattern of European penetration of the subcontinent was limited and determined by the structure of Indian commercial society.[23] In other words, colonialism did not completely remake the subcontinent, but was constrained by indigenous structures. To call this indigenous origins, however, is a misnomer. The agency for the making of colonialism still lay with Europeans, and the indigenous society merely channelled or set limits upon European actions.

Bayly has used indigenous origins in a second sense to show that

[23] Bayly, *Rulers*, *Townsmen and Bazaars,* ch.6.

Indian social groups lent their support to the emerging Company and later colonial state.[24] This I believe is the correct understanding of the concept. However, he fails to explain why various South Asian actors supported the Company state. This omission is reflected in such phrases as 'collaborating classes', implying that groups who supported the rising colonial state were merely cooperating with a colonial project which was still fundamentally European. The result is that colonialism in South Asia is once again something made by Europeans, save for the caveat of 'native' assistance.

I offer a new interpretation of the indigenous roots of colonialism from the standpoint of labour and the political economy of production. My interpretation is one in which south Indian social groups—for fundamental reasons of their own—played significant roles in the rise of the Company state and in the making of colonialism. There was a powerful coincidence of interests and political projects between the Company—later colonial—state and the indigenous supporters of this state, which may also explain why colonialism in South Asia was so resilient and long-lasting.

The Company state was unique within the south Indian political order. It had an unusual ability to incorporate and to give political power to a variety of groups, many of which were disenfranchised within the indigenous order. This was why weavers were attracted to the Company and its territories in the final decades of the eighteenth century. The Company lent its political support to weavers in their conflicts with merchants, and for this support weavers remained with the Company even though the Company was steadily eroding the conditions for their subsistence. Thus even weavers—by migrating to Company territories—unwittingly played a role in the making of colonialism.[25]

Weavers were not the only group to be attracted to the Company state. In the final decades of the eighteenth century, merchant financiers of production—who were being squeezed between the expansion of state power and the claims of producing groups—too turned to the Company for support and received backing in their conflicts with both producers and new centralising state formations. These merchants, in turn, became crucial supporters of the Company state and this support was critical for the rise of English power. These merchants, however, were only the first group to back the Company. More generally, the Company state was able to come to dominance because it was able to

[24] See C.A. Bayly, *Indian Society and the Making of the British Empire* (Cambridge, 1988), ch.2.

[25] See my 'Weavers, Merchants and States', ch.4.

extend political power, and thus win the backing of several important and powerful indigenous social groups.

These propositions will be demonstrated shortly for the case of cloth merchants, but first it must be noted that merchants as a whole had a complex relationship to the English East India Company. Lakshmi Subramanian has shown that while major segments of the merchant community in western India were backers of Company power, no less important merchants were virulently opposed to this power. The lines of cleavage divided neatly, with merchants who competed with the Company opposing it and those whose activities complemented the Company supporting it. Scholars have found similar configurations for other regions in South Asia, but it should be stressed that no one has systematically analysed the link between merchants, or other groups, and the Company state, from the standpoint of their relationship to producing classes. This relationship was transformed with the rise of Company power in South Asia, with profound consequences for the path of economic development in the nineteenth century.[26]

Cloth merchants in the indigenous political order

I have described elsewhere in some detail the nature of relations between weavers and cloth merchants in late pre-colonial south India.[27] For those familiar with the position and power of merchants in early-modern Europe, the situation in south India will be understood to be very remarkable indeed. Weavers in south India worked as independent artisans. They owned their own looms and worked in their own houses free of outside supervision or interference. Although independent, weavers were by no means self-sufficient. They were dependent upon advances of working capital for the purchase of materials. There were a number of sources for this capital, but in this period cloth merchants were by far the most important. These merchants made advances to many weavers in order to obtain the large quantities of cloth they required for their trade. The most striking feature of the advance system, and of the relationship between weavers and merchants, was the power wielded by weavers.

When the advance was made, an oral contract was struck between weaver and merchant. This contract stipulated the size of the advance,

[26] Lakshmi Subramanian, 'Capital and crowd in a declining Asian port city: the Anglo-Bania Order and the Surat riots of 1795', *Modern Asian Studies*, 19 (1985), pp 205-37; P.J. Marshall, *Bengal: the British bridgehead* (Cambridge, 1987), pp.166-8; Bayly, *Indian Society*, ch.2.

[27] See my 'Weavers, Merchants and States', ch.3.

the quality and price of the cloth to be woven, and the date of delivery. Much of the power of weavers derived from an asymmetry in this contract. Both weavers and merchants were free to cancel the contracts at any time. But while the weaver bore no cost for cancelling (he simply had to return the advance to the merchant), the merchant forfeited his advance if he cancelled. This steep penalty effectively ruled out the option of cancelling and obligated the merchant to receive all cloth produced by the weaver.

As a result of this asymmetry, weavers possessed the freedom to accept advances at will and sell completed cloth to any buyer. For instance, in the mid 1780s weavers in Vizagapatnam produced cloth using merchant advances, but sold their cloth to private traders who paid higher prices.[28] Such weaver freedom, coupled with the high demand for south Indian cloth, gave weavers great power to set cloth prices, which, naturally, adversely affected merchant profits.

The asymmetry of contract, along with high cloth demand, also made it difficult for merchants to enforce cloth quality standards. Confident of receiving high prices for even poor quality cloth, weavers did not hesitate to add to their incomes by reducing the quantity and quality of yarn that they used. Even if a piece of cloth found no buyer, the asymmetry in the contract guaranteed that the merchant who had financed its production was always available as a buyer of last resort. Consequently, near the end of the century much of the cloth which merchants received was thin, flimsy and of terribly poor quality. A Company servant at Cuddalore remarked that 'no private merchant can ever have weavers so much under command as to oblige them to put the proper quantity of thread in each piece'.[29]

There were also other areas of conflict between weavers and merchants. The most serious of these was the problem of outstanding debts by weavers. The lack of institutionalised and legally enforced systems for debt repayment made it extremely difficult for merchants to recover debts. Both weavers and merchants were fully aware of this and the English East India Company records are replete with complaints from merchants about the losses they suffered from unpaid weaver debts.[30]

The inability of merchants to collect debts was due in part to their inability to restrict the mobility of weavers. Weavers were some of the

[28] MPP, 1784, vol. P/240/59, pp.1043-4, IOL.

[29] South Arcot Collectorate Records, Cuddalore Consultations, 1786, vol. 86, pp.96-9, TNA.

[30] MPP, 1768, vol. P/240/27, p.63 and pp.838-9, IOL; MPP, 1776, vol. 115B, pp.327-42, TNA.

most peripatetic inhabitants of south India. It was not uncommon for them to pick up and move when they heard word of better prospects or if they faced oppression by merchants and even states. The mobility of weavers made weaver debts to merchants insecure and it was not uncommon for weavers to run off with merchant advances. In 1781, for instance, weavers fled Masulipatnam after receiving merchant advances as Hyder Ali's cavalry was approaching.[31]

The strength of weavers was also the product of some fundamental merchant weaknesses. Merchants, in contrast to weavers, were not able to close ranks and limit competition between themselves. But more importantly, merchants were excluded from the state within the south Indian political order. Unlike many parts of Europe where the economic power of merchants was supplemented by political power, in south India merchants had no access to the powers of the state. In this political configuration, weavers were able to assert a great deal of authority and independence.

In fact, rather than supporting merchants in their conflicts with weavers, states often did the opposite. Rulers in south India frequently protected weavers and actually checked the authority of merchants. For instance, in 1787, a zamindar at Ingeram ordered merchants to cease their practice of carrying weavers away from their villages and placing peons over them to extract debt repayment. The zamindar further instructed that this was no longer to be done without his permission and future all merchants who had claims on weavers were to submit these claims to him. He would then settle accounts and render justice.[32]

At the end of the eighteenth century, cloth merchants also found themselves increasingly in conflict with states in south India. These conflicts resulted from the severe fiscal crises of the period which led states to enter the world of commerce, as was described earlier. Cloth was one of the favourite items of state commerce and a number of states entered the cloth trade. For example, in the 1790s a number of zamindars in the Northern Circars were cloth dealers.[33] Cloth was also one of the most important items in state monopolies and cloth monopolies were some of the most prevalent. When entering the cloth trade states took over merchant functions such as making advances, which they were forced to do in order to get a lien on cloth, and receiving and sorting the completed cloth. As a consequence, merchants found themselves either pushed out of the cloth trade or increasingly in competi-

[31] MPP, 1781, vol. P/240/52, pp.139-40, IOL.
[32] MPP, 1787, vol. P/241/3, p.3187, IOL.
[33] MPP, 1789, vol. P/241/15, p.3137, IOL.

tion with powerful state trading enterprises. And, more often than not, cloth merchants were the losers in these battles as they were squeezed between the claims of weavers and the ambitions of late-eighteenth-century state forms.

The position of cloth merchants in the social and political order of late-eighteenth-century south India was transformed after the rise of the Company. I have shown elsewhere that by combining economic and political authority the English East India Company profoundly transformed its relations with weavers.[34] With the rise of the Company, cloth merchants were incorporated into the Company state, creating another potent combination of political and economic power. More than a century of conflict between the Company and cloth merchants was set aside and replaced by a formidable alliance.

Cloth merchants in the Company political order

After 1790, relations between weavers and merchants began to change. The new relations were first apparent in areas under the political control of the English East India Company. In these places, some of which were major weaving centres in south India, the balance of power shifted away from weavers towards merchants. A new and more militant class of merchants was being created, and, with the expansion of English power, this new breed came to be found all over south India.

The above changes were intimately connected with the rise of English Company power. The ascendance of the English was a political revolution in south India as it gave merchants, for the first time, political expression to their economic power. The first beneficiaries were cloth merchants. With the support of the Company state, cloth merchants restructured their relations with weavers and used the powers of the state to reduce the power and income of weavers. The system of contracts was transformed; weaver mobility was reduced; debts were collected with greater rigour.

An early casualty of these changes was weavers' power to set cloth prices. Weavers were stripped of their ability to pass on increases in costs in the form of higher prices for cloth and, as a result, weaver incomes began to fall below subsistence level. In 1798, for instance, weavers in the Northern Circars found that their returns to weaving were falling due to increases in the prices of cotton and copper coins. Unable to force merchants to pay more for cloth, and facing a crisis of subsistence, five hundred weavers assembled at the Madapollam fac-

[34] See my 'Weavers, Merchants and States', ch.4.

tory to seek the assistance of the English. The weavers, however, found scant sympathy or support for their plight.[35] By 1820, the power of weavers had declined so much that merchants in Trichinopoly encountered no resistance from weavers when they slashed cloth prices.[36]

Merchants weakened the bargaining and price-setting powers of weavers in several ways. Perhaps the most important was monopolising the labour of weavers, which was done with the assistance of the Company's political power. In Ingeram the merchants divided weaving villages between themselves and agreed to make advances only in the villages they were allocated. Initially the weavers welcomed the scheme, believing that by receiving advances from only one merchant they would be harassed less by merchants and their brokers. But they quickly discovered that their bargaining power was reduced and sought to remove the system, just as they earlier opposed the Company attempts to monopolise their labour. Once again their efforts failed.[37]

In Vizagapatnam the Company supported the merchants in their efforts to reduce the power of weavers by appealing to Vizeram Rauze, the local Raja, to place restrictions on the cloth trade. Of particular concern to the Company and the cloth merchants were private traders, whose demand reduced the quantity and quality of cloth that weavers supplied the merchants. The Company also requested that high duties be levied on private cloth, and that the cloth varieties demanded by the Company merchants not be allowed to leave the district. Vizeram Rauze assented to only the latter request, and issued orders restricting the trade in the Company's cloth varieties. The Company also attempted to persuade the Raja to give directions to weavers to make cloth according to Company standards, but no such order was ever issued.[38]

Merchants also forced weavers into their exclusive employ by compelling them to take their advances. The power of the Company state was essential for such actions. In 1788 merchants—with Company approval—used peons in the Northern Circars to carry away weavers and force advances on them. Similarly, in 1792 the Company noted that weavers in Godavari were not working for merchants voluntarily, but under compulsion.[39]

[35] Godavari District Records, 1798, vol. 830, pp.24-46, APSA.

[36] Trichinopoly District Records, Board of Revenue Correspondence, 1820, vol. 3678, pp.203-4, TNA.

[37] Godavari District Records, 1798, vol. 830, pp.24-46, APSA.

[38] MPP, 1783, vol. P/240/57, pp 1827-1831, IOL; MPP, 1784, vol. P/240/59, pp.1045-7, IOL; MPP, 1785, vol. P/240/60, pp.101-2, IOL.

[39] MPP, 1788, vol. P/241/9, pp 3100-1, IOL; Godavari District Records, 1792, vol. 830, pp.13, APSA.

The merchants were also able to use the authority of the Company state to collect weaver debts more effectively and rigorously. In Ingeram, merchants placed peons over weavers to recover outstanding balances.[40] And again, the Company pressured indigenous states to support merchants in their conflicts with weavers. In Madapollam the Company instructed local zamindars to assist merchants in recovering outstanding weaver debts.[41]

There were numerous complaints from the weavers that the merchants were too severe in their collection of debts, and they appealed to the Company to ease their situation.[42] But with the incorporation of merchants into its state, the Company ceased to act as a check on merchant authority, and the weavers began to receive far less support from the Company. For instance, in 1795 a merchant used peons to carry away some weavers in Arni, a town in the Company's jagir. The weavers petitioned the Company to intervene and prevent such action, but the Company's Revenue Collector for Arni—arguing that the dispute was beyond his purview—refused to support the weavers' petition.[43] This was very much in contrast to earlier Company actions in support of the weavers in their conflicts with the merchants.

It must be reiterated that the power of the Company state was central to the transformation of relations between merchants and weavers. Lending support to this claim is the fact that while weaver power was declining in Company territories, weavers continued to be in a strong position in areas untouched by Company political power. Throughout the 1790s cloth merchants operating in Tanjore, a Maratha principality, had many problems recovering weaver debts, received poor quality cloth, and were often precariously close to suffering great losses. In Tanjore merchants could not exert any authority over the weavers as the district was not under Company political rule.[44] Merchants encountered similar difficulties in Ramnad, which was under the political authority of the Raja of Ramnad. Merchant profits on cloth produced there were always uncertain and the merchants felt it was hardly worth their while.[45]

[40] MPP, 1788, vol. P/241/4, pp.26-7, IOL.

[41] MPP, 1789, vol. P/241/14, p.2470, IOL.

[42] Godavari District Records, 1798, vol. 847, pp.141-2, APSA; Godavari District Records, 1798, vol. 830, pp.24-46, APSA.

[43] Chingleput Collectorate Records, 28 August 1795, vol. 446, TNA, as summarised in the *Guide to the Records of Chingleput District* (Madras, 1934), p.69.

[44] Tanjore Collectorate Records, 1795, vol. 3325, pp.29-30, TNA.

[45] Tanjore Collectorate Records, Nagore Factory Records, 1793, vol. 3323,

The incorporation of merchants into the Company state was a critical factor in the rise of English East India Company power. In exchange for the Company's political backing, merchants lent support to the English East India Company state. The precise nature of this support remains to be specified in greater detail, but it is likely that the Company relied upon these merchants to penetrate Indian society, which is suggested by the Company retreat on the elimination of merchant intermediaries for the provision of cloth.[46] The alliance between Company and merchant has been shown here for the case of conflicts between cloth merchants and weavers. However, there are indications that the labour of many types of producers—not only that of weavers—was difficult to command and control, and that other merchants, not only cloth traders, experienced similar problems. Merchant capital was active in advancing capital for agricultural production and there is evidence that contracts between merchants and peasant cultivators too were asymmetric in the same fashion as contracts between weavers and merchants.[47] Similarly, spinners were able to use their mobility in the late eighteenth century to break contracts and run off with advances of cotton and money. Thus the conflicts between merchants and weavers which have been described here were also characteristic of relations between merchants and many other types of producers.

In many ways the position of dominant agrarian groups in late eighteenth-century south India was analogous to that of merchants. There is extensive evidence, as documented by Burton Stein and others, that the centralising drive of states came into conflict with the interests of dominant agrarian classes. There is also evidence that these dominant agrarian groups faced enormous difficulties commanding and controlling labour. The Company state was able to resolve these problems by empowering these classes in their conflicts with both states and producers. In turn, this access to the Company state led agrarian elites to become key supporters of the Company.[48] This change in the political power of those who commanded labour is fundamental to understanding the economic impact of colonial rule.

Conclusion

It is widely recognised that the nineteenth century was characterised by

---

pp 5-10, TNA.

[46] See my 'Weavers, Merchants and States', ch.4.

[47] Ibid., pp.122-3.

[48] For insight into the position of agricultural labour see Washbrook, 'Land and labour'.

low levels of investment in South Asia, both in comparison to pre-colonial levels and cross-nationally. Typically the low investment levels have been attributed to a shortage of savings or a lack of capital. For nearly one hundred years nationalist writers have claimed that the savings shortage was created by the British drain of wealth from the subcontinent. In a similar vein, David Ludden implies that the heavy land revenue demand of the colonial state reduced the investment fund.[49]

These views are problematic on both empirical and theoretical grounds. It is widely acknowledged that after 1850 price inflation diminished the burden of the land revenue demand. However, the evidence suggests that the increase in investment did not match the decline in the colonial state's share. Crispin Bates has found that rates of investment in central India were very low in the second half of the nineteenth century. However, this was not due to a shortage of savings. Profits were being made in agriculture, but landed groups simply did not invest these profits.[50]

There are also theoretical problems with the nationalist explanation. By identifying the problem as one of savings these writers have assumed a classical accumulation process in which the level of investment is determined by the quantity of savings. However, since the work of Keynes, we know that the causality may actually run in the reverse direction: it is the level of investment that determines the quantity of savings. In such a Keynesian accumulation process, investment demand —not savings—is the crucial variable.[51]

The political transformations described in this essay suggest a profound change in the position of investment within the political economy of South Asia.[52] In the late pre-colonial period propertied classes were

[49] For a summary of nationalist economic history, see Amiya Bagchi, *The Political Economy of Underdevelopment* (Cambridge, 1982), ch.4. David Ludden, however, also comments on the demand for investment. He points out that the structure of land revenue assessment acted as a disincentive to investment and agricultural improvement. In addition, he argues that the social institutions which facilitated investment in earlier centuries broke down in the nineteenth century. See his *Peasant History in South India* (Princeton, 1985), pp.141-9.

[50] Crispin Bates, 'Class and economic change in central India: the Narmada Valley 1820-1930' in Clive Dewey (ed.), *Arrested Development in India* (New Delhi, 1988), pp.241-82.

[51] It should be pointed out that a low level of savings in the nineteenth-century Indian economy is consistent with a Keynesian accumulation regime: low rates of investment resulted in low levels of output or income and consequently the quantity of savings was small.

[52] While many analysts believe that the demand for investment is influenced

excluded from the state. Thus they had no political mechanism by which to command and control labour. Furthermore, as we have also demonstrated for weavers, producers possessed great capabilities for resistance. Labour was in a strong position to demand a sizeable share of the social product.

This configuration of class forces created a very powerful inducement to invest. Lacking political power, propertied classes found that the only method they had to attract and command labour was by offering labour either a high return or a security of returns. These were achieved by investing. First, by increasing the productivity of labour, investment made it possible to give labour the higher returns it demanded. Second, investment increased the reliability of production systems making possible more secure returns. Thus in the pre-colonial period, investment and command of labour were linked, which created a powerful inducement to invest. And all available evidence suggests that investment levels were high in the late pre-colonial period.[53]

After being incorporated into the Company state, propertied classes no longer had to invest in order to attract labour. These classes now were able to use the power of the state to command and control labour. Thus the link between investment and command of labour was broken, which led to economic stagnation in the nineteenth century. Therefore, the accumulation crisis in nineteenth-century India was not created by low savings, but rather by a lack of investment demand.[54]

---

by politics (for example, as one of the determinants of Keynes' 'animal spirits') it remains a largely unexplored topic in the economics literature.

[53] See Muzaffar Alam, 'Agrarian uprisings'; Bayly, *Rulers, Townsmen and Bazaars*, ch.2; Stewart Gordon, 'The slow conquest: administrative integration of Malwa into the Maratha empire', *Modern Asian Studies*, 11 (1978), pp.1-40. To command labour was, of course, not the only motive to invest in the pre-colonial period.

[54] David Washbrook has drawn a different connection between the power of labour and investment. He has argued that the smashing of labour allowed propertied classes to increase profits in the nineteenth century by squeezing labour rather than by the riskier path of investing. The argument presented here makes no claims about the determinants of investment demand in the nineteenth century. Rather it points out that the political transformations wrought by colonialism eliminated a very powerful inducement to invest. See his 'Progress and problems: South Asian economic and social history c.1720-1860', *Modern Asian Studies*, 22 (1988), pp.57-96.

Chapter 6

CASTE SOCIETY AND UNITS OF PRODUCTION IN EARLY-MODERN SOUTH INDIA[1]

David Ludden

In the eighteenth century, South Asia may have produced a quarter of world manufacturing output, predominantly textiles.[2] Recently, Prasannan Parthasarathi made a breakthrough in the study of early-modern manufacturing by showing that in south India, cloth production depended upon countless, local exertions of power by weavers, merchants, and state elites.[3] Scholars therefore need to study localities in South Asia to understand manufacturing in the early-modern world economy. Why did the mercantile activities that connected south Indian textile producers to world markets focus on some localities and not others? How did articulations with world markets sustain output in these localities? How was productive power organised locally? How did manufacturing and commercialism affect local society and politics? In searching for answers to these questions, we can extend Parthasarathi's idea that weaving castes acted like flexible but effective labour collectives. For it seems that in production localities generally, caste organised the productive powers that sustained the early-modern growth of manufacturing in south India. Exertions of power that formed the crux of textile production arose from the general working of caste

[1] Research for this paper was funded by the Social Science Research Council (with a grant from the Ford Foundation) and by the National Endowment for the Humanities.

[2] Paul Bairoch, 'International industrialization levels from 1750-1850', *Journal of European Economic History*, 11 (1982), p.296. Building on such evidence, André Gunder Frank argues ('The world economic system in Asia before European hegemony', *The Historian*, 56, 2 (1994), pp.260-76) that the centre of the world economy lay in Asia during the early-modern period 'and only shifted to Europe after 1800' (p.260). In the early nineteenth century, after English machine textiles began to hit the world market, Indian cloth still increased its share of West African textile imports: see Philip D. Curtin, 'The tropical Atlantic in the age of the slave trade', in Michael Adas (ed.), *Islamic and European Expansion: the forging of a global order* (Philadelphia, 1993), pp.186-7.

[3] Prasannan Parthasarathi, 'Weavers, merchants, and states: the south Indian textile industry, 1680-1800', unpublished thesis, Harvard University, 1992.

society.

Using data on 159 villages—at the tip of the Indian peninsula, in the Tirunelveli Kattabomman District of Tamilnadu—preserved in the 1823 *Census and Dehazada of the Province of Tirunelveli*, this chapter describes the creation of production localities by clusters of castes that organised early-modern manufacturing in local configurations of social power. To understand articulations of caste and economy that made locality units of manufacturing work in early-modern south India, we need a long-term view of a landscape composed of many interacting localities. For the evolution of any one locality involves many others. In their interaction, politically potent clusters of *jati* groups formed local units of production, and these formations involved both material and cultural determinations.

The relationship of caste as a cultural phenomenon to its many economic and political meanings forms the necessary background to any social history of economic development in South Asia. It is clear from our census data that jati ritual status did not determine occupation or residence in early-modern Tirunelveli. Almost all castes lived in almost every part of the region in 1823, and there was significant occupational and wealth diversity within castes. Material wealth and ritual status probably did correspond to one another at the extremes of *varna* ranking, as they did in the Baramahal, in 1797, where Brahmans had the highest per capita food consumption, and Chamars, Potmakers, and Karumbars had the lowest (see Table 1).

But Baramahal data also indicate that Muslims (including the Muslims called Labbais) and foreign Marwaris, who would have had a loose relationship with the caste ritual order, had high material status and played important economic roles. The *Baramahal Records* divide caste groups into separate labouring, commercial, and landed castes, which reveals a wealth hierarchy based on class rather than caste. Among landowners, great wealth variations would have separated the best-fed Brahman families from the poor peasants categorised in 'inhabitants'. Among labourers, consumption differentials came not from ritual status but from economic specialisations.

In Tirunelveli, the economic and ritual position of a caste differed significantly with locality; this reflected social mobility and economic growth, as we will see. Untouchables were were not always landless or bonded labourers. Privileged *mirasidar* landowners were not always Brahmans or Vellalas. By 1823, untouchable Pallas and Pariahs entered many economic niches and *mirasi* land rights were bought by many jatis. A local combination of high-caste landlords and untouchable

Table 1. *Food consumption by caste: the Baramahal in 1797*

Percentage	(a) of population	(b) of food consumed	Ratio (b/a)
Brahman	6.7	15.0	2.2
Merchant/Marwari	6.0	11.2	1.9
Muslim	3.3	5.5	1.7
Lubbay	5.3	6.7	1.3
Barber/washerman	1.3	1.3	1.0
Chair/chamar	2.7	1.3	0.5
Potmaker/burder	2.0	1.4	0.7
Kurumbar/shepherd	4.0	2.2	0.6
Tank digger	0.7	0.9	1.3
Weaver/Kaikkolar	4.7	4.3	0.9
Inhabitants	63.3	49.0	0.8

Source: *The Baramahal Records*, sect.IV, *Products* (Madras, 1912), pp.107-8, from Prasannan Parthasarathi, iWeavers, merchants and states: the South Indian textile industry, 1680-1800', dissertation, Department of Economics, Harvard University, 1992, pp.103-5.

labourers did typify agricultural production in the Tambraparni valley from medieval times to 1823.[4] But irrigated cultivation—even the most productive wet farming—did not depend on this caste combination alone. Mirasidars did not farm only irrigated land or do so only with landless labourers. Ritual forms and prescriptions seem to have organised social interactions and power culturally as caste society transformed itself and its material environment over the centuries.[5]

[4] See David Ludden, 'Agrarian commercialism in eighteenth-century south India: evidence from the 1823 Tirunelveli Census', *Indian Economic and Social History Review*, 25, 4 (1988), pp.493-519. Reprinted in Sanjay Subrahmanyam (ed.), *Merchants, Markets and the State in Early Modern India* (Delhi, 1990), pp.215-41.

[5] See David Ludden, *Peasant History in South India* (Princeton, 1985). In this paper, I use the term 'medieval' to refer to the period of south Indian history spanning the first millennium C.E. and lasting until roughly 1200. 'Post-medieval' is a vague term that covers the period c.1200-1600. 'Early-modern' covers the period c.1600-1850 and the regimes of the Madurai Nayaks, the Nawab of Arcot, and the English East India Company in the southern Tamil country. See David Ludden, *Peasant History*, and 'World economy and village India, 1600-1900: exploring the agrarian history of capitalism', in Sugata Bose (ed.), *South Asia and World Capitalism* (Delhi, 1990), pp.159-77.

Hierarchy and partition

Despite mounting evidence to the contrary, new historical theory has fortified old ideas about the static quality of India's pre-colonial political economy. One set of historians depicts a massively immobile, subsistence-oriented agrarian economy, isolated from urban economic and political change.[6] Another explains subaltern resistance in colonial times by reference to the traditional moral economy of self-reproducing village societies.[7] Such theoretical commitments to the immobility of India before colonialism make the well-documented diversification of social formations in South Asia impossible to explain, or even acknowledge; they make major transformations in agrarian society, over centuries before 1800, impossible to imagine. But this form of theory has another, contrary purpose—to render pre-colonial India stable and unified, and thus to highlight the enormity of change after 1800. It underlies a combination of history, social science, and cultural studies that organises the world around colonialism, and to that end, turns traditional India into a sedentary, self-reproducing social formation, a stable, unified culture.

Evidence shows however, that from ancient times, India saw countless movements of people in and out of the localities of social reproduction, where the internal dynamics of stability and change were constantly propelled by exogenous forces. If we could spend a year east of the Indus, before 1800, we would see a society on the move. Consider warfare. Abul Fazl's *A'in-i Akbari* and other sources support speculation that nearly 20 per cent of the people in Akbar's empire depended 'wholly or partly on the pursuit of arms', which meant travelling to

[6] See Fernand Braudel, *Civilization and Capitalism, 15th–18th Century*, vol.I, *The Structures of Everyday Life: the limits of the possible* (New York, 1981). Also Bose (ed.), *South Asia and World Capitalism*, on the work of Immanuel Wallerstein.

[7] For discussions, see Braudel, *Civilization and Capitalism*, pp.31-104; David Ludden, 'Orientalist empiricism and transformations of colonial knowledge', in C.A. Breckenridge and Peter van der Veer (eds.), *Orientalism and the post-Colonial Predicament* (Philadelphia, 1993), pp.250-78; and David Ludden, 'India's development regime', in Nicholas B. Dirks (ed.), *Colonialism and Culture* (Ann Arbor, 1992), pp.247-87. For examples, see David Arnold, *Famine: social crisis and historical change* (Oxford, 1988), and 'Famine in peasant consciousness and peasant action: Madras 1876-8', in Ranajit Guha (ed.), *Subaltern Studies: writings on South Asian history* (Delhi), pp.61-115; Ramachandra Guha, *The Unquiet Woods: ecological change and peasant resistance in the Himalayas* (Delhi, 1989); and Ranajit Guha, *Elementary Aspects of Peasant Insurgency in Colonial India* (Delhi, 1983)

fight. Regions of the Ganga plain and the Deccan were characterised by seasonal military migrations that were part of peasant subsistence.[8] Agriculture was not sedentary in much of India. Seasonal migrants, people fleeing war and drought, army suppliers and camp-followers, artisans moving to find work, and peasants looking for new land, traders, nomads, shifting cultivators, hunters, herders, and transporters would have accounted for perhaps half the population of India in the eighteenth century. Mobility was at least as characteristic of pre-modern India as sedentarism.

So it is useful to imagine pre-modern India as a terrain of perpetual movement, where social, political and economic order only emerged in the context of constant, pervasive conflict and adjustment. Vertical conflicts in the social relations of inequality and hierarchy generated patterns of social subordination. Horizontal conflicts among social groups created schisms, partitions, fragmentations and segregations among groups. Caste society as a whole and its constituent jatis were shaped in the process. Locally, as the process of containing and resolving conflict created social order, it always involved non-local powers. Non-local power played a constant, critical role in the local working of caste society, and in south India, this power radiated from temples and courts. Religious and political elites in these centres of power envisioned the localities of social reproduction as components of their own domain, as units of an orderly system established by their own moral authority. But these temple and court elites exerted their power in a social world that they did not control: elites engaged local concatenations of power that could not be reduced to regulation by temple and court. In pre-modern centuries, a vast array of local actors exercised structural powers to transform local society, changing their own material world and the terms of their social transactions. Temple and court ritual adapted to the fractious dispersion of social power in which jatis created economic regions.[9]

[8] The quote and the *A'in* statistical inferences come from Irfan Habib's review of Dirk H.A. Kolff, *Rajput and Sepoy: the ethnohistory of the military labour market in Hindustan, 1450-1850* (Cambridge, 1990), in Irfan Habib (ed.), *Medieval India* 1: *researches in the history of India, 1200-1750* (Delhi, 1991), pp.210-11. For an extensive treatment of this theme, see David Ludden, 'History outside civilization and the mobility of South Asia', *South Asia* 17, 1 (1994), pp.1-23.

[9] On social powers or capacities, agency and structure, see Alex Callinicos, *Making History: agency, structure and change in social theory* (Ithaca, 1988), and Anthony Giddens, *Central Problems in Social Theory: action, structure and contradiction in social analysis* (Berkeley, 1979).

Forms and codes of conduct that contained and channelled conflict in localities and regions of social change developed in transactional systems connecting castes, gods and kings. Vertical transactions constituted kingdoms and empires, as they also modelled social relations in and among jatis in segmented regions of state power.[10] Transactional systems that ordered caste society and state politics simultaneously took hierarchical forms that produced not only social inferiority in relations of command but also dignity in social relations of economic specialisation and inequality. Chronicles (*vamcavalis*) 'make it clear that honors and emblems [were] only meaningful when given by a superior, a king or deity',[11] so that subordination was also dignification: '[a]cting on behalf of one's lord...is a relationship established by the actual, though always partial, sharing of the substance of sovereignty...in the form of titles, emblems, land, and sometimes even pre-eaten rice'.[12] Gifts by human and divine lords dignify as they rank jatis, internally and externally.

Nicholas Dirks shows how temple and state gift transactions in Pudukkottai constructed Kallar jati formations in historical patterns of migration and conflict. Dirk Kolff makes a similar point for north India when he argues that a peasant soldier's service *naukari* status rested on a relationship with a lord; Kolff goes further to argue that there was a complementarity in 'North Indian peasant culture...between home, marriage, and ascriptive status on the one hand, and pastoralism, *naukari* and ascetic achievement on the other'.[13] The cultural logic of personal social ranking by royal honour and state service provided a flexible, dynamic element in the historical formation of caste society, which helps to explain differentiations and elaborations of what Thomas Zwicker called 'dignities of difference'[14] and the regional construction of what Burton Stein calls segmentary state forms in peninsular India. Because in vertical and horizontal formations of conflict and transaction 'we can see direct links (as well as instructively inexact fits)

[10] Burton Stein, *Peasant State and Society in Medieval South India* (Delhi, 1980). Arjun Appadurai and Carol Breckenridge, 'The south Indian temple: authority, honour and redistribution', *Contributions to Indian Sociology,* 10, 2 (1976), pp.167-211. Nicholas B. Dirks, *The Hollow Crown: ethnohistory of an Indian kingdom* (Cambridge, 1987); Ludden, *Peasant History.*

[11] Dirks, *Hollow Crown*, p.103.

[12] Ibid.

[13] Kolff, *Rajput and Sepoy*, p.95.

[14] Thomas Zwicker, 'Morality and Etiquette in the Reproduction of Hierarchical Caste Relations in South Asia', Master's dissertation, Department of Anthropology, University of Pennsylvania, 1984.

between the segmentary structure of lineages, subcastes, and castes on the one hand and the emerging structure, at the regional level, of the pre-colonial old regime state on the other'.[15]

Inside medieval south Indian kingdoms, a transactional system that ordered fractious, dispersed social powers, by linking individuals and groups with the power of kings and gods, expanded its influence in the first millennium A.D. The social logic of caste evolved in these kingdoms; its seems to have taken root first at the pinnacle of an already stratified society, in transactions among military men and local patriarchs. It seems to have taken hold first in irrigated, rice-growing, riverine areas, where inscriptions record the rise of a medieval hierarchy focused on Brahmans and Vellalas, temples and courts. From the tenth century onward, many representations of caste hierarchy appear in epigraphy of royal transactions and proclamations.

But states did not dictate caste order. Local actors built political formations whose reproduction and expansion constituted hierarchy in society. The expansion of medieval states, like their decline and replacement after 1300, certainly did involve purely coercive machinations by military élites; but, from medieval to modern times, states in southern India rested on a growing number of diverse, overlapping and vested political segments formed by local jati clusters, in which conflict was ordered by transactions with kings and gods. Incompatible forms of jati order coexisted inside states. Medieval states contained contrasting jati sub-regions: most dramatically, caste society in the riverine, rice-growing areas contrasted starkly with dry and pastoral areas.[16] Such contrasts multiplied after 1200, because the medieval states of the first millennium did not dominate all the land or people in the peninsula: large areas and populations lay outside these agrarian states and caste societies. The colonisation of such exterior regions accelerated social mobility and involved rampant jati war. Many stories of this period depict wars that pitted militant, migratory, farming jatis against hunters and pastoralists. Subduing the forest-dwellers—commonly Karumbars in the Tamil country—became a necessary condition for effective kingship.[17]

During this critical post-medieval period in the history of caste society—c.1200 to 1700—groups once associated with hunting, pasto-

[15] Dirks, *Hollow Crown*, pp.153-4, referring to Stein, *Peasant State*.

[16] James E. Heitzman, 'Gifts of Power: temples, politics, and economy in medieval south India', PhD thesis, Department of History, University of Pennsylvania, 1985.

[17] Ludden, *Peasant History*, p.49ff.; Dirks, *Hollow Crown*, p.90.

ralism, robbery and threats to settled society became dominant jatis in new areas of agricultural colonisation. South and east of Madurai, Maravas and Kallars carved out domains at the expense of Vellalas, and they created new forms of jati order, incompatible with those in medieval core areas, which remained dominated by Vellalas and Brahmans.[18] The Vijayanagar empire in the far south comprised a system of political mediations for jati wars around Madurai; and it was not until the sixteenth century and the rise of Madurai Nayakas that a stable political structure emerged in state segments created during centuries of caste war.

In the Madurai domain the logic of post-medieval social conflict created a logic of early-modern political order. The new order was partitioned horizontally among dominant jati groups and spatially among sub-regional state segments. Incompatible forms of jati order were spatially segregated by the partitioning of dominant caste domains. Kallars and Maravas divided Pudukkottai, north and south; Maravas and Telugus divided the dry-lands of Tirunelveli, east and west.[19] Medieval core, irrigated, rice-growing areas of Vellala-Brahman dominance retained forms of caste society distinct from those developing in dry millet-growing areas of post-medieval colonisation. Even today, dominant castes that rank high in dry villages rank low in wet villages.[20] Shanars, who rank low in wet and dry areas, built domains for themselves south of the Tambraparni river. Palla and Pariah untouchables, who were bonded servants for high-caste families in wet areas, became independent farmers in the dry region north of the Tambraparni.[21] During centuries of agrarian colonisation, farming jatis created new social forms by conquering hunters and pastoralists; they avoided subordination to established dominant jatis by building new domains for their own dominance separated spatially from old ones.

Vijayanagar and Nayaka royalty institutionalised the already partitioned spatial segments of the new political system in ritual transactions with court and temple in Madurai. The vamcavalis show this for Telugu and Marava *palaiyakkarars* in Tirunelveli; and Dirks described it in Pudukkottai.[22] The resulting sub-regional 'little kings' used transactions of fealty and gifting to build authority inside their own state segments.

[18] Ludden, *Peasant History*, pp.49-67; Dirks, *Hollow Crown*, pp.71-107, 139-55.

[19] Ibid., p.142; Ludden, *Peasant History*, maps 15 and 16.

[20] Dirks, *Hollow Crown*, pp.73-4.

[21] Ludden, *Peasant History*, pp.59-67.

[22] Ibid., pp.49-52; Dirks, *Hollow Crown*, pp.55-203.

The replication of transactions with Madurai formulated jati hierarchy in segments of the state and in segregated regions of jati order; 'the political development of regional hegemony led to the development and elaboration of particular forms of subcaste organisation...among the dominant Kallars of Pudukkottai'.[23] Territorial segregation enabled incompatible forms of jati order—constructed by different clusters of castes—to coexist in segments of one polity. In segments of the state system, the same logic of deference and subordination that produced little kings under big kings produced local order based on vertical transactions among jati leaders and kings.

Politics and production

The politics that built regions of kingship and jati dominance organised labour that built the agrarian landscape. State expansion and fragmentation paralleled agricultural expansion and colonisation. Migratory colonisation opened political frontiers and production frontiers at the same time. The horizontal partitioning of the political landscape divided systems of land and labour control. Vertical transactions of fealty and transcendence generated capital for investment and power to command labour. There is thus no practical distinction between the cultural, political, social and economic history of caste. Similarly, there is no practical distinction between the transactional logic of caste and commerce. For the horizontal and vertical transactions of jati society generated commercial resources. As dominant farming jatis conquered the peninsula, they expanded production frontiers in spatially-partitioned domains of labour control defined by transactions in tribute among centres of trade.

The dominant caste domains around Madurai were built by the late sixteenth century and remain spatially intact even today. But inside regions, caste society continued to change, and resulting conflicts were mediated by transactions with kings and gods. In pursuit of livelihoods, families moved around and settled in localities that became increasingly differentiated in their caste composition and economic character. Caste livelihood strategies and labour power, in the context of physical mobility and systems for the orderly jati integration into new localities, stimulated the manufacturing sector. For the physical mobility of caste groups and their ability to be integrated quickly into new economic settings brought skill, labour and capital into localities, expanding their productive capacities.

[23] Ibid., p.153.

The transactional linkage of all localities to temples and kings in the political system formed a logic for the integration of caste groups in any locality, which in turn fuelled the growth of manufacturing and commercial centres. Caste leaders followed the pattern of little kings, paying tribute to higher authorities and paying to endow temple rituals, to establish themselves in the local hierarchy. Immigrant caste groups could thus enter into a new locality and new set of economic relations fairly easily: the rules and cost of entry were well-known throughout India. Such migrations and resettlements generated local production in response to market demands; and a portion of the return went into the vertical flow of tribute to kings and gods. The commercial character of state revenue is obvious by the seventeenth century, when commercial financing and forward contracting provided tributary income for Nayakas of Madurai. Some men who transmitted tribute to Nayakas and to Rajas of Ramanathapuram fit perfectly the image of 'portfolio capitalists' drawn by Sanjay Subrahmanyam and C.A. Bayly; the most prominent of these patriarchs, the Medai Delavoy Mudaliyar, effectively ruled Tirunelveli under the Nayakas.[24] After 1730, this class of actors became larger and more diverse, as Europeans struggled to control the tributary system. Uttumalai Raja, in Tirunelveli, for instance, found cash payments of tribute through commercial middlemen to be necessary for his local authority.[25] Trade of all sorts increased to help finance the increasing scale of cash payments to rulers.[26] Likewise, commercial activity at all levels came to rest on the relations of authority that were established by tribute payments.

The 1823 *Census and Dehazada of the Province of Tirunelveli* is a tally of taxable assets and caste groups that accounted for state revenue in the political economy of tributary commercialism in early-modern Tirunelveli.[27] English East India Company officers who designed the census, conceived of India as a land of villages, and taxable assets in revenue villages were the central objects of census enumeration. Yet

[24] Sanjay Subrahmanyam and C.A. Bayly, 'Portfolio capitalists and the political economy of early modern India', *Indian Economic and Social History Review*, 25 (1988), pp.401-24, reprinted in Sanjay Subrahmanyam, *Merchants, Markets and the State in Early Modern India* (Delhi, 1990). Ludden, *Peasant History*, pp.69-70, 89, 99, 189.

[25] Dirks, *Hollow Crown*, p.92. The Arabic word *tohfa* is used for 'tribute' in this text, to suggest the innovative character of such payments.

[26] For details, see Ludden, 'Agrarian commercialism'.

[27] See Ludden, 'World economy and village India'; Frank Perlin, 'Proto-industrialization and pre-colonial South Asia', *Past and Present*, 98 (1983), pp.30-95; Subrahmanyam and Bayly, 'Portfolio capitalists'.

from our perspective, we can appreciate that the economic landscape recorded in 1823 was more complex and dynamic: it was built over centuries, by migration and settlement, by labour, by commercial linkages, by transactions across political partitions along networks of movement and communication, and by ritual that formed political hierarchies and dignities of social difference.[28] The East India Company ascended the apex of the state system in 1801 and accounted for assets as best they could. The 1823 census of Tirunelveli is a most successful effort of this accounting project. It flattens out census villages for cold, statistical dissection, but we can use its data to bring local elements of the regional economic system back to life.

The most powerful local actors in the regional economy, duly recorded in the census, were Mirasidars of the Tambraparni basin. From medieval times, these Vellala and Brahman landowners extended their control of irrigated land, low-caste labour force and political power in the region. The riverine tract of paddy cultivation embodied their power. But labour relations that characterised the Tambraparni were not reproduced elsewhere, even where irrigated farming did expand. The expansion of agrarian frontiers outside the medieval Tambraparni heartland during post-medieval colonisation engendered labour relations of a different sort, organised by different dominant jatis—Nayakas, Reddiyars and Maravas—whose combination of conquest and farming distinguished their subculture of labour control from that of Tambraparni Brahmans and Vellalas.

The economic landscape recorded in the census thus arose from labour relations constructed in the history of caste politics; and caste politics were in turn conducted in a changing economic climate generated by labour organised by dominant caste power. The residential settlement patterns that we can see in the 1823 census data were often the product of relatively recent migrations, as people moved and settled in places of opportunity. Caste society thus continued to build the economic landscape in the early-modern period. Just as untouchable labour under mirasidar control had made the medieval river valley into a ribbon of green, and just as militant peasants had created a land of rice,

[28] Rituals generated symbolic capital whose accumulation was a component of commercialism and a cultural force in the growth of the market economy. Religious gatherings and institutions of all kinds were major economic phenomena. This justifies treating religious establishments as components of the commercial economy, as I do below. The first major work on this theme was Burton Stein, 'The economic functions of the medieval South Indian temple', *Journal of Asian Studies*, 19 (1960), pp.163-76.

millet and gardens north and south of the Tambraparni in post-medieval centuries, caste groups moving into centres of employment and investment produced an urbanising economy of trade and manufacturing in the eighteenth century.

Production localities

Irrigation highlights the long history of agricultural development that underlay urbanisation. As the major means to raise land productivity, irrigation fuelled economic urbanism—which I measure for each 1823 census village by calculating the ratio of assets listed in Table 3 to total farm acreage.[29] Table 2 displays the urban-rural continuum, in which irrigation is most intense at the urban end of the spectrum.[30] On average, urban sites altogether have 3.54 times more of the sample area's irrigated land than of its total farmland. Small towns have a similar ratio (3.18), but rural sites have ratios down from 2.42 to 0.04. The low proportion (3 per cent) of uncultivated wetland (*tarisu*) in urban centres indicates the intense utilisation of wetland in urban areas. Wells also

Table 2: *Economic differentiation in four Tirunelveli Taluks, 1823*

	Census villages		Population		Econ.index	Pop./100 acre	
	No.	%	Average	%	Average	Total	Wet
Urban sites	36	22	2,253	34	5.87	116	229
Major centres	6	4	4,813	17	4.28	101	280
Big towns	15	9	1,492	13	4.52	103	193
Suburbs	15	9	454	4	8.81	145	214
Small towns	8	5	427	2	2.32	63	158
Rural sites	115	72	1,492	62	.73	24	121
Big villages	16	10	2,633	25	.78	23	152
Small villages	22	14	1,446	19	.69	20	123
Hamlets	77	48	398	18	.72	30	57

Notes: Percentages are of the sample total. The last two columns show population per 100 farm acres. The taluks are Tenkasi, Shankarankoil (without zamindaris), Brahmadesam and Shermadevi. Index values measure concentrations of 44 dehazada items (Table 3) in each village compared to farm acres. Farm acres include all revenue classifications, including waste. 'Wet' means 'classified as irrigated'. (See Ludden, 'Agrarian commercialism' for details.) *Source*: See note 30.

[29] See Ludden, 'Agrarian commercialism'.

[30] The source for Tables 2 to 6 is: Tamil Nadu Archives, Revenue Department Sundries no.39, 'Census and Dehazada of the Province of Tirunelveli'.

concentrated in urban settlements. So it is clear that urban sites of manufacturing and trade grew in proportion to local water, paddy and food.

Sixty per cent of all state revenue came from irrigated land, some of it collected in cash from speculators who received government grain for retail sales, the rest collected in kind for sale in government granaries. State revenues from temples, customs, land and other sources also passed through urban centres, where it could be invested in irrigation, trade and revenue contracting, all of which expanded the state's financial base. Service groups, artisans, merchants and labourers sought work where investments in irrigation poured water on the land. Urban buyers generated demand for rural products and labour, as urban financiers collected and transmitted government revenue to enhance portfolios that included land, grain, temple endowments, and other assets.

Because taxes, profits and temple endowments generated the wherewithal for local investments for irrigation, and because the availability of labour, food and resources in market centres would have lowered the cost of local irrigation, development, urbanisation and irrigation reinforced one another. This was not a one-way causal relationship. Statistically, in fact, irrigated arable is not a good predictor of economic urbanism. Large urban centres have lower proportions of wetland in their borders than big towns.[31] Many trade and manufacturing assets lie in localities with little irrigation. Many small villages contain large irrigated tracts but few trade and manufacturing assets.[32] Irrigated places in 1823 were rural and urban; they could have been either small agricultural villages or major trade and manufacturing centres. Spreading water on the land did not suffice to make a place a centre of manufacturing and trade.

Economic urbanisation depended on extensive economic relations with many localities in networks of trade and power. Five of the six

[31] Large urban centres had less than twice the extent of wet arable (as a proportion of the sample area) than they had total farm acres; while smaller urban centres and towns had four times as much. The smallest type of rural settlements in fact had a higher proportion of wet arable to farm acreage (2.42) than did large urban centres (1.86), and three times than did larger rural localities (0.82); the reason for this being that larger rural areas embraced proportionately more dry land, despite having roughly the same index of concentration of trade and manufacturing assets as small rural areas, which supported more people per farm acre because of their higher proportion of irrigated land. Ludden, 'Agrarian commercialism', Table 5.

[32] Ten census villages in the Tambraparni tract had very high proportions of irrigated farmland (over 90 per cent), but no looms at all recorded in their borderds. See Pattamadi, discussed below.

large urban centres in our sample lay in the medieval core political territory of Tirunelveli, in tracts watered by the Tambraparni and Chittar rivers, at the heart of the regional transportation system. One, however, Shankarankoil, lay in a tract askew of central corridors with poor soil and wretched irrigation: its population—like that of most major urban centres, I think—could not have fed itself with local cultivation alone.[33] Altogether, large urban centres have 17 per cent of the sample population but only 9 per cent of cultivated wetland. They have only 18 cultivated wet acres for every 100 people, whereas 40 is the average for rural areas, 55 for small rural areas. However intense their local rice-farming might have been, urban centres must have fed themselves by buying food from their hinterlands. Agricultural villages would have sent grain to urban centres. This food, like the investments that built local irrigation, came into urban centres because of their position in networks of accumulation and exchange.

The political partitioning of south India was an important determinant of any locality's economic position, because the segments of states constituted central place hierarchies. Four of six urban centres were taluk headquarters, with long histories of regional political significance. Major urban centres and big towns together had 30 per cent of the sample polulation, only 21 per cent of its cultivated wetland, but 80 per cent of government headquarters (*katcheries*), 44 per cent of town custom stations, 63 per cent of road custom stations, and 53 per cent of state granaries. Government grew in market centres and markets grew in states. So urban centres developed as concentrations of consumption, public activity, trade and redistribution. Urban centres and big towns, with 30 per cent of the sample population, had 43 per cent of principal temples, 48 per cent of *mandapams*, 76 per cent of *chattrams*, and 56 per cent of the major annual festivals; they had 58 per cent of all two-storey houses, 51 per cent of terraced houses, and 53 per cent of tile-roof houses in the sample region.

The urban growth of trade and manufacturing affected many aspects of local life. Urban sites (Table 2) held about one-third of the sample population. They had much higher population densities and quite different caste compositions from small towns and rural census villages. Table 3 indicates, however, that only one set of manufacturing assets was concentrated very dramatically in urban centres—gunny frames. This reflects the fact that major urban centres contained a high proportion of high-cost production for long-distance trade; they held 70 per

[33] For more detail, see Ludden, *Peasant History*, Maps 8 and 10.

Table 3: *Ranked average indexes of concentration for village economic index items, by locality groups*

Rank	Item	Average index value: Urban places	Small towns	Rural places
1	Gunny frames	24.74	.00	.04
2	Toddy shops	14.72	.34	.18
3	Arrack shops	14.06	.91	.22
4	Brazier shops	9.67	3.68	.29
5	Carts	8.60	3.43	.77
6	Asses	8.32	1.81	.72
7	Annual festivals	7.60	3.34	.45
8	Terraced houses	7.52	2.41	.91
9	Muslim looms	7.39	.00	.49
10	Kaikkolar looms	7.16	3.67	.26
11	Total looms	6.83	2.32	.40
12	Sugar mills	6.60	2.07	.62
13	Betel bazaars	6.51	5.65	.80
14	Goats	6.35	.41	.80
15	Silversmith shops	6.30	2.30	.62
16	Bleaching places	6.23	.55	.86
17	Pallar looms	6.19	2.19	.63
18	Jack trees	6.06	4.53	.62
19	Shanar looms	5.76	3.62	.77
20	Public buildings	5.57	4.17	.79
21	Silk looms	5.54	.00	.14
22	Potter works	5.30	4.21	.80
23	Horses	4.92	.98	.80
24	Coconut trees	4.89	2.78	.86
25	Lime kilns	4.79	.00	.88
26	Razor cases	4.76	3.10	.76
27	Total population	4.65	2.32	1.01
28	Bazaars	4.63	1.54	2.16
29	Houses	4.58	2.45	.97
30	Periodic festivals	4.51	3.86	2.13
31	Religious buildings	4.12	2.86	.99
32	Buffaloes	4.05	3.81	.96
33	Sheep	3.90	1.54	1.04
34	Rock wells	3.88	1.21	.81
35	Mat frames	3.73	.00	.59
36	Ploughs	3.43	2.98	1.05
37	Oil mills	3.30	4.07	.85
38	Bulls	3.16	2.35	1.04
39	Cows	3.12	2.67	.99
40	Carpenters' yards	2.74	2.53	.93
41	Dirt wells	2.36	3.89	.89
42	Mango + tamarind trees	2.20	2.51	1.03

Note: Index items with urban averages below sample average are omitted. Index values are item averages for locality groups. *Source*: See note 30.

cent of all silk looms and 78 per cent of all Kaikkolar looms; 94 per cent of silk looms were in major urban centres or big towns.

By contrast, major urban centres and big towns, with 30 per cent of the sample population, had only 64 per cent of all taxed looms, 46 per cent of the silver-shops and 61 per cent of the brazier-shops. Urban sites had significant concentrations of trade and manufacturing assets, but the production system—and textile production in particular—involved the combination of activities and assets that were dispersed throughout networks in which urban centres were nodes of accumulation and exchange. It is reasonable to assume that assets accounted for in the 1823 census were commercially active and therefore taxed—they constitute a set of assets registered at the intersection of the commercial economy and the state taxation system. Some of these assets (and their associated production activities) were distinctly rural: only 38 per cent of all carts and Muslim looms in the sample, and only 11 per cent of Shanar looms and 20 per cent of Palla looms were registered in urban sites.

The activities of textile production—cotton-growing, cleaning, spinning, weaving, dyeing, packing, transport and finance—were spread throughout the central place hierarchy. Weaving was concentrated in the 21 of 159 census villages which had a higher share of the sample's total number of taxed looms than of its population. These 21 weaving centres include all six major urban centres, three big towns and two small suburbs, but also one small town and five small villages. Even small rural localities sustained commercial weaving, in part from local demand and in part from trade along the urban-rural continuum that connected villages to long-distance trade. Concentrations of Muslim and Kaikkolar weavers of high-quality cloth appear in five small villages.[34] Moreover, tiny hamlets—which altogether account for a little more of the sample population (18 per cent) than major urban centres (17 per cent)—contain many more of some types of taxed commercial assets: oil mills (28 to 12), betel gardens 45 to 4), betel bazaars (26 to 5), carpenters' yards (67 to 32), potters' works (66 to 25), periodic festivals (105 to 68) and bazaars (141 to 118), not to mention milk-cows and buffaloes, ploughs, bullocks and commercial trees (coconut, supari, jack, mango, tamarind and palmyra).

Because commercial and manufacturing activities were spread across the urban-rural continuum, urban and rural localities were not

[34] For instance, Minakshipuram, a tiny settlement of 166 people near Tirunelveli town, had 103 'Moor looms'. See also the case of Karisattan, below.

distinguished by the presence of taxable commercial and manufacturing assets, but rather by the scale of accumulation and by the preponderance of farming assets in their boundaries. No part of the region—even the most rural areas—lay outside the commercial economy. Even the smallest rural villages were differentiated from one another in their economic character by their position in regional networks of economic specialisation. Compare Pattamadi, with 552 residents in the Tambraparni valley, two miles from Seranmahadevi (taluk headquarters), and Karisattan, with 450 residents in the dry land seven miles from Shankarankoil. At first sight, Pattamadi would seem to be the more commercially active: it has 98 waterworks, 47 religious buildings, a major annual festival, 14 periodic festivals, a customs station, 17 terraced houses and 41 merchant houses, all sustained by trade along the active road between Tirunelveli town and Seranmahadevi, and by the 21 per cent of its total arable acreage irrigated from the Tambraparni,. Yet this village and its 81 mirasidars seem to have lived by working the transit trade, farms and trees alone. Virtually no manufacturing assets appear in its census record, the exception being a sugar mill; and in addition to irrigated land, it boasted 22,732 taxable trees, mostly palmyras.

By contrast, only eight per cent of arable in Karisattan was irrigated. It had only 556 taxable trees and was clearly not a market centre, though it did have three periodic festivals, one bazaar, one betel bazaar, one arrack shop and two merchant houses. But Karisattan had one iron forge, 13 Kaikkolar looms, one carpenter's yard, two potters' works, and two bleaching places for cloth; and one milch cow for every two inhabitants (compared to one for every eight in Pattamadi) and two sheep and goats (compared to none in Pattamadi). The people in Karisattan clearly produced a lot to sell.

Who the people were in these two villages helps to explain their economic differences. In Pattamadi, a Pandya Vellala stronghold, all but two mirasidars appear as non-residents.[35] Pandya Vellalas were 21 per cent of the population; Pallas and Pariahs together were 50 per cent; both being about twice the average percentage for sample villages, which is typical for a Tambraparni village. Pattamadi's abundant palmyras were surely tended by its large Shanar population (at 18 per cent about twice the census village average). No Pandya Vellalas lived in

[35] The 1823 census records 81 mirasidars for this village, but only two mirasidar houses. By contrast, Karisattan had 51 mirasidars and 54 mirasidar houses. On meanings of 'mirasidar' in colonial records, see Ludden, *Peasant History*, pp.101-15.

Karisattan, but instead a small group of migrant Chola and Tulu Vellalas. The untouchable castes amount to only 17 per cent of its population, well below the sample census village average (24 per cent). Most resident Karisattan jatis had histories of migration—Kaikkolars, Chetties, Reddiyars, Totiyars and Maravas—and along with the immigrant Vellalas, they constituted 60 per cent of the village. Karisattan's bleaching places were obviously worked by its large group of resident washermen (at four per cent, four times the sample average). Its population of Kaikkolar weavers (16 per cent) was eight times greater that the average of the sample census villages.[36]

Caste and economy

In Pattamadi and Karisattan, we see two localities with different social and economic profiles, one at the ancient core of the region and the other on its periphery, built as production environments by distinctive caste clusters. Pattamadi and Karisattan typify the pattern of production localities in Tirunelveli recorded in the 1823 census: local caste clusters reflect distinctive social formations of economic organisation. These arose historically because family decisions to move and settle in particular places distributed labour and capital among places within networks of human mobility, trade and power. The historical combination of specialised caste migration and settlement strategies, the spatial clustering of castes endowed with complementary assets, the availability of ritual and social techniques for organising power among caste groups, and ready communication along the urban-rural continuum made the early-modern economy responsive to its world market environment.

Family strategies and the formation of caste clusters are clearly visible in census data, which describe jatis of many different kinds. Important economic differences among castes appear in their spatial distributions, which can be taken (very roughly) to represent aggregate family preferences and the outcome of residential settlement strategies. Some castes formed large populations, embraced many occupational distinctions, and spread across the entire region, all along the urban-rural continuum (Tables 4 and 5). Other large jatis concentrated only in one region or at one end of the urban-rural spectrum. For instance, Vellalas and Brahmans—who together dominated the political economy of the Tambraparni valley, where they had a much bigger demographic share than elsewhere—demonstrate different residential preferences. Brah-

[36] This average pertains to the 140 villages in the sample with more than 100 inhabitants.

mans lived much more often in urban sites; and among Brahmans, Smarta Telugus (who migrated into the region in post-medieval centuries) had a much stronger tendency to live in more urban sites than Smarta Tamils or Sri Vaishnavas. On the other hand, (native) Pandya Vellalas spread over the entire region in exactly the same pattern as the population generally; as did the immigrant Tondaimandala Mudalis;

Table 4: *Castes enumerated in all four taluk returns, with headings, in order of appearance in 1923 Census tables*

	Total	%		Total	%
Brahmans			*Sudras continued*		
Smarta Telugu	2,177	1.3	Intermixed Sudra	447	.3
Smarta Tamil	6,187	3.7	Panchalar/artisan	6,064	3.7
Sri Vaishnava	1,367	.8	Cuddashelkaran	125	.1
Mudivar Tadvati	551	.3	Potter (Koshavar)	1,031	.6
Shiva Bhaktar	510	.3	Barber (Ambatan)	2,019	1.2
Vishnu Nambiyar	221	.1	Washerman (Vannan)	1,707	1.0
Total	12,499	7.5	Dyer (Shoyakaran)	200	.1
Religious Establishment			Total Sudras	83,620	50.4
Oduvar or Gurukle	382	.2	*Muslims*		
Hundi Thauthen	477	.3	Pattulu	520	.3
Vyraver	885	.5	Lubbay	7,508	4.5
Ochen & Mulacaren	653	.4	Total	8,028	4.8
Dasi or dancing girl	757	.5	*Christians*		
Total	3,950	2.4	Parava	59	.0
Sudras			Shanar	361	.2
Pandy Vellala	16,294	9.8	Pariah	469	.3
Karaikkattu Vellalas	1,428	.9	Total	1,244	.8
Sholleah & Tulu V.	550	.3	*Inferior Sudras*		
T. Mudaliyars	803	.5	Elava	2,041	1.5
Chetties	2,740	1.7	Shanar	17,493	10.5
Villay Jeddiyan	1,256	.8	Cunniyan	122	.0
Vaniyan	2,902	1.8	Korava	220	.1
Patnulkar + P.	1,684	1.0	Total	21,528	13.0
Kaikkolar	5,160	3.1	*Low Caste*		
K. Maravas	9,100	5.5	Palla	21,293	12.8
Kotaly Maravas	5,040	3.0	Vallava	132	.0
Panan	199	.1	Pariah	8,727	5.2
Chalupan	245	.2	Shinimaun/Chuckler	2,028	1.2
Continued next column			Total	32,596	19.6

Notes: Totals for each caste category may include castes not listed here. Census village averages are for villages with populations over 100. The 159 villages are in four taluks: Tenkasi, Shankarankoil (without zamindaris), Brahmadesam, and Shermadevi. K = Kondaiyankottai; P = Pattashalaiyan; T = Tondaimandala; V= Vellala. *Source*: See note 30.

Table 5: *Percentage of caste population by type of locality*

	Urban areas				Rural areas			All	All
	A	B	C	D	E	F	G	Urb	Rrl
Total population	17	13	4	2	25	19	18	34	62
Number of castes	9	15	6	2	26	18	24	30	68
Brahmans									
Smarta Telugu	35	15	1	1	13	19	16	51	48
Smarta Tamil	27	22	9	4	10	10	18	58	38
Sri Vaishnava	16	19	4	0	13	38	10	39	61
Mudivar Tadvati	29	6	13	3	16	22	10	48	48
Shiva Bhaktar	62	13	1	2	7	8	7	76	22
Vishnu Nambiyar	19	20	5	3	18	12	23	44	53
Total	28	18	6	2	14	15	16	52	45
Religious Establishment									
Oduvar or Gurukle	32	24	7	3	12	11	10	63	33
Hundi Thauthen	30	19	1	1	20	11	19	50	50
Vyraver	7	11	2	2	24	22	31	320	77
Ochen/Mulacaran	25	27	1	2	15	16	14	53	45
Dasi	45	19	1	1	15	12	8	65	35
Total	29	19	2	2	17	14	18	50	49
Sudras									
Pandya Vellala	19	15	9	33	19	14	21	43	54
Karaikkattu Vellala	49	2	2	0	8	9	29	53	46
Chola/Tulu Vellala	8	0	0	1	1	15	75	8	91
Tondaimandala Mudali	14	17	4	1	28	19	17	35	64
Chetties	25	20	1	1	13	25	15	46	53
Villay Jeddiyan	14	20	0	0	34	18	14	34	66
Vaniyan	10	14	5	4	29	18	20	29	67
Patnulkar + Pattashalaiyan	75	14	0	0	1	8	2	89	11
Kaikkolar	70	5	0	4	10	8	2	75	20
Kondaiyankottai Maravas	5	10	2	2	44	18	20	17	82
Kotaly Maravas	18	34	6	4	7	13	17	58	37
Panan	20	31	4	9	13	17	7	55	37
Chalupan	9	26	51	0	5	3	7	86	15
Intermixed Sudras	18	13	1	0	12	34	14	32	69
Panchalar or artisans	19	12	6	2	24	17	18	37	59
Cuddashelkaran	19	31	0	0	1	7	42	50	50
Potters (Koshavar)	15	15	5	1	19	16	29	35	64
Barbers (Ambatan)	20	17	4	2	21	19	17	41	57
Washermen (Vannan)	12	12	18	2	23	17	17	42	57
Dyer (Shoyakaran)	50	21	15	3	1	2	9	86	12
Total Sudras	18	13	4	2	25	20	17	35	62

[Key: A = large centres; B = big towns; C = suburbs; D = small town; E = large; F = medium; G = small; Urb = urban; Rrl = rural.]

Table continues.

Table 5 continued.

	Urban areas A	B	C	D	Rural areas E	F	G	All Urb	All Rrl
Muslims									
Pattulu	53	9	4	0	19	8	8	66	35
Lubbay	30	6	1	2	33	14	14	37	61
Total	32	6	1	2	32	14	13	39	59
Christians									
Parava	24	17	0	8	5	36	10	41	51
Shanar	0	0	2	3	57	36	1	2	94
Pariah	67	23	0	2	4	0	4	90	8
Total	38	13	1	2	25	18	3	52	46
Inferior Sudras									
Elava	11	20	5	2	28	13	20	35	61
Shanar	2	14	2	1	37	36	19	18	82
Cunniyan	35	19	27	4	7	0	7	81	14
Korava	22	5	2	2	26	26	17	29	69
Total	5	14	2	1	35	24	19	21	78
Low Castes									
Palla	6	15	6	2	27	18	27	27	72
Vallava	25	23	0	0	27	5	20	48	52
Pariah	19	18	6	1	19	17	20	43	56
Shinimaun or Chuckler	1	3	1	1	36	33	24	4	93
Total	9	15	6	2	26	18	24	30	68

Key: A = large centres; B = big towns; C = suburbs; D = small towns; E = large; F = medium; G = small; Urb = urban; Rrl = rural.
Notes: Totals for each caste category may include castes not listed here. Census village averages are for villages with populations over 100. The 159 villages are in four taluks: Tenkasi, Shankarankoil (without zamindaris), Brahmadesam and Shermadevi. *Source*: See note 30.

whereas immigrant Karaikkattu Vellalas were split between very rural and strong urban preferences, and Chola and Tulu Vellalas much preferred hamlets like Karisattan.

Other large jatis that migrated into the region were split on similar lines. Among Maravas, the Kondaiyankottais and Kotalis favoured rural and urban settings, respectively, which in effect meant that relatively few members of the much larger Kondaiyankottai group lived in Zamindar (formerly Poligar) fort towns: Uttumalai, Surandai and Chokkampatti. Shanars had very strong rural preferences. Pallas (the largest landless labour caste) settled in the same spatial pattern as did the population as a whole, but eschewed urban centres, which suggests a distinct caste profile for urban labour. The small landless labouring jati, Pariahs, show a stronger tendency to live in urban sites, which often have high Pariah percentages—for instance, Seranmahadevi (16 per cent) and Ambasamudram (8 per cent)—suggesting that Pariahs played more active roles than Pallas in manufacturing.[37]

Small, specialised caste groups, which comprise about half the total sample population, show the most marked urban and rural preferences. This is critical for understanding the role of caste in the early-modern economy. For it seems that there were social mechanisms for fissioning and inventing castes that produced countless small, specialised groups. Most very small castes in the census are not listed in these tables, because only castes that appear on all four taluks census tables that comprise our sample are included here. Some of these omitted jatis appear only on one taluk census return and some only in a few villages. Castes omitted from my listings can thus be presumed to have been significant only in small areas or localities, at least in official perceptions, which were clearly related to political and economic considerations.[38] Keeping this in mind, it is interesting that only two serious deviations appear in percentage distributions of the number of caste groups and total population along the urban-rural continuum (Table 4): these appear in urban centres and small rural areas.

The proportion of castes in major urban centres is much smaller than the proportion of people counted in urban centres; and a significantly higher percentage of all castes than of population appears to have lived in small rural villages. This indicates that a great many very small jati groups lived only in small rural settlements. A few tiny castes that demonstrate strong rural preferences do appear on our list: Vyravers, Chola and Tulu Vellalas, and Chucklers. But most small jatis in my listing are in urban settlements: non-Brahman temple specialists ('the religious establishment'), Karaikkattu Vellalas, Chetties, Patnulkaran and Pattashalaiyan silk-weavers, Kaikkolars, Chalupans, Cudashelkarans, Panans, Dyers, Pattulu Muslims, Pariah Christians and Cunniyans. Small castes were much more likely to be enumerated if they were seen by state officials as significant for urban society, the political core of the state and economy. Large urban centres were composed disproportionately of small, specialised caste groups involved in state

[37] See the discussion below of the disporportionately large number of small castes listed for urban areas.

[38] See Ludden, 'Agrarian commercialism'. There was clearly a heavier emphasis on counting and distinguishing caste groups in urban centres, one reason being the problems of social control created by low-caste workers, for which see R.E. Frykenberg, 'On roads and riots in Tinnevelly: radical change and ideology in Madras Presidency during the nineteenth century', *South Asia*, 4, 2 (1982), pp.34-52.

politics, trade and manufacturing.

The census figures give a glimpse of the complex and moving social world of residential decisions that defined locality units of production. In rural areas, the major dominant castes (Vellalas, Maravas and Brahmans) and the major landless labourer caste (Pallas) usually comprise the majority of the population. But concentrations of artisans (weavers, potters, Panchalars), merchants (Chetties, Villay Jedians), and subordinate farming castes (Shanar, Pariah and omitted jatis) are common. If we analyse the caste composition of census villages, starting with rural ones and moving towards major urban centres, we see more and more frequent local concentrations of jatis that we would expect to relocate readily into locations of market opportunity; and we also see higher numbers of these castes in census village populations. But this is a gradual progression, like the rising slope of manufacturing assets up the urban-rural continuum. For opportunities in trade and manufacture were also concentrated in small rural settlements, like Karisattan, with its cluster of Kaikkolars and washermen, working in the textile industry.

A dry urban suburb, Vagaikulam (population 837), just south of Brahmadesam, had the highest village percentage of Panchalar artisans (17 per cent) in our sample, a high concentration of brass works, and many Shanar looms, lime-kilns and betel bazaars. A small rural village, Pottalpudur (population 504), six miles north-west of Brahmadesam, had the next highest percentage Panchalar population (12 per cent), with concentrations of mat and gunny frames and oil mills. The highest village proportion of Chalupens also appears in two urban suburbs: in one, near Seranmahadevi (Vellankoil, population 294) Chalupens were 16 per cent of the population; in the other, six miles east (Kilachevel, population 656) they were 12 per cent; and both had huge numbers of gunny frames.

Decisions by specialised caste groups to move into specialised settlements activated the manufacturing economy, most prominently the weaving industry.[39] In the 1740s, the Madras Council complained that 'weavers when disgusted leave lighted lamps in their houses and remove to some other part of the country, so that whole towns are deserted in a night'.[40] The demographic outcomes of weaver mobility can be startling. Kaikkolars were a majority of the population (56 per cent) in Turtikulam Devasthanam (population 312), an urban suburb of

[39] See Christopher John Baker, *An Indian Rural Economy: the Tamilnad countryside, 1880-1955* (Oxford, 1984).

[40] K.N. Chaudhuri, *The Trading World of Asia and the English East India Company, 1660-1760* (Cambridge, 1978), pp.252-3.

Uttumalai town, and prominent in the major urban centres of Ambasamudram (33 per cent), Shankarankoil (20 per cent) and Tenkasi (12 per cent). Tenkasi's many Muslim looms and 29 per cent Muslim population suggest that a third of its population engaged in cloth trades. A quarter of Viravanallar's 4,833-strong urban population were silk-weavers (Patnulkarans and Pattashalaiyans), who worked a local concentration of silk looms. The weaving industry also involved regular movement among settlements. Of course, cotton, silk, dyes, looms, bleaches, thread, gunny sacks and cloth circulated among sites, each produced and use in specialised places. Weavers and loom-owners also moved for work across village lines. In Tenkasi and some other Muslim weaving centres, like Ravanasamudram (near Brahmadesam, population 489) and Kallidaikurichi (population 4,651), the resident Muslim population would have been sufficient to work the looms counted in those places. But where Muslim looms were most concentrated in proportion to population, in the urban suburbs of Vallankoil and Minakshipuram (population 996, near Tirunelveli town) there were no Muslims resident in the census village at all.[41]

Caste clusters

Caste settlement-strategies produced patterns of jati residential association that defined the social composition of production localities. Using 1823 census data to deduce the logic behind the formation of jati clusters, I assume that if jati populations were randomly distributed, there would be no significant correlations between any two castes across the villages in the sample; if they were evenly distributed, all village caste populations would correlate with one another and also with total population. Then I compute correlations with Pearson's 'r' measures of linear relationship, so that a maximum correlation of 1.0 between two jatis means that an increase in the population of one caste would be matched exactly by a proportionate increase in the other, for 117 villages in my sample with populations greater than zero. Looking at the correlation data,[42] we see in Table 5 that all jatis correlate significantly with total population: normally all jati populations in a village increase in some proportion to village population. Significant correlations among jatis

[41] The category of 'Moor Looms' in the 1823 census probably refers to looms for which Muslims were liable for taxes. See Ludden, 'Agrarian commercialism'. It is thus possible that outside Muslim loom-owners paid taxes on looms in the village.

[42] All data on which this paper is based are available from the author on request.

thus do not necessarily suggest caste residential associations that need explaining: they may simply derive from normal associations between all jati populations and total population. To find indications of caste decision-making about jati residence that created clusters of jatis and patterns of association, we look for non-significant or negative correlations and also for high positive correlations.

In Table 6, I have erased non-significant correlations because their values are not important, but blank cells indicate more or less random associations that deviate from the normally positive, significant correlation between jati population and total population. So blank cells reflect jati strategies of residential settlement that produced dissociation or segregation among castes. Blank cells indicate caste groups detached spatially or isolated residentially from one another. Conversely, correlations between any two jatis much higher than that between either caste and total population reflect a positive association stronger than normal, which can also be taken to reflect a caste logic of residential decision-making: I have flagged high correlations in Table 6.

Table 6 shows Brahman correlations, which indicate broader patterns. (A table of all correlations would need 50 rows, and 50 columns.) The table reiterates that Brahmans are not all alike, not even Smartas. Only Smarta Tamils correlate with population density, village economic types, and wet cultivation. The small population of Mudivar Tadvatis was very prone to settle in drier areas, as reflected by their correlation with total farm acres, a figure dominated by dry acreage; but they also settled in dry urban areas (Table 5). Brahmans correlate quite well with one another, but not in every case: Smarta Tamils and Smarta Telugus emphatically do not. This would be the result of post-medieval partitioning of Smarta territories along the Tambraparni river, which seems to parallel the partitioning by Telugu Nayakas and Maravas of the dry periphery to the north. The medieval alliance of Vellalas and Brahmans that dominated the political economy of the Tambraparni valley is clearly visble in 1823 residential patterns, in which Smarta Tamils cluster with Pandya Vellalas and Pallas. But migrations in the post-medieval period brought Smarta Telugus into the region in political alliance and residential association with immigrant Vellalas—Tondaimandalam Mudaliars—whose leader, the Medai Delavoy, encouraged allies among Vellalas and Telugu Brahmans to migrate south. In this migration, it seems that Smarta Telugus were granted land in villages outside Smarta Tamil control, where they remained until 1823: for none of the Vellalas are as segregated from one another as are these two Brahman groups. In addition, Smarta Telugus tend slightly more

Table 6: *Brahman correlations in 1823 Census tables*

	Sm. Tel.	Sm.Tml.	Sri Vai.	M. Tadv.	S.Bhak.	V.Nam.	Total
Population	.3205	.2261		.2477	.3883	.3214	.5106
Density		.2667					.2192
Wet acres						.2603	.2544
Total acres				!.2670			
Urbanism		.3589			.3144	.2526	.4333
Wet/dry		.2236				.2308	
Brahmans							
Smarta Tel.				!.3613		.2193	.3998
Smarta Tml.			!.4082			!.3753	!.8192
Sri Vaishnava		!.4082					.4915
Religious Establishment							
Ochen/Mula		!.2916		!.2608	!.6756	!.3329	.4265
Dasi				!.2482	.9268		.3358
Total				!.3032	!.8930	.2374	.4011
Sudras							
Pand. Vell.	.2522	!.3430	!.2637		!.5114	.3200	!.5839
K.K. Vell.					!.6125	.3102	.3226
T. Mudali	!.3889	!.3317		!.4439	.3605	.2681	.5033
(Vellalas)	.2758	!.2836	.2042	.1837	!.5379	!.2777	!.5481
Chetties		.2390	!.3857		.3512		.3917
Vil.Jedy.	!.4393						
Silk weavr.	!.4670						
Kaikkolar	.2601			!.2956	!.7764		.3929
Panan		.3564	!.3639				.3156
Pancha	!.4161	!.2693		!.2844	!.4020	!.3639	!.5707
Potters	!.3454			!.3302	.2539	.2608	.3975
Barbers	.3124	!.3215	!.2364		.2772	!.3931	!.5446
Washermen					.3225	.1763	.2377
Total	!.3359					.2786	.3672
Muslims							
Pattulu	.2877				!.4094	.2830	.3881
Lubbay						!.3268	.3421
Inferior Sudras							
Elava		!.2487				.2431	.2891
Cinnyan		!.2658				.2450	.3141
Korava							.2824
Low Castes							
Palla		!.2434			.2522	.2713	.4142
Vallava					!.5758		
Pariah		!.2396	.3257		.2177		.3716
Chuckler		!!-.2379					
Total		.2325	.2375		.2663	.2666	.4190

Table continues.

Table 6 continued.

Notes: Only significant correlations are presented in this table. Cells with non-significant correlations are omitted: they are, under Sudras, Chola/Tulla Vellalas, Vaniyans, Cuddashelkaran and all Maravas; all Christians; and, under inferior Sudras, Shanar. Valid cases = 117 (0/0 divisions produce invalid cases); ! = correlation by column higher than with total population; !! = negative correlation; density = population per farm acre; wet acres = total nanjai; total acres = total farm acres; wet/dry = total wet/total dry acres. For caste and jati names see earlier tables; in the column-headings (Brahmans), Sm. Tel. = Smarta Telegu; Sm.Tml. = Smarta Tamil; Sri Vai. = Sri Vaishnava; S.Bhak. = Shiva Bhakta; V.Nam. = Vishnu Nambiyar; the total is for all Brahmans. Vellalas = Pandya, Karaikkattu, Chola, Tulu and Tondaimandala. Economic type as in Table 2, coded for this computation in ascending order in the urban-rural continuum: 1 = hamlet; 2 = mid-size village area; 3 = large village; 4 = small town; 5 = big town; 6 = urban suburb; 7 = major urban centre.

than Smarta Tamils to live in urban centres (Table 5) and are much more positively associated with weavers and merchants, indicating that they played a role in the rise of commercial centres, all across the urban-rural continuum, during post-medieval centuries.

On this evidence, several conclusions can be drawn that pertain to the social construction of economic locations. A medieval Tambraparni cluster of castes (Tamil Brahmans, Pandya Vellalas and Pallas) persisted in irrigated farming areas until 1823, though like other castes, Brahmans and Pandya Vellalas did settle in proportion to total population everywhere. Post-medieval immigrant groups still remain clustered together in 1823, in part because they jointly settled open land and in part because dominant castes partitioned the landscape politically by building up their own jati clusters, in regions under their control, as in Pudukottai. As a result, Smarta Telugus are much more closely associated with Tondaimandala Mudalis than with Pandya Vellalas, and not at all with Smarta Tamils, who cluster more with Pandya Vellalas than with other Vellalas.

Commercially- and occupationally-specialised jatis are often immigrants into the region and into localities; in a sense, their mobility makes them perpetual migrants, over the long-term. All these migrant castes are more closely associated with one another than with dominant castes or the medieval Tambraparni cluster of castes, although exceptions to this rule occur when a small group like Chetties concentrated in an area dominated by Pandya Vellalas and Smarta Tamils. Immigrant clusters populated whole regions of migratory settlement, for clusters of castes opened whole regions together, as the Telugus did in northern

Tirunelveli.[43] Also, since dominant political powers—the Medai Delavoy, the Madurai Nayakas, the Nawab of Arcot and the English East India Company—migrated into the region with natural allies and powerful patronage, we expect to see residential associations among their allied groups, and we do. Urbanisation brought immigrant and commercially-mobile jatis together into clusters. Telugu castes, Muslims and Parava Christians thus have high correlations with artisan and merchant groups, which have strong correlations with one another. Urban and rural jati populations differed significantly in the proportion of Brahmans, non-Brahman temple specialists, merchant and artisan groups, and even untouchables, for Pariahs are more prominent than Pallas in urban areas (Table 5).

Numbers in the 1823 census that represent local clusters of caste populations are remnants of colonial accounting and traces of the social history that formed local units of production. A small portion of manufacturing output from these localities entered world markets, but the internal dynamics of caste society that organised localities for production gave the entire eastern peninsula the powers to respond to overseas demand that made south India a world manufacturing centre in the early-modern period. Locally, caste society organised labour and capital for production. The mobility of caste groups and political struggles over centuries had carved up the landscape for coherent clusters organised around the exploitation of opportunities in particular locations. The hierarchy of caste dominance in each location was part of its organisation as a segment of the state and allowed political assets to be mobilised for productive purposes. At the pinnacle of local society, patriarchs within dominant caste groups, like the Medai Delavoy Mudaliar (though most men like him worked on a much smaller scale) served a hinge role connecting localities to wider networks of economic and political power. In this context, specialised caste families moved over the landscape in response to opportunities for investment and employment during the rise of demand for regional manufactures after 1700. A politically powerful local financier would invest to attract these specialists—weavers being prominent among them—who were then integrated into local society by established patterns of patronage and ritual participation. Localities that thrived as units of manufacturing became stable residential settings for requisite combinations of workers, financiers, artisans, traders and service castes, whose output combined with that of others in regional networks of trade. The 1823 census

[43] Ludden, *Peasant History*, pp.50-2.

records a moment in that history. Soon after, economic conditions that sustained most of the local textile manufacturing units of south India disappeared, and the economic adaptability of caste society faced the domination of industrial capitalism.

Chapter 7

NOBLE HARVEST FROM THE SEA: MANAGING THE PEARL FISHERY OF MANNAR, 1500-1925[1]

Sanjay Subrahmanyam

> We have seen that Ceylon is a place with a glorious past; its once magnificent cities are now but a mass of crumbled and half buried ruins; its native dynasty has passed away forever; one institution alone has descended to us unchanged by the vicissitudes of three thousand years—the Pearl Fishery.[2]

Introduction

From the Venetian Marco Polo (1254-1324) on his return from the court of the Great Khan in the closing years of the thirteenth century, to Leonard Woolf (1880-1969) of the Bloomsbury group of London intellectuals, who visited and described it in 1906, the pearl fishery in the Gulf of Mannar has attracted a fair amount of attention over the centuries.[3] 'Dit edel zee gewas'—this noble harvest from the sea—was how the Dutch East India Company's factor Floris Blom in 1694 described the pearls that in March and April each year were extracted from the narrow stretch of water between the Tamil coast in southern

[1] I am grateful to the Calouste Gulbenkian Foundation, to the Indo-Netherlands Cultural Exchange, and to the School of Oriental and African Studies, for funding research on which this paper is based. Thanks are due to Ramachandra Guha and Peter Reeves for comments on an earlier draft.

[2] Henry W. Cave, *The Book of Ceylon, being a guide to its railway system and an account of its varied attractions for the visitor and tourist*, pt.iii, 'The Pearl Fishery' (London, 1908), p.641.

[3] See, for example, S. Arunachalam, *The History of the Pearl Fishery of the Tamil Coast* (Annamalai, 1952); James Hornell, 'The Indian Pearl Fisheries of the Gulf of Mannar and Palk Bay', *Madras Fisheries Department Bulletin*, XVI (Madras 1922), the two best-known accounts in this century. From the late nineteenth century, see G. Vane, 'The pearl fisheries of Ceylon', *Journal of the Ceylon Branch of the Royal Asiatic Society*, X, 34 (1887), pp.14-40, and Edgar Thurston, 'Pearl and Chank Fisheries of the Gulf of Mannar', *Madras Government Museum Bulletin* 1 (Madras, 1894). We should, of course, not forget Georges Bizet (1838-1875) whose opera *Les Pecheurs de Perles* appeared in 1863!

India and northern Sri Lanka.[4] Blom, like some of his fellow-employees in the service of the Dutch Company (VOC), had a particular interest in the 'harvest'; for between 1658 and 1796, the Dutch controlled the pearl fishery as its administrators, and have left behind in the process a rich corpus of documents on the subject. Before the Dutch, the Portuguese had to an extent controlled pearl-fishing in the region, and after the Dutch it was the turn of the English, who took the fishery over from them in 1796 and administered it through the nineteenth and early twentieth centuries. One can scarcely find an enterprise then that encapsulates the phases of European 'expansion' in Asia better than the fishery, which passed through the hands of each of the great colonial powers in Asia of the early modern and modern periods. And yet, the pearl fishery has equally been seen often enough as unchanging and primitive in character, withstanding the 'vicissitudes of three thousand years' without losing an iota of its pristine, romantic, character.

It should be stated at the outset, however, that it is not as an exercise in comparative colonial administration, that the present essay is conceived. Rather, it is for me an exploratory foray into the history of the pearl fishery from the point of view of resource management, focusing on the different participants in the venture—who included, but did not exclusively comprise, the Portuguese, and the Dutch and English East India Companies. I intend to argue that certain long-term trends are visible in the manner in which the fishery was managed and organised, which have a bearing on why it entered into a crisis of productivity in the early years of the present century, a crisis symptomatised above all by the collapse in 1912 of the Ceylon Company of Pearl Fishers Limited. But the fishery is interesting not merely as a case study in the management and mismanagement of a renewable resource. It is also important because pearl-fishing was an economic activity which, by its very nature, depended on co-ordination, and could not be left to the decisions of individual actors.

In this sense, the 'harvest' metaphor of Floris Blom is partly a misleading one. Save in certain complex systems of water-management for agricultural purposes, one rarely comes across such a level of immediate interdependence (or of direct externalities) across individual pro-

[4] Algemeen Rijksarchief, The Hague (henceforth ARA), Overgekomen Brieven en Papieren (henceforth OB), VOC.1543, fl.652, 'Rapport van het voorgevallene in de peerlvisserije gehouden voor de derdemael bij d'E. Compe op de banken van Aripo', Commandeur Floris Blom, Oppercoopluyden Joan van Keulen en Alexander Bergaigne, 8 May 1694.

ducers in the agricultural sphere as in pearl-fishing.[5] Equally, in the sphere of manufacturing—say, weaving—co-ordination between producers was scarcely necessary beyond a certain minimal level (for example, to ensure the uniformity of a textile type, when faced with an order). True, the uncontrolled utilisation of certain other public goods of a renewable character such as forest, fisheries and pasture, following the logic of individual revenue-maximisation, may lead, as ecological historians have insisted in recent years, to a possible 'Tragedy of the Commons'.[6] The same is true for fisheries in general, and Arthur McEvoy, in defining the 'Fishermen's problem', does no more than state and demonstrate through a case study the fairly standard proposition that, 'In a competitive economy, no market mechanism ordinarily exists to reward individual forbearance in the use of shared resources'.[7] But as we shall see, despite the very ambiguous nature of the property relations in which it was located, the pearl fishery was never part of a 'competitive economy' in any sense; rather, partly because of its geographical location and partly because of the prestigious nature of the product itself, it had long been a privileged sphere for state interference. It is therefore scarcely surprising that the state plays a major role in the discussion that follows.

It may be useful, however, to begin by considering the nature of the 'beast' itself. *Margaritifera vulgaris*, the Indian pearl oyster or pinctada, is a species closely related to both scallops and mussels. It is a bivalve mollusc, usually less than three-and-a-half inches in height as well as in length. The ordinary life-span of the Indian pearl oyster is thought to be around five years, shorter than that of some other species

[5] On co-ordination in water-management, see, for example, Emmanuel Adicéam, *La géographie de l'irrigation dans le Tamilnad* (Paris, 1966), pp.174-81; *passim*; more recently, Robert Wade, *Village Republics: economic conditions for collective action in South India* (Cambridge, 1988).

[6] Cf. Madhav Gadgil and Ramachandra Guha, *This Fissured Land: an ecological history of India* (Delhi, 1992); and earlier Ramachandra Guha, *The Unquiet Woods: ecological change and peasant resistance in the Himalaya* (Delhi, 1990). Finally, the papers collected in David Arnold and Ramachandra Guha (eds.), *Nature, Culture, Imperialism: essays in the environmental history of South Asia* (Delhi, 1995), which includes one essay on fisheries (though not on the pearl fishery), namely Peter Reeves, 'Inland waters and freshwater fisheries: some issues of control, access and conservation in colonial India'.

[7] Arthur F. McEvoy, *The Fisherman's Problem: ecology and law in the California fisheries, 1850-1980* (Cambridge, 1986), p.11. Also see, in the Indian context, John Kurien and T.R. Thankappan Achari, 'Overfishing the coastal commons: causes and consequences', in Ramachandra Guha (ed.), *Social Ecology* (Delhi, 1994), pp.218-44.

of oyster, such as the Australian. Oysters have been described as 'sedentary animals, mere passive machines for eating and reproducing'; thus, they almost totally lack sensory organs. There are two sexes of oyster, both of which produce pearls. The spawning seasons are at their height in April-May and September-October, which coincide closely with the pearl-fishing seasons as already defined by about 1500.[8]

Writers on pearl-fishing in the Gulf of Mannar have adopted a particular terminology since the nineteenth century to describe the intricacies of the pearl-producing process. A key term here is 'spat', meaning the advanced larvae of the oyster, which are fully-formed but still free-swimming, unlike the oyster itself. Such larvae settle in collectives on particular banks, to form a pearl-bed, and once settled are thought to lead a relatively sedentary existence, awaiting as it were the process of irritation created either by a foreign body intruding into the oyster, or a particle deposited by the oyster itself. Around these bodies, there form, through the accretion in concentric layers of shell substance, one of three forms of pearl: the gem-pearl, the cyst-pearl and the muscle-pearl. Less prosaically perhaps, the matter was summed up in the late nineteenth century by Sir Edwin Arnold, a visitor to Tuticorin:

> Know you, perchance, how that poor formless wretch—
>   The Oyster—gems his shallow moonlit chalice?
> Where the shell irks him, or the sea-sand frets,
>   This lovely lustre on his grief.[9]

Visitors like Arnold were always impressed by the dangers of pearl-fishing, nor merely for that formless wretch, the oyster, but for the divers, starved of oxygen, but courageously battling sharks, both real and imagined, with the aid of 'shark-charmers', who for their part prudently stayed ashore to collect a modest fee by the end of the morning's work. Less favourably, they were struck by the singular lack of hygiene and overpowering stench of putrefaction that attended the process once the oysters had been brought ashore and sold in heaps by auction. As Thurston noted, cholera was a frequent occurrence that accompanied pearl-fishing; in 1889, the Ceylon fishery where he was present had to be abandoned as a consequence. His account is a striking one, and confirms what Dutch observers already describe in the 1660s:

> [The process] is resorted to of leaving the oysters to putrefy in the sun, and subsequently extracting the pearls from the residue after it has been submitted

[8] Hornell, 'Indian pearl fisheries', pp.116-24.

[9] From his *India Re-visited* (1887), as cited in Thurston, 'Pearl and chank fisheries', p.7.

to repeated washings to free it from the prevailing maggots, pulpy animal matter, sand &c. This process of putrefaction is greatly aided by flies—big red-eyed blue-bottles. At the Ceylon pearl fishery, which I was sent to inspect on the termination of my work at Tuticorin, the merchants complained at first of the scarcity of flies; but, later on, there was no cause for complaint, as they were present not only in the kottus, but in other parts of the camp, in such enormous numbers as to form a veritable plague, covering our clothes with a thick black mass, and rendering the taking of food and drink a difficult and unpleasant process until the evening, when they went to rest after twelve hours of unceasing activity.[10]

The ease with which the fishery could be abandoned was no coincidence. Pearl-fishing had a particularly notable attribute: it was a shifting activity, which followed the location of the most productive pearl-banks in a particular season, and hence rarely was conducted twice consecutively at the same location. The pearl-fishing camp until the late nineteenth century was thus a sort of mobile improvised town, set up at short notice before the fishery, and dismantled equally rapidly once the fishery was over. To be able to create and service an artificial urban centre of this sort, which by the second half of the sixteenth century could apparently host as many as 50 to 60 thousand people, required that the economic and political system have a great deal of flexibility.[11] Not only did the population have to be housed and fed, large sums of money had to be moved to purchase the pearls, and security provided to merchants and others. Part fair and festival, part industry, and part pageant, the enterprise was in many respects unique. As late as 1905, when the camp had largely lost its shifting character, and come to be located semi-permanently in Marichchukkaddi, on the north-west coast of Sri Lanka, the governor of the island, H.A. Blake, described it thus in a letter:

The annual camp at Marichchukkaddi is a town built entirely of 'cadjan', or palm matting, and wattles, and containing about 40,000 people, divers and boat-owners from India, divers and boat-owners from the Persian Gulf, pearl merchants and shopkeepers from India and Ceylon, pearl gamblers, and loose characters who manage to escape detection and come down with the boats, carrying coolies, water-drawers, and all the other human material of a town in being.[12]

[10] Thurston, 'Pearl and chank fisheries', p.23.

[11] *The Travels of Pedro Teixeira*, trans. W.F. Sinclair, introduction Donald Ferguson (London, 1902), pp.177-9.

[12] Governor H.A. Blake to the Rt. Hon. Alfred Lyttleton, Kandy, 14 June 1905, *Despatches Regarding the Leasing of the Pearl-Fisheries of Ceylon* (Colombo, 1906), pp.327-8, in Cambridge University, Centre of South Asian

A romantic image, no doubt, reminiscent in good measure of the gold-mining boom-towns of popular fiction; Blake goes on in much the same vein in this letter to describe how the 'boutique' of a wealthy merchant was attacked on the very first night of his visit to the camp, by a 'determined band of Indian dacoits', who 'carried off money and property to the value of Rs.34,000'. But at the same time, such a set of images conveys an important message: it is clear that for all its peculiarities the pearl fishery allows us an opportunity to open doors into the economic and political system of the early modern period, to see it in its complexity, and also witness competing structures of rights and power jostle with one another. To take merchants alone, W.C. Twynam, in 1890,[13] listed among those present at the pearl fishery that year the following groups:

> Jains and Arabs from Bombay; Mohammedans from Nagore, Kailpatan, Keelakarai and Tondy; Komaty Chetties from Negapatan and Kumbakonem; and Chetties and petty traders from Ramnad, Madura, Jaffna, Paumben &c; also boutique-keepers from Batticaloa, Mannar, Jaffna, Trincomalee, Colombo etc.

Nearly two hundred years before, in 1694, Floris Blom and his colleagues too had referred to a complex network of trade and finance in explaining a rise in the price of pearls. Thus:

> This dearness of the pearls is caused by the arrival of many merchants from the lands of the Mogol, Madure, Tansjouwer et cetera, with great capitals, each of whom wanted the jewels most strongly, and who have bid so high and made purchases that many experienced native merchants swear that on some varieties they will make a loss rather than a profit....[14]

Complex and sophisticated at a relatively early stage of its existence then, one struggles to extricate the pearl fishery from its own image, to pose its evolution as an activity over time.

The great lottery

We may begin our survey five-and-a-half centuries before Thurston, Blake and Twynam, and over 350 years before Floris Blom, by considering an early description of the pearl fishery (written perhaps half a

---

Studies (henceforth CSAS), E.L. Pawsey Collection, no.8, 'Pearl Fisheries of Ceylon, Reports, 1867-1907' (bound). For an evocative description of the fishery of 1906, see Leonard Woolf, *Growing: An autobiography:of the years 1904 to 1911* (London, 1970), pp.87-98.

13 See W.C. Twynam, *Report on the Pearl Fishery held at Marichchukkaddi during 1890* (Colombo, 1890), p.3; in CSAS, E.L. Pawsey Collection, no.8.

14 ARA, OB, VOC, 1543, fl.651v, 'Rapport van het voorgevallene...'.

century after Marco Polo) in the *Mirabilia Descripta* of Friar Jordanus (c.1330). The friar reports on this activity as a most peculiar wonder of the region, following his description of Silem (Ceylon):

> Between that island and the main land are taken pearls or marguerites, in such quantity as to be quite wonderful. So indeed that there are sometimes more than 8,000 boats or vessels, for three months continuously [engaged in fishing]. It is astounding, and almost incredible, to those who have not seen it, how many are taken.[15]

The numbers of vessels and the duration of the fishery are indeed 'incredible', so much so that we should probably not take Friar Jordanus at his word on the point. The broad thrust of his description is nevertheless acceptable, confirming that by the Venetian Polo, and being confirmed in turn by later observers. In the early sixteenth century, the first Portuguese reports are available to us, and these are still more specific in their detail. At this time, the coast of Tirunelveli was under the control of a branch of the ruling house of Venad, the Tiruvadi rajas. Two major urban centres existed from which pearl-fishing was organised. One was Kilakkarai, not far from Rameswaram at the north-eastern limit of the fishery coast, and the other was a centre designated by the Portuguese as 'Cael' (Kayal), at the mouth of the Tamraparani river. The latter was probably not a single urban node but a combination of two: Kayalpatnam on the one hand, and Palaiyakkayal on the other. One of the early Portuguese accounts, that of Duarte Barbosa (c.1518) offers us the following description:

> Nigh to this Island [of Mannar] there is in the sea a shoal, covered by a depth of ten or twelve fathoms of water wherein are found pearls both great and small in extreme abundance. Of these, some are shaped like a pear. The Moors and Gentiles of a city named Cael, pertaining to the King of Coulam [Kollam], used to come hither twice in the year to fish for them.... The little pearls belong to the pearl-gatherer and the great ones to the King, who keeps his factor there. They pay him as well certain fees to obtain his permission to fish.[16]

The two fisheries, the 'great' and 'little' (in Portuguese, *pescaria grande* and *pescaria pequena*) were held respectively in April-May and September-October. The major investors in it, as it appears from Barbosa's account, were both Cetti merchants and 'Moors', the latter being the Tamil-speaking Sunni (and largely Hanafite) Maraikkayars resident in such centres as Kayalpatnam, Kilakkarai, and Vedalai. Members of

[15] Friar Jordanus, *Mirabilia Descripta: the wonders of the East*, trans. Henry Yule (London 1863), p.28; also see p.43.

[16] Mansel Longworth Dames (ed.), *The Book of Duarte Barbosa*, vol.II (London, 1921), pp.116-17.

this community also acted as the agents of the Tiruvadi raja, in taxing the pearl fishery. Thus, as Barbosa has it:

> A wealthy and distinguished Moor has long held the farm of the duties levied on seed-pearls (*aljofre*). He is so rich and powerful that all the people of the land honour him as much as the King. He executes judgement and justice on the Moors without interference from the King. The fishers for seed-pearl fish all the week for themselves save on Friday when they work for the owner of the boat, and at the end of the season they fish for a whole week for this Moor, whereby he possesses great abundance of seed-pearl.[17]

While the Maraikkayars and Cettis acted as the financiers and fiscal mediators, the actual diving for pearls was done by other groups, most notable among which were the Lebbais (a low-status Shafi'i Muslim community), and the Paravas, very largely a fishing community. Portuguese interest in the region allowed the last-mentioned of these groups to challenge Maraikkayar dominance by converting to Christianity, and seeking the aid of the Portuguese state apparatus, by then based at Cochin and Goa.[18]

In the 1520s, a series of conflicts raged in the waters around Sri Lanka between the Portuguese state and private traders (or *casados*) it patronised, and Mappila Muslims from Kerala. The Maraikkayars, as allies of the Mappilas (with whom they frequently intermarried) were also, willy-nilly, a part of these differences. The Portuguese seem to have made the pearl-fishing fleet itself a target of its attacks in these years, rendering life economically unviable for both Maraikkayars and Lebbais, and Paravas. In the mid-1530s, therefore, the notables of the Parava community (the so-called *pattankattis*) nominated one of their number, the *jati talaivan* Vikrama Aditya Pandiyan, to negotiate a mass conversion to Catholicism under the auspices of the Cochin church. The numbers who converted may have been as high as twenty thousand, perhaps even higher. The jati talaivan assumed the new name of Dom João da Cruz, and on the basis of its role as patron to the Paravas,

[17] Ibid., p.123.

[18] For a set of detailed studies, see Georg Schurhammer, *Gesämmelte Studien*, vol.II: *Orientalia* (Rome, 1963). For the most recent synthesis, see Jorge Manuel Costa da Silva Flores, 'Os Portugueses e o Mar de Ceilão, 1498-1543: trato, diplomacia e guerra', Mestrado thesis, Universidade Nova de Lisboa, Lisbon, 1991; for an older summary vision, to be re-read in the light of Flores's work, C.R. De Silva, 'The Portuguese and pearl-fishing off South India and Sri Lanka', *South Asia* (N.S.), I, 1 (1978), pp.14-28. For the Paravas, also see the general study by Patrick A. Roche, *Fishermen of the Coromandel: a social study of a seafaring caste of the Coromandel* (New Delhi, 1983).

the Portuguese Crown began to claim rights over the fishery as well.[19]

From the 1520s, as the Portuguese built a trading nexus between western Sri Lanka (the kingdom of Kotte) and southern Coromandel, a Crown factor was appointed to the pearl fishery coast (*costa de pescaria*), a post probably first held by a certain João Flores. The role of these factors in enabling the Crown to establish its rights over the fishery was considerable; it was also aided by the fact that in these years, political control of the hinterland was disputed between the Tiruvadi rajas and a new force in regional politics, the Madurai Nayaka Visvanatha, claiming legitimacy through his attachment to Vijayanagara. Visvanatha's forces appeared on the fishery coast in the 1540s, hoping to gain total control of it, and while they largely succeeded, some elements like the Portuguese were already too entrenched. For one, by the mid-1540s the Paravas had been given a further dose of Counter-Reformation Christianity by the Society of Jesus, whose presence on the coast was practically inaugurated in 1543 by the formidable Francisco Xavier, and a new settlement—Punnaikkayal—had been created, dominated by them.[20] Jesuit letters report frequent clashes in these years between the Paravas and the *badagas* (Telugu soldiery of Visvanatha), and it appears that in the final analysis the Madurai Nayakas had to settle for a compromise. The Portuguese-Parava combine was left to dominate the fishery, with the Nayakas being given certain limited rights.

The new equilibrium in the mid-sixteenth century is described at some length by the Portuguese financial superintendent (*vedor da fazenda*) Simão Botelho, writing in the 1550s.[21] He mentions two fisheries a year, one near Kilakkarai and the other on the other side of Gulf, in Karadiva in Sri Lanka, revenues from both of which were collected by the Portuguese captain and factor, who patrolled the waters with a fleet of small vessels (*catures*). Collections were said to be around 7,500 *xerafins*, but in imminent danger of diminishing. Also mentioned by Botelho is a simmering conflict between the captains and the Jesuits,

[19] Cf. George Schurhammer, 'Die Bekehrung der Paraver (1535-1637)', in *Orientalia*; also Schurhammer, 'Letters of D. João da Cruz in the National Archives of Lisbon', in Schurhammer, *Gesämmelte Studien* IV: *Varia* (Rome, 1965).

[20] For details, including a useful description of pearl-fishing in the epoch, see George Schurhammer, *Francis Xavier: his life, his times*, trans. by Joseph Costelloe, vol.II (India, 1541-1545) (Rome, 1977).

[21] Simão Botelho, 'O Tombo do Estado da Índia' (1554), in R.J. de Lima Felner (ed.), *Subsídios para a história da Índia Portuguresa* (Lisbon, 1868), pp.244-6.

which was eventually resolved in the next decade by the simple expedient of abolishing the post of captain and factor, and using the Society of Jesus as Goa's representative on the coast. Thus, in the 1580s, when the Portuguese traveller Pedro Teixeira visited the area, he found an arrangement rather different from that described either by Barbosa or by Botelho. For one, the practice of the 'little' fishery of September-October no longer existed, and there was thus only one fishery in April and May. But also, a well-defined *modus vivendi* now existed between the Nayaka of Madurai, 'lord of their land', and the Jesuits, 'who manage everything here'.[22] The former received the proceeds of one day's fishing in the season as his right, and left the actual management of the enterprise to the Paravas and the Society of Jesus, who in turn were supposed to pass on the bulk of the taxes to the Portuguese administration at Cochin or Goa.

Some figures exist for what the pearl fishery actually yielded to the Portuguese in the years they controlled it. See Table 1.[23] These figures

Table 1: *Portuguese revenues from the pearl fishery, 1525-1634* (in *pardaus* of 300 *reis*)

Year	Amount	Year	Amount
1525-43	7,500	1585	9,000
1552	3,200	1605	25,000
1574	5,000	1611	24,184
1581	5,000	1634	1,853

are somewhat misleading, for they suggest that the fishery was becoming more and more valuable as a taxable resource, when this was far from being the case. In fact, accompanying the increase in taxes was a greater and greater gap between fisheries, with one crucial period being the early seventeenth century, It was claimed in these years by the Jesuits that the oysters in the fishery's banks were simply not ripe, or that there were other reasons why no fishing could be conducted. This eventually contributed to (even if it did not cause) a rift that arose between the Jesuits and Goa, leading to the expulsion of the former from the fishery coast in 1605. But things did not improve even then. In

[22] *The Travels of Pedro Teixeira*, pp.178-9; also see José Wicki, 'Duas relações sobre a situação da India Portuguese nos anos 1568 e 1569', *Studia*, 8 (1961), pp.151-3.

[23] Vitorino Magalhães Godinho, *Les Finances de l'État Portugais des Indes Orientales* (*1517-1635*) (Paris, 1982), p.111.

a letter from the Portuguese king to his viceroy, written in 1611, it was claimed that 'the fishery has not been conducted for the last six years on account of the disturbances that there have been among those Christians'.[24]

When the Jesuits returned to the coast in the early 1620s, these troubles continued. Claims and counter-claims may be found in the Portuguese archives of the epoch. One version had it that the fishery was in fact being conducted secretly, but that the proceeds were being appropriated by the Jesuits. In another view, the pearl banks had from the late sixteenth century simply ceased to be productive. From numerous enquiries that were conducted, some under the auspices of a Portuguese captain appointed to reside at the town of Tuticorin from around 1630, no clear single account emerges. In 1634, when a fishery was actually conducted, the attendant violence and factional fighting among the Paravas led to a situation where Goa actually sent a fleet the following year to the region, to 'castigate' the Parava headmen and burn down some of their villages.[25]

Relatively little can be said therefore in concrete terms about how the pearl fishery was actually managed during the first half of the seventeenth century. One Portuguese writer from the 1630s, António Bocarro, suggests that the situation in the Gulf of Mannar in these years was highly charged, on account of political difficulties between the Madurai Nayaka and the Marava Setupati of Ramnad, and that this impinged on the fishery.[26] Unlike the late sixteenth century then, any power which wished to administer the pearl fishery in the latter half of the seventeenth century had to contend not only with the Paravas and the Nayaka, but the Maravas and their allies, the Maraikkayars, whose fortunes began to revive about this time.

[24] Letter from Philip III to the viceroy at Goa, Rui Lourenço de Távora, 20 February, 1610, in R.A. de Bulhão Pato (ed.), *Documentos Remetidos da Índia*, vol.I (Lisbon 1880), p.342, '...se não fazer a dita pescaria de seis annos a esta parte pelas inquietações que houve n'aquelles Christãos'.

[25] For the events of this period, see Historical Archives, Panaji, Goa, Monções do Reino, 19-C, fls.1166-77; Monções do Reino, 20, fl.45v; for the context, also see P.S.S. Pissurlencar (ed.), *Assentos do Conselho do Estado*, vols.I and II (Goa 1953), vol.I, pp.258-9, 364-5; vol.II, pp.16-18, 84-90. Finally, for a rather exaggerated Portuguese description of the fishery in the seventeenth century, see *Ribeiro's History of Ceilão*, ed. and trans. P.E. Pieris (Colombo, 1909), pp.163-7, where João Ribeiro claims that 3,000-5,000 *champanas* took part in a fishery lasting over forty days!

[26] António Bocarro, 'Livro das plantas de todas as cidades, fortalezas, e povoações do Estado da Índia Oriental', in A.B. de Brangança Pereira (ed.), *Arquivo Português Oriental* (N.S.), vol.IV, pt.III, sec.1 (Goa 1938), pp.368-9.

In 1658, the Dutch East India Company conquered most of the Portuguese possessions in Sri Lanka, and also expelled the Portuguese from the fishery coast. In the same year, the Dutch signed treaties with the Madurai Nayaka and the Marava Setupati, which set the stage for a new phase in the management of the Mannar fishery. The Dutch claimed that as successors of the Portuguese, they had the same fiscal rights over the pearl fishery, as well as the same right to patronise the Paravas as a community (despite the fact that the latter were Catholics and the Dutch usually Protestants). As the VOC conceived it in this period, the season was to begin with an inspection of the pearl-banks, to be carried out by a number of Dutch officials in collaboration with Parava and Maraikkayar notables. Samples were to be taken, and if found satisfactory, a fishery was to be held. The duration of the fishery would vary, however, depending on the richness of the sample. Once it had been decided to hold a fishery, a site had to be chosen—which could be either on the northern or the southern shore of the Gulf. If the latter, the camp would be in VOC territory and matters would be greatly simplified. If the former, the camp could fall either in Ramnad or Madurai, and the co-operation of the relevant ruler—the Setupati of Ramnad or the Nayaka of Madurai—would have to be solicited.[27]

To the Dutch, the pearl fishery was a massive harvest which had to be co-ordinated, and in which various rights of differing antiquity needed to be reconciled. These rights were created by different means. Some pertained to state authority: thus, the Dutch East India Company had rights by virtue of its control of coastal Sri Lanka, the Madurai Nayakas and the Marava Setupatis by virtue of their control of sections of the fishery coast. Others belonged to the communities which participated 'traditionally' in the fishery, above all the Paravas and Maraikkayars, who had to be consulted in its management. Still others were vested in institutions, such as the Ramesvaram temple.[28]

All these rights were defined in terms of a unit of operation peculiar to the pearl fishery, namely the diving stone. These stones were the object that was taxed by the Dutch; they weighed between five and six kilograms, and had a hole driven through their centre through which a

[27] ARA, OB, VOC.1256, fls.446-56v, 'Rapport der Peerlvisserij de eerstemaal bij tijden van d'E. Compe. gehouden op de bancken van Manaer tusschen Aripo en 't dorp Condatie...', by Jan van der Laen etc., 22 May 1666; also ARA, OB, VOC.1273, fls.1449-51v, report by Van Rheede to Van Goens, 22 June 1669.

[28] See for example, ARA, OB, VOC.1543, fls.664-65v, 'Vrigelaten steenen en vaertuijgen van den Naik van Madure, den Teuver, nevens de pattangatijns van Jaffanapatnam, Manaar en Tutucorijn' (1694).

knotted rope was passed. The diver, clad in a breech-clout, was lowered from a boat while standing on the stone, with the rope being used to draw him up at the end of a dive. The boats themselves, vessels called *tonis* , were owned by men termed *campanottis*, belonging in the period largely to the Parava and Maraikkayar communities. The divers for their part seem largely to have been Paravas (Christian converts as well as non-Christians) and Lebbais. If they died in the course of the fishery, the tax was reduced, and this was termed a 'half-stone'

The first pearl fishery involving the Dutch, concerning which we have information at any level of detail, is one held in 1666. It was probably the first one held after 1658 on the southern shores of the Gulf of Mannar, though one had been held in 1663 on the Tuticorin side of the Gulf, concerning which little is known. In comparison to the 1663 fishery, which yielded a revenue of Dfl.18,000 to the VOC, the 1666 one was far more lucrative, producing revenues of Dfl.68,473. It began on 22 March 1666, and the number of vessels involved was 270, far smaller than was to be the case later in the century. From the correspondence of the period, we gather that the relatively low level of participation (even in comparison with Pedro Teixeira's late-sixteenth-century estimate of 400 to 500 boats per fishery) was on account of two factors: first, poor relations between the Dutch and the Madurai Nayakas, who claimed a right to one day's proceeds in the fishery, which the VOC disputed; second, the fact that the Paravas were none too eager to co-operate with the Dutch in the operations either.

The poor quality of the relations between the Madurai Nayakas and the Dutch was reflected not only in diplomatic dealings but in the actual use of force. As a Dutch document from 1669, giving the 'Reasons and Causes of the commencement and continuation of the Madura War, conducted on the defensive, on the part of the Hon. Company', put the matter, the fault lay with the Madurai Nayaka's government, and the fact that 'the peoples who inhabit the countries of Madura are by nature servile, lazy, distrustful, miserable and consequently low, cunning, faithless, lying, greedy, possessing least of all virtues as regards to honour and shame, overbearing in prosperity, slavish in adversity, cruel, merciless, only by compulsion good or beneficient'.[29] In this situation of moral abjectness there arrived the Dutch Company, which having defeated the Portuguese in 1658, 'succeeded to their rights over the coast, as well as to their authority over

[29] Public Record Office (henceforth PRO), London, Colonial Office (C.O.) 54, no.166, sec.3, fls.110v-111, translation into English of a report by Laurens Pijl to Rijklof van Goens (1669).

the sea-ports, the Christians, the Pearl-fisheries, and all thereunto appertaining, in fact to all that the Parruas first had, and the Priests and the Portuguese afterwards possessed'. This situation was however not accepted by the Madurai governor at Palaiyamkottai, Barmiliappa Pillai, whose tyranny is alleged by the Dutch to have led the 'native Heathen and Moorish merchants of any capital' to commit suicide, so that they were found 'hanging on trees near their own houses and gardens, which proved that they preferred hastening their own deaths to remaining longer in subjection to and exposed to the unfeelingness of the local governors'!

Dutch hostility and self-righteousness thus contributed their share to violent confrontations, when a fishery was actually held in 1669, on the Tuticorin side of the Gulf. In all, 555 tonis took part on this occasion, and the tax collections amounted to some Dfl.132,000 (and after expenses had been deducted were still in the region of Dfl.120,000). We are able to observe on this occasion, with some closeness, the system of taxation followed. Diving stones were divided into three categories: Christian (which paid the least tax), Heathen or Hindu (which paid somewhat more), and Muslim or Moorish (which paid the most). These stones were designated on the basis of the diver's identity, not that of the campanotti; thus, a single boat could contain stones of all three 'religious denominations'. On this particular occasion, the number of stones was slightly over five thousand.

However, the fishery apparently had to be called off halfway, as violence escalated. Even if the Dutch consoled themselves with the proverb that 'half an egg is better than an empty shell', it seemed matters had to be settled once and for all. Pitched battles involving artillery were conducted between the Dutch stronghold of Tuticorin, and the neighbouring Nayaka outpost of Melur, and the Company claimed a military triumph by the end of that year. However, it appears to have been a pyrrhic victory, for the Dutch eventually came around to conceding to the Madurai Nayaka and the Marava Setupati their 'traditional' rights (which were in fact less than a century old!). Moreover, the fishery of 1669 was followed by a long hiatus, for no recorded pearl fisheries took place on either side of the Gulf until the late 1680s. In 1690, when a fishery was finally held, it was of unusually long duration (that is, forty-seven days instead of the normal twenty-four, and involved 349 vessels); it was suggested by one observer that this was an 'abuse' on the part of local Dutch Company employees, who could have shortened the duration and increased the number of boats, thus swelling the VOC's revenues. This fishery yielded Dfl.63,000, that is to say, markedly less than those of the late 1660s, as is recorded in a detailed report prepared on the occasion by Hendrik Adriaan van Rheede, the celebrated Dutch administrator and naturalist, who was present on the scene.[30]

Van Rheede's report, submitted to the Directors of the Company in January 1691, points to the existence of a total of forty-seven pearl-banks, distributed as follows: Kollam to Punnaikkayal, 9; Punnaikkayal to Patnamadduru, 22; Patnamadduru to Rameswaram, 6; Mannar to Kalpitiya, 9; Kalpitiya to Negombo, 1. These banks, he stated, all lay from one to three miles distance from the shore, and were located at a depth of from six to twelve fathoms of water. Van Rheede also went on to describe the actual process of diving, the economic relations between the camapanottis and the divers, and other issues that space does not permit us to develop here. His is also one of the earliest accounts to discuss the cyclicity of regeneration of pearl-banks, which he states took three years to form, were at their best in the sixth and seventh year, and thereafter began to disintegrate. Pearl-fishing, in his description, involved two stages. First, around October, an assaying expedition was sent out under Dutch supervision (but including several expert 'native informants') to sample the oysters in each bank. The value of the pearls yielded by a sample of a thousand oysters from each bank was ascertained: if this fell below 48 *panams*, no fishery was held in that bank. Depending on the number of banks whose yield exceeded this cut-off value, and the extent to which they exceeded it, the duration of the fishery would be determined. The location of the banks would in turn determine where the pearl-fishing camp was set up, whether it would be on both sides or only one side of the Gulf, and where precisely it needed to be from the viewpoint of access to the banks. The normal duration of a full fishery was reckoned at three *valy*, or twenty-four days, which formed a standard against which fisheries were measured.

Van Rheede's description is fleshed out some years later, in 1694, when we have the first Dutch census of the pearl fishery.[31] This census was conducted at the pearl-fishing camp, at the time of the registration

[30] 'Extract uyt de missive door den Commissaris-Generaal, Hendrick Adriaan van Reede, heere van Mydreght etc., geschreven aan de vergaderingh van de seventiene uyt Tutucorin, in dato 16 January 1691', in Pieter van Dam, *Beschrijvinge van de Oost-Indische Compagnie*, Book II, pt.ii, ed. F.W. Stapel (The Hague, 1932), pp.412-33.

[31] ARA, OB, VOC.1543, fls.655-63, 'Lijste der Thonijs steenen ende persoonen den 24en maart 1694 in de peerlvisscherije op aripo opgenomen'.

(*uitschrijving*) of the tonis. This process took place four to five months after the assaying, and in the interim the Company usually sent out messengers to all the major ports along the south-west and south-east coasts of India and coastal Sri Lanka, with placards announcing the dates of the fishery and the location of the camp. If the fishery was held on the southern shore of the Gulf, the Dutch flag was flown, but otherwise a flag was flown for the Nayaka of Madurai or the Setupati ruler of Ramnad, depending on the camp's precise location. On the strand, an area was demarcated and cordoned off, and toll-booths set up at the entrances to the camp. All commodities—foodstuffs and cloth being the major items—were taxed on entry; at the same time, the toll-keepers were to ensure that no pearls left the camp save with official sanction.

The 1694 census lays bare the complex character of the fishery, and shows us both its importance as an employer (over 11,000 persons were employed on the boats alone), and the extended geographical nexus of which it was a part. In this year, tonis from thirty-three different ports participated, including at least four centres north of Point Calimere, and three in Sri Lanka. Table 2 summarises the geographical distribution of boats by port of origin, and also lists the divers and other personnel on board the vessels. The divers are categorised for tax purposes on the basis that we have discussed earlier, into Muslims, Hindus and Christians. As emerges fairly clearly, each boat carried some thirty persons on average; also two in seven on board any vessel were divers. Other features that emerge are the dominance of Christian and Muslim

Table 2: *The fishery in 1694: boats, men and divers by place of origin*

Place	Boats	Men	Divers	Christian	Hindu	Muslim
Tuticorin	83	2,653	751	672	8	71
Kilakkarai	52	1,532	433	12	36	385
Jaffnapatnam	33	759	213	158	22	33
Mannar	33	787	221	176	23	22
Kayalpatnam	30	996	284	26	27	231
Punnaikkayal	23	751	216	213	–	3
Adiramapatnam	16	364	101	20	39	42
Periyapatnam	14	291	81	28	9	44
Karaikal	13	323	90	2	1	87
Manappad	12	467	135	126	–	9
Other	76	2,234	607.5	257	39	311.5
TOTAL	385	11,157	3132.5	1690	204	1238.5

Table 3: *The fishery in 1698: boats, men and divers by place of origin*

Place	Boats	Men	Divers	Christian	Hindu	Muslim
Tuticorin	68	1,925	534	519	4	11
Punnaikkayal	25	691	192	190	–	2
Mannar	21	488	134	127	1	6
Jaffnapatnam	15	411	114	110	–	4
Vaippad	9	225	62	62	–	–
Mukkuru	9	112	31	29	1	1
Virapandiyapatnam	8	258	72	66	1	5
Veruppad	8	200	55	55	–	–
Palaiyakkayal	7	188	52	52	–	–
Other	7	213	59	56	–	3
TOTAL	177	4,711	1,305	1,266	7	32

divers over their Hindu counterparts; also the close relationship between ports dominated by two communities, the Paravas and the Maraikkayars, and the fishery. In the former category of Parava-dominated ports are Tuticorin and Punnaikkayal, in the latter are Kilakkarai, Kayalpatnam, and Adiramapatnam.

Information similar to that presented in Table 2 is available from the Dutch records for two later years—1698 and 1708.[32] Of these, the first is somewhat atypical, but also interesting, for a violent quarrel between the Paravas and Maraikkayars led campanottis from the latter community, under the leadership of the Periya Tambi Maraikkayar (the title of the leading Maraikkayar from Ramnad), to boycott the fishery.[33] Table 3 shows how the fishery appears in the face of a Marakkayar boycott. It is of course clear that no boats from such ports as Kilakkarai and Kayalpatnam played a role in the latter fishery. But it is equally of significance that even Lebbai divers employed by Parava campanottis chose to abstain from the fishery; thus the number of Muslim divers from even Tuticorin falls sharply.

The third fishery from this period for which we have detailed infor-

[32] ARA, OB, VOC.1605, fls.1050-52v, 'Lijste der thonys, steenen en persoonen in d'maand April anno 1698 op de peerlvisscherije van aripo opgenomen'; VOC.1756, fls.1177-88, 'Lijste der vaartuijgen personen duyckers en steenen die in de peerlvisscherije van Tutucorijn Anno 1708 zijn bevonden'.

[33] For details, see David Shulman and Sanjay Subrahmanyam, 'Prince of poets and ports: Cîtakkâti, the Maraikkâyars and Ramnad, ca.1690-1710', in A.L. Dallapiccola and S. Zingel-Avé Lallemant (eds.), *Islam and Indian Regions*, (2 vols. Stuttgart, 1992), vol.I, pp.497-535.

mation is that of 1708. This was by far the most successful of the three in terms of participation, even though it was attended by some trouble, on account of the Parava-Maraikkayar differences that we have mentioned above (which were exacerbated by the fact that the camp on this occasion was in Madurai territory). Almost as sizeable in terms of initial participation as the 1669 fishery mentioned above, the fishery of 1708 attracted tonis from a total of forty-one ports, and yielded somewhat over Dfl.106,000 to the VOC. The profile of this fishery, then, was as in Table 4. This, when compared with that for 1694, suggests a

Table 4: *The fishery in 1708: boats, men and divers by place of origin*

Place	Boats	Men	Divers	Christian	Hindu	Muslim
Tuticorin	122	3,759	1,044	878	33	133
Kilakkarai	73	2,209	618	60	112	446
Kayalpatnam	37	1,196	332	54	39	239
Mannar	32	952	264	224	14	26
Jaffnapatnam	29	861	241	207	4	30
Sundarapandiyapatam	28	762	209	81	32	96
Punnaikkayal	25	727	204	201	–	3
Karaikal	20	632	177	3	9	165
Periyapatnam	19	504	140	71	19	50
Adiramapatnam	14	335	91	38	12	41
Tondi	10	234	65	33	24	8
Other	119	3392	937	530	92	315
TOTAL	528	15,563	4,322	2,380	390	1,552

fairly stable distribution of boats by port of origin, and also a reasonably stable balance in the relative proportions of Christian Parava, Lebbai and Hindu divers. As before, Tuticorin and Kilakkarai dominate the proceedings by far, and the only port significantly to increase its participation is Sundarapandiyapatnam. Also of significance, although not captured in this table because of its summary character, is the somewhat greater participation of campanottis from distant ports like Naguru, Tranquebar and Porto Novo in Coromandel, and Anjengo on the Malabar coast.

After this fishery of 1708, there was a considerable gap before another successful one could be held. In 1711, the Dutch factors reported that 'the pearl-fishery on the Aripo banks brought little up', while in the following year too no success was reported. In fact the next fishery which, so far as we are aware, enjoyed any success, was one in 1724, followed by one the very next year; both were held in

Kondachi Bay, on the southern (Sri Lankan) fringes of the Gulf of Mannar.[34] These two fisheries were once more followed by a rather extended hiatus, when the banks yielded little or nothing; and by the 1740s the Dutch began to lose interest in the enterprise, which seemed to have become an annual ritual exercise in futility. It was in these years that they began to resort to an expedient, namely the creation of a revenue-farm for the fishery, given out to the jati talaivan of the Paravas of Tuticorin, a certain Dom Gabriel Gomes. According to the memoir left by Jan Schreuder, Dutch governor of Ceylon, for his successor in 1762, this innovation was to be credited to the Baron van Imhoff, who had 'clearly demonstrated to what risk, indeed to what disadvantage the Company was exposed', if it conducted the fishery directly.[35]

Table 5 summarises Dutch revenues from the pearl fishery from the early 1660s to the mid-eighteenth century, including the returns on the first few years of the Gomes farm.. The first years were hence successful indeed, and in the triennium 1747-9, fishing was conducted on both shores of the Gulf, with the Arippu fishery accounting for the lion's share of returns. Subsequent to this, as we gather once more from Schreuder's memoir, a fishery was also held in 1750, but for six days only, and yielding a mere 6,960 florins. Again a fishery is reported in 1753, and still another in 1754, the first a moderate success, but the latter an abysmal failure. A hiatus then ensued until the mid 1780s, for a variety of reasons that we shall detail below.

Table 5: *Dutch revenues from the pearl fishery, 1663-1749* (in Dutch florins)

Year	Amount	Year	Amount
1663	18,000	1708	117,000–119,000
1666	64,000–68,000	1724	143,000
1669	132,000	1725	150,000
1690	73,000	1746	57,200
1694	81,000	1747	316,800
1698	28,000	1748	577,680
1699	92,000	1749	884,100

[34] ARA, OB, VOC.2026, fls.845v-47, report by Gualterus Woutersz to Joannes Hertenberg, Governor of Dutch Ceylon, 6 May 1725.

[35] *Memoir of Jan Schreuder, Governor of Ceylon, delivered to his successor Lubbert Jan Baron van Eyck, on March 17, 1762*, trans. E. Reimeirs (Selections from the Dutch Records of the Ceylon Government, No.5) (Colombo, 1946), p.81.

Thus, at the end of the first century of Dutch administration, two features stand out. First, the substantial fluctuations in the revenues collected, as well as the long gaps between fisheries. On the other hand, it is also worth remarking that when a fishery was held, it accounted for a very substantial proportion of the revenues of the Dutch Ceylon government, indeed second only to the income from cinnamon. These revenues were largely derived from the tax on diving stones, but this was not the only source of income. In 1725, for example, of a total income of 53,149 rix-dollars, some 7,940 rix-dollars came from sources other than the stone tax, of which the most lucrative (6,300 rix-dollars) was the farm on 'money-changing' given out to a Maraikkayar notable.[36] The stamp tax on cloth sold at the pearl fishery camp, and the tax on the 'bazaar' were of lesser significance, but were nevertheless farmed out from as early as 1666 to Parava or Maraikkayar notables.

From company to state

In the second half of the eighteenth century, as we have briefly mentioned above, the pearl fishery entered into difficulties. In 1767 and again in 1768, when attempts were made to hold fisheries first near Tuticorin and then at Arippu, violent disputes broke out between the Dutch and Virappa Pillai, the representative of Muhammad 'Ali Walajah, Nawab of the Karnatak at Arcot, who now claimed rights over the northern littoral of the Gulf of Mannar. The Nawab argued that the revenues of the pearl fishery in fact belonged to him, besides other privileges, such as the tax-free stones, the right to an entire day's catch, and the oysters brought up from one dive a day per diver.[37] The Dutch emissary to the Nawab's court, Peter Sluysken, attempted to settle for a limited right, namely twenty boats for the Nawab in every fishery. The following conversation ensued, in Sluysken's account, with the Nawab posing a leading question:

> [He asked] 'Which nations inhabited those lands formerly? Men who wore turbans or hats?' It was now my turn to reply. I said, that the Company was very sensible of the marks of friendship which the Nabob had shewn them, and had taken that circumstance into full consideration. That hats had not been so long in use as that country had been inhabited and that therefore the former inhabitants of the country must have been men without hats.
>
> The Nabob then asked, whether the former natives of the country were white or black?
>
> I said I did not know, so many hundred years had gone by under circum-

[36] ARA, OB, VOC.2026, fls.845v-47, 'Rapport'.
[37] ARA, Hoge Regering van Batavia, I.04.17, no.589.

stances similar to the present.

H.H. then said that the White were natives of Europe and the Black of India.[38]

The tactic of asserting rights through the notion of the 'original inhabitant' was eventually stone-walled by the Dutch representative, who bluntly told the Nawab's son in a later conversation that 'it was well known how the Dutch Company had acquired its right of possession, and it was also well known how H.H.'s father had obtained his right'. Sluysken's mission thus failed in a sense, but status quo was maintained until the 1780s, when the Nawab sought to reopen the negotiations, by now acting quite clearly at the behest of the English East India Company. The English had already conducted the fishery of 1784, the first after 1768, which yielded them a gross revenue of Rs.42,447. In the years 1786 and 1788, two Englishmen, James Dott and James Buchanan, ostensibly acting as ambassadors of Arcot but in fact the agents of Fort St. George, dealt with VOC representatives at Colombo, and arrived at an understanding of sorts. The treaty signed by Dott in February 1786, stipulated the following:

The pearl-fishery at Tuticorin will be publicly auctioned to the highest bidder, and the price at which it has been purchased will be divided between the Noble Company and the Nawab, as Lord of Madurai and Lord-Suzerain of the Marava country, in two equal portions, after all expenses have been deducted. To the farmer will be ceded all the rights that may exist over the bank or banks that he has farmed. He will do with the oysters and the pearls that he extracts what he will, and shall in consequence conduct this operation in the freest manner, and so that no one may interfere in it. All other usages and customs, contrary to what has been established in this article, will be revoked and abolished.[39]

However, this treaty said nothing about two related issues: first, the pearl fisheries to be held to the south of the Gulf of Mannar, and second, the chank (or conch-shell) fishery. Both questions were raised by the Nawab's representative, Buchanan, in his protracted negotiation with the VOC in 1788. The new treaty thus divided the proceeds of the chank fishery as well, and also granted the Nawabs a quarter of the 'neat profit' of the Mannar and Arippu pearl fisheries.[40]

In the 1780s and 1790s, therefore, decades that should be seen as

[38] PRO, CO.54, no.166, sect.5, fls.206-206v, 'Mr van Sluijsken's Journal of His Mission to Madras, September 1770'.

[39] Treaty of 25 February 1786 in J.E. Heeres (ed.), *Corpus Diplomaticum Neerlando-Indicum*, vol.VI (1753-1799) (The Hague, 1955), pp.567-71.

[40] ARA, Hoge Regering van Batavia, I.04.17, papers of the embassy of James Buchanan, 1788.

marking the transition from Dutch to English control of the pearl fishery, a characteristic instrument—namely revenue-farming—was adopted. The fisheries of 1787 and 1792 conducted off the Madurai coast, and the ones held in three successive years from 1796 to 1798 on the Sri Lankan side, were all farmed out. In 1796, the farmer was a certain John Jervis, who repudiated his contract though, forcing the Company to conduct the fishery directly in the arrangement usually termed *amani*.[41] In the next two years it was hence decided to resort to local capital, and the farmer was the Jaffna-based Kondappa Cetti, whose father Vaidyalinga Cetti acted as surety. According to the papers of a later investigation carried out into corruption in the fishery's functioning, the system that was now put in place differed in large measure from that in use in the fisheries of the late seventeenth and early eighteenth centuries. The farmer in 1797 was required to pay a fixed rate of 1,850 Porto Novo *pagodas* per boat, for the use of 150 boats over 30 days. If the number of days of fishing increased, the rent would go up proportionately. The fishery on this occasion began on 3 March and ended on 19 April, and it was claimed that 5,036 boat-days were put in, yielding a rent of 310,533 pagodas. In addition, the Company received a crop of oysters from certain boats that did not satisfy regulations, which yielded an additional revenue of some 18,960 pagodas. The Company was pleased with the return, and the fishery superintendent, Robert Andrews, was allowed to continue the same arrangement the next year at Kondachi Bay, with the same revenue-farmer. This time, rents per boat were raised, participation dropped somewhat, but the fishery nevertheless yielded 380,742 Porto Novo pagodas.

In the next year, 1799, there was a substantial innovation. The justification for the new regime was explained by the Governor of Ceylon, Frederic North, to the Secret Committee of the Court of Directors of the East India Company as follows, in a letter of June 1799.

> Your Honourable Court already knows that the Pearl Oyster Banks of Mannar were farmed, during the Three (*sic*) Fisheries preceding the last, to a rich Merchant of Jaffnapatnam, by the Governor of Fort St. George, for a very considerable sum of money (exceeding during each of the two years the sum of Three Lacs of Pagodas). This sum was regularly paid into their Treasury, so that, on that account, no Fault whatever was imputable to the Renter, the Exercise however of his Right, I have the scruple of asserting produced the greatest Damage to the Banks, Damage which the Government could not well foresee, which it

[41] Colvin R. De Silva, 'The pearl fisheries of Ceylon, 1796-1837', *Ceylon Literary Register*, II, 10 (1932), pp.433-42; also Colvin R. De Silva, *Ceylon under the British Occupation 1795-1833: its political, administrative and economic development*, vol II (Colombo, 1962), pp.501-10.

was nearly impossible for its self and its agent on the spot to prevent, and which, had our Tenure of that Island been as unstable as it was then supposed to be, would probably never have been felt or detected.[42]

In the new arrangement, three Commissioners—Hugh Cleghorn, John McDouall and Lt. George Turnour—were sent out to Mannar to conduct the fishery: boats (implying rights to fish) were 'sold' individually, with the fishery being directly supervised by the three Commissioners. There were, however, accusations thereafter of large-scale fraud, so that not only the Commissioners of 1799 but even Andrews fell under a cloud. The corruption investigation, whose papers occupy several volumes, has the characteristic flavour of such enquiries in the period, revealing a sub-stratum of suitably Machiavellian 'native interests' which manipulated the Commissioners and in fact covertly controlled the entire operation. Governor North took this as a sign of the venality to be associated as a norm with Madras-trained officials ('the wretches brought from the Coast by Mr. Andrews', as he put it), of whom he identified McDouall as the factional leader. These men, who rendered the Company 'lukewarm services, of sullen literal obedience', were, he felt, aided and abetted by Indian mercantile interests, chief among whom in the fishery of 1799 was a certain Narayanasvami Nayakkar, a merchant of Coromandel who was the factotum of John McDouall. The major testimonies against Narayanasvami were those of three rival merchants—Nagalinga Pillai, Ponnayya Pillai and Cinnayya Pillai—one of whom went so far as to declare to a commission of enquiry that 'Narrain had all power at the Fishery; and as all Merchants waited on him upon business, and not on the Commissioners, he was more revered and looked up to than them in all respects'.[43] This led Governor North to look deeper into the earlier fisheries, and he came rapidly to the conclusion that even worse practices had been followed on these occasions. He wrote to the Company's Secret Committee in January 1800:

The Data upon which I ordered the Enquiry into the last Fishery were trifling, unconnected and irrelevant in comparison of those which I send you concerning the Fisheries of 1797 and 1798. Among those you will see many precise

[42] Oriental and India Office Collections, London (henceforth OIOC), Board's Collections, F/4/130, no.2402, pp.5-6. I am grateful to C.A. Bayly for pointing out the existence of these papers to me.

[43] OIOC, Board's Collections, F/4/131, no.2404, 'Proceedings and Report of the Commissioners appointed...to examine into the administration of the late Pearl Fishery at Condeatzie, 1799', Testimony of Ponnayya Pillai, Colombo, 16 November 1799, p.394.

depositions taken upon Oath, from the only Persons who could have absolute knowledge of the Facts, Persons unconnected by Habits, and without any previous communication, all agreeing with each other in the essential Points of more than Five Hundred Boats having fished during both the Fisheries in lieu of one hundred and fifty...[44]

It is significant that a major source of complaint, and of disaffection against the new Cetti dominance, was a certain Maraikkayar notable, Abdul Qadir Sahib, described in the Company records as a 'Moorman of Kilcarry'. Testifying before Governor North, he suggested that the Cettis were in league to control not only the fishery but associated farms, such as that of the toll-booth ('Banksall') in the fishery camp. The investigation dragged on for several years, and in the interim the next two fisheries were once more directly conducted (in 1801 and 1803). In 1804, it was Kondappa Cetti again who took on the farm, and as before he was required to use 150 boats for a period of 30 days. All these fisheries between 1792 and 1805 were, incidentally, held on the Sri Lankan side of the Gulf.

The fisheries of the late eighteenth century, like those of the early nineteenth century, were evidently makeshift affairs, and no 'fishery policy' is at all discernible on the part of the Company's Ceylon government. There was a good deal of wavering between two possible methods: direct administration, and farming-out, with a leaning towards the latter being discernible on close observation. This is more or less in keeping with the manner in which revenue administration in general was conducted in these years. In 1806, for example, Governor Thomas Maitland decided to strike what he thought was a middle course between dealing with a single revenue-farmer and individual boat-owners. Thus, he had his private secretary, a certain Mr. Wright, rent out the right to fifty boats for thirty days' fishing to a single individual (at 1,500 Porto Novo pagodas per boat), laying down a condition that the latter could not sub-rent boats save with Wright's approval and a large advance. The informational advantages of this were stressed by Maitland, as follows:

The evident gain from adopting this line was that Government had all the advantage of the Aumany Fishery, and the Renter became neither more nor less than the Black Agent of Government who by his Knowledge of the habits of the Natives managed the letting of the Boats in a manner infinitely more con-

44 OIOC, Board's Collections, F/4/131, no.2404, Letter from Governor North to the Secret Committee, Colombo, 17 January 1800, pp.14-15; also see his earlier letter of 5 October 1799, F/4/130, no.2403, pp.20-22, 26-8.

genial to their Habits than could have been done by a European....[45]

The identities of the revenue-farmers gradually evolved from what they had been under the Dutch; in 1808, when the fishery was rented out, bids came in from Kondappa Cetti, Kadamba Lingam Pillai, Habib Muhammad Maraikkayar, Ramasvami Nayakkar, and Virappa Cettiar, with a stray bid being made by the (possibly burgher) firm of M/S De Fries and Co.[46] Again, in 1814, when a different system, namely of renting out rights to five boats in a lot for six days was tried out, the thirty renters listed are dominated by Cettiars, following by Maraikkayars, with only one European participant—a certain Mr. Williams.[47] When once more, in 1816, the system of renting out the entire fishery was resorted to in Arippu, there were only two tenders, one from a certain Jaffnapatnam Gopala Cettiar and the other from Habib Muhammad. The former's tender was accepted, with unhappy consequences, when Gopala announced that 'he had made an erroneous calculation; that the Merchants would not come forward to support him, and that he was unable to compleat the Installment'.[48] Besides the Jaffnapatnam Cettis mentioned above, others involved in the first decade of the nineteenth century on the Indian end of the pearl fisheries were a certain Gregory M. Baboom, a merchant from Madras, later a certain Cinnayya Mudaliyar, in 1807 one 'Drachysamy' Cetti and his agent, Hari Prashad, and so on.[49] Later, the involvement of Nattukottai Cettis in the fishery grew more and more marked, reaching a height in the mid-nineteenth century. The earlier dominance by Parava and Maraikkayar interests is thus no longer so visible; the link between control of labour (here, divers) and the investment of capital had turned relatively fragile.

But further changes lay in store once into the nineteenth century. The spirit of *raiyatwari*, so much in the air in these years, could not leave the fishery's administration untouched, as is evidenced in a debate that took place in the 1830s and early 1840s. Its first stirrings may be heard as early as 1824, during the administration of Sir Robert

45 PRO, C.O.54, no.22, Governor Maitland to Lord Viscount Castlereagh, Colombo, 21 May 1806, fls.30v-31.

46 PRO, C.O.54, no.27, Extract from the Minutes of the Council held at Colombo, 22 January 1808, fls.247-48.

47 PRO, C.O.54, no.53, Aumani Fishery Accounts, 6 April 1814, fls.71-72.

48 PRO, C.O.59, no.28, Robert Brownrigg to the Secretary of State the Earl Bathurst, Colombo, 11 February 1816 (unfoliated).

49 *Guide to the Records of the Tinnevelly District, 1796-1835* (Madras, 1934), passim.

Wilmot Horton, who was advised that the Dutch had systematically over-fished the banks in the earlier century, and that this was the reason why there had been no fisheries possible after 1820. Nevertheless, the importance of the fishery was underlined by pointing to its actual revenue yield after 1799, which appeared as in Table 6.[50]

Table 6: *Pearl fishing revenues in British Ceylon, 1799-1820*
(in pounds sterling)

Year	Gross	Charges	Net
1799	29,808	6,684	23,124
1801	13,970	2,045	11,924
1803	14,486	940	13,546
1804	63,381	1,932	61,449
1806	33,862	1,095	32,767
1808	80,695	1,881	78,814
1809	24,379	586	23,793
1814	76,318	2,283	74,035
1820			2,899

There were at least three positions in the debate within the colonial government and the European community in Sri Lanka, as it turned out, in the 1830s. The most extreme view was of those who argued that the state should leave the fishery entirely to private individuals, since otherwise it constituted a 'monopoly'—and was hence objectionable. It was principally against this view that James Steuart, a former inspector of the pearl banks, and Master Attendant at Colombo, wrote a brief polemical work in 1843, which is in fact the first monograph to have been written on the pearl fishery. Steuart argued that the monopoly was of 'general benefit to the community', since the fishery was a peculiar natural phenomenon, and hence not to be equated to other monopolies. As he wrote towards the end of his essay:

> We would not be supposed to be favourers of monopoly, or of exclusive rights and privileges of some of the community to the injury of others; nor do we approve of trading Government. But when a beneficient Providence blesses a country with a peculiar benefit, it is right in the Government of that country jealously to preserve and monopolize such natural advantage for the good of its people generally, and not be induced to sacrifice it to popular clamour or delu-

50 PRO, C.O.59, no.28, G. Brande, Colonial Audit Office, to Sir Wilmot Horton Esq., 12 October 1824.

sive theory.[51]

Steuart's defence of state interference was thus straightforward; since the fishery involved assaying, a decision on the extent of fishing, and supervision to prevent 'cheating', a co-ordinating body was required. And yet, this co-ordinating body could have been as much governmental as commercial. It seems that at this point of time, Steuart was not altogether averse to the idea of farming out the fishery to a single capitalist, rather than auctioning the right to take part in the fishery to individual campanottis, a practice that had apparently been followed off and on in the first three decades of the nineteenth century. His arguments, though perverse, are a refreshing change from other nineteenth-century writings which argued that Indians were conservative in their investment and oddly 'risk averse'. Thus:

...when we take into consideration the reckless habits and gaming propensities of the natives, and that speculations in pearl fisheries on a limited scale, are as uncertain as those in lotteries, the morality of both being exceedingly questionable, it becomes doubtful whether the bringing of such speculations within the means of the poor, is not a public injury rather than an unmixed good...

Or again, adopting a tone at once paternalistic and conservative in respect of wealth and status:

Nor should we make a merit of that, which tends to deprive the wealthier natives of the legitimate influence of their property; to bring down an uncertain speculation within the means of the thoughtless poor; to place temptation before a people too prone to risk their substance on any game of chance.[52]

It is still more curious to find Steuart, a mere decade later, having wholly reversed his position on at least one of the issues. In a letter from Colombo to the Colonial Secretary in December 1854, he wrote:

From experience gained at many pearl fisheries, I am clearly of the opinion, that the renting of even a large one to one or two wealthy capitalists is objectionable: for they invariably sell the boats to sub-renters at considerable profit, and I can see no reason why the Government should not endeavour to secure such profit to its Treasury.[53]

Of course, here too Steuart had evidence to back up his claim. As early as 1799, Lieutenant-Colonel David Robertson had in a report to

[51] James Steuart, *An Account of the Pearl Fisheries of Ceylon* (Cotta, 1843), pp.30-1.

[52] Ibid., pp.29-30.

[53] CSAS, E.L. Pawsey Collection, no.7, 'Pearl Fishery Reports, Miscellaneous (1854-1896)'.

Henry Dundas (which Steuart published as an appendix to his 1843 book, without however drawing the appropriate conclusions!), made precisely this point in respect of the three fisheries of 1796-8. His reconstruction of the proceeds of the fisheries is shown in Table 7, using the three-fold classification of Government Rent, Premium (at which the revenue-farmer 'sold' the boats to individual campanottis) and Gain of the Adventurers (that is, of the entrepreneurs, divers and crew all together):[54]

Table 7: *Shares in the pearl fisheries, 1796-8*
(in Porto Novo pagodas)

	1796	1797	1798
Rent	98,426	330,620	380,748
Premium	49,463	110,203	95,187
Gain of Adventurers	148,389	220,411	118,983
Total	296,778	661,234	594,918

Such a division, apparently so disadvantageous to speculators, was clearly unacceptable in the 1850s, and a new system was hence put in place, as evidenced by the papers from the tenure of George Vane as Superintendent of the Pearl Fisheries, dating to the years from 1855 to 1860.[55] Vane's writings are characterised throughout by a strong polemic *against* renting, which he associated with over-fishing in a manner reminiscent of the position taken at one stage by Governor North in the late eighteenth century. Thus:

> Fish, snakes and chanks destroy an enormous number of young oysters. Currents and drifts of sand carry away into the deep water or cover beds of oysters. But in my opinion, the frequent lapse of fisheries may be attributed to the system under which, years ago, the banks were fished, namely, the *renting* to one or two persons the right of fishing with from 100 to 300 boats daily, with no control over the proceedings of the renter and divers but that of restriction to certain limits and the hours of fishery.[56]

Instead, alleging that 'the renting system is the much desired object of rich Chetties, who, I believe, would now make a large pecuniary sacrifice for its reintroduction', he moved to shore up a strongly *dirigiste*

[54] Steuart, *An Account of the Pearl Fisheries of Ceylon*, pp.88-9.
[55] *Papers relating to the Pearl Fisheries in Ceylon & c.*, (Selections from the Records of the Bombay Government, New Series, no.LXXXVI), (Bombay 1865), esp. pp.1-28, annexures 29-50.
[56] 'Report by Mr. Vane', in ibid., p.6.

system, wherein the state's role grew considerably. The fishery, as before, was to be announced after a sample had been taken in October or November, but the number of boats was to be kept limited to a maximum of 100, save in special circumstances. Boat-owners were to present themselves at the start of the fishery to the Superintendent, who would first choose among them on the basis of the quality of the vessel, and then take a lottery among the boats that had 'qualified'. Each boat was to carry twenty-three persons, including a fixed crew of ten divers and ten assistants ('munducks'). Furthermore, a division of oysters was to be made every day on the return of the fleet to the fishing camp: the government would receive three-quarters and the remaining quarter would be divided between campanotti, divers, and other crew.

Vane's system was an extraordinary mixture of invented tradition and drastic innovation. The division in shares between state and boat-owners and crew was clearly wholly different from what had obtained under the Dutch, where we have seen that the principal state revenue came from taxes on diving-stones and not from a sharing of the daily 'harvest' of oysters. The claim of a three-quarters share for the state is already visible in the period that Steuart wrote, and may have gone back to the direct (*amani*) fisheries of the 1830s, but is unlikely to have been much older than that. At the same time, the regulations in Vane's time were designed to clamp down on certain sorts of innovation.

The division between campanotti and crew was fixed, and it was expressly forbidden to pay divers wages in money 'instead of allowing them their share of oysters, according to the established customs'. Still more curious was a provision by which divers had to remain employed by the same campanotti through the whole fishery, those doing otherwise being subject to punishment for 'deserting from the boats'. Both labour mobility and the emergence of a wage-based market were thus legislated against.

These provisions remained in place during the early part of the tenure of W.C. Twynam as Superintendent of the fisheries, with the further change that the number of boats remained well below the limit prescribed by Vane, as we see from the report on the fishery of 1877.[57] The number of vessels in this year was kept down to fifty per day, with a total squadron of one hundred divided into two sections, to fish alternately. The bulk of these vessels were from Kilakkarai (61, to be precise), with the participation of Tuticorin and other Parava centres having dropped drastically by now. The same was true of the force of

[57] CSAS, E.L. Pawsey Papers, no.8, *Report on the Pearl Fishery of 1877*, by W.C. Twynam (Colombo, 1877).

divers, who in the latter half of the nineteenth century and early twentieth century seem to have come very largely from the Lebbai community. Indeed, Twynam seems to have been forced—against his own inclinations—by a shortage of divers in 1877 to keep the number of boats within limits. He was later quoted as being a strong opponent of the theory of 'over-fishing', quite the contrary to Vane in fact.[58]

It was during Twynam's tenure that the realisation dawned on British officials that they had largely destroyed any incentive that had existed for private participants in the fishery by means of their heavy taxation of the proceeds, together with the doing away of tax-free stones and boats to influential members of the Parava, Maraikkayar, and other communities. As a consequence, in the course of the 1880s, the share of government was redefined, to two-thirds of the daily catch—though this new division was equally to be blandly termed as 'according to immemorial custom' a few decades later![59] At the same time, the desire grew to manage the fishery as a resource in a 'scientific' manner, which is already evident in some of Steuart's own writings, and which we see for example from the report submitted by E.F. Kelaart in 1857, 'On the Natural History of the Pearl Oyster of Ceylon'. Kelaart followed this report up with two others in the next two years, and this scientific interest reached a new height in 1867 with the Report of the Commissioners Appointed to Inquire into the Sea-Fisheries of Ceylon.

But while science marched on, the extraction of oysters did not cease either. Taking the period from 1800 to 1925, we note that some thirty-nine fisheries were held, besides three minor ones. For the most part, these were held on the Ceylonese side, with the Tamil coast hosting fisheries only in fourteen years. The fisheries between 1800 and 1925 yielded an average revenue of Rs.160,000, but this concealed enormous fluctuations. The highest return in the pre-1850 period was from the fishery of 1814, which produced a revenue of as much as Rs.1,051,876; the next year's fishery, however, yielded returns of no more than Rs.5,842, and the year after Rs.9,266. Figures from the latter half of the nineteenth century show that the problem can be broken up in terms of two components: the extent of oyster availability, and the average pearl yield of the oysters themselves. Moreover, we observe a

58 William Twynam, *Report on the Ceylon Pearl Fisheries, 1899*, quoted by J. Pearson in *Reports on the Pearl Fishery of 1925* (Colombo 1926), p.9 (CSAS, E.L. Pawsey Papers, no.13).

59 James Hornell, 'The pearling fleets of South India and Ceylon', *The Mariner's Mirror*, XXXI, 4 (1945), p.230.

certain cyclical bunching effect, so that fisheries tend to come together in certain periods, with rather large gaps between them. The picture for the nineteenth and early twentieth centuries thus was as in Table 8:[60]

Table 8: *Number of oysters fished in the Ceylon fishery, 1835-1925* (in millions)

Year	Oysters	Year	Oysters
1835	16.06	1881	27.34
1836	16.01	1884	0.64
1837	2.54	1887	31.35
1855	6.74	1888	22.05
1857	32.45	1889	38.99
1858	16.48	1890	33.68
1859	9.53	1891	44.31
1860	3.60	1903	41.18
1863	11.,69	1904	41.04
1874	1.70	1905	81.58
1877	6.85	1906	67.10
1879	7.65	1907	21.22
1880	35.24	1925	15.78

A quick glance through Table 8 reveals a rather startling change between two sub-periods, namely 1835-84 and 1887-1925. In the first of these, some 195 million oysters were fished from fifteen fisheries, while in the second over 438 million oysters were fished in a mere eleven fisheries. Whether one calculates this as an average per year, or per fishery, there is evidently a *trebling* in the intensity of the exploitation of the pearl fishery between these two sub-periods. In the last section of this paper, it is the causes and consequences of this change that will occupy our attention.

Mysteries and miracles

One of the major problems preoccupying writers from Steuart and Kelaart onwards was what they regarded as the cyclical character of the fishery, which limited its optimal exploitation. Their thoughts on this subject were somewhat analogous to those writers on forestry in colonial India, who addressed the problem of 'sustained yield' from such renewable resources. In fact, where the pearl fishery is concerned at least, the roots of this preoccupation can be traced back to Van Rheede,

60 *Reports on the Pearl Fishery of 1925*, Appendix, p.40.

or even further, to the Jesuits on the fishery coast in the early seventeenth century. Steuart in his work denied that over-fishing had any part to play in failures of the fishery, strenuously defending the former Governor, Sir Robert Wilmot Horton, against the charge of having 'scraped and ruined' the banks. When putting forward his own interpretation, he retreated into a notion of the mysteries of nature. Thus:

> The success of pearl fisheries in the Gulf of Manaar, depends primarily upon natural events beyond the control of man.... We may presume from past experience, that unsuccessful intervals will continue to recur. We cannot promote or facilitate the production of pearl oysters. We cannot cause the spawn to settle down upon nourishing ground. These are events beyond the control of man. The winds, the waves, and the uncertain currents of the ocean, carry the embryo over unlimited space. It is only when, in the infinite wisdom of the Creator of all things, the oyster brood descends upon banks suited to nourish and support its—that it comes within our limited power to watch its advancing age, and to fish up the respective deposits in succession as they approach the proper age....[61]

Such metaphysics was, however, not the order of the day in the late nineteenth century, when the idea that was increasingly gaining hold was that with proper management, the fishery could be made entirely predictable, and be caused to yield pearls every year. In the gap between the fisheries of 1891 and 1903, protagonists of this viewpoint found sympathetic support in the Government of Ceylon, and especially in the person of the Governor, Sir Joseph West Ridgeway, whose term went on from 1896 to 1903. To focus briefly on Ridgeway (1844-1930), we may note that he had become an accomplished career administrator after having joined the army in 1860, and served in the Afghan war of 1879-80. He was then appointed Under-Secretary (Foreign Department) in the Government of India from 1880 to 1884, and later went on to become Governor of the Isle of Man (1893-5) before taking up his Colombo position. Not only this, Sir Joseph West Ridgeway had a sharp eye for business and exploration, holding the post after 1910 of President of the British North Borneo Company, besides being Vice-President of the Royal Geographical Society. If his political ambitions remained unfulfilled (he stood twice for parliament on the Liberal ticket, but lost, in 1906 and 1910), his social standing (the Athenaeum, Boodle's and the Naval and Military Clubs), his titles (K.C.B. in 1891, G.C.M.G. in 1900, and G.C.B. in 1906), and his familial connections (two brothers the Bishops of Chichester and Salisbury respectively) were all largely impeccable.

[61] Steuart, *Pearl Fisheries of Ceylon*, p.25.

It was at Ridgeway's behest that Sir William Herdman, F.R.S., Professor at the University of Liverpool and a marine biologist of repute, was brought in to investigate the fishery, together with his assistant James Hornell. Herdman arrived in Ceylon in January 1902, and eventually completed his massive, five-volume report only in 1906.[62] His principal conclusion was that the mortality of the pearl oyster could be controlled, even though he did note that overfishing was a distinct possibility under certain circumstances. His major recommendation was to follow the practice of 'cultching', namely the spreading of an artificial layer of dead coral, rock fragments and rubble, which would provide young oysters a surface on which they could attach themselves. The idea was derived from the oyster farms at Arcachon in France, where whitewashed tiles were used, in relatively shallow water, to facilitate the production of edible (rather than pearl) oysters.

Interestingly, Herdman's recommendations came at a time when the Mannar pearl fishery had resumed production, after a hiatus of over a decade. Ridgeway was most enthusiastic about the possibilities, as we see from his farewell speech before the Legislative Council, in which he declared that,

> Professor Herdman gives a definite explanation of the causes exercising pernicious effects on the pearling industry, and he formulates a number of remedial, or rather cultural measures which he believes will bring prosperity and eliminate a large number of the unfruitful years.

The contrast was thus drawn between Herdman's 'very complete and valuable work', and the earlier situation when 'we had no scientific data to go upon', and even worse 'nothing was known regarding the oyster, its habits and natural enemies, or for the reasons for its appearance and disappearance at particular localities'. Short shrift was thus given to all earlier work from Kelaart to Thurston, and the pre-history (before Ridgeway and Herdman) of the fishery was summed up as follows:

> The pearl fisheries in the Gulf of Mannar have been for centuries a lucrative source of revenue to the Government of this Island. During the one hundred and seven years of British rule over £1,000,000 nett revenue has accrued to the Colony from these fisheries, representing an average annual income of some Rs.150,000. But the income is precarious; for instance, during the period

[62] W.A. Herdman, *Report to the Government of Ceylon on the Pearl Oyster Fisheries of the Gulf of Mannar* (5, vols., London, 1903-1906); *The 'Ceylon Hansard', containing the debates of the Ceylon Legislative Council during the session of 1903-1904* (Colombo, 1904), Appendix, pp.111-15, 'Pearl Fisheries and the Marine Biological Department'.

named there have been three long gaps, viz., from 1837 to 1855, from 1864 to 1873, and from 1891 till the present year. Two centuries ago the Commandant of Jaffnapatam, writing for the instruction of the Political Council of that town, stated that 'the pearl fishery is an extraordinary source of revenue on which no reliance can be placed, as it depends on various contingencies, which may ruin the banks or spoil the oysters', and a similar statement would accurately describe the experience of the British administration.[63]

On the other hand, Ridgeway's beliefs concerning the newest findings, and his immense faith in Herdman's science, had rather crucial consequences. Almost as soon as he left the government, a proposal was put before his successor Sir H.A. Blake, that the pearl fishery be leased out to a registered company, which would undertake its commercial exploitation. The matter was debated at length, and with great vigour in the Ceylon Legislative Council, many of whose members were violently opposed to leasing the fishery out. The Ceylon government's position was that it was anomalous for the state to take charge of a productive enterprise; for, in fact, this was the business of private capital.[64] A curious reversal had thus taken place between the mid-nineteenth century and the early twentieth century. But in fact the reversal was not quite complete. In the mid-nineteenth century, the issue had been of direct state exploitation versus Cetti capital. In 1904-1905 capital was to come from a London-based company, the Ceylon Company of Pearl Fishers Limited. Further, the chairman of the company was the Right Honourable Sir Joseph West Ridgeway, and its scientific adviser, Sir William Herdman. The first general manager of the company was Herdman's former assistant, James Hornell. There was thus a happy meeting of capital, government and science in the enterprise.

The lease obtained by the Company of Pearl Fishers was of twenty years' duration. In each of these years, the company was to pay a rent of Rs.310,000, whether or not a fishery was held. In addition, they were to buy a pearl-extracting apparatus recently developed by the Marine Biological Department, a government trawler, and to engage, moreover, to spread 500 tons of cultch a year, besides a sum of between Rs.50,000 and Rs.150,000 annually on 'experimental and cultural work'.[65] Though the company was formally founded only in March 1906, the profits of the fishery that year (administered by government)

[63] *The 'Ceylon Hansard'*, 1903-1904, p.111.

[64] *The 'Ceylon Hansard', containing the debates of the Ceylon Legislative Council during the session of 1906-1907* (Colombo, 1908), pp.x-xii (address of Sir H.A. Blake, 22 November 1906), and pp.88-90.

[65] CSAS, E.L. Pawsey Papers, no.8, *Lease of the Ceylon Pearl Fisheries* (Colombo, 1907).

nevertheless went to it. The directors of the company who signed were a certain J.H.M. Shaw and W.H. Phillips, and the names of Sir Joseph West Ridgeway and Sir William Herdman do not appear on it. Nor do we know how much they invested in the company's initial issued capital of £90,000. As a later investigator wrote:

> So rosy, in fact, were the prospects that no prospectus was issued to the public; I am informed by the Secretary that the original capital was all privately subscribed. The shares were only obtained by the general public at a later date through the medium of the Stock exchange, where they sold at a high premium.[66]

In fact, in the first two years of the company's existence, dividends of some £50,000 were paid on the issued capital, an astonishing rate of return as contemporaries saw it. But after 1907, the company's luck turned. The next year, Thomas Southwell was named scientific adviser, and he assured the company that the fishery could be made perennially productive, if—instead of the cultching scheme proposed by Herdman and Hornell—wire-netting were used to protect the pearl banks from predatory fish, and a concrete breeding tank (or oyster hatchery) were set up in northern Ceylon. Joseph Ridgeway in turn dutifully conveyed these projects to the shareholders in their annual meetings, even though another marine biologist was later to describe the oyster hatchery scheme as 'biologically speaking, a most amazing proposal to lay before a body of shareholders as a business proposition'.[67] Finally, in 1911, after four barren years, the company faced bankruptcy, leading Ridgeway to declare that 'the failure of this venture has been one of the greatest disappointments of my life'. The shareholders, for their part, blamed not the former governor, but Hornell and Southwell. The marine biologist Joseph Pearson was to write in 1925:

> The shareholders took alarm at the 'failure' of the Marine Biologist to produce a pearl fishery for their benefit, and in their colossal ignorance of what could be achieved by the application of scientific methods to a commercial problem, the shareholders demanded something in the nature of a miracle.[68]

It is nevertheless interesting that Pearson, who supervised the 1925 fishery in large measure, continued to argue that overfishing had noth-

[66] H. Lyster Jameson, 'An examination of the causes that have led to the failure of the biological work recently undertaken on the Ceylon pearl fisheries', *Journal of Economic Biology*, VII, 1 (1912), p.15.

[67] Ibid., p.18. Also see West Ridgeway's speech to the shareholders as reported in the *Financial News*, 7 November 1906.

[68] CSAS, E.L. Pawsey Papers, no.13, *Reports on the Pearl Fishery of 1925* (Colombo, 1926), p.10.

ing to do with the gap of seventeen years that followed the fishery of 1907. He went so far, in fact, as to state that it was 'impossible to overfish the pearl banks so as to leave no oyster reserve', even though in 1925 he permitted less than 16 million oysters to be fished, lower than in any other successful fishery since 1879. He may have thought himself vindicated, for despite this caution there was to be no pearl fishery in the waters of Sri Lanka again until 1958.[69] In the second half of the 1920s, relatively minor fisheries continued to be held off the coast of Tamilnadu, as indeed has since been the case, with intervals, since that date.

In lieu of a conclusion

This chapter has been principally concerned to analyse the management of the pearl fishery of Mannar under different regimes, focusing in particular on the alternation between commercial modes of exploitation (be it revenue-farming, or the Ceylon Company of Pearl Fishers) and the more-or-less direct administration by a variety of regimes, Some long-term trends have been visible in the fishery, but also certain fluctuations over a shorter horizon. The first substantial change immediately precedes the productivity crisis of the late sixteenth century, and is signalled by the abandoning of the practice of two fisheries in favour of just one, in the months February to April. This practice of a single fishery continues in the latter half of the seventeenth century and the early eighteenth century, when the fishery is seemingly revitalised under a system wherein the Dutch levy a tax on the means of production rather than on the product. This system, of the tax on stones, evidently left a greater incentive with divers and campanottis than the system subsequently adopted, wherein the product was taxed either directly by the state or indirectly by state-supported revenue-farmers.

It is noteworthy that the years from about 1740 to 1890 are also those when the Parava community moves away from involvement in the pearl fishery. This shift has been portrayed by a historian of the Paravas, Patrick Roche, as a result of the move from *jati tolil* to *velai* (or corporate communal economy to wage-work). Roche thus argues that whereas the Portuguese and Dutch had excluded Maraikkayars and Lebbais (whom he terms 'Kayalars') from the fishery, the British regime opened the activity to all groups; in brief it was competition and

[69] *The 1958 Pearl Oyster Fishery, Gulf of Mannar* (Colombo Fisheries Research Station, Bulletin no.11) (Colombo, 1961).

the market that reduced Parava interest in the fishery.[70] My reading of the history of pearl fishery, while focusing less on Tuticorin and more on Ceylon as compared to that of Roche, would be somewhat different. It would seem that in the course of the nineteenth century, the fishery as an employer came to be of much reduced importance. This was not because the market was allowed to intrude; on the contrary, we have seen that the British regime at times sought actively to limit wage-work, and limit the mobility of labour from one employer to another. Only after about 1890 did participation begin to pick up, and this was aided by the importation of contingents of 200 to 300 Arab divers by the British government for each fishery. Again, this was characteristic, for men like Hornell (who was a great supporter of the use of Arab divers) persisted in seeing diving as an activity defined by community, and hence saw the matter as the substitution of one community by another. To him, the Paravas were a shiftless lot, who 'will do little or no work till they have got rid of their earnings in drink and in entertainments and are penniless once again'. The Lebbais were better men on account of their 'abstemious lives consequent upon fairly faithful observance of the Prophet's laws'. But best of all were the Arabs, who were 'more willing to obey my orders and follow suggestions than either the Paravas or the Kilakarai Moormen—a result due naturally to their higher intelligence'.[71]

The argument has often been made with respect to other natural resources—fisheries in general, or forests—that the processes of the nineteenth century accelerated their depletion, upsetting a sort of balance between humans and these resources that had existed over the centuries and leading gradually to a 'Tragedy of the Commons'. The debates conducted in the Ceylon Legislative Council and elsewhere on the conduct of the pearl fishery are testimony to the fact that such thinking existed already in the early twentieth century. It is summed up by the member of the Council from Kalutara, E.W. Perera, who in a debate of 1925, declared:

> The Company [of Pearl Fishers] paid no attention whatever to the pearl banks. They tried to get as much as possible out of them and scraped the spat and subsequently sold out. I do not know whether spat were scraped out by machinery, but the banks remained unfertile for several years. That is a matter of detail.
>
> After that the Secretary of State issued a circular to the effect that no Governor of a Crown Colony should be the Director of a company which was floated in connection with the industries of the Colony of which he had been

[70] Roche, *Fishermen of the Coromandel*, pp.83-4.
[71] Hornell, 'The Indian pearl fisheries', pp.64-5, 146.

Governor. The stable door was closed after the horse had been stolen.[72]

Of the fact that the Ceylon Company of Pearl Fishers represented a unique combination of naïvete and greed, there seems little doubt. Their touching trust in the power of science sets the shareholders of the company apart from the speculators of the eighteenth or early nineteenth centuries. But can we go beyond that, to conclude, for example, that the setting aside of 'local knowledge' and 'community control' of resources in favour of a *dirigiste* state regime meant the ruin of the fishery, and thus that a distinctly inferior form of resource management was chosen over a superior one? There are several problems with adopting this line of argument in its most simple form with respect to the pearl fishery. First of all, systematic state interference had begun early here, and cannot be tied directly to the Industrial Revolution and post-Enlightenment constructions of the relationship between universal, scientific knowledge and local knowledge. Indeed, the brutal setting aside of the Maraikkayars in the sixteenth century by the Jesuits and their Parava clients already represents a rather drastic shift in the nature of community control, even if it was later successfully contested.

Thus, when we accumulate the mass of contemporary testimonies from different periods, it emerges that there was no pre-1750 Golden Age to be contrasted with what came afterwards. There was instead a drift from a political regime—that of the Portuguese, whose main claim to control the fishery was through their patronage of a community, namely, the Paravas, to another political regime—that of the Dutch—which combined such a privileged relationship with the Paravas with a claim that control over water stemmed from control over land, here coastal Ceylon. However, this claim to a resource in water, based on the control of land, meant that the competing claims of other littoral powers—the Nayakas of Madurai, the Setupatis of Ramnad, and eventually the Nawabs of Arcot—had to be accommodated. Eventually, under the English East India Company, as both margins of the Gulf of Mannar came for the first time under a single power, this issue was seemingly resolved. Privileges and rights in the fishery vested in local potentates and even temples were abolished by the time Company rule in India gave way to the Crown in mid-century; from now on the play of forces rested largely at the level of capital, and the key question was of the state's relationship to the 'private' sector in the management of a 'public' resource.

[72] *Debates in the Legislative Council of Ceylon 1925*, compiled by F.G. Toussaint and V.C.C. Dewapurarathna (Colombo, 1926), p.47.

It is perhaps worth emphasising in this context that the approach derived from the 'Tragedy of the Commons' and the 'Fisherman's Problem' sits somewhat askew of the peculiar trajectory of the pearl fishery. Such approaches as these stress the deleterious effects of unbridled competition, which may lead to the running-down of the resource, with the implicit contrast being between the stable moral economies of communities and the self-destructive logic of selfish individualism. The problem in the case of the pearl fishery, as we have seen, seems rarely to have stemmed from the rapacity of individual boat-owners who were hardly eager to take the last oyster off the banks lest their competitors do so. Rather, here the problem appears, in the final analysis, to be associated paradoxically enough, with the nature not of competition but of *monopolies*, most conspicuously the Ceylon Company of Pearl Fishers Ltd. This may not be without its lessons in other contexts where the principal choice is not (as romantics fondly imagine) between the community and the individual as 'primitive economic agent', but between legally- and institutionally-regulated competition, and an unchecked and untrammeled concentration of economic power.

Chapter 8

THE LOGIC OF THE ARTISAN FIRM IN A CAPITALIST ECONOMY: HANDLOOM WEAVERS AND TECHNOLOGICAL CHANGE IN WESTERN INDIA, 1880-1947[1]

Douglas E. Haynes

That a variety of forms of organisation and technology exist side by side in the Indian economy has long been a commonplace in the academic literature on the subcontinent. Recent scholarship has now relinquished the view that small-scale units with relatively simple techniques of production and divisions of work should be seen merely as 'survivals' of a 'traditional', 'semi-feudal' or 'pre-capitalist' past. What has been emphasised instead is that such units are often critical parts of the larger economy, shaping it as well as being shaped by it[2]. Nowhere perhaps has the polymorphic character of Indian capitalism been more dramatically illustrated in recent years than in the textile industry, where power-loom workshops employing limited amounts of wage-labour have not only been able to continue production into the 1990s, but have begun to capture a dominant share in the cloth market from the large mills. Much of the vitality of the power-loom sector can no doubt be attributed to the industrial policies of the post-colonial state, particularly in the area of labour legislation. But the fact that the power-looms first emerged during the colonial period, when little such regulation was in place, suggests that the developing structure of Indian capitalism itself encouraged and reinforced small-scale production. In

[1] An initial draft of this article was presented at the Annual Conference on South Asia at the University of Wisconsin at Madison in November 1992. I wish to thank participants in this session and others who offered comments on my session, including Marcia Frost, Alice Clark, Mattison Mines, David Ludden, Frank Conlon, Shelley Feldman, and especially Anand Yang. I would also like to thank Tirthankar Roy, Sanjay Subrahmanyam and Burton Stein for comments on a subsequent draft of this essay. and other work. Any shortcomings of the essay in its present form, of course, are entirely my own responsibility.

[2] An important formulation of this position is Jairus Banaji, 'Capitalist domination and the small peasantry: Deccan districts in the late nineteenth century', *Economic and Political Weekly*, XII (August 1977, special number), pp.1375-1404.

fact, up to the very end of British rule, artisan households, headed by master craftsmen and employing handlooms, continued to produce a significant portion of India's cloth. Such units were hardly pre-capitalist relics; indeed, most had become thoroughly penetrated by merchant capital.

In order to explore how a great range of organisational forms for producing textiles managed to sustain themselves within the context of the emerging economy of the colonial period, this essay examines two kinds of artisan organisation in western India during the late nineteenth and early twentieth centuries. The first of these is what might be called the dependent artisan-household, that is, a kind of productive organisation unit that primarily utilised family labour but depended upon merchant-capitalists for its finance, raw materials and marketing. The second is the artisan workshop (*karkhana*), a firm headed by a master-weaver employing relatively small amounts of extra-familial labour (from four to as many as fifty workers). In this essay I explore the logic of these two kinds of industrial organisation by looking primarily at their adaptations to new technologies that became available during the late colonial period. What, I ask, accounts for the differential rates of adaptation of these innovations by these two kinds of organisation? And why did actors in both kinds of organisation tend to adopt techniques that preserved the craft character of production?

Maintaining a kind of dual focus on artisan 'firms' and on the larger structures in which these firms participated helps to resolve what at first sight seems to be a major contradiction between the perspectives of the existing primary sources and the interpretations of modern scholars. Colonial officials and Indian social reformers, frustrated by the reluctance of handloom weavers to adopt certain technical innovations or to organise themselves along co-operative lines, changes that they believed to be in the weavers' interest, commonly categorised artisans as an inherently conservative set of actors who balked at the introduction of any kind of change. By contrast, historical work done in the last few years has insisted that the artisan economy was a dynamic one, undergoing constant changes during the last century of British rule.[3] This new scholarship has indeed discovered important shifts in

[3] For instance, Christopher J. Baker, *An Indian Rural Economy, 1880-1955: The Tamilnad countryside* (Oxford, 1984), ch.V; Tirthankar Roy, 'Relations of production in handloom weaving in the mid-thirties', *Economic and Political Weekly* XXIV (28 January 1989), pp.PE.21-34, and 'Size and structure of handloom weaving industry in the mid-thirties; *Indian Economic and Social History Review* XXV (January-March 1988), pp.1-24; Konrad Specker,

methods of cloth production and marketing among Indian weavers. But it has arrived at its conclusions largely by charting broad long-term patterns of change, not by examining the decision-making processes that might have produced such patterns. The kind of reconsideration of artisan behaviour necessary to explain the signs of dynamism in the artisan economy, but still account for what colonial officials took as evidence of conservatism, has not taken place.

A closer examination of handloom weaving reveals the shortcomings of any attempt to measure artisan activity by any abstract standard of 'conservatism' or 'progressiveness'. Many artisans did indeed make steady adjustments to the changing character of the larger economy. But such adjustments were always conditioned by the relationship of the artisan producers to the structures of regional capitalism. Organised on a family basis, exposed to constant vicissitudes in demand for cloth, and lacking resources to fall back upon, most dependent artisan households were preoccupied with making ends meet. Weavers were selective in adopting innovations that might improve productivity, not because of any intrinsic aversion to profit-seeking, but because they lacked the access to the market that they needed to translate any increased production into improved prospects for family subsistence and prosperity. By contrast,the larger workshops, which often possessed the ability to cultivate markets to absorb any increased volume and to do away with unneeded labour when such markets could not be found, tended to adopt some of the same technologies swiftly and rather painlessly. But their strategies, too, were strongly affected by the volatility of demand for cloth. They too stayed away from heavy investments of fixed capital that would hurt their firms' ability to adjust to fluctuations in consumption.

In short, the economy of western India promoted the reproduction of small-scale units with rather simple divisions of labour, organisations that to a considerable extent continued to be based upon craft principles.[4] As a result, the artisan economy followed its own patterns

'Madras handlooms in the nineteenth century', *Indian Economic and Social History Review* XXVI (April-June 1989), pp.131-66; and Peter Harnetty, '"Deindustrialization" revisited: The handloom weavers of the central provinces of India, c.1800-1947', *Modern Asian Studies* XXV (July 1991), pp.445-510. Tirthankar Roy, *Artisans and Industrialization: Indian weaving in the twentieth century* (Delhi, 1994) is the most systematic treatment of the theme in English.

[4] By craft here I mean productive organisations which use machines that can be adopted to a variety of products and in which the skilled worker plays a major role in determining the shape of the product manufactured. The division

of change, patterns independent of those associated with the textile industries of Bombay and Ahmedabad which were emerging at the same time.

The macro-context

Literature on artisan cloth production during the colonial period has been dominated by the debate over the 'deindustrialisation' of India. But neither position in this debate has fully captured the complexity of changes in the artisan economy taking place during the latter half of the nineteenth century. No doubt, some significant areas of artisan cloth production 'survived' the competition of mill-made textiles; overall, the handloom sector maintained a market share of roughly one quarter of India's cloth consumption as late as the mid 1920s. Those involved in the industry were constantly developing new markets and adjusting their methods of making cloth. At the same time, however, the position of most handloom weavers clearly was becoming one of increased insecurity and of dependence upon merchant-capitalists. It is therefore important to go beyond the implicit assumption in much of the deindustrialisation debate that the health of the handloom sector can best be measured by determining the numbers of weavers or the volume of cloth they produced.[5]

Nowhere perhaps was the shifting character of the artisan economy more marked than in western India. As Table 1 indicates, virtually all the largest weaving centres in the Bombay Presidency during the early twentieth century were ones that had experienced significant growth during the late nineteenth century. Since weaving in dispersed villages appears to have declined during this same period, the table seems to reflect the growing 'urbanization' of the handloom industry.[6] Artisan

---

of labour in such organisations tends to be relatively simple. In other words, I am using the term in roughly the same sense as it is used in Michael J. Piore and Charles F. Sabel, *The Second Industrial Divide: possibilities for prosperity* (New York, 1984), pp.5-6. Piore and Sabel contrast craft production with 'mass production', the aim of which is 'to decompose every handwork task into simple steps, each of which could be performed faster and more accurately by a machine dedicated to that purpose' (p.19). As the term is used in this essay, craft production can be compatible with certain kinds of power-driven machines and production for the market.

[5] As much of the work listed in footnote 3 has in fact begun to do.

[6] In using the term 'urbanization', I mean the increasing tendency of weavers to live and work in larger marketing-production centres, centres which served as the headquarters of merchant-capitalists dealing in cloth. The Indian census definition of town is not so important to my own analysis (though all of the

Table 1: *Estimated numbers of looms in key handloom centres in the Bombay Presidency*

District & town	Early	c.1875	1910	1929-32
Sholapur				
Sholapur	NA	6,465	10,000	(1932) 7,500
Dharwar				
Hubli	(1843) 2,263	4,982	8,000	(1929) 3,512
Nasik				
Malegaon	NA	2,441	7,019	(1932) 5,500
Yeola	NA	2,000	3,425	(1932) 3,000
Bijapur				
Guledgud	(1851) 1,800	2,386	3,150	(1929) 3,500
Thana				
Bhiwandi	NA	650-700	3,125	(1929) 2,000
Ahmednagar				
Sangamner	NA	1,000	3,015	(1929) 2,000
Ahmednagar				
Ahmednagar	(1820) 213		3,000	
+ Bhingar [1]	(1850) 1,322	1,800-2,000		(1929) 3,500
Dharwar				
Ranebennur	400+	NA	2,775	(1929) 2,060
Gadag-Betgeri	(1844) 1,507	1,399	2,390	(1929) 3,250
Bijapur				
Ilkal	500	NA	1,275	(1929) 3,025
Ahmedabad				
Dholka	NA	(1887) 2,500	400 [2]	(1929) 710

[1] Figures either for Ahmednagar only or for Ahmednagar and Bhingar. [2] Estimate for the whole of Dholka taluka. *Notes*: For years shown in parentheses, 1875 figures represent those at the time of the Gazetteer; those for 1929-32 are best estimates in the year shown. NA = not available.

cloth-producers tended to congregate increasingly in larger weaving centres where ample supplies of yarn and good marketing facilities were available. In Gujarat, about which the table tells us little, significant concentrations of weavers in urban places had developed as early as the seventeenth century. During the nineteenth century, the region

centres in Table 1 fit census definitions). The figures in Table 1 do not suggest any conclusion on the issue of 'deindustrialisation', both because they are confined to certain centres (and do not give overall figures) and because they reflect only the later part of the colonial period.

experienced a sharp drop in rural weaving, though several urban centres, such as Dholka and Ahmedabad, also declined. Overall, weavers were removing themselves from localised networks of exchange to live and work in larger centres of production with distant markets.[7]

Change was most dramatic in Maharashtra, which appears to have been previously only a minor area of cloth production. There major new centres of production emerged, such as Sholapur, Ahmednagar, Bhiwandi and Sangamner. In contrast to Gujarat and northern Karnataka, the two other major regions of the presidency, the weavers in these centres generally came from outside the traditional artisan communities of the area. Many were immigrants who moved from famine-prone regions of northern India and Andhra to settle in the new centres and ply their trades after the mid-nineteenth century. Two main streams of migration developed. The first was the movement of Muslim weavers, known as Momins (or Julahas) from the United Provinces to centres along or near the Agra-Bombay highway, such as Dhulia, Malegaon, Yeola and Bhiwandi. The other was the migration of Hindu Padmasali weavers from Hyderabad state to towns in the east of the Bombay Presidency such as Sholapur, Ahmednagar and Pune. In several towns in the region the Momins and Padmasalis came to positions of virtual control in the weaving profession, displacing such local communities as the Koshtis.

Weavers and merchants in these centres were also shaping new kinds of connections with the international economy. One very significant development was the growing reliance upon modern industry for

[7] The table includes the ten largest weaving centres in 1910 and two other interesting centres, Ilkal and Dholka. The data in the table have been gathered from the settlement reports of various talukas in the Bombay Presidency, various District Gazetteers of the Presidency, from information collected by P.N. Mehta in preparing his report on handloom industries in Bombay, collected in Maharashtra State Archives, G.D. 1910, vol.98A, comp.820, pt.II; S.V. Telang, *Report on the Handloom Industry in the Bombay Presidency* (2nd ed Bombay, 1933); N.M. Joshi, *Urban Handicrafts of the Bombay Deccan* (Pune, 1936); and *Report of the Bombay Economic and Industrial Survey, 1938-40*, vol.I (Bombay, 1938-40), p.59. The rigour with which various estimates were collected varied widely, so these figures can only provide a rough idea of weaving populations. When it is possible to compare Mehta's figures (listed as 1910 estimates in the table) with other figures available at the same time, it is clear that his estimates for larger centres are somewhat high (generally around 10 to 15 per cent). The loom estimates for smaller centres were somewhat more meticulously collected. Despite the roughness of all these figures, they consistently point to the expansion of urban weaving in Maharashtra and northern Karnataka between the late 1870s and 1910.

supplies. Most artisans began using yarn from European or Indian spinning mills during the early to mid-nineteenth century. By the late nineteenth century, the traditional spinning industry was virtually non-existent, and weavers obtained their yarn either from Europe or from Indian spinning factories. Indeed, there were a number of mills in inland areas of the Bombay Presidency whose main function was to produce yarn for handloom workers. Artisan cloth producers became linked to the international economy in other ways as well. Silk-weavers increasingly depended on imports of raw silk from China; *zari* (gold thread) workers imported gold, silver and silk from abroad; and by the early twentieth century, the vast majority of weavers had taken to using foreign dyes, particularly aniline and alizarine dyes made in Germany.

Such changes of course significantly reduced the employment of those artisans who had once specialised in the preparation of the weaver's raw materials, but they also influenced the conditions faced by the weavers themselves. Handloom producers increasingly were affected by prices and the availability of supplies in international markets. At times, fluctuations in these markets could force the artisans out of business altogether. During World War I, the period of the most dramatic crisis of supply in the handloom industry, lack of access to foreign yarn and to German dyes drove many weavers to the larger cities of the Bombay Presidency to seek industrial work.[8]

The development of large-scale textile factories obviously also had an effect on markets for artisan cloth. Weavers no doubt had to abandon many fields in which they could no longer compete. But at the same time, they sustained some old markets and generated new ones. In general, artisans tended to give up the production of medium and coarse medium-count clothing, where the mills reigned supreme. But they were able to control other markets. By the beginning of the twentieth century, they tended to make either very coarse cloth for peasants and agricultural labourers, who considered the produce of handloom weavers superior to mill-made manufactures; or they wove more elaborately-designed cloth for more prosperous consumers, using silk or high counts of cotton yarn. Usually, handloom weavers fared

[8] See the various District Gazetteers of the Bombay Presidency and the Annual Administrative Reports on various districts in the Presidency, especially during the war years. These are found in the files of the Revenue Department (R.D.) in the Maharashtra State Archives. Morris D. Morris of course recognised long ago the significance of international sources of yarn for handloom weavers. See, for instance, his 'The growth of large-scale industry' in Dharma Kumar (ed.), *Cambridge Economic History of India*, vol.2 (Cambridge, 1983), esp. pp.576-7, 669-71.

better in women's clothing than in men's wear. Tirthankar Roy has elaborated further: artisans, he suggests, tended to manufacture cloth that could be draped whole over the body rather than clothing that required further stitching, and they made textiles with intricate border designs and not cloth needing sophisticated finishing processes.[9] The sari in particular remained the province of the handloom weaver until well into the twentieth century. No doubt export markets of western Indian producers declined, but artisans of the region increasingly produced cloth for more distant internal markets. The cotton-growing tracts of Khandesh and Berar emerged as especially important centres of consumption for producers in both Maharashtra and northern Karnataka.

By the end of the nineteenth century, artisans in western India made cloth for highly differentiated, often regionally focused, markets for specific products. Silk-weavers of Guledgud produced blouse pieces for sale in Maharashtra and Berar; artisans of Yeola manufactured silk saris mainly for the cotton-growing tracts and for Bombay weavers in Ahmednagar made coarse coloured *nagari* saris of nine yards length for tribals in Khandesh and Gujarat; weavers in Bhiwandi produced high-quality cotton cloth of fine yarn principally for buyers in Bombay. Within these general types, the demand for different designs appears to have been in continual flux, requiring the producers to alter their patterns regularly. The limited, specialised and fluctuating character of consumption in these kinds of cloth proved conducive to artisan manufacture, which required little capital investment and the ability to customise products to suit small groups of customers. In other words, the nature of cloth markets encouraged a kind of 'flexible specialisation'.[10] By contrast, mass-producing mills with elaborate divisions of labour, heavy investments of capital, and inflexible technologies were at a serious disadvantage in meeting these needs of consumers.

But while handloom weavers found sizeable fields of consumption

[9] Roy, *Artisans and Industrialization*, ch.4.

[10] See Charles Sabel and Jonathan Zeitlin, 'Historical alternatives to mass production: politics, markets and technology in nineteenth-century industrialisation', *Past and Present*, 108 (August 1985), pp.133-76. In borrowing this model, I stress one key feature of the concept, that is, the employment of high-skill, general-purpose machines that could make products customised to small and changing markets. Sabel and Zeitlin stress that such firms were flexible in another sense: they constantly adjusted their techniques of production in new circumstances. The notion of flexibility in this sense is only partially followed in this essay, since I stress differing degrees of innovation among different organisations.

for their cloth well into the twentieth century, their position in the larger market was an insecure one. The demand for the two kinds of textiles they produced—very coarse cloth used by poor consumers and that of luxury and imitation luxury products used by middle- and upper-class consumers—was almost always unstable. Both of these kinds of production were consistently subject to strong seasonal fluctuations. Country folk made most of their purchases of cheap cloth during the marriage season and after the harvest had been collected, times when they had some cash to spend. But coarse cloth was in rather limited demand during other parts of the year. Luxury production similarly fluctuated with the coming and going of the marriage season. There were also longer-term variations, such as those produced by crop failures and by drops in international prices of cotton or sugar. In bad agricultural years, the peasants' first step in coping with reduced incomes was to cut back on all non-grain purchases. During the famines of 1876-77 and 1896-1900, weavers felt the effects of shortage well before most agriculturalists and were often the first to enter relief works.[11]

Most of these emerging features of the artisan economy—the growing distance of weavers from the sources of their raw materials and their markets, their vulnerability to severe annual and cyclical oscillations in demand, the variations in supply and price of raw materials, and the concentration of weaving in larger centres—were changes that promoted the penetration of the handloom industry by merchant-capitalists. Weaving families frequently came to develop contractual relations with moneylenders and traders who provided yarn or credit and who sold most of the artisan-produced cloth.

The key feature of these dependent relations, as Tirthankar Roy has argued, was that of 'tied sale',[12] that is, artisans regularly entered into

[11] In the earlier famine, for instance, demand was reported to be so slack in Sholapur that weavers had to abandon their usual occupation and seek work in the relief works; in Yeola, the demand 'so entirely failed that Government had...to advance materials to the weavers and buy up their work to save them from starvation'. The Yeola report went on to state that 'these people have probably felt the scarcity more than any other class in this Collectorate'. Maharashtra State Archives, 'Administrative Report of Sholapur District, 1876-7' in Revenue Department (hereafter RD) 1877, XIX, comp.1195; 'Administrative Report of Nasik District, 1876-7' in RD 1877, XVI, comp.1151, p.202. This general picture is confirmed through a reading of a wide variety of materials on the Bombay Presidency during the famine years, such as the Annual Administration Reports of the various districts in the presidency and the files of the RD (Famine) in the Maharashtra State Archives.

[12] Roy, *Artisans and Industrialization,* ch.3.

advance contracts that required them to dispose of their cloth to particular dealers, usually at prices far below the market prices for these goods. But tied sale could take a number of forms. In some cases, semi-independent weaving families negotiated contracts with merchants for each bundle of cloth produced. In others, weaving families developed long-term dependent ties with specific merchants. In still others, artisans worked for wages in small workshops of master weavers who sold the final product on the market. Finally, there were some cases where such workshops were themselves in dependent relationships with other master-weavers or merchants.

In the remainder of this chapter, I will emphasise what I believe to be the most significant organisational forms in western India (in terms of volume of production by artisans): the dependent artisan households and the independent master-weaver workshops. Focusing on these two forms allows us to arrive at some general conclusions about the relationship between artisan firms and the larger market for artisan-produced cloth.

Dependent artisan households

By the early twentieth century, there were several tens of thousands of weaving artisan households in the Bombay Presidency. The *Bombay Economic and Industrial Survey* estimated in 1940 that there were altogether 70,000 to 100,000 looms in the province.[13] Of these, the vast majority were controlled by individual artisan families who carried on production within their homes. P.N. Mehta, writing in 1909, estimated that 75 per cent of the weavers in the Bombay Presidency fell in one of two categories. The first was composed of 'independent' weavers not permanently indebted to any 'sowkar' (moneylender) but with little staying power during slack seasons. These weavers, Mehta argued, 'cannot afford to keep their production for any length of time, and must sell at a sacrifice even of part of their labour wages. They are often compelled to take yarns on loan to keep them going. They thus fall into straitened circumstances'. The second, about twice as numerous, had developed debts on the pledge of their looms with individual cloth-dealers for whom they had to work until the debt was paid off.[14] Both types of weaver, Mehta pointed out, tended to become heavily reliant

[13] *Report of the Bombay Economic and Industrial Survey Committee*, Vol.I, p.58.

[14] P.N. Mehta, 'Report on the Hand Loom Industry [of the Bombay Presidency]' in India Office Library, P/W 137 (1909), p.1.

on merchant capitalists for the perpetuation of their subsistence.

In the terms of Marxian analysis provided by Jairus Banaji in his study of commodity expansion in the western Indian rural economy during the same period, such forms of economic relationship reflect the *formal* subsumption of labour to capital, a system by which capitalists manage to appropriate surplus value of labour 'outside the framework of a specifically capitalist mode of production'. Banaji associates at least three significant features with formal subsumption: (1) the processes of labour tend to be 'technologically continuous' with those in pre-capitalist industry; (2) labour processes remain external to the movement of capital and production retains its small-scale decentralised character (as opposed to becoming centralised under the control of capitalists); and (3) capitalists achieve control over labour through advancing raw materials or tools or appropriating 'surplus value in the form of interest' without becoming involved in direct supervision over labour.[15] Expansion of the capitalists' earnings thus occurs less by technical transformations of production methods than by an intensification of the exploitation of small producers through the pressure of interest rates and advance claims over the final product. For Banaji the critical point is that despite the preponderance of small producers under such circumstances, it is the capitalist who 'reconstitutes the process of production by enabling the reproduction of labour power...and repro-

[15] Banaji, 'Capitalist domination and the small peasantry', p.1376. Banaji contrasts 'formal' subsumption with the 'real' subsumption of labour, a form of production relations in which the capitalist processes of labour are fully introduced. He also distinguishes between 'preformal' and 'formal' subsumption. In preformal forms of subsumption, the small producer can retain some control and ownership over the means of subsistence but is nonetheless subjected to capital. In the latter the small producer is completely expropriated but is 'nonetheless retained in former process of production and subjected to exploitation by capital on a more continuous or intense basis, i.e., with capital disposing of the power to reconstitute the process of production from one cycle to the next'. The dependent weaving households discussed here actually range from those based upon 'preformal' to those based upon 'formal' forms of subsumption. But as Banaji points out, the distinction between the two is not particularly important; both allowed capitalist 'exploitation' through the establishment of claims upon the small producer. I depart from Banaji's view of these forms of relations as 'stages' of capitalism which 'tend to lead' from one to the other over time. For a somewhat analogous concept, see Brian Fegan's use of the concept of 'rent capitalism' (initially formulated by Hans Bobek) in 'The social history of a Central Luzon barrio', in Alfred W. McCoy and C. de Jesus (eds.), *Philippine Social History: Global Trade and Local Transformations* (Honolulu, 1982), pp.95-8.

duction of the means of production...'.[16]

The position of the artisan household is strongly analogous to that of the middle-peasant household which constitutes the primary subject of Banaji's study.[17] Artisans generally owned their own tools and often their own homes. The artisan family determined the division of labour within the household. Usually the male head of the household did the weaving. Boys took up the profession around the age of 15. Women in the household rarely wove themselves; instead they did the essential work of preparing the yarn for the loom, stretching threads of yarn in the appropriate order for the warp, and winding yarn for the weft. Children often assisted in these tasks. The women of the family were also responsible for a range of critical domestic tasks: cooking, cleaning and taking care of small children. Weaving households hesitated to hire outside labour, since this would raise the costs of production significantly without any necessary impact on income. However much outside factors impinged upon handloom weavers, it was ultimately the weaving family that gave shape to the processes of labour.[18]

But while artisan households in western India possessed a certain autonomy in the actual processes of work, most did not exercise control over the disposal of their goods. Since they generally lacked the knowledge of the Bombay yarn market or the markets for finished cloth, they easily fell into dependence upon merchant-capitalists who provided them with raw materials or finance, and who purchased the final products of the looms. Fluctuations in market conditions enhanced the weaving family's dependence, making any attempt to accumulate savings difficult. Weavers who chose to market their goods independently, ran the risk of not being able to sustain their own production and subsistence. Mehta captured the precarious nature of the position of artisans in the market:

> It is grievous to find many weavers in the Deccan and other places procuring yarn sufficient only for the weaving of one saree. They and their family waste time in preparing such short warps and gaiting them up to the looms. The cloth is woven and the further work of preparing and weaving has to be stopped till the cloth is sold.... The cloth has to be disposed of to make provision for the family and to buy a further supply of yarn with which to continue work. Only

[16] Banaji, 'Capitalist domination and the small peasantry', p.1389.

[17] Banaji in fact briefly discusses the nature of artisan production in this essay. See 'Capitalist domination and the small peasantry', pp.1383 and 1397.

[18] See Haynes, 'Relations of production among handloom weavers in the Bombay Presidency', paper presented at the conference on 'Cloth, the World Economy, and the Artisan', Dartmouth College, April 1993.

precarious wages could be earned by such a system.... Wasteful as are their manufacturing methods both in time, wages and material, they [are] worse off in selling their goods. They have to leave work and spend some hours in finding a suitable customer; and failing to find one, they have to go to the local merchants who knows too well how they are situated and invariably strikes up a bargain in his own favour.[19]

Faced with such risky, time-consuming and unrewarding efforts, many weavers either resorted to borrowing money from the moneylender-yarn merchants, or obtained small amounts of work by entering into contracts that offered the merchants cloth at low prices throughout the year. In the process, they lost control of their ability to sell their products to the highest bidder, falling subject to the domination of the moneylenders. It thus often became the merchant-capitalists who made it possible for the process of production to be reconstituted from one cycle to the next.[20]

In most cases, a kind of putting-out system developed. The weaving household would get an advance of yarn from the dealer, often for a very small amount of material, perhaps just enough to make one sari. In return, the weaver would agree to provide the merchant with the finished cloth at a given price. Since weavers tended to make such agreements during slack periods when they were most desperate, their negotiating power was usually very limited. Even when they just sought to buy yarn, they were in a weak bargaining position. According to Mehta, when the artisan got 'yarn on credit from a merchant who buys his cloth, the merchant who by experience knows exactly the quantity of yarn required for the cloth, adjusts the price of the yarn so as to leave hardly sufficient wages to the weaver and his family when payment for the cloth is made'.[21] Without the advances provided by the merchant, however, the artisan family generally lacked the ability to sustain its productive activity.

Usually the merchant-moneylender would take upon himself the responsibility of disposing of the final product. But since the capital he invested was generally rather small—in some cases only as much as the cost of the yarn he had purchased—his risks were actually quite limited. If a sudden contraction occurred in the market, he was able to pull back quickly without losing a sizeable investment. His profit was thus achieved not by enhancing the productivity of the artisans working un-

[19] Mehta, 'Report on the Hand Loom Industry', pp.1-2.

[20] The wording is a paraphrase of Banaji, 'Capitalist domination and the small peasantry', p.1376.

[21] Mehta, 'Report on the Handloom Industry', p.1.

der his domination, but by raising the price of yarn he sold to the weaving family and/or by depressing the payments for the final product to as near subsistence level as possible. The system thus facilitated substantial profits for the merchant during good times, and limited losses during the bad. At the same time, these arrangements perpetuated the weaving family's poverty and its reliance upon capitalists.[22]

The merchant-capitalists in such cases were usually businessmen who combined a variety of functions; they were often yarn-dealers, moneylenders, and cloth merchants as well as men involved in the control over labour. Success in the cloth business required connections to a variety of commercial and capital networks: yarn networks stretching back to the mills of Bombay and of Manchester; financial networks linking the individual moneylender to larger indigenous bankers and ultimately to the modern banking houses of India's provincial capitals; and cloth networks culminating in the major consumption centres of the Presidency. Contracts thus did much more than create a relationship between two individuals; they were agreements that linked weavers to the much larger structures of the regional economy. The weavers themselves participated in these greater structures only indirectly, through the mediation of the merchant-moneylenders.

The decision-making behaviour of weaving households bore the stamp of their subjection to the hostile and insecure conditions of western Indian capitalism. With only a very restricted access to the markets in yarn, capital and cloth, artisan producers had a *limited* ability to perpetuate their own economic activity, if they did not rely on the sowkars. The structural position of the family constrained its ability to transform its situation, forcing it under most circumstances to concentrate on matters of its own subsistence rather than upon the expansion of its production and profits. The small-production economy thus continued to reproduce itself over time.

D. Narayana Rao, writing in 1929 on Madras weavers, provided a simple but useful picture of the logic of cloth-producing households in India. Because these households were organised on a family basis, he suggested, they sought primarily to enhance a kind of 'wage' that was marked by the difference between the sale price of the cloth and the cost of yarn (rather than as a return to each unit of labour). The amount of work the family applied to a particular cloth, Rao argued, 'does not really count with him [the weaver] except in so far as he has to make allowance for the minimum subsistence wage of the family'. Rao

22 These kinds of relations are discussed in greater detail in Haynes, 'Relations of production'.

insisted that if the weaving household could be guaranteed regularity of employment, facilities for marketing, and raw materials at a cheap rate, the weaver 'would doubtless be prepared to increase production by working more hours at his loom' or by adopting technical improvements, even if this meant reducing the amount of 'wages' that he took on each cloth. 'The real difficulty with him', he went on, 'is the higher cost of yarn supplied to him, want of continuous employment, and absence of facilities of marketing'.[23]

The importance of maintaining all family members combined with the inability to control market forces could lead to behaviour that would be destructive for a larger business employing non-family labour.[24] This is perhaps best illustrated during times of crises. For artisans of the Bombay Presidency, crises generally occurred when merchant-capitalists discontinued making advances of yarn or of money due to sudden decreases in demand for their wares or sharply increasing costs of raw materials. At such moments, weaving families were often released from their position of dependency only to compete in an extremely unfavourable market climate. While some weavers responded to such circumstances by leaving the profession altogether or by migrating to other areas, others stepped up their production in the desperate hope that greater numbers of buyers would make up the loss in price per piece.

During the 1930s, for example, weavers in the Bombay Presidency were often faced simultaneously with sharply lower prices for their cloth, higher prices for yarn, increased competition with the mills in certain areas of production, and the tendency for merchants in many parts of the presidency to stop furnishing advances. The response of many was to abandon the profession altogether; several centres reported sharp declines in the number of looms still working. But in some towns artisans seem to have tried to maintain or even accelerate their level of production, apparently in hopes of raising family earnings more through the sheer number of cloths sold rather than the profits

[23] D. Narayana Rao, *Report on the Survey of Cottage Industries in Madras Presidency* (Madras, 1929), p.78.

[24] Some of the discussion of artisan logic is influenced by discussions of the proto-industrial family in Europe. See Hans Medick, 'The proto-industrial family economy', in Peter Kriedte, Hans Medick and Jurgen Schlumbohm, *Industrialization before Industrialization: Rural industry in the genesis of capitalism* (trans. Beate Schempp) (Cambridge, 1981), pp.38-64. Obviously, I depart from Medick in seeing the logic of the family economy as being a product of an intrinsic 'rationality' of the small producer, and instead attribute this logic to the structural circumstances faced by the artisan.

realised on each. All over the Presidency, newly 'independent' weavers, often those who had once served as outworkers for yarn merchants, were reported to be involved in a cut-throat competition with each other to dispose of their goods to cloth-dealers, behaviour that undoubtedly drove prices down further. Some went around to local markets trying to sell their cloth directly to consumers, thus avoiding middlemen altogether. But because their holding power was so limited, this also contributed to a decline in prices.[25] Without the links to markets possessed by the merchants, moreover, many weavers continued to produce goods whose demand was in decline, unable to capture the developing tastes for new products in distant centres of consumption.[26] In other words, the depression precipitated both a deepening of the family's own self-exploitation and its submission to more intense exploitation by cloth-dealers.

Understanding the logic of household production is critical to appreciating why weaving families made certain technical adjustments in their methods of cloth manufacture virtually unnoticed by colonial officials, but did not make others that the authorities thought most essential to the improvement of the weavers' lot. In general, weavers demonstrated little interest in making changes that only promised improvements in productivity without guaranteeing markets or the security of employment. But they readily made changes that immediately widened the gap between the price of cloth and the price of yarn or that improved the demand for their product.

There seems, for instance, to have been little reluctance to adopt mill-made yarn during the later nineteenth century; available records seem to suggest that weavers took to using such yarn almost as soon as its price fell below that of the yarn spun by Indian agriculturalists. In some interior regions, the high transport cost of mill-made yarn, a material far more bulky than cloth itself, had kept its prices too high for local weavers to consider its use until well into the nineteenth century. But once railways were constructed in these areas, this obstacle was removed, and weavers quickly embraced factory yarn, putting indigenous spinners out of business in the process. In Dharwar, this adapta-

[25] *Report of the Bombay Economic and Industrial Survey Committee*, Vol.II. Especially see the short sections on handloom weavers in the reports on Belgaum, Ahmednagar, Nasik and East Khandesh. Also see Joshi, *Urban Handicrafts of the Bombay Deccan.*

[26] For the marketing difficulties of weavers during the depression, see especially, *Report of the Bombay Economic and Industrial Survey Committee*, Vol.I, pp.104-5; Vol.II, *Ahmednagar*, pp.9-11.

tion apparently restored the weavers' competitiveness in certain lines of cloth; after the railways were built into the Bombay Karnataka, local cloth was reported to be holding its own with imported textiles. Unfortunately, the *Dharwar Gazetteer* reported, the prices of grain (and hence the cost of subsistence) generally went up as well with the advent of railways, and so the new margin of profit associated with cheaper yarn usually did not allow the weaver to maintain any improvement in his standard of living for long.[27]

Similarly, weavers all through the Bombay Presidency quickly adopted the use of European dyes, particularly aniline and alizarine dyes, with little prompting from the colonial administration. The use of German dyes emerged in the presidency during the last decade of the nineteenth century and the first decade of the twentieth century. The new techniques were far easier and far less time-consuming to prepare than pre-existing methods. They allowed weavers to reduce their payments to dyers significantly and to meet an expanding demand for coloured cloth in the Indian countryside that seems to have sprung up in response to the new colours. In a number of cases, weavers chose to learn dyeing processes themselves, thus eliminating their dependency on labourers external to the family.[28] The shift to new dyeing processes was so complete that when the supply of German dyes was cut off during World War I, the older techniques for making vegetable dyes could not be recovered, no doubt because many traditional dyers had left the profession.[29]

Both of these changes promised to increase the family 'wage' by lowering the costs of the weavers' raw materials, but without requiring significant new investment on the part of the household. One might argue in fact that the new dyeing processes, by sometimes reducing reliance on outside labour, were better suited to production units organised on a family basis than the older ones had been. Neither of these changes, of course, could have taken place without the support of the merchants who supplied the yarn or the dyes, and who ultimately disposed of the cloth on the market.

[27] *Gazetteer of the Bombay Presidency: Dharwar District* (Bombay, 1877), p.377. The *Gazetteer* suggested that it was the pressure of grain prices more than the improved access of consumers to imported cloth that pressed upon weavers whenever railways were built into an area.

[28] An extensive discussion of dyeing in the Bombay Presidency can be found in Maharashtra State Archives, General Department (G.D.) 1896, vol.25, comp.196, pt.II.

[29] See the administrative reports for various districts in the Maharashtra State Archives, R.D. for 1916 and 1917.

Artisan households in western India, even those maintaining a very marginal standard of living, also seem to have adapted to changing tastes and demand for new designs. In this case, the adaptations were probably prompted by cloth dealers who discovered new markets, and who then commissioned weavers to produce goods for them.[30] With the assurance that their products would likely find a sale, perhaps in larger volume than before, many artisans readily made shifts in what they produced.

But these signs of innovativeness seemingly stand in contrast to the weavers' responses to the introduction of superior loom technology by the Industries Department of the Bombay Presidency. Efforts to enhance the production of the handloom began in western India during the first decade of the twentieth century. Missionaries associated with the Salvation Army in Bombay and the American Marathi Mission in Ahmednagar, designed new kinds of automatic looms that increased the efficiency of weaving as much as 100 per cent. Hopes for these looms initially ran high; the colonial government in fact allocated sizeable grants to these organisations to support their research. The administration also conducted experiments with a Japanese loom. The machines, however, proved to be too expensive for the ordinary weaver. They were too complicated for most artisans to repair without extensive training, and they were often unsuited to the kinds of cloth available in the market. Few weavers showed any enthusiasm for the new looms.[31]

By the second decade of the century, the government had lost faith in most of these innovations, and had decided instead to promote the simply fly-shuttle slay. A device which the weaver propelled between two hammers on either side of the loom by pulling a cord, the fly-shuttle improved the rate of weaving from 40 up to 70 per cent over the traditional throw-shuttle method. Seemingly it suffered few of the disadvantages of the more complex automatic looms. The capital required for purchasing the fly-shuttle loom and accessories was relatively small running from Rs.10 to Rs.25. The new techniques could usually be mastered in a short time; one workshop owner claimed that his labourers learnt to work the shuttle at top speed within half a month. These advantages seemed so obvious that some officials expected the

[30] For instance, 'A Note on Ilkal Saris', note prepared by the Handloom Weavers' Co-operative Society, Bangalore, c.1992.

[31] For instance, Maharashtra State Archives, G.D. 1912, comp.820, vol.84, p.191.

majority of weavers to adopt the mechanism almost immediately.[32]

These expectations, however, were not fulfilled; instead the adoption of the new attachment was slow and hesitant among weaving households. By 1928, nearly two decades after the fly-shuttle was first introduced, the majority of handloom weavers in the Bombay Presidency still did not use the device.[33] From the first, officials blamed this failure on the 'conservatism, prejudice and ignorance'[34] of the weavers, a theme that they would reiterate many times over the following decades. But the colonial documents themselves suggest that, rather than searching for the explanation of the weavers' behaviour in intrinsic cultural characteristics, it is necessary to consider a variety of other constraints.

One reason that the fly-shuttle did not prove immediately popular was that it was somewhat difficult to adapt to higher qualities of cloth. Often artisans felt that the loom could not handle certain kinds of yarn or weave intricate designs. No doubt producers of coarse cloth were quicker to take up the new techniques than those dealing in the highest kinds of cloth, especially silk, even though the difficulties of applying the fly-shuttle to finer varieties were not insurmountable.[35] The administrators demonstrating the new looms, however, rarely had the technical ability themselves to suggest how the new looms needed to be altered to suit different varieties of cloth. Many weavers, on the other hand, seem to have seen little point in devoting their innovative energies to the processes of experimentation and learning necessary to adopt the manufacture of high quality cloth to the fly-shuttle loom.

A regularly recurring obstacle was the reluctance of the merchant-capitalists to provide financing for the new looms or yarn to those who used them. In Belgaum, it was reported that the 'sowkars' disliked new kinds of loom and refused to provide yarn to those who used them.[36]

[32] For a discussion of the fly-shuttle looms, see the letter of R. Ewbank to Govt., 23 December 1911, in Maharashtra State Archives, G.D. 1912, comp. 820, vol.84, pp.122-4; also see *Proceedings of the Co-operative Conference in Poona, 1911*, p.28.

[33] See Telang, *Report on Handloom Weaving*, Appendix A.

[34] W. Pomfret to Registrar of Co-operative Societies, 26 December 1912 in Maharashtra State Archives, G.D. 1912, vol.84, comp.820, pp.162-3.

[35] For instance, Maharashtra State Archives, G.D. 1912, vol.84, comp.820, pp.124, 143; *Annual Report Relating to the Establishment of Co-operative Societies in the Bombay Presidency, 1912-13*, p.14.

[36] Letter of Collector of Belgaum, 28 February 1912, in Maharashtra State Archives, G.D. 1912, vol.84, comp.820, p.199. See also pp.162-3 of the same compilation.

Some merchants were clearly hesitant about financing innovations when the risks in the industry were so high.[37] They had, after all, traditionally pursued a strategy of limited investment, hoping to achieve profits by the repeated number of times these investments were realised in the form of cloth. There seems to have been a high degree of variability from place to place in the willingness of capitalists to provide the financing needed by those using the fly-shuttle looms. Of course any innovations were doomed if the sowkars responded by refusing to give advances of yarn.

But even when there was no apparent resistance from the capitalists, many weavers were reluctant to take up the fly-shuttle. One serious difficulty was the lack of a comparable technology in warping and winding. With the fly-shuttle slay, a weaver could no doubt increase his output if he worked the same amount of time; but this could only be achieved if non-weaving members of the family somehow could prepare considerably more yarn for the loom than they had done previously. If the weavers themselves chose to devote more of their time to the preparation of yarn, then the goal of increasing the firm's productivity would have been substantially undermined.

By the 1920s news kinds of warping machines had been developed, but these techniques did not usually prove adaptable to weaving households. These machines were too expensive to be purchased by individual families, and they proved to be of little advantage to weavers who purchased only enough yarn for weaving one or two saris at a time. Most of the new machines were adopted by small enterprises that specialised in the preliminary processes. But for the small producers, contracting out work to warping specialists meant increased costs, since they had traditionally had their warping and winding done by unpaid family labour. Operating close to the margin of subsistence, very few weaving households in the presidency utilised such warping firms. Frustrated by the failure of the fly-shuttle to achieve an improved standard of living by itself, some colonial officials reluctantly concluded that 'if material improvement in the economic condition [of the weavers] is to be effected, attention must be concentrated on preparatory processes'.[38]

[37] *Report of the Bombay Economic and Industrial Survey Committee, 1938-40*, vol.I, p.99.

[38] Discussion of the dilemma in preliminary processes can be found in Mehta, 'Report on the Handloom Industry', pp.9-10; *Minutes of Evidence taken before the Indian Industrial Commission, 1916-8*, vol.IV (Bombay, 1929), p.340. The quote comes from *Report of the Director of Industries, Madras,*

The objection to the fly-shuttle most commonly stated by the weavers, however, was fear of overproduction. Weavers regularly expressed concern that the demand for their cloth was too limited for them to be sure of a market for any increased output, and that any increased production would cause a fall in prices and hence in earnings. Since households rarely possessed the ability to cultivate far-flung markets themselves, there seemed to be a high likelihood that they would find no buyers for any increased output, at least at acceptable prices. To many weavers, the most likely consequences of the introduction of the fly-shuttle loom appeared to be either that they would work shorter working hours to produce the same output, or that they would produce an increased output that would realise lower prices. In neither case did they hold out much hope that family earnings would increase.[39] No doubt, many weavers also feared a long-term danger to employment prospects among their communities stemming from the innovation.

The fly-shuttle also did not help with the most important dilemma of the weavers—how to withstand the periods of the year when demand was most limited. There was little reason to believe that more work would come their way during bad seasons if they adopted the attachments. Indeed, it may have seemed possible that higher production by each loom during good times might tempt the merchant-capitalists to rely on few dependent weavers during the bad. Without more work during slack times, the weavers would still be vulnerable, still be tempted to negotiate contracts that would leave them a meagre subsistence. It is likely that many weavers believed that any increased gains from the fly-shuttle might simply allow merchant to depress piece-rates further. Thus the weak position of the weavers in the market tempered their willingness to embrace the fly-shuttle.

Eventually many thousands did take up the new mechanism, though often many years after colonial authorities first introduced it in the presidency. Shifts to the fly-shuttle among household firms seem to have been most complete in centres like Malegaon, where demand was more regular than in most weaving places of the presidency. Once a certain number of weavers producing a particular kind of cloth switched to the fly-shuttle, there was undoubtedly much pressure on others to follow

1927-8 (Madras, 1928), p.37.

[39] See *Report of the Bombay Economic and Industrial Survey Committee, 1938-40*, Vol.I, p.98; Joshi, *Urban Handicrafts of the Bombay Deccan*, pp.104-6. This view is also discussed in D.M. Amalsad, *Handloom Weaving in the Madras Presidency* (Madras, 1925).

suit if they were not to be undercut. Thus, it is not surprising, as Table 2 indicates, that the adoption of the fly-shuttle tended to be highly concentrated in a few centres. There were other towns specialising in different products where very few weavers used the attachment.[40] No doubt part of this contrast stems from the tendency of artisans making the finest quality of goods not to use the innovation. Ilkal and Yeola, for instance, were largely centres producing high quality silk. But such a tendency does not explain the patterns in towns like Dharangaon, Bhingar, and Hubli, where much, in some cases all, of the cloth produced was cotton. No doubt the numbers from just one moment in time mask the painful experiences of those who hesitated to adopt the new technology. In Malegaon, for instance, most weavers were initially reluctant to use fly-shuttles. But after several years, Momin weaver households rather quickly adopted the new methods, no doubt with the

Table 2: *Types of looms used in various urban centres, 1928*

	Throw-shuttle	Fly-shuttle
Sangamner	800	1,200
Bhingar	700	200
Yeola	2,800	200
Malegaon	200	3,800
Dharangaon	2,000	200
Parola	1,200	500
Ahmedabad	750	10
Dholka	700	10
Surat	1,800	200
Sholapur	200	6,000
Kamatgi	100	700
Ilkal	3,000	25
Gulegud	2,000	1,500
Gadag	3,200	50
Gajendragad	2,000	50
Ranibennur	2,000	60
Hubli	350	12
Gokak	700	25
Bhiwandi	3,000	1,700
Pune	500	300

[40] The table comes from S.V. Telang, *Report on Handloom Weaving Industry in the Bombay Presidency*, Appendix A. Telang provided information on 40 centres; I have included the 20 largest.

support of their merchant-capitalist patrons. Deccan weavers, largely from the Koshti and Sali communities, did not respond to this competition quickly. By the 1930s, the Momins of Malegaon were in a position of dominance in the local industry, and many families from the other castes had moved to other professions.[41]

All of this suggests no inherent opposition to new technology, as colonial officials supposed. For the most part, dependent weaver households did indeed take up new techniques that promised to advance the family livelihood. But not all innovations seemed to hold such a promise for many weavers. Because the weavers possessed only a limited independent ability to sustain the reproduction of their own activity, the prospects for an improvement of productivity did not necessarily imply the improvement of family welfare. At the same time, merchants involved in the business generally refrained from investments in new kinds of technology that would have necessitated a change in the means by which they pursued profit. In short, the nature of regional capitalism bolstered rather than undermined the significance of the family economy.

The workshops

Artisan workshops, or *karkhanas*,[42] were organised on a very different basis from that of the dependent artisan households. The dominant feature of these firms was their reliance on extra-familial labour. Karkhanas could contain anywhere from four to sixty looms. In the smaller firms, the matter-weavers generally did at least some weaving themselves. In the largest firms, however, members of the owners' family confined themselves entirely to management and marketing. Workshops recruited most of their labour on a piece-rate basis from the weaving communities. In Sholapur, the western Indian city with both the largest number of karkhanas and the largest workshops, *karkhanadars* found a plentiful supply of labour among Padmasali migrants from Andhra Pradesh, who came to the city with weaving experience

[41] Joshi, *Urban Handicrafts of the Bombay Deccan*, pp.103-4. An alternative explanation for this pattern is found in Tirthankar Roy, 'Learning to Survive: acceptance of innovations in Indian weaving', paper presented at the conference on 'Cloth, the World Economy and the Artisan', Dartmouth College, April 1993. Roy attributes the concentration of innovation largely to collective traits of particular caste groupings.

[42] The term karkhana could be used in reference to any artisan establishment, but its more common meaning seems to have been a larger workshop employing significant amounts of labour from outside the karkhanadar's family.

but no looms or property of their own. Often they agreed to contractual relations which gave them an advance and wages in return for their agreement to work for the karkhanadar. They tended to live in the workshop itself, sleeping and eating next to the looms that provided their livelihood.

Most karkhanas in the Bombay Presidency were products of an evolution from independent weaver households rather than of investment by individuals outside the weaving communities altogether. Most were owned by Padmasalis or Momins who had been particularly successful in business. In interviews I conducted in Sholapur and Ahmednagar, a number of Padmasali master-weavers told me family histories of how their fathers or grandfathers had come to Maharashtra in the early twentieth century, purchased a loom after two or three years of work as a labourer, then begun to buy further looms with accumulated savings. It is not clear why such individuals were able to overcome the structural obstacles that frustrated the majority of their co-community members. No doubt such success was a product of enterprising behaviour, special knowledge of market conditions, and good fortune. It seems likely that many of these firms developed after an unusually good series of years that allowed their founders to develop some savings. Several master-weavers told me that they had created their karkhanas in the early or mid 1920s, a time that seems to have been especially kind to weavers. Clearly, this evidence of mobility suggests no inherent obstacle to entrepreneurial activity among weaving families.

Not all large workshops were free from dependence on merchant-capitalists. R.G. Kakade, who did a survey of the industry in Sholapur during the late 1930s, found that about half of the firms with more than six looms were owned by *asamis* or outworkers, who worked on contract for other karkhanadars or for particular cloth dealers (by contrast only five out of seventy-five firms with less than six looms were classified as fully 'independent'). Even a few larger firms with as many as 30 looms fell into the asami category.[43]

Karkhanadars who were not working as outworkers had several advantages over the dependent weaver households. First, they were generally able to acquire capital and raw materials at more favourable rates than smaller operators. In Sholapur, for instance, bigger workshop owners were to wring from yarn-providers significant concessions on yarn prices and on the timing of payments because of the size of their

[43] R.G. Kakade, *A Socio-Economic Survey of Weaving Communities in Sholapur* (Poona, 1947), pp.40, 42.

dealings. The smaller operators, Kakade reported, were forced to offer higher prices for yarn, to pay even more when they purchased on credit, and to settle frequently for yarn of inferior quality. The large independent karkhanadars were also in a position to bargain for the best cloth prices in the market; with more substantial resources they could buy large quantities of yarn when prices were low, and wait to sell until prices of cloth were favourable. Dependent weaver households, as we have seen, were often desperately in search of yarn for the next sari, and often had no alternative but to turn to their usual capitalist-patron, even if he offered far from the best available prices for cloth in the market.[44]

A second distinguishing feature of the large independent workshops was the form of labour arrangements within them. Kharkhanadars paid lower wage rates than local mills. Usually, moreover, they paid a piece-rate for work done, and thus had only to reduce the total amount of work they gave to their employees to cut the total size of their wage payments. This left them better able to withstand rapidly fluctuating markets than firms that paid daily wages. In some cases, they hired entire weaving families, paying for the work of women who performed preparatory processes along with the wage to male weavers. This was no doubt an arrangement that allowed for reduced payments to labour.[45] Many firms, however, had much of their warping and sizing work done by outside firms specialising in preliminary processes.[46] In Sholapur, these warping firms were in keen competition with each other, and had cut their rates steadily. In the dependent weaving household, as already mentioned, contracting work out to warping establishments meant extra expenses since it meant paying for work done by otherwise unpaid family labour.

An especially important characteristic of labour organisation that differentiated the karkhanas from artisan households was their ability to release workers they did not require. The karkhanas did not face the burden of ensuring survival of all labourers in the firm as the weaving family had to do. Labourers in the karkhanas of Sholapur did not expect regularity in employment, and often travelled back to their native places during slack times, perhaps to work in agriculture. When business picked up again, the master-weavers were usually able to hire labour anew. Clearly such arrangements allowed regular adjustment

[44] Ibid., p.55.
[45] Ibid., p.51.
[46] Ibid., p.25-6.

both to seasonal fluctuation and long-term crises.[47] In effect, arrangements with asamis permitted the same kind of adjustment: the khankardar could contract work to outworkers during busy seasons, then fall back upon his own labour when there was less demand. Though further research is needed, it seems likely that many of the karkhanas were not so much enduring units of production but constantly shifting combinations of machines and labour, adding and subtracting the number of looms they employed and the number of outworkers they engaged as their business expanded and contracted.[48]

Thirdly, the independent karkhanas tended to enjoy a superior position in the cloth market. Not only did kharkhanadars have better holding power, but they usually possessed better access to knowledge about market conditions, since they disposed of larger amounts of cloth and often opened their own shops to sell their wares. A few of the kharkhanadars, such as the Irabatti family in Sholapur, became major cloth-dealers. As the size of their firms grew larger, merchants in other centres often came to them directly with orders; in some cases, long-lasting business relationships developed. Growth of the firm seemingly allowed kharkhanadars to divert time from actual labour to understanding market conditions. This was an expenditure of time that the dependent weaver household, living from sari to sari, could not afford.[49]

The bigger workshops thus were often better able to adjust to changes in the larger economic world and to introduce new products and patterns that suited the tastes of consumers. L.V. Tikkekar, a kharkhanadar of Sholapur, reported to the Bombay Provincial Banking Enquiry in 1929 that his firm and others had left the production of coarse goods due to mill competition, but had simply shifted to the manufacture of finer kinds of cloth that were in high demand. When pressed by the committee about whether he was worried about the mills moving into these new lines as well, Tikkekar expressed confidence that if that somehow happened, his workshop would just shift the patterns it produced again and make some other varieties of cloth consumers wanted.[50] Such confidence seemingly stemmed from an aware-

[47] Ibid., p.49; and interviews conducted with weavers and merchants in Sholapur.

[48] I have drawn some of my language and analysis here from discussions of subcontracting in nineteenth-century Europe and America by Sabel and Zeitlin, 'Historical alternatives to mass production', p.149.

[49] Interviews; and Kakade, *A Socio-Economic Survey*, for instance, p.81.

[50] See testimony by L.V. Tikkekar to the Bombay Provincial Banking Enquiry, 1929-30, Maharashtra State Archives, File 29/Sh.

ness of sizeable regional markets that remained unsatisfied.

On the whole, the karkhanas of Sholapur made a major transition in the type of sari they were producing during the 1920s and 1930s. Workshops such as that of the Irabatti family stopped making nine-yard saris of the *chargomi* brand, and began producing higher quality saris such as the *maheswari* sari, which was increasingly in demand in the Konkan.[51] The imitation of goods produced in other centres was a particularly prominent form of innovation in Sholapur. Product change occurred among weaver households as well, but this was an extremely risky business unless it was prompted by cloth-sellers with strong connections to cloth markets.

Each of these three features enhanced the ability of big independent firms to reproduce themselves. Kakade found in his study of Sholapur during the late 1930s that only 22 out of 75 firms smaller than six looms had survived longer than 5 years. By contrast, 24 of 30 firms larger than this had been in existence five years or longer. He found only three (4 per cent) of the smaller firms to be 'expanding'; by contrast, 13 (43 per cent) of the larger ones were increasing their business.[52]

Because of their distinctive attributes, the karkhanas reacted very differently to crises to the weaver households. Of course, one such 'adaptation' was simply to go out of business when the firm ceased to be profitable; this was an option the weaving family did not have (though it could, of course, move to some other profession). During the depression years, workshops in some towns simply dissolved themselves, releasing their workers to seek employment in agriculture or in the cities. In some of these cases, however, one-time workshop owners became heads of weaver household firms, and still tried to sell cloth on a smaller scale.[53]

But many karkhanas adjusted in other ways. During the 1930s, a number of workshop owners shifted their production increasingly to new types of cloth and tightened their hold on labour. This period seems to be one in which master-weavers were rapidly moving towards the production of finer kinds of cloth and of 'imitation' goods. Karkhanas also sharply reduced wages they paid their labourers. Kakade reported a steady reduction in weavers' wages throughout the 1930s; by 1938, wages had declined between 48 per cent and 59 per cent since

[51] Kakade, *A Socio-Economic Survey*, p.84.
[52] Ibid., p.43.
[53] See *Report of the Bombay Economic and Industrial Survey Committee*, vol.II. See especially volumes on Ahmednagar and Nasik.

1925, depending on the kind of cloth made.[54] Many cut back on the size of their work-forces. A number apparently made attempts to 'rationalise' production, for instance, by reducing patronage services such as the provision of a hookah to workers during breaks, imposing fines for inferior workmanship, and charging workers for expenses connected with living in the karkhana, such as the use of privies and municipal water.[55] In effect, kharkhanadars responded to the depressed conditions by attempting to drive their labour costs lower. While weaving household firms adapted to the 1930s in part by increasing the 'self-exploitation' of family labour, the karkhanas adjusted by attempting to intensify the exploitation of their hired labourers.

Because of their arrangements for labour and their superior access to the markets, the kharkhanadars seem to have had little reluctance to adopt many of the technical innovations that weavers in dependent households accepted hesitantly, if at all. Unlike the weaver households, they did not have the same fear of overproduction when they introduced methods that would increase the productivity of labour. With their market contacts, they could often hope to dispose of any increased volume. But failing that, they could always dismiss excess workers. In general, however, kharkhanadars avoided investments in large plants that would have reduced their ability to adjust to fluctuating conditions. Instead they put their money into small-scale, relatively cheap, general-purpose machines that could be added (and possibly subtracted) in small units at a time and that did not require changes in the division of labour.

One such innovation was the fly-shuttle loom. Kharkhanadars in Sholapur actually began to introduce the fly-shuttle in their factories years before government made the attempt to popularise it. The Irabatties, for instance, already had converted entirely to the fly-shuttle when the Industries Department decided to switch its proselytising efforts from 'automatic' looms to the fly-shuttle around 1911. Indeed, it seems to have been the demonstrated success of the initial ventures pioneered by the kharkhanadars of Sholapur that convinced the department that the fly-shuttle was superior to the various projects it had been sponsoring up to that point.[56] The colonial government's later image of itself as the catalyst of change in the industry effectively edited it out

[54] Kakade, *A Socio-Economic Survey*, p.49.

[55] Ibid., p.49. Much of the paragraph is based upon material gathered in oral interviews.

[56] Ibid., p.30; letter of R. Ewbank to Govt., 23 December 1911, Maharashtra State Archives, G.D. 1912, comp.820, vol.84, pp.122-4.

the part that local kharkhanadars had played in the spread of the fly-shuttle in western India. By 1915, when the government was still struggling to introduce the new loom elsewhere, almost all the workshops of Sholapur had adopted it.

Another interesting example is that of the power-loom, which weavers in Bhiwandi, Surat, Malegaon and Sholapur began to employ during the 1920s and 1930s. Until the end of World War I, the small-scale capitalist simply had not been in a position to apply power to his business; a large plant requiring substantial amounts of fixed capital had been essential to generate the power to drive the looms. But with the development of small electric motors and the simultaneous provision of electricity to certain Indian towns, the power-loom became accessible to kharkhanadars with relatively modest capital. Most commonly, they purchased used power-looms from mills that were either upgrading technology or going out of business. These looms were relatively inexpensive, costing on average several hundred rupees, and could be bought in small quantities. One Momin kharkhanadar from Bhiwandi that I interviewed said he initially purchased two power-looms in the early 1930s, then bought two more after he had learnt how to make his initial machines run successfully. By World War II, his firm had grown from a small handloom enterprise with several looms to a larger firm employing dozens of labourers. The use of such power-looms increased productivity considerably. Not only did each loom produce more, but one worker could sometimes be responsible for two machines.[57]

In some cases weavers employing power-looms took up new kinds of specialisations, such as the production of art silk cloth (that is, cloth using synthetic threads). In others, the power-looms made inroads into fields of production once dominated by the handlooms, such as the manufacture of fancy *patals*, saris of high-count yarn, and even saris with gold and silver thread borders. According to Kakade, power-loom goods were preferred by consumers because they were 'more attractive from the viewpoint of border, design, fashion and fancy in colours than either the handlooms or the mills'. At the same time, the power-loom workshops were better able than large factories to manufacture goods in desired dimensions and to produce speciality items. In other words, the power-looms possessed the same advantage of being able to produce customised goods for small, changing and specialised markets

[57] *Report of the Bombay Economic and Industrial Survey Committee*, vol.II. See volumes on Thana, Nasik and Surat districts.

that had always characterised the handlooms.[58]

In Bhiwandi and Surat, the power-loom karkhanas had begun to displace the handlooms by the end of the 1940s; handloom workers, especially, the weaver household-firms within these towns, found it difficult to compete. Bhiwandi, with its geographic position close to Bombay, had the spècial advantage of regular access to electricity supplies and the ready availability of used looms from the Bombay mills. The new looms did not spread so quickly to other towns, including Sholapur, where reliable sources of electricity came only much later. At least one kharkhanadar in Sholapur, however, developed oil-driven machines to keep a portion of his looms working; the remaining looms were all handlooms.[59]

Here again, the kharkhanadars adopted new technology without any prompting from the provincial government. If anything, colonial officials regarded the power-loom as a pernicious development that threatened the handloom producers they were trying to protect. These officials seemed to overlook the fact that the power-looms were a development from within the pre-existing industry, generated largely by members of the weaving communities. Only this oversight allowed the officials to maintain a general image of artisans as actors blind to the advantage of technical change.

But the kharkhanadars did not introduce just any innovations. They added new technology slowly, avoiding heavy investments that would place their firms at risk in the small and rapidly fluctuating markets for the kinds of cloth produced outside the mills. This strategy allowed them to retain the flexibility that was so critical in these fields. Machines from the fly-shuttle loom to the power-loom thus reproduced forms of labour process based at leased in part on craft lines. The workshops of 1940 still preserved a division of weaving labour similar to that which had existed in 1900.

In effect, a sharp division between what might be called 'weaver's capital' and industrial capital persisted. Bombay industrialists refrained from entering into most fields of production controlled by the small producer. Members of the weaving communities, with experience largely in gearing their production to the micro-markets for western Indian women's clothing, abstained from organising their enterprises along mass-production lines. Both sectors possessed their own distinctive forms of dynamism without showing any tendency to evolve from

[58] Kakade, *A Socio-Economic Survey*, pp.79-80.

[59] See testimony by L.V. Tikkekar to the Bombay Provincial Banking Enquiry, 1929-30, Maharashtra State Archives, File 29/Sh.

one to the other.

Conclusion

The approach of dependent weaver households and of karkhanas to new techniques is not only significant in itself; it provides an illustration of the larger business strategies these different kinds of units developed in the context of the expanded commodity production in western India during the late nineteenth and early twentieth centuries. Weaver households were certainly driven by considerations of 'family economy', in part because their position of dependence on merchant-capitalists regularly frustrated their attempts to create any surplus above subsistence needs and also because this position kept them distant from the markets they needed to cultivate in order to generate stable or expanding sources of income. While they introduced changes of product and work method, these changes were conditioned by their need to reproduce family livelihood and by their imperfect ability to manipulate the market for cloth.

The karkhanas, by contrast, often possessed the ability to adjust to changing circumstances by reducing the costs of labour within the firm in radical ways or by shaping new markets. The master-weavers in these firms were in a better position to adopt a more entrepreneurial approach to their businesses. The term 'entrepreneurship' may in fact actually be inappropriate here, since in fact they had developed mechanisms for passing much of the risks involved in expanding their operations on to their own work-forces.

But it would be a mistake to overemphasise the differences between the two kinds of firms and not recognise certain commonalities. Indeed, if one shifts the comparison from the level of the production unit to that of the capitalist—that is, if one compares the merchant-capitalist relying on weaving households for his cloth to the weaver-capitalist running his own workshop with hired labour—strong similarities in strategy appear. Both kinds of actors combined control over production decisions with involvement in the market, but both did so in a way that allowed disengagement when conditions were unfavourable. Both in effect shifted much of the burden of participation in a volatile market to their labour forces; both cultivated their profits more by turning over their investments in yarn rapidly than by investing large amounts of capital in large factories. On the whole, weaver-capitalists, with their long tradition of involvement in cloth production, were more ready to put money into new techniques than were the merchants financing weaver households. But still they did so cautiously, buying one or two looms at a time. On the whole, they invested in divisible technologies, that is, in small, relatively inexpensive machines that essentially replicated the same function as the older looms. The new technology tended to preserve the pre-existing division of weaving work within the karkhanas.

In short, the weaving industry as a whole continued to be characterised by a kind of flexible specialisation with similarities to that prevalent in some European industries during the early phase of industrialisation.[60] The flexibility of artisan manufacture stemmed not just from the smallness of production operations and the relative simplicity of technology but also from the ability of capitalists to depress the earnings of labour sharply when market conditions were unfavourable. Such flexibility was well suited to the special conditions of certain segments of the cloth market, such as the market in women's saris and blouses, where producers had to shape their products to relatively small, changing pools of demand. Mass production in the mills, by contrast, tended to be better adapted to the larger, less specialised and more stable demand in goods such as men's shirts, and pants,[61] where something like a national market seems to have emerged. Thus, different forms of organisation should not be seen as reflecting different stages on a common trajectory of development. It would be more correct to argue that capitalism in India was developing a polymorphic character, with different structures adapting themselves to different niches in the larger economy at the same time.

This study certainly supports the contemporary reassessment which suggests that the 'crafts' sector could be a significant contributor to economic vitality.[62] I have argued here that the weaving industry, and particularly the firms of weaver-capitalists, possessed their own kind of dynamism, one that did not fit neatly with colonial assumptions about economic development. But the findings of this study also warn against any attempt to romanticise small industry and the 'informal economy'. As I have shown, small weaving households and larger karkhanas allowed especially extensive exploitation of artisan labour. Not only did capitalists in both contexts possess considerable ability to depress

60 Sabel and Zeitlin, 'Historical alternatives to mass production'.

61 However Rajnarayan Chandavarkar warns us against exaggerating the size and stability of the cloth market for the mills in *The Origins of Industrial Capitalism in India: business strategies and the working class in Bombay, 1900-1940* (Cambridge, 1994).

62 Piore and Sabel, *The Great Industrial Divide.*

the earnings of their workers, but also they exposed these workers to the worst consequences of market instability. Today, these tendencies, are, if anything, accentuated, as smaller firms in India and elsewhere are able to escape the labour regulation and union organisation faced by larger firms. To a great extent, this development runs directly contrary to the logic of Marx, who expected that it would be the continuing development of mass production that would lead capitalists to intensify their pressures on the work-force. As both scholars and policy-makers in a number of societies focus on small firms as the best hope for economic growth, it is important to keep in mind that such firms have often simply facilitated alternative forms of domination over labour, forms that may more easily escape the scrutiny of the state and of labour organisers.

Chapter 9

SEARCHING FOR THE *SARDAR*: THE STATE, PRE-CAPITALIST INSTITUTIONS AND HUMAN AGENCY IN THE MARITIME LABOUR MARKET, CALCUTTA, 1880-1935

G. Balachandran

The broker or *sardar* is a hoary chestnut in Indian labour history. No account of the recruitment of workers for mines, factories, or plantations is complete without him. Chiefly a supplier of labour, in some contexts such as the jute mills of Calcutta, the sardar played a wider role. At work he oversaw, regulated, and disciplined the men and women under him. Outside work, he was a moneylender; he might even own the workers' housing and the shop(s) where they bought their necessities. He was also a neighbourhood leader or *dada*, a status he maintained both through the exercise of force, and that of rather more symbolic forms of power and authority. Employers, including the colonial state, felt they could not do without the sardar, while contemporary British sources regarded *sardari* (or equivalently, in their view, *dasturi*) as an ancient institution which would not easily go away. Sardars were also no strangers in anti-colonial movements. The Indian National Congress, for instance, was quick to see their potential as local party mobilisers, fund-raisers, and leaders, while some of the early trade-unions, too, often drew upon the leadership of these elements.[1]

Scholarly interest in sardari is part of the wider preoccupation with the persistence of pre-capitalist or pre-modern institutions in colonial India. The prevalence of sardari and, more generally, of other 'pre-capitalist' institutions and forms of authority used to be traditionally regarded, on the left, as denoting the inability of the colonial state and expatriate capital to carry out a 'bourgeois revolution'. But in more recent times, an argument has been made that this also represented a cultural failure arising from the workers being in the grip of 'pre-capitalist' ideas and attitudes, and consciousness of kinship and com-

[1] R. Chandavarkar, *The Origins of Industrial Capitalism in India: business strategies and the working classes in Bombay, 1900-1940* (Cambridge,1994), pp.195-8.

munity.[2] Other historians of the Indian working-class have tended to attribute the survival of sardari, both narrowly and in its wider relationships, to its utility to employers in an industry where the required level of skill was very low, and the potential costs of supervision high.[3] One might also venture, in similar vein, that workers too regarded sardari as a form of mediation between areas of excess supply and excess demand for labour in a poorly organised market with severe information problems; besides, the relationship between the workers and the sardars was too deep and wide-ranging to be easily eliminated or replaced, even should the workers want it, by more formal links and institutions.

There is a circularity in the relationship which the culturalist argument postulates between the consciousness of the workers and the persistence of pre-bourgeois institutions. Besides, the success of human agency in transforming attitudes and institutions into some recognisably modern and capitalist ones seems to be the only yardstick by which its efforts are judged. Therefore, the efforts of workers to negotiate the many constraints and possibilities arising in a tangled context where the institutions and agents of capitalism are imbricated in a pre-capitalist setting are of little interest. Largely unconcerned with the wider issues of collective human agency, let alone the difficult question of overlapping collective identities, the functionalist-economic argument shares with Marxists and Marxian culturalists a teleological vision of change, but differs from the latter in assuming the universality of maximising behaviour. Few functionalist historians are troubled by the potential variety of the interplay, to make a stylised distinction, between individual rationality, group loyalties, and hierarchical institutions founded on power. Rather than get drawn into the endogenous dynamics of the relations between workers, their many bosses, and the worlds they populate, some have preferred to invoke exogenous influences such as trade, new competition, change in factor availabilities, etc., to account for technological-institutional change in work organisation and in the labour market. Thus the longer-term decline of sardari, say in the Bombay cotton-textile industry, could be regarded, in this light, as an institutional process accompanying the changes in manufacturing technology and work organisation which Japanese competition, chiefly, provoked.

In short then, neither view is much interested in the actual course of evolution of 'pre-modern' institutions in a modern setting. In the one

[2] D. Chakrabarty, *Rethinking Working-class History* (Princeton, 1989).

[3] M.D. Morris, *The Emergence of an Industrial Labour Force in India: a study of the Bombay cotton mills, 1854-1947* (Bombay, 1965).

view, if sardari, for instance, betokened pre-capitalist ties and attitudes, the workers' efforts to mitigate or otherwise modify its working did not make news. In the other, the decline of pre-capitalist institutions is mirrored by the rise of capitalist ones, and the process of displacement is usually understood in functionalist terms. It is not surprising, in the circumstances, that interest in the institution of sardari, or more generally pre-capitalist institutions in modern settings, is rarely matched by a systematic (and sympathetic) attempt to study its (their) evolution through time.

This chapter attempts partly to repair this gap through a study of the changing method of recruitment, mainly at Calcutta port, of Indian seamen for British shipping over roughly half a century from 1880. The working class is identified primarily with industry, and the most influential labour histories have been of the industrial working class. In India, particularly, the 'services' sector has rarely attracted the attention of working class historians, and maritime labour is no exception. This is perhaps no surprise. Work on board ships might appear as a form of casual employment even to historians familiar with the rapid turnover of labour in Calcutta's jute or Bombay's cotton mills. The numbers of seamen employed at any one time, particularly in the more 'organised' ocean-going sector, may not compare favourably with employment in jute or cotton. These numbers would be considerably larger if one includes river craft and coastal vessels. But the latter were mainly in the 'unorganised sector', where the nature of employment was perhaps even more casual than on ocean-going vessels, methods of recruitment and work supervision quite diverse, and few reasons existed to expect a palpable sense of working class identity to emerge.

Maritime labour was among the most militant sections of the Western working class, particularly in the early part of this century. The men themselves did not lose their potential for militant action even when their unions turned pragmatic and accommodationist.[4] Few historians would, however, give Indian seamen high marks for militancy or proletarian consciousness. They shared many subjective experiences in common with the factory workers of Bombay and Calcutta, and it is a moot point whether these were weakened or reinforced during long periods of absence at sea. In addition, the more casual nature of sea employment encouraged the retention of ties with land. While stereotypes can be misleading, it was common until the 1930s for Indian sea-

[4] Frank Broeze, 'Militancy and pragmatism: an international perspective on maritime labour, 1870-1914', *International Review of Social History*, 36 (2), 1991, pp.165-200.

farers to spend up to half their working lives on land, and mainly in villages. This did little to ensure the continuity vital to effective trade union activity. Although trade-unions made considerable headway among Indian seamen during the interwar years, the former remained 'moderate' in their leadership, perspectives, alliances, and affiliations. Yet, chiefly through their own efforts, and despite official and employer opposition, Indian seamen managed to secure important changes in the way they were hired and, though jobbery did not altogether cease, the virtual elimination of at least one level of intermediaries in the process of their recruitment. How did this happen, and what lessons do their experiences hold for Indian working-class history?

I

The employment of Indian seamen on foreign ships until the middle of the nineteenth century, was confined chiefly to periods of war in Europe when the availability of local seamen for merchant shipping dropped, or to replacing arriving European crews decimated in India by disease and death. But from mid-century on, thanks to the repeal of Britain's navigation laws, the gradual ascendancy of steam over sail, the opening of the Suez Canal, and the rising cost of employing European labour, Indian seamen were increasingly engaged as crews on international, chiefly British, merchant shipping. By 1891, there were nearly 24,000 Indian seamen in the British mercantile marine who accounted for a tenth of all crew on British ships. This number more than doubled to 52,000 by 1914, while the proportion of Indian crew on British merchant ships rose to 17.5 per cent. Thanks to the economic instability of the interwar years, Britain's declining share in world shipping, and the general slump in maritime employment, the number of Indian seamen on British ships fell to 36,000 on the eve of World War II. But they now accounted for nearly a quarter of those employed on British ships.[5]

The above numbers do not, however, indicate the real strength of India's maritime labour force. Apart from those who served on indigenous shipping and on board vessels of other nationalities, these numbers also excluded men who would normally seek employment on

[5] C. Dixon, 'Lascars: the forgotten seamen', in R. Ommer and G. Panting (eds.), *The Working Men who Got Wet*, (St. John's, Newfoundland, 1980), p.281; R. Hope, *A New History of British Shipping* (London, 1990), pp.383, 392.

British vessels, but who were not currently on board a ship. The latter category would have been quite large, since Indian seamen were engaged on six-month or one-year agreements, and they typically allowed long intervals to elapse between two engagements. Thus, according to one, though no doubt exaggerated, estimate, there were as many as 2,35,000 seamen registered on the books of the country's principal seamen's unions in 1935.[6]

There were three departments on board a steam vessel carrying passengers: the engine, the deck, and the saloon. The last department was very small or non-existent in a vessel devoted exclusively to carrying cargo. Although all Indian seafarers tended to be referred to as *lascars*, particularly in British merchant shipping legislation and by Board of Trade officials entrusted with enforcing it, on board a vessel this term referred only to those working on the deck. Men in the engine room were either firemen, donkeymen, or coal-trimmers, while those in the saloon might be stewards, bakers, cooks, pantry-keepers, etc. The Indian crew of each of these departments also had their own cook or *bhandari*. Apart from these three departments, *seacunnies* or *sukhanis* (Indian quartermasters or helmsmen) were hired separately from the other crew, and occupied a strategic position on board a vessel. Indian crews in the engine and deck departments were led by a *serang*, who might be regarded as a boatswain, and who was often the highest ranking Indian on board a British vessel. The deck serang might be assisted by as many as three *tindals* on larger vessels. In later years, tindals also began to appear among engine-room crews. The crew in the saloon department was usually under the charge of a chief steward or butler.[7]

The serang was frequently a man of considerable seafaring experience. As a work-leader or foreman, he was closely in touch with his European officers, communicating their orders to his crew, and ensuring that they were carried out. Since few European officers could speak the languages of their Indian crew, and since often, the serang had more experience at sea than many a junior officer on board, he was a key link in the efficient running of the vessel. As far as the ship's officers were concerned the 'serang was the crew', and he was expected to command the unquestioned obedience of the men under his charge. For this reason, the serang was also regarded as the mainstay in the recruitment of Indian crew for merchant vessels, and the changing method of engagement of Indian seamen owed, to an extent, to the

[6] D. Desai, *Maritime Labour in India* (Bombay, 1940), p.20.

[7] For convenience, these men are also usually referred to as serangs in the text.

changing consciousness and sense of opportunity of the serang.

II

Until 1859, crimps and boarding-house keepers, referred to often as *ghat serangs*, were the main agents through whom Indian seamen found employment. The East India Company and its successor regime too utilised the services of crimps, at Rs.10 per crew member in the 1850s, to man their navies.[8] In some cases, the Registrar of Merchant Seamen, an office created earlier in the decade to regulate crew engagement, acted as an intermediary between the ship's captain and the crimp, accepting payment from the former to do so.[9] The latter practice was officially discouraged, and crimping outlawed under the Merchant Shipping Act of 1859. While small indigenous vessels in the coastal trade and inland river steamers were not covered by the 1859 (and subsequent) legislation affecting crew regulations, the hiring of Indian seamen for foreign-going ships was thereafter entrusted to shipping brokers licensed by the port authorities in Calcutta and Bombay, where the overwhelming majority of the crews were engaged. But there was little change on the ground, since those who were crimps in the earlier system were licensed as shipping brokers in the new one.[10] There were brokers in the smaller ports as well, though full crews were rarely shipped from any of them. Alone among the major companies, the British India Steam Navigation Company (BISN) did not engage its crews through licensed shipping brokers. Accounting for nearly half the crew engaged in Calcutta, the BISN's large requirement for Indian crews enabled it to employ its own ghat serangs and ghat butlers for the purpose. Although no different from brokers in the roles they discharged, ghat serangs and butlers were paid employees of the BISN.

Once the licensed shipping brokers or ghat serangs were informed about a ship's crewing requirements, they mustered a few serangs before the ship's officers, or often chose the serangs themselves. It was then mainly up to the broker and the serang to choose the crew. In later years, particularly after the plague outbreaks of the 1890s, Indian seamen engaged to serve on British or Indian ships were expected to pass a medical examination after which they were gathered at the shipping office or on the vessel to sign the articles of agreement.[11] This proce-

[8] National Archives of India (NAI), GI, Home Miscellaneous, 25 February 1859, 10-12 A.

[9] NAI, GI, Home Miscellaneous, 18 June 1858, 41-4 A.

[10] Ibid.

[11] This paper deals only with Indian crews aboard British ships, who ac-

dure was usually supervised by a Shipping Master or his deputy whose responsibility it was to 'open' an agreement and explain its contents to the crew. While literate seamen signed their names to signify consent, others did so by touching the shipping official's pen. Thereafter the crew was notionally paid its advance, which was usually a month's wage, and advised to report to the ship in time for sailing which could be two days to a week from the date of engagement. The brokers were responsible for ensuring the presence of the selected crew on board when the ship sailed, and were liable for the refund of the advances drawn by absent members of the crew. For their pains, brokers received in compensation from the shipowners or their agents between half to one rupee for each crew member shipped, and 5-7.5 per cent of the wage advance paid to them.

Shipping brokers covered themselves against losses arising from absent crews by drawing on the security of the keepers of sailors' boarding-houses. Immediately after signing the articles, a seaman was obliged to deposit the wage advance he had just received in a bag held by a representative, sometimes called a 'runner', of the broker. Some time thereafter, often the same evening, the broker's representative would call on the crew member to hand over the advance wage, this time, however, in the presence of a surety. Although family members could stand surety, and were paid a part of the advance wage when they did so, few seamen had family in Calcutta. Besides, according to one broker, the problem with encouraging family sureties was that 'courtezans...and such other friends of ill-repute will immediately step in as wives, daughters and brothers of these men, and would entice the seaman to remain as much as possible in their own company'.[12]

It was commonly the boarding-house keeper who offered surety for the advance wage paid to a member of the ship's crew. In the process, the advance ended up with the boarding-house keeper who, apart from claiming a commission of a rupee or two for having stood surety, used the remainder to settle the seaman's debts to him. The boarding-house keeper charged, in 1879, a fixed sum of six rupees from an ordinary

---

counted for the bulk of Indian seamen on foreign-going vessels. Indian seamen hired to serve on foreign vessels flying flags other than the Union Jack were signed on (or off) in the presence of a consular official of the country concerned. The Indian government's shipping offices usually had but a small role to play here, unless, as happened rarely, such a role was delegated to them.

[12] NAI, GI, Finance and Commerce Department (FC), Statistics and Commerce Branch (SC), May 1886, 640-50 B, minutes of 28 February 1884, 'paper' presented by the Bombay broker Darashaw Ruttonjee Chichgur on the 'results of his enquiries into the ghat serang system in Calcutta'.

seaman for board and lodging, and, in addition, advanced money for tobacco and other necessities.[13] On paper the shipping broker had a staff of *sircars*' to handle wage advances and mobilise the crew and their effects for a voyage. In practice, however, the latter function came to be performed increasingly by boarding-house keepers who had an incentive, given the fixed amount they charged for board and lodging, to keep turning boarders over on a regular basis.

By the early 1880s, there were widespread complaints of abuse and corruption connected with the engagement of seamen in Calcutta. Of particular concern to shipowners hiring crews in Calcutta was the fact that the men who finally sailed with the vessel were frequently inferior to those originally engaged to serve on it. Although preliminary inquiries revealed that brokers were not really required for engaging crews in Calcutta, and that their close links with boarding-house keepers represented a major opportunity for corruption, government officials were inclined, on the whole, to blame instances of bribery and the shipping companies' labour recruitment problems on the villainy of the serangs. The Board of Revenue of the Bengal government claimed that the 'condition of thraldom of the native lascar' was due to the operations of the ship's serang, the ghat serangs, boarding-house keepers, and other crimps, and not due to the licensed brokers against whom 'complaints were rare'.[14] Supposing serangs also to be owners of the boarding houses at which seamen stayed and ran up debts between engagements, some in the government proposed setting up a 'Native Sailors' Home' under official auspices. But largely for reasons of its cost, the idea died a quick death, and even an earlier practice followed by the Calcutta Police of supervising privately-owned seamen's boarding-houses through licensing and regular inspections which had been abandoned by 1870, could not be revived.[15] Before long, however, the reported practice of replacing experienced seamen with inexperienced substitutes became a minor scandal in Calcutta, and protests from the Chamber of Commerce became more strident. But rather than attributing these and other ills to serangs, the Chamber sought the elimination of brokers and ghat serangs, the replacement of brokers' cash advances to seamen by a system of advance notes encashable after the

[13] NAI, GI, FC, Separate Revenue Branch (SR), 555-7 B, report of the Deputy Commissioner of Police, Calcutta, enclosed with Shipping Master to Secretary, Board of Revenue, Lower Provinces, no.216-s, 11 July 1879.

[14] Quoted in NAI, GI, FC-SC, May 1886, 640-50 B, report of the official committee, para.32.

[15] NAI, GI, FC-SR, March 1880, 555-7 B.

vessel sailed, reorganising the shipping office along the lines of similar offices in Britain, and the introduction of the Bombay system of Continuous Discharge Certificates containing a detailed record of each crew member's sea experience.

The Calcutta Chamber's complaints became the subject of inquiry by an official committee comprising port officials, representatives of shipping companies, and the Superintendent of the Presidency Jail. Among the witnesses it heard was D.R. Chichgur, Bombay's sole shipping broker. The latter volunteered to take over the brokerage role in Calcutta, and his case was supported by a Captain Brebner, Calcutta's new shipping master, who had earlier been an assistant shipping master in Bombay. But whether or not so intended, Chichgur's intervention, by putting brokers under a very benign light, greatly assisted the cause of the Calcutta brokers. Other shipping officials in Calcutta and representatives of all the shipping companies, with the solitary and insubstantial exception of the P&O which hired its crew mostly in Bombay, also wanted brokers retained since otherwise it would be impossible to ship crews from the port. The committee, far from reporting against the system of licensed brokers, rejected the view that the latter were to blame for the poor quality of seamen shipped. The brokers' 'power over (the) men seeking work...[was] limited by a variety of circumstances', while the quality of the crew was poor because 'demand was greater than supply'.

The committee followed government officials in laying the blame for the ills pointed out by the Calcutta Chamber squarely at the door of the serangs. The latter exercised 'undoubted authority over the lascar'. Once the serang was selected, 'the choice of the crew is left to him'. He demanded and got a *salami* from them which was the 'custom of the country', and other payments besides. Since the men found it in their interest to be on good terms with the serang, they 'cheerfully submit to being mulcted in the pocket'. The serang also collected the crews' wages from them for redistribution according to his own judgment of their worth, and in the process lined his own pocket. Hence, it was in his interest to replace experienced seamen signed on at relatively high wages with inexperienced substitutes who agreed to go to sea for a lower wage.

In contrast, the committee gave licensed shipping brokers a clean chit. They were honest men. Ignoring suggestions that the position of the engine-room serang was a purchasable commodity in Calcutta and that the deductions which serangs made from the crew's wages were at least partly meant for brokers and ghat serangs, the committee insisted that complaints against shipping brokers were rare, and never proven. In any case, as these men came from a 'higher and more educated class', the 'balance of integrity' was in their favour. The committee also adopted without question employers' assumptions about the unreliability of Indian crews. Not surprisingly, therefore, it endorsed the role which shipping brokers performed, of mobilising crews for sailing, as being essential to the shipping business. Accepting the brokers' contention that they needed three sircars to mobilise the crew of one vessel, the committee argued that if brokers were abolished as the Calcutta Chamber of Commerce demanded, their role would have to be performed by the Shipping Office at a higher cost. The committee also endorsed the brokers' practice of claiming the men's advance immediately after it was paid, as the best arrangement possible under the conditions. The only substantive reform it suggested was the introduction of the Bombay system of Continuous Discharge Certificates by means of which seamen were registered with the shipping office, thus providing a readily available record of their careers at sea. The certificate would also help affirm the individuality of the crew member since he alone would be responsible for the entries made in it concerning his conduct, character and work. Moreover, as these certificates became the basis upon which crew members were selected, they offered, in the committee's view, the possibility of detaching the lascar from the influence of his serang.

Though the serang had never been a popular figure with officials and shipping companies, the 'tyranny of the serang' became henceforth a staple of the official discourse on Indian seamen, and the representation which the committee attempted in its report became the basis for the stereotypes which dominated the official imagination on the subject for the next two generations. On quite a few occasions thereafter, the Government of India and port officials received complaints, often from Board of Trade officials in London, that bribery and corruption prevailed on a large scale in the engagement of Indian seamen. After conducting routine inquiries into these complaints, Indian authorities ritually affirmed that while serangs exacted large sums from the crew, *dasturi* was the custom of the land and was to be found in all forms of employment. No action they took would 'assist in any appreciable degree in freeing lascars from the control of their serangs', nor was it clear that the 'freeing' would, 'if attainable, be beneficial to the men'.[16] While the corruption of serangs was regarded as an undisputed fact, com-

[16] NAI, GI, Commerce and Industry Department (CI), Merchant Seamen Branch (MS), Aug. 1905, 1-10 A, despatch no.43, 3 August 1905.

plaints that brokers or European officers of ships charged bribes from the former were usually greeted with disbelief. Even when investigations revealed the truth of the allegations about ships' officers demanding and getting bribes from serangs, the Indian government insisted that 'the general weight of the evidence goes to prove that it is, as a rule, the serang who extorts money and only occasionally the officer'.[17] In this instance too, little evidence was found to implicate the broker.

III

There were several reasons for the distrust and suspicion with which shipping companies and officials viewed the serang. No doubt, the absolute command over his crew, which these sources usually attributed to the serang, was a major advantage in the day-to-day running of a vessel. A good serang was an asset which European officers valued greatly and, although regular turnovers were the rule, companies preferred known serangs who were sometimes hired repeatedly to serve on the same vessel, or under the same officers. Few European officers could even identify their Indian crew, let alone attempt to overcome barriers of language and race to forge direct relations with the men bypassing the serang.[18] Hence they had necessarily to give the serang a free hand to manage his crew.

But the serang's status among the crew, whether real or imagined, was also a source of threat to the companies, since it carried with it a formidable potential for combined action. As the Chairman of the 1884 committee noted, no doubt with some exaggeration, about a crew engagement he had had occasion to observe,

> the men are drawn up in a line, the serang acts as a spokesman in their behalf ...[and] whatever he bids them do, they do; if he accepts for them the terms offered, they agree; but if he demurs, they also hesitate; if he absolutely refuses, they all move in a body out of the shipping office.

It was widely believed that the lascars were meek and submissive before the serang because, among other reasons, they depended on him for their employment on board a ship. Sometimes it was suggested that the serang commanded obedience because he was the 'headman' of the village to which his crew belonged. Images of the lascar as the serang's 'victim' were also common. But beyond this, little was known or ven-

[17] NAI, GI, CI-MS, March 1914, 5-20 A, despatch no.14, 12 March 1914.
[18] NAI, GI, Legislative Department, June 1896, 89 A, app.33, Bombay Shipping Master's letters, nos.65 and 231.

tured about relations between and amongst Indian crews. For the most part, it made practical sense for the shipowners to disregard the greater internal differentiation among Indian crews and assume their corporate character, of which the serang was the principal embodiment.

One may speculate about the influence these employer perceptions of lascars crews and their internal relationships exerted on the actual manner in which the latter worked themselves out. One might argue, too, that particular representations of the ties between the lascar and the serang implicit in the state's feeble and occasional efforts to weaken these ties may have worked perversely to reinforce some of them. Besides, even though the degree of collective activity differed between sailing vessels and steamships, everyday life even on the latter nevertheless did involve recognising the group aspect of the seaman's identity in numerous little ways. This recognition was much greater in the case of lascar gangs, not least because of the racial divide and its seeming impenetrability to the ship's officers. The colonial state too made the lascar's group identity the basis for some of its initiatives, one of which, for instance, held all members of an Indian crew collectively liable whenever any contraband was discovered in their quarters on board.[19]

For the most part, shipping companies were sensitive to the thin line which separated group activity, and industrial group identity of any kind, from the 'shop-floor' unity of the workers. Shipowners employing Indian seamen, as employers everywhere in the nineteenth century, tended to react with alarm to the slightest evidence of 'combination'. Trade unions did not become a regular part of the Indian seaman's experience until the interwar years. Yet, the complaints which shipping companies and officials alike made from the 1880s about lascars uniting to protect their rights appeared more plausible because race already set these men apart and together.[20] As racial and class suspicions merged, any pretensions the shipping companies' may have had of paternalistic concern for the lascar evaporated. Their protests against the state's attempts at paternalism in relation to Indian seamen also acquired a sharp edge, resentful employers and shipping officials (many of whom would typically have spent several years with one or more shipping company before landing a port job) tending now to emphasise the lascars' ability to resist being imposed upon, and otherwise look after themselves. A particular source of apprehension was the men's 'air of...independence', which they could afford to cultivate

[19] NAI, GI, FC-SC, Oct. 1889, 512-20 A; October 1892, 566-75 A.

[20] NAI, GI, FC-SR, March 1884, 386 A; CI-MS, November 1905, 1-11 A.

more easily because they lived and worked in groups.[21] To the extent the serang held the key to a group's cohesion, his role gained further importance, and the officers' dependence upon him grew. For this reason, valued as he might be for his contribution to the smooth running of a vessel, the serang's mediatory role in relations between the crew under his charge and their employers also often made him a focus of countervailing power and authority. This duality of position and status was an enduring source of uneasiness in relations between the serang and his bosses.

The serang's reputation for entrepreneurship, although not without profit to employers since it probably helped keep wages down, also did not endear him to those intimately acquainted with shipping.[22] Serangs (as also tindals and other better paid members of the crew) were known to carry out a brisk trade, sometimes in partnership with their ships' junior officers and with the assistance of the rest of the crew, in the ports to which they voyaged. Cabbages and onions to Colombo and Galle, fowl to the Straits, coconuts, bone china, crockery, and glass and fancy items to India, birds to Marseilles, and Indian curios to other European ports were some of the goods which bemused shipping officials reported serangs and other Indian crew as carrying.[23] These goods often took up the already small space meant for the Indian crew which had, partly as a result, to make do with cramped, poorly ventilated and unhygienic quarters. Shipping and customs officials claimed serangs also masterminded the smuggling of contraband goods, chiefly of tobacco, on board their ships. In a few cases, serangs were also alleged by their employers and by shipping officials to short supply crews' rations and pilfer surplus stocks for sale in the market. Whether these allegations, which on one occasion led to the government reducing crews' rations to the ultimate benefit of the shipping companies, preceded or followed the low esteem in which the serang was held is impossible to say. But it is important that the reader be alive to both possibilities.

21 See for example the letter from the Bombay Chamber of Commerce to the Government of Bombay, 15 June 1904 in NAI, GI, CI-MS, November 1905, 1-11 A.

22 NAI, GI, SC-CT, August 1892, 494-531 A; in particular, see J.E. O'Connor's note, 28 July 1892.

23 NAI, GI, SC-CT, Aug.1892, 494-531 A, statement of the Health Officer of the Calcutta Port; SC-CT, March 1901, 135-42 A, statement of the Port Officer, Bombay; Legislative Dept., June 1896, no.89 A, app.33, letters of the Bombay Shipping Master, who claimed serangs also traded in 'monkeys, snakes, and even small deer'.

Finally, the serang seems to have suffered on account of verbal associations. The ghat serang had a poor reputation historically, and sources in Britain, where many of the complaints against serangs originated, were prone to confuse the two types of serangs. This may have owed partly to the fact that some ghat serangs had earlier been employed as serangs on ships.[24] Whatever the reason for it, the fact of this confusion was not always clear to these sources' official interlocutors in India. Hence, whenever complaints from Britain mentioned ghat serangs as recipients of bribes from Indian seamen, exasperated officials in India responded by observing that ghat serangs had been replaced since the 1860s by licensed shipping brokers, and tended to assume, following the report of the 1884 committee, that the complaints were about serangs making money at the expense of the men who served under them. It did not occur to any official that while the term ghat serang may have vanished from official vocabulary following the 1859 legislation, the assistants of Bombay's licensed broker were still referred to as ghat serangs, and that in popular usage the term was used generically to represent intermediaries in the maritime labour market.

A further source of confusion may have been the pattern of recruitment and work supervision which prevailed in indigenous vessels and small steamers plying in coastal trade and in inland rivers. These vessels did not come within the scope of the Indian merchant shipping legislation, and the place of the licensed shipping brokers was usually taken by the serang who hired the crew and oversaw their work on board. Since these vessels had few officers other than the Captain, the serangs here, many of whom held government licences secured after passing some qualifying tests, discharged a wider range of responsibilities. They also collected (and in a few cases even negotiated) wages on behalf of the entire crew, and so had considerable discretion over their distribution. As a report of the Bengal Trade Unions Federation noted, the relation between the crew of inland vessels and their serang was 'almost that of an employee and employer'.[25] Powerful as some serangs on ocean-going ships were known to be, few officials, whether from the union or from the government, went so far in describing the ascendancy which the former had over their crew.

[24] Royal Commission of Labour in India, *Evidence*, vol.5, pt.2, Bengal (excluding coalfields and the Dooars), oral evidence of Captain R. Liddell, Marine Superintendent, British India Steam Navigation Company Limited, E-4338.

[25] Nehru Memorial Museum and Library (NMML), AITUC papers, file 48, report of the Bengal Trade Unions Federation, December 1933.

It is appropriate to note at this juncture that the knowledge which employers or the colonial state possessed about Indian seamen was not founded on any detailed investigation or study. The relatively limited numbers involved, the transient nature of maritime employment, and the fact that local authorities did not fear them, in their capacity as seafarers, as a major threat to public order meant that at least until the 1920s, Indian seamen ranked low in the investigative priorities of the colonial state. As long as capable seamen were forthcoming in adequate numbers, shipowners too were rarely concerned to find out where their men came from, their occupations while on land, how they lived in the major port cities whilst awaiting engagement, or about how they were engaged. Our knowledge on these questions, paradoxically enough, owes more to the defensive intervention of the seamen's unions than to the regulatory or coercive role of the state. In this sense, perhaps, knowledge about the seamen's conditions in ports, and on land generally, constituted part of the 'technology' of labour's resistance to capital, rather than that of the state, or of the rule of capital.

It is not the intention here to argue that serangs were, as a group, non-extortionate of habit, or that they were proletarians bound by ties of class solidarity to the crew they commanded. Indeed, seamen's unions were only too conscious of the serang's potential for corruption if the elimination of brokers was not accompanied by the setting up of a more transparent system of engaging crews.[26] Nor is it the case that there were no intermediaries in the labour market who made money at the expense of the workers. But the serang was not, in most instances, the sardar.[27] If the colonial state made him into one, it was chiefly because it held a particular set of assumptions about the organisation and functioning of Indian labour markets. Some of these assumptions, or variants of them, may have been valid in the specific contexts where first they were made, but the validity of the others, such as the identity of intermediaries and their relation to workers and the work process, could conceivably vary across industries. It is perhaps worth remarking

[26] NAI, GI, CD-Shipping, March 1925, 1-28 A, memorandum of the Indian Seamen's Union, 6 February 1923.

[27] Seamen's unions did not entirely deny that serangs took bribes or cuts from a seaman's wages. But in their view, licensed shipping brokers and ghat serangs were the main culprits, and reforming recruitment practices had to begin with the elimination of these intermediaries; see for example the evidence of the seamen's unions to the Royal Commission on Labour in India, vol.5, pt.1, pp.242-3; and pt.2, E-1090-1101; and the resolutions passed by the Indian Seamen's Unions in NAI, GI, CD-Lascar Seamen Branch (LS), June 1922, 1-30 A.

here that historians who implicitly follow the colonial state in accepting the overarching assumption of labour market institutions and practices being invariant over space, may also be wont to overlook the possibility of their changing through time.

IV

As it happened, the market for Indian maritime workers and the manner in which they were recruited underwent some important changes in the quarter century after the First World War. The interwar years witnessed major changes in the domestic and external contexts within which Indian maritime labour functioned. The growth of political activity and consciousness in the major Indian towns, and the emergence of trade unions and other labour organisations were important elements of this change. In addition, the general priority accorded to labour issues by government and non-official opinion alike rose following the founding of the International Labour Organisation (ILO). But important as these changing contexts were, they were to a considerable extent mediated and articulated by the agency of the workers, and their organisations.

It is not necessary to enter in any detail into a discussion of the seamen's unions which existed in the major port cities of India.[28] Suffice it to note that seamen's associations were among the earliest bodies 'in the nature of trade unions to appear in Bengal'. According to an official of the Bengal government Industries Department, the early appearance of seamen's organisations and their 'recurring birth in the absence of any actual strike-history' originated in the 'direct contact of the men themselves, afloat and in home waters, with Western trade unionism.' Though this influence was first discernible in Bombay, it soon spread to Bengal, some Calcutta seamen coming to possess 'tickets' entitling them to 'what they call trade-union benefits in England'.[29] It was not until 1919, however, that the ground was laid for sustained trade union activity in Calcutta with the founding of an Indian Seamen's Union by one Manfur Khan, a serang who also owned a boarding-house. Immediately after its founding, the union organised a boycott of brokers. But this could not be sustained, and the union itself languished in Manfur Khan's absences on coastal voyages. In July 1920, this union merged with the Indian Seamen's Benevolent Union in to form the Indian

[28] On this see F. Broeze, 'The muscles of empire: Indian seamen and the raj, 1919-1939', *Indian Economic and Social History Review*, 18, 1 (1981), pp.43-67.

[29] NAI, GI, CD-LS, June 1922, 1-30 A, note by the Department of Industries, Government of Bengal, September 1921.

National Seamen's Union, which was renamed the Indian Seamen's Union (ISU) in March 1921. One of the union's earliest initiatives was to wage a successful strike for higher wages. The seamen most actively involved in the union were serangs and stewards, though by the time it was founded, the ISU had a core of 300 to 400 men of all ranks who took part in its activities. Like other labour unions in India at the time, maritime unions too were led by influential outsiders. According to an official report on seamen's unions, many of these leaders were really there as 'outside patrons', a sub-editor of *Bengalee*, the financial manager of another paper, the *Amrita Bazar Patrika*, the Deputy Legal Remembrancer of the Bengal government, and a retired Presidency Magistrate figuring among the ISU's seven vice-presidents. Other outside leaders included the Municipal Commissioners of wards in which the docks were situated, one or two owners of seamen's lodging-houses, and a barrister by the name of Muhammed Daud. Daud, who gave up his practice as a pleader during the non-co-operation movement, affiliated the ISU to the Bengal Provincial Congress—ISU being the first union to do so—and to the All-India Trade Union Congress.[30]

It is customary to view the presence of outsiders in their unions as a sign of the workers' lack of autonomy. To a large extent, this was the case. But the report cited above also notes the establishment by one Shaikh Samir, described as a lascar broker, of the *Anjuman-i Jehajian* in 1920. Samir's aim was apparently to weaken the ISU since its 'objects regarding lascar recruitment were unpalatable to the broker interest'. Samir's union held out an attractive package of monetary benefits for members, and offered better terms in respect of advances and absentee penalties. The union made some initial headway on the strength of such offers, but soon ceased effectively to exist. Nor should it be overlooked that many outsiders failed to gain the workers' confidence, or to be accepted as their leaders. Outside leaders were also not immune to challenge by others from within the union or outside. To some extent, these challenges were resolved partly through recourse to the plebiscitary agency of the workers themselves. For instance H.S. Suharawardy, who later became Chief Minister of Bengal, was a victim of such agency. As his political fortunes grew on the strength of a conservative sectarian platform, his support among Calcutta's largely Muslim seamen waned, and despite some employer support, the Seamen's Association of India he founded languished in the wilderness. The gainers were Muhammed Daud and Aftab Ali, the latter a

[30] NAI, GI, CD-LS, June 1922, 1-30 A, note by the Department of Industries, Government of Bengal, September 1921.

coal trimmer and union activist, who in 1923 jumped ship in America, living there for three years before returning to resume his trade union activities in India.[31] Daud remained a leader of Calcutta seamen employed on foreign-going ships until the late 1920s. But he lost the leadership of inland mariners and waterside workers because, in the words of a Bengal Trade Unions Federation report, he was identified too closely with a 'clique of masters, serangs [of inland vessels], and drivers'.[32] The new leadership appears to have worked closely with Aftab Ali.

Seamen's unions were generally moderate in their ideology, leadership, and affiliations. Yet, agitating to secure the elimination of labour market intermediaries, and their replacement by an employment bureau run with active union participation, remained an important plank of their platform through much of the interwar period. Although the early stirrings of trade union activity among Indian seamen were not lost on the authorities, the abuses inherent in the system by which they were recruited came into public focus partly as a result of the initiative of the International Labour Organisation; in particular the 1920 Convention on the Employment of Seamen. Nor did the unions entirely succeed in securing a fully open or transparent method of recruitment. Yet their intervention had two important effects on the course of events. First, it ensured that seamen had a voice in determining the manner in which the Seamen's Recruitment Committee (1921-22) represented the organisation of their market and the system by which they were recruited.[33] This, as the outcome of the 1884 committee and subsequent official inquiries showed, was no small achievement. Secondly, as we discuss below, the Clow Committee's findings made little impression upon provincial authorities and shipping officials, especially in Calcutta. But pressure from the unions helped ensure, on the whole, that the committee's recommendations, some of which were later endorsed by the Royal Commission on Labour in India, were not entirely swept under the carpet by local officials.

V

The Indian government decided against ratifying the 1920 ILO Con-

[31] K. McPherson, *The Muslim Microcosm: Calcutta, 1918-1935* (Wiesbaden, 1974), p.37, 131; Broeze, 'Muscles of empire', pp.54-6.

[32] NMML, AITUC papers, file 48, report of the Bengal Trade Unions Federation, December 1933, p.5.

[33] This committee is referred to in the text as the Clow Committee, after its chairman Sir A.G. Clow, I.C.S.

vention on the Employment of Merchant Seamen, resolving instead to examine the methods of seamen recruitment to definitely ascertain 'whether abuses exist and whether those abuses are susceptible of remedy'.[34] This resolution was followed by investigations in Bombay and Calcutta by small three-member committees comprising representatives of the government, seamen, and shipping companies.

These investigations revealed a shocking state of affairs in Calcutta. The two firms of shipping brokers, which had been carrying on the business for many years, and the ghat serangs of the British India Steam Navigation Company, were found by the committee to have systematically extorted money from the seamen they hired. They could afford to do so, since only they received 'accurate information' about a ship's crew requirements. This information was important when a ship was in port, and absolutely vital when it was not.[35] In the words of the Calcutta committee, it was the 'exception for any serang to go to sea who has not given a substantial bribe to the broker or to the ghat serang'. Butlers (as serangs of the saloon department were called) paid Rs.50 to the broker or his assistants, while each saloon boy paid Rs.2 or Rs.3. Bribery occurred on a far larger scale in the hiring of crew for the engine and deck departments. Here the broker received bribes ranging from Rs.200 to Rs.500, while the ghat serang's bribe ranged from Rs.300 to Rs.1,000. The bribe could even exceed Rs.1,000 in cases where there was an 'opportunity...of smuggling opium or other excisable articles'.[36]

The serang had, of course, to recover these payments from the wages of the men under him. The actual practice of doing so varied between crews of the engine-room and those on the deck. In the latter department, each of the 'upper men', with the exception of the tindal, paid their serang a one-time lump sum at the start of the voyage. This, in 1921, could amount to Rs.40 each. The tindals typically paid Rs.10 each, though they might, on occasion, even receive some payment from the serang. The *khallasies* or deck-hands paid according to a graduated scale, each man settling his wage with the serang before going on board the vessel. The difference between this and the wage the seaman had

[34] Government of India, Central Legislative Assembly resolution, 26 September 1921.

[35] Appendix B, Report on the Preliminary Inquiry in Calcutta, para.13; according to this report (para.4), one reason why there was more corruption in Calcutta than in Bombay was that brokers at the former centre were often required to ship crews for vessels which were not in port.

[36] Report of Preliminary Inquiry in Calcutta, paras.7-8.

contracted with the company was known as the 'increase'. This 'increase' was very low (sometimes even negative) in the case of old and experienced hands, while younger and less capable men paid a larger proportion of their pay to the serang. It was consequently in the serang's interest to load his crew with inexperienced or incapable men from whom a higher 'increase' could be charged. But against this, the serang had to balance the requirements of ability and efficiency, since otherwise he might earn the censure of the chief officer and endanger his chances of being re-engaged on the vessel. The local committee managed to examine the private account books of two deck serangs. In one case, the increase amounted to Rs.88 out of a total monthly wage bill of Rs.330. The ghat serang had been paid Rs.250, while other payments (to clerks in the shipping office, etc.) came to Rs.16. Such a large 'increase' was apparently exceptional, and according to the committee, the serang on this ship had incurred a large expenditure on a lawsuit arising from his previous voyage. In the other case where the broker had been bribed Rs.200 and the shipping-office clerk Rs.5, the increase worked out to Rs.48 on a monthly wage bill of Rs.252. The 'upper men' on this ship, together, made an one time payment of Rs.74 to the serang.[37]

In the case of engine-room crews, the practice was somewhat different. The tindals assisted the serang in paying the broker's bribe, the first tindal paying up to Rs.200, and the second tindal about Rs.100. In addition they might pay small sums (say Rs.10) to the serang. The crew of the engine department (firemen and coal trimmers) all paid the serang in the same scale, the total payment usually amounting to a month's pay in a six-month voyage.[38]

These numbers might suggest, on the face of it, that the serangs too made money at the expense of their crew. In reality, however, according to the committee, this was not the case. In addition to the bribe, brokers insisted on serangs placing with them a deposit of Rs.60 to Rs.100, 'for the privilege of being on...[their] books', and for considering their claim to a ship. Typically, serangs borrowed the amounts needed to pay the bribe and the deposit from moneylenders, who charged the 'invariable rate...[of] 150 per cent a year'. Since a long interval of several months might elapse between the time the money was borrowed and its repayment at the end of the voyage, the effective cost to the serang of finding a ship could amount to more than twice the payments he had made to the broker or the ghat serang. So that, accord-

[37] Ibid., paras.9-10.
[38] Ibid., para.10.

ing to the committee, despite the 'increase' which he could lay his hands on, the serang made very little money, or was sometimes out of pocket if he made only one voyage. The serang's hope of saving any money thus depended on his being re-engaged for a second and subsequent voyage, the bribe payable upon such occasions being lower than that charged for the original engagement.[39]

The conventional wisdom among shipping officials in India, epitomised for example in the 1884 report, was that apart from hiring seamen, brokers were needed to administer the system of advances in a way as to minimise the risk of a seaman absconding with his advance, and of having to hire a substitute in his place. In practice, however, the broker did not bear the entire risk of the advance wage. In the first place, the earlier practice of nominal cash advances having ceased, the broker gave each seaman on articles a promissory or 'advance note' equivalent to a month's wage. Almost immediately thereafter, the broker's *dalal* or boarding-house keeper (or *mahajan*; sometimes the two roles were united in the same person) encashed one half of the advance note, at a commission. The broker was not liable to pay the other half until the ship sailed with the seaman on board. But seamen tended to cash the other half with local moneylenders at a charge of one anna per rupee on the full value of the note, or two annas per rupee on the outstanding loan.[40] In this way the moneylender took over half the risk of the seaman absconding with his advance wage. The broker himself stood to lose only the half a month's pay he had advanced in cash to the seaman, though as the Calcutta committee pointed out, even this risk was often undertaken by the keeper of the lodging house at which the seaman resided.[41]

Following these findings, the two committees met together to con-

[39] Ibid., paras.11-12; the report was silent regarding the 'increase' charged by the serang on the second voyage.

[40] It is not clear whether, in the event of a seaman not joining a ship after cashing the advance note, the moneylender was liable for the whole of the advance wage. Such a liability can be viewed as a means of compensating the broker for the 'moral hazard' arising from the moneylender's willingness to cash the advance note ahead of the ship's sailing, and might explain the manner in which the moneylender calculated his discount charges. While there is no evidence that such was indeed the case, it would be surprising if, in the face of repeated dealings between brokers and moneylenders who held conditional claims on them, the former did not hold the latter liable for a seaman's absence in some way. Please note here, that at two annas per rupee for, say a month, the effective interest rate works out to 150 per cent. Typically, ships sailed within a week of signing on their crews.

[41] Report of the Preliminary Inquiry in Calcutta, para.6.

sider remedial measures. This larger committee, which was headed by Sir A.G. Clow, Controller of the Labour Bureau, Government of India, was joined by N.M. Joshi (AITUC) and Sir Frank Carter, neither of whom had been involved in the local committees. The inclusion of N.M. Joshi meant that labour was represented in the Clow Committee by three members. Carter, a Bengal legislator, represented shipping interests in Calcutta.

Although, according to the Clow Committee's unanimous report, corruption was not unknown in Bombay, the bribery which attended the recruitment of seamen in Calcutta was nothing short of 'systematised extortion'. In its view, not only were Calcutta's brokers superfluous in the roles assigned to them, they were also the source of almost all the corruption which attended the recruitment of seamen in the port. The committee therefore recommended dismissing the licensed shipping brokers and the BISN's ghat serangs, and ending the existing system at the 'earliest possible moment'.[42] Instead it proposed the setting up of an employment bureau to organise the recruitment of shipping crews. The bureau was also to prepare a register of serangs and seamen available for employment. Serangs registered with the bureau were to be selected either by the Superintendents of the shipping companies, or the ships' masters, or directly by the bureau. Since, according to the committee, Calcutta crews did not form 'self-contained groups' closely attached to the serang, it proposed engaging ordinary seamen by roster. However, the serang would retain the right to make 'reasonable objections' against any man, and to select one or two members of his crew. The other responsibility which the brokers were supposed to fulfil, that of making advances and ensuring that seamen reported to the ship in time for sailing, was to be entrusted to seamen's unions, co-operative societies, or to respectable individuals. The latter category did not, in the committee's explicit view, include Calcutta's brokers.[43]

VI

The Clow Committee's report represented a major shift in the way the organisation of the maritime labour market in Calcutta, the role of intermediaries in it, and most importantly, the relations between ordinary seafarers and the serang were perceived. Fundamental to the

[42] Report of the Substantive Committee, paras.1-3; the full report may be found in NAI, GI, CD-LS, June 1922, 1-30 A, pp.27-59.

[43] Para.11.

reforms which the Clow Committee proposed for Calcutta was the view, shared by the seamen's union if not adopted at its urging, that the port's seafaring community was largely made up of individual workers coming together for individual engagements under a serang.[44] Although seafarers might be linked to the serang in other webs of hierarchical relationships which might, in some cases, affect the composition of crews, the latter's selection and regulation on board were largely independent of them. In this sense, Calcutta crews resembled a modern industrial work-gang; and the serang, regardless of any earlier connections he might have with individual members of his crew, was more akin to a foreman than to a sardar. Nor was the serang, according to the Clow Committee and its defenders, the major source of corruption in the prevailing system of shipping crews; indeed, but for the broker, the serang 'would cease to exact bribes'.[45] As can easily be imagined, these perceptions were critical to any possibility of a more transparent method of engaging crews in Calcutta.

The Indian Seamen's Union, the pre-eminent organisation of Calcutta seafarers, was enthusiastically in favour of the Clow reforms, in particular the suggestion to set up a bipartite employment bureau. Failing that, the union was willing, if it was 'unavoidable', to accept an employment office run by the state. The ISU believed a state-run bureau should be set up with a 'good deal of precaution', and placed under the charge of a senior official of a British seamen's union experienced in the working of the National Maritime Board. But rather than allowing the effectiveness of such an office to depend on the 'personality' of the person who headed it, as officials proposed, the union echoed the Genoa Convention and the views of its representatives on the Seamen's Recruitment Committee in demanding that the employment bureau's work should be overseen by a bipartite advisory committee.[46]

In contrast, the Committee's strongly-worded report aroused great

[44] For evidence that the unions held to this view, see NAI, GI, CD-Shipping, March 1925, 1-28 A, memorandum of the Indian Seamen's Union, 6 February 1923.

[45] NAI, GI, CD-Shipping, October 1927, 104-s(4), 1-6 A, note by Clow, 16 December 1925.

[46] NAI, GI, CD-LS, August 1922, 1-7 A, letter from President, Indian Seamen's Union, Calcutta, to Secretary, Marine Department, Government of Bengal, 31 July 1922; Seamen's Recruitment Committee, Report of the Substantive Committee, paras.5 and 13; Joint Secretary, Indian Seamen's Union to Government of Bengal, 6 February 1923; also see the letter of the Indian Seamen's Union, Bombay, 28 July 1922, in the same file.

consternation in the Government of India.[47] The report's frank description of the existing practice of recruitment and its drastic recommendations for change virtually paralysed the authorities into inaction for many months. Several rounds followed of slow and extensive consultations with the provincial governments, shipping interests, and the labour unions. Although the Bengal government could no longer deny the existence of corruption in the engagement of crews in Calcutta, it continued to drag its feet in the matter of reform.[48] The Calcutta Port Officer was opposed to any change in the system of recruitment, arguing on the one hand that the remedy for bribery lay in the men's own hands, and on the other that 'the Indian seaman, far from being the innocent victim has...shown himself thoroughly capable of taking care of his earnings....' The Chamber of Commerce and the shipping companies were lukewarm to the Committee's suggestions, the latter suggesting that while corruption ought to be eliminated, nothing the government did could possibly save the men from themselves.[49] Some reorganisation of the engagement of seamen in Calcutta was, however, unavoidable, and rejecting the recommendations of its own labour department in favour of a full-fledged recruitment office, the Bengal government set up an employment bureau as part of the shipping office of the port. Captain H.F. Darvell, who in his own words had 'twenty-one years of close association with Lascar seamen ashore and afloat', was appointed as Shipping Officer to implement and oversee the new system of recruitment.[50]

From the outset, Darvell was sceptical about the need for reform, and about the practicability of the Clow proposals. In a series of letters to his superiors in the Bengal government, Darvell stoutly defended the licensed brokers, arguing that they undertook a variety of duties on behalf of the shipping companies or their agents, which were not touched by the committee's report. Such duties included drawing up portage bills, and sorting out crews' accounts, the latter being usually complicated by the seamen serving on many vessels during the pend-

[47] For details, see Broeze, 'Muscles of Empire'.

[48] For instance, its observations on the report of the Clow Committee were sent an year and a quarter after they were sought by the Indian government; see NAI, GI, CD-Shipping branch, March 1925, 1-25 A, letter from Secretary, Government of Bengal, 15 August 1923.

[49] NAI, GI, CD-Shipping branch, March 1925, 1-25 A, office note, 5 October 1923; letter of the Calcutta Port Officer, 19 July 1922.

[50] The above quote and the following paragraphs are based on NAI, GI, CD-Shipping, October 1927, 104-s(4), 1-6 A; Darvell's letters are on pp.3-15 of this file; all emphases in the original.

ency of an agreement, advances they received in foreign moneys, commodities supplied by employers, fines and forfeitures, etc. Since few companies had clerks to do the accounting, brokers were indispensable to the business of shipping in Calcutta. The committee had also greatly underestimated the work the brokers performed in rounding up crews for voyages and, often, despatching them by rail or ship to outer ports where their ships might be berthed. To carry out these tasks, Darvell claimed, the brokers employed a staff of 50 'undoubtedly well-trained and organised' men. In the new arrangements proposed by the committee, he argued, these costs would fall on the shipping office which would have to employ and train a similar number of men. This would prove a 'long and difficult task' for the employment bureau. He therefore favoured retaining the brokers, and placing them under the overall supervision of his office.

Darvell also rejected the union's argument, which the committee accepted, that seafarers at the port were independent individuals not 'attached' to any particular serang. This was, in his opinion, a 'misinformed' view. He also doubted the committee's finding about the extent of corruption by the brokers. The bribe of Rs.1,500 which the committee referred to

> might possibly be an authentic occurrence...[but if] the particulars...had been fully obtainable...it would be discovered that such sums have been paid—not to the Brokers themselves *but to their senior underlings*, these men being thoroughly versed in every item of a smart Serang's pickings whilst on service....

In Darvell's view, the Committee was also wrong to believe that the money serangs borrowed on the eve of their voyage was meant to pay the broker's bribe. These loans were really intended, he argued, to finance the trade in goods, including contraband, which serangs routinely carried out on their voyages.

The risk that the committee's proposals might, if implemented, help strengthen unionism among seamen was, for Darvell, another strong argument against them. Already, the Indian Seamen's Union was trumpeting the creation of the employment bureau as a reward for its efforts. The bureau was so closely associated with the union in the men's perceptions, that they even addressed him as the 'Officer-in-Charge of the Union Bureau'. The bureau's presence enabled the ISU to improve its position with seamen, its officials often forcing him to grant them interviews which they then made 'as public as possible'. The union had been sufficiently emboldened by recent developments to seek office premises within the bureau, but would have no truck with any arrangement which made the bureau seem a 'sleeping partner' of the union. Even so, union officials were now present in strength with pamphlets and other propaganda at the time of the crews' signing on, interfering with the engagement of crews, and doing everything to 'impress the seamen with the importance of their position...'. The Quarter-Masters' Union already levied a fee from all sukhanis engaged to serve on a vessel. Should the lower ratings follow this example, 'in...a few years some lakhs of rupees' would lie in the union's hands, 'and the Port of Calcutta would have in existence a Seamen's Union well provided with Funds'.[51]

The Marine Department of the Bengal government endorsed Darvell's views. D. Gladding, Deputy Secretary in the department wondered 'what will happen to Shipping if the Unions make much progress...'. He believed the committee had over-reacted to stray instances of bribery, and that its proposals were not accounted for as much

> by the local facts as by two forces, and the Government of India's estimate of them, *viz.*, the International labour organisation and Mr. Daud. We are rather out of touch with the former in Bengal but we see a good deal of the latter. Have not both these forces been overestimated?[52]

On the other hand, in the view of Gladding and other Bengal officials, the Committee had underestimated the degree of 'attachment' existing between the serang and the crew. The latter was a 'useless collection of individuals' in the absence of a serang 'commanding a sort of social obedience' from them. At the same time he feared that the committee's recommendations would undermine the 'corporate subservience' of the crew to their serang, and lead to an 'actual deterioration in the running of ships'. Finally, the Marine Department rejected the idea of employing crew by roster, as the Clow Committee proposed, since it could not be implemented without sacrificing the principle of 'selection'. The present system, the department affirmed, ensured the 'survival of the fittest'.[53]

In the end, the views of the Bengal government prevailed over the recommendations of the Clow Committee and the Indian government's

[51] Throughout the 1920s, the sukhanis were organised into a separate union. Once in 1920, the sukhanis' union attempted to wrest control of their recruitment from the brokers. These efforts did not succeed; see NAI, GI, CD-Shipping, October 1927, 104-s(4), 1-6 A, Clow's note,

[52] NAI, GI, CD-Shipping, October 1927, 104-s(4), 1-6 A, p.1 of the file.

[53] Ibid., Gladding's letter, 5 December 1925; and 31 May 1926; both Gladding and Darvell claimed support of the shipping companies for their arguments.

general attitude of support to them. The proposal to maintain registers of other ratings was not adopted, while the register of serangs which Darvell had begun preparing was made little use of in the actual selection process. The licensed brokers' services were not dispensed with. Despite the Clow Committee's explicit opposition, the business of administering advances and ensuring the presence of the crew at the time of sailing continued to be entrusted to them. However, half the advance wage was now paid to the men in cash, and the other half by means of an advance note. The only change brought about in regard to crew engagements, apart from closer supervision by the shipping office, was the publicity given by the latter to demands for crews, especially for serangs, by ships. While this may have helped diminish the influence of brokers in some cases, many agents and companies continued to rely on their services both for general engagements, and especially for hiring urgently needed replacement crews. Since shipping companies depended on brokers for many tasks, including the all important one of finding them men in an emergency, few ventured to bypass them in any systematic way. While government and shipping company officials maintained before the Royal Commission on Labour that these changes had helped eliminate corruption to a great extent, the unions were far from satisfied. The measures so far implemented were, in the latter's estimation, 'absolutely meaningless'.[54]

Finally, it took another initiative by the Indian Seamen's Union before the curtain was brought down brought down on the institution of licensed brokers in Calcutta. Apparently, as later events showed, the brokers adopted new methods to 'recoup themselves for the loss of perquisites' under the new arrangements.[55] Complaints abounded of brokers demanding Rs.500 to Rs.800 to promote an ordinary seaman to the rank of a serang, while the seamen they engaged, or advanced wages to, were expected to pay the brokers up to Rs.25 each as salami. Brokers also began to charge a bribe to arrange for the issue of new Continuous Discharge Certificates (or nullies) to aspiring seamen. By now this certificate had virtually become a badge of identity for Calcutta's seamen, and few could hope to find engagement on board a vessel

[54] NAI, GI, CD-Mercantile Marine II branch, January 1931, 32MMII/30, 1-31 B, resolution of the Indian Seamen's Union, 17 November 1929; Royal Commission of Labour in India, *Evidence*, vol.5, pt.2; oral evidence of H.F. Darvell (beginning on p. 260), Capt. R. Liddell, Marine Superintendent, BISN (p.296), and Mahbubul Huq and Aftab Ali of the ISU (p.80); vol.2, pt.1, Government of India memorandum relating to seamen, pp.328-9.

[55] NAI, GI, CD-Mercantile Marine branch II, Jannuary 1931, 32 MMII/30, 1-31 B, note by S.N. Banerji, 27 November 1929.

without one. From the late 1920s following the urging of seamen's unions and of the ILO, maritime administrators in many parts of the world began to restrict the registration of new seamen as a means of reducing unemployment amongst seafarers. With the ISU making a similar demand in India, the authorities in Calcutta too began to regulate the issue of nullies. The new restriction now afforded some scope for bribery, which licensed brokers were quick to seize.

Even the new system of advances afforded brokers ample opportunity for profit. Once the seaman was in the possession of an advance note, the broker allowed him to cash the note at a discount of about 6.5 per cent. As ships normally went to sea within a week of engaging their crews, the rate of interest which the brokers charged on their advances amounted to nearly 350 per cent. Earlier, brokers had used the agency of boarding-house keepers (mahajans) to discount these notes, splitting the profits evenly between them. But no longer wishing to share the discount charges with the latter, they began to undertake the discounting business themselves. By seizing control over the discount market, brokers were also able to enforce their salami demand more stringently.

Matters came to a head in 1929.[56] In October that year, the ISU came across some evidence of one broker, S.K. Ghosh, having demanded and obtained bribes from three seamen for the issue of new nullies. Following this, the union decided, on 17 November, to organise a boycott of the broker. The boycott proved successful, lasting several days, and forcing agents and companies who conducted their business through Ghosh to go to other brokers. In response, Ghosh filed a libel charge against the ISU General Secretary Aftab Ali for having alleged that he charged a commission or *batta* on advance notes. The mahajans, whom Ghosh had alienated by taking over their discount business and by not promptly discharging the advance notes they presented, deposed in Ali's favour. The latter also managed to produce a draft partnership agreement between Ghosh and his close relative K.C. Roy Chowdhury, Labour member of the Bengal government who was then representing Indian labour at an ILO session in Geneva. According to this draft agreement made in 1922, Ghosh agreed to share his brokerage profits with Roy Chowdhury in return for the latter exerting to get him a broker's licence. Though Ghosh denied all knowledge of the agreement, P.C. Mitter, the Calcutta advocate who framed the agreement at Ghosh's instance, confirmed its existence. The case itself was dismissed on jurisdictional grounds, but it had aroused enough contro-

[56] The following paragraphs are based on ibid.

versy in the background of the union's successful boycott of the broker, for the Indian government to appoint a formal inquiry. The results of the inquiry went against Ghosh, following which the government revoked his licence to practise as a broker. Ghosh appealed against the decision on the plea that besides hailing from the same town as Aftab Ali, the inquiry officer Khan Bahadur Mohammed Mahmud was motivated by 'communal bias'. He also charged the union with 'cherishing' and working towards 'Soviet' and 'Bolshevik' ideals. But to little effect.

The findings against Ghosh greatly weakened the position of Calcutta's shipping brokers. Buoyed up by its success against Ghosh, the Indian Seamen's Union kept up its campaign against the other brokers, who suffered another devastating blow when the Royal Commission on Labour recommended their abolition.[57] The Industries and Labour Department favoured implementing this recommendation, while officials in the Commerce Department wanted the brokers to be persisted with as they had rendered valuable service during the war and could prove an useful bulwark against seamen being 'subject to...new kind of abuses due to the tyranny of the Unions...'.[58] But the climate of opinion had shifted decisively against Calcutta's brokers, and in 1934, the authorities decided against renewing their licences.

VII

As noted earlier, the elimination of licensed shipping brokers did not mean the end of intermediaries in the maritime labour market. Nor did it mean the end of corruption in the recruitment of Calcutta crews. There is some suggestion that the vacuum left by the brokers led somewhat, as the unions had anticipated, to a strengthening of the serang's role in the engagement of crew, particularly in Bombay.[59] The serang's position had still to be purchased in Calcutta, and many men with long years of experience at sea failed to make the grade because they could not afford the bribe. Nor was the selection of ordinary crews for engagement entirely fair or above board. Despite some reforms in that direction and the union's efforts, a roster-based system of recruitment giving preference to seamen who had been out of work the longest was never really implemented. Companies' agents and officers,

[57] Royal Commission on Labour in India, *Report*, recommendation no.158.

[58] NAI, GI, CD-Commerce Department, Mercantile Marine branch, October 1934, 22MMII (2)/34, 1-2 B, office note, 30 August 1934.

[59] Desai, *Maritime Labour in India*, pp.31-2; J. Mowat, *Seafarers' Conditions in India and Pakistan* (Geneva, 1949), pp.14-8.

clerks in shipping offices, and even union officials were alleged at various times to have taken bribes in return for influencing the selection of crew. Methods of recruitment always remained a step or two behind the consciousness of India's maritime workers, and union protests remained an abiding feature of the maritime labour scene in India.

But the 'systematic extortion' by institutionalised agents highlighted by the Clow Committee had largely become, on the eve of World War II, a thing of the past. The elimination of licensed shipping brokers in Calcutta was a major step forward, and arguably, but for this, the other changes which followed in the next decade, including the adoption of an 'open muster system', may well have taken far longer to materialise. More so as the union's fight against brokers was waged partly on the terrain of representation, and its success helped affirm the idea that Calcutta's seamen were individuals who came together for engagements under a serang to whom they did not necessarily owe any 'corporate subservience' springing from ties outside the maritime labour context. The Clow Committee adopted a different representation from its predecessors of the relations between serangs and the crew in Calcutta chiefly because of the union's intervention. It is instructive to underline here, in passing, that back in the rarefied corridors of the government, some of the assumptions refuted by the Clow Committee returned to hold up action on its recommendations.

The form of bourgeois consciousness which the Indian Seamen's Union articulated was perhaps altogether novel in the context of Calcutta's working class. Readers may however object that this consciousness may not have been shared by a majority of the union's members. Employment of Indian crews on board British ships could often resemble a form of indenture. As such it is not perhaps the best example of a purely 'capitalist' form of labour organisation. Yet it is instructive, in addressing this objection, to reflect on the wider question of the seeming paradox of 'pre-capitalist survivals' in a capitalist setting. This paradox is sometimes attributed to the 'needs of capital'. There is some evidence in the present case that licensed shipping brokers represented a cheap option for the smaller companies, and that Calcutta's shipping officials thought nothing of stressing this point. But the existence of this paradox is also sometimes attributed to human agency, in the failure of the Indian working class to come into being from under the 'debris' of its pre-capitalist moorings. This failure is sometimes seen to be best exemplified in the nature and functioning of working class organisations.

Revolutionary neither in intent nor by disposition, the Indian Seamen's Union was an unlikely exception to the latter generalisation. If trade unions comported themselves in the image of the state, the ISU did so in some amusing, even farcical, ways. Its officials were in the habit of writing (or acknowledging) 'demi-official' letters whose style was a poor imitation of the letters they may have received from the government. The president of the union was prone, rather in the style of the viceroy's or the secretary of state's despatches, to refer to the union's 'executive committee' as '*my* committee', or sometimes even as '*my* council'. Some may see this as an 'everyday' form of trivialising authority by appropriating its symbols and usages, but clearly nothing was farther from the intentions of union officials. On the contrary, in mimicking the state, union officials were attempting to appropriate its authority to enhance their own standing in the men's eyes. Officials in the government were aware of this tendency and, even while deploring it, were often not averse to making use of it.

Against this background, one may further ask whether the union's affirmation of bourgeois individuality was also not opportunist. So it may have been. But the significance of the union's perception, or argument if one prefers, lay more in itself, than in its fit with reality. For that matter, the state's contrary representation of the relations between serangs and other crew members was not based on any study or investigation. Rather, it derived from a more general perception of the sources and relations of power and authority in indigenous society. As any possibility of reform came to turn on the extent to which 'traditional' relations of power and authority were reflected among Indian crews, officials grew more emphatic in stressing the former's 'corporate' character, while the union grew more deliberate in refuting it.

So to the final point. If the ISU's stand, or that of the state, was opportunist or unrepresentative, then one is forced to ponder the possibility of agency being at work even in defining or setting out the particular form of the wider paradox discussed in these concluding paragraphs. If this was indeed the case, the paradox itself perhaps deserves another look, especially after relocating it in contexts of conflict and contestation involving capital, the state, and the working-class.

Chapter 10

THE TATA PARADOX

Claude Markovits

Business firms in India have not received much attention from economic historians. Most of the literature available belongs to the genre of firm histories, the writing of which has generally been commissioned by the firms themselves and therefore is often apologetic in nature, if not even hagiographical. Of modern Indian business firms however, the House of Tata is undoubtedly the one which has received the most extensive coverage. One might well ask why add a few more pages to the already abundant literature on this best-known and most studied of all Indian firms. I cannot claim to have discovered anything really new about the Tatas. However I find the existing literature, although informative and often insightful, either too much informed by an 'heroic' conception of entrepreneurship, or too exclusively preoccupied with microanalysis of the specific growth process of particular companies, like the Empress Mills or Tata Iron and Steel Co (TISCO). It is not my intention to belittle the extraordinary feat of entrepreneurship represented by the emergence of such a firm in the specific context of colonial India. But I think one has to go beyond that kind of statement. Some synthetic survey of the firm across a time span of over a century, aiming at situating it within the general context of Indian entrepreneurial history and attempting to link it to macro-economic trends appears to be needed.

I must therefore clearly state at the outset that the 'Tata paradox', or rather paradoxes which are the theme of this paper, have a meaning only within a political economy framework which has become largely dominant in historical studies of Indian capitalism, without however having acquired the status of a 'paradigm', since no global consensus can be claimed for it. This framework owes a lot to the work of economists such as A.K. Sen and Amiya Bagchi. A crucial element in this approach is the distinction made between indigenous and expatriate firms operating in colonial India. Bagchi has mainly stressed the institutional disadvantage of the former in relation to the latter in terms of access to the state and participation in worldwide trading and financial networks, ultimately tracing its origins in the racial bond of affinity between British rulers and British businessmen.[1] On the other hand, Tomlinson has drawn attention to some advantages Indian firms had over their British competitors, particularly in the jute market, in relation to supply factors, due to the existence of 'informal' credit networks, largely caste- and kinship-based, which allowed them more direct access to rural producers.[2] In spite of their widely divergent views, it seems to me that both authors would agree that to differentiate between indigenous and expatriate firms in the Indian colonial context is meaningful, a view that 'pure' economists would certainly find strange. It is doubtful in any case whether such 'pure' economists would find in India many 'firms', British or Indian, which would fit in with the often-quoted definition of the firm as a profit-maximising agent, endowed with a known and given technology and operating subject to a well-defined market constraint.

This definition of the firm posits as universal characteristics certain features of modern Western industrial firms. Leaving aside the question of technology, when applied to Indian firms it raises two different sets of questions. The first one pertains to profit-maximisation. In a well-known analysis of North Indian merchant firms in the eighteenth century, C.A. Bayly has argued in favour of a 'Chayanovian' model, stressing the similarities between merchant and peasant families, in particular the emphasis on reproduction of the family.[3] He sees Indian merchant firms as informed by a logic of kinship which does not necessarily enhance profit-maximisation, but makes credit, identified with family prestige, the crucial notion. According to him, this specific logic can run contrary to the logic of profit-maximisation in dictating, for instance, marriage alliances which do not necessarily contribute to an enlargement of the firm's assets. It is interesting to note that this kind of behaviour can be found in modern Indian industrial firms. Thus the great Ahmedabad industrialist Kasturbhai Lalbhai is known to have created companies with the stated purpose of endowing nephews of his, without very definite calculations about expected profits.[4] Of course it remains a moot point whether one can validly generalise from all this and put forward a theory of the 'Indian' firm as non-profit-maximising.

[1] A.K. Bagchi, 'European and Indian entrepreneursip in India, 1900-30', in E. Leach and S.N. Mukherjee (eds.), *Elites in South Asia* (Cambridge, 1970), pp.223-56.

[2] B.R. Tomlinson, 'Colonial firms and the decline of colonialism in eastern India 1914-1947', *Modern Asian Studies*, 15, 3(1981), pp.455-86.

[3] C.A. Bayly, *Rulers, Townsmen and Bazaars* (Cambridge, 1983), p.376.

[4] See D. Tripathi, *The Dynamics of a Tradition. Kasturbhai Lalbhai and his entrepreneurship* (Delhi, 1981), p.76.

However, serious doubts are in order regarding a definition of the firm as a profit-maximising agency in the Indian context. Serious reservations have also been expressed by students of Indian firms regarding the nature of the market constraints. Morris D. Morris in particular has stressed the high degree of uncertainty regarding the market due to lack of infrastructure and paucity of reliable information.[5] In India, therefore, the market constraint does not appear to have been 'well-defined' but in a state of constant flux which hindered rational calculations of cost.

Of all firms operating in colonial India, the firm of Tatas is probably the one which would come closer to that definition, since it was less informed than most Indian firms by a logic of the family and kinship and operated under market constraints which tended to be better defined than for most firms (the steel market is not dependent on the vagaries of the monsoon as is the market for cheap cotton cloth, and the parameters which regulate it are somewhat open to rational types of calculations). But I am not here going to examine Tatas in the light of different 'theories of the firm', an exercise for which in any case I am not competent. Rather, I am interested in exploring what I perceive as a paradox in relation to the above-mentioned 'political economy framework' and its possible wider implications, treating 'paradox' as a sort of heuristic device.

My point of departure is what I call the Tata paradox, basically that of a firm which displayed characteristics of both the indigenous and expatriate ones, in addition to some which appear largely unique, and which therefore tended to straddle the boundary between those two types of firms.

If the Tatas are compared with other large Indian firms, the following features will be noticeable. First, the character of the firm was strictly 'non-family', as manifested in particular in the employment of professional managers on a scale unknown in most other large Indian firms, but more common in expatriate firms. Thus the role of Sir Bezonji Dadabhai Mehta, who had started his career in the railways, in the success of the Empress Mills in Nagpur is well known.[6] Though a Parsi, he was not a direct relation of the founder of the firm, J.N. Tata, and yet the latter trusted him with the management of his first major venture, a fairly rare occurrence in the mostly Hindu Indian business

[5] See D. Kumar (ed.), *The Cambridge Economic History of India*, vol.2 (Cambridge, 1983), p.556.

[6] F.R. Harris, *Jamestji Nusserwanji Tata. A chronicle of his life* (Bombay, 1958, 2nd edn.).

world, where family connections were of such crucial importance; Burjorji J. Padshah, another Parsi, who was not a relation, played a very similar role in the development of TISCO and of the electric companies.[7] How much of this was due to differences in family structure between Parsis and Hindus is not a point I shall consider here. Secondly, the firms' financial structure was characterised by a greater degree of reliance on the stock market than in most other large Indian firms; and by a marked divorce between ownership and control, the former being widely diffused among individuals and companies,[8] while the latter was clearly concentrated in the hands of a few members of the Tata family (rather than in the family as a corporate entity). Moreover, from 1914 onwards, the Tatas enjoyed a close and almost institutionalised relationship to the colonial state such as no other Indian firm ever matched, reinforced by the constant hiring of retired ICS officers as Board members or managers,[9] a practice which was not widespread amongst other big Indian firms. (Of course the latter could not offer such attractive conditions as the Tatas, not only in terms of salaries but also of work environment.) Thus the Tatas almost overcame the 'racial' barrier which prevented most Indian capitalists from gaining social acceptance by the British rulers.

This does not mean that the Tatas did not also display some traits which were characteristic of other big Indian firms. For instance their approach to labour problems was not, in spite of well-publicised welfare measures,[10] fundamentally different from that of other big Indian employers of labour.It is true that the success of the Empress Mills in Nagpur is often attributed in part to a particularly enlightened policy of wooing labour in a region where Tatas were the first large-scale industrial employers.[11] But gradually the Tatas seem to have aligned their labour policy with that of most industrial firms operating in India. TISCO in particular is known for its bad record of labour relations,[12]

[7] Ibid., p.189.

[8] When TISCO was formed in 1907, the total Tata stake was Rs.25 lakhs, about 121 per cent of the total capital subscribed. See C.M. Lala, *The Creation of Wealth.. A Tata story* (Bombay, 1981), p.24. There was a total of 8,000 investors in the company.

[9] Such as John Peterson who was Director-in-Charge of TISCO in the mid-1920s, or Sir Ardeshir Dalal who joined the Tata board in 1931. Lala, *The Creation of Wealth*, pp.97 and 196.

[10] See a list of 'firsts' in labour welfare in ibid., Appendix A, p.203. The eight-hour working day was introduced in TISCO as early as 1912, while it was enforced by law only in 1948.

[11] Harris, *Jamsetji Nusserwanji Tata*, p.44.

[12] There were strikes at TISCO in 1920, 1922 and 1928 (which lasted from

and the anti-union bias in Jamshedpur was strong. It should be noted that in this field the line between Indian and British firms was rather blurred: labour practices in India were largely shaped by the structural characteristics of the labour force and employers' strategies did not play such a large role as is often assumed.[13]. In their financial practices as well, in spite of a reputation of honesty, the Tatas were not above resorting to methods which one associates more with Marwaris, if one is to believe the widely-diffused rumour about the existence of a private firm through which much of the profits of their companies was siphoned off without the knowledge and approval of the shareholders. This is not meant to suggest that British businessmen in India were more honest than Indian businessmen: it is just that their ways of dealing with shareholders were different. The Tatas' marketing network appears also to have been built according to 'Indian' rather than 'British' principles, although I have not come across a detailed study of Tata dealerships.

However, in some other ways Tatas were a unique firm in the context of colonial India, particularly in their approach to technological innovation and in their pattern of diversification. They tended as a rule to adopt the latest technology available, and not to follow slavishly British practices, as most Indian firms did. Their knowledge of world conditions was unparalleled in Indian industrial circles which still looked to Manchester and Birmingham as the Meccas of textile and iron technology. In cotton textiles it is true that, to look after the technical side of the Empress Mills, they hired Lancashire men, such as James Brooksby and Robert Roscoe, thus following the general trend among Indian millowners.[14] However, those two technical men proved to be exceptionally capable and innovative. They were largely responsible for the adoption of the ring frame,[15] a pioneering experiment at the time, since Lancashire mills did not yet use it on a significant scale. They adapted this new technology to the specific needs of the Indian textile industry, particularly the spinning of the coarser counts of cotton which were grown in India and which the throstle could not spin. In

---

when the anti-management union collapsed and 'happier relations ensued'. Lala, *The Creation of Wealth*, pp.120-2.

[13] R. Chandavarkar, *The Origins of Industrial Capitalism in India. Business strategies and the working classes in Bombay, 1900-1940* (Cambridge, 1993).

[14] On the role played by Lancashire men in the birth and development of the Indian cotton textile industry, see my 'Transfert de technologie de Grande-Bretagne en Inde: le cas de l'industrie cotonnière (1854-1920)', in *Cahiers du Centre de Recherches Historiques*, 4 (1989), pp.43-58.

[15] Harris, *Jamsetji Nusserwanji Tata*, pp.30-1.

striving for technical innovation and excellence, the two Britons always had the full support of J.N. Tata. When setting up the TISCO steelworks, the Tatas also gave preference to state-of-the-art technology while striving to adapt it to local conditions, and this attitude was a key factor in the technical success of the venture. It compares favourably not only with that of most Indian cotton-mill owners, but also with that of the Scottish managing agents of the Calcutta jute mills. Most of the technical personnel which helped start the Jamshedpur steelworks had been recruited at high cost in America and Germany.[16] Britons formed only a small part of the staff, and that kind of cosmopolitan approach was unknown in India at the time.

Other unique features of Tatas were their almost exclusive concentration on industrial activities, as well as the pattern of diversification of the latter. Regarding the first point, one should beware of simplifications. The Tatas never eschewed finance and trade, on principle. The founder of the firm, J.N. Tata, used to lend monies for many years, but then found investment in real estate in Bombay a more profitable proposition,[17] and the firm seems never to have returned to moneylending on a significant scale. In the same way, the Tatas' large venture in the China trade, which played a significant role in the primary accumulation of capital by the firm, was entrusted to a cousin of J.N. Tata, R.D. Tata,[18] and although a success in financial terms, became something of a side-show in relation to the firm's manufacturing ventures. In any case, the success of TISCO and its continuous expansion stretched the managerial resources of the firm to the utmost and prevented it from expanding much in other fields.

However, the pattern of diversification of the activities of the firm was not totally opportunistic like that of most large Indian firms, but followed a certain industrial logic. The product-mix of the Tata conglomerate prior to 1947 was wide-ranging, since, apart from the two core activities of cotton textiles and steel, it encompassed real estate, hotel management, electricity production, construction (Tata Construc-

[16] The following description of the TISCO works in 1911 shows this: 'At the time of Mr. Fraser's visit Sakchi was an extremely cosmopolitan place. Mr. Wells was general manager, and his chief assistants in the management, as well as the blast furnace superintendent and his staff, were all Americans. The crew of the steelworks and their superintendent were Germans. The superintendent and crew of the rolling mills were English.... There were a certain number of Austrians, Italians and Swiss, while Chinese were working as carpenters and in the pattern-shops'; ibid., p.202.

[17] Ibid., p.67.

[18] Ibid., p.93.

tion which was ceded to Walchand in the 1930s), cement production (the three Tata cement factories were amalgamated with others to form the Associated Cement Companies in 1936), tinplate (as a minority partner in a joint venture with Burmah Shell operating in Jamshedpur next to TISCO), oil and soap. If the link between cotton textiles and steel is not obvious, since the major linkage of textile machinery production was not represented, nevertheless it is clear that steel in its turn led to tinplate and at a later stage to trucks, and electricity production in the Ghats was geared to the needs of the cotton mills of Bombay. Actually the pattern of diversification went even beyond a simple logic of the firm to become the first attempt at some kind of systematic economic planning in the Indian context. The firm of Tatas thus came to fill a vacuum and to take upon itself some of the economic functions which were those of the state in a Listian conception which was, before 1914, still anathema to the British rulers of India.

However, this did not lead to a direct clash with the colonial state but rather resulted in a process by which the firm of Tatas and the colonial state became closely enmeshed. This is perhaps the most paradoxical aspect of the whole Tata saga, the fact that an Indian firm was capable of manipulating the colonial state to ensure its growth even before the adoption of a policy of 'discriminating protection' which at a later stage was a significant boost to the growth of many Indian firms. How crucial the help of the colonial state was at different stages to the growth of TISCO is well-known. Let us simply recall here Lord Curzon's decision of 1899 to change the rules regarding the granting of mining concessions,[19] Lord George Hamilton's constant encouragement to J.N. Tata's scheme which played such a role in overcoming bureaucratic obstacles,[20] the manifold help given by the government at the time of the setting up of the steelworks, the guaranteed purchase by the Indian Railways of part of the production,[21] and the role of various

[19] Ibid., p.153.

[20] In 1900, on a visit to London, J.N. Tata had a long interview with Lord George Hamilton, who was then the Secretary of State for India. Lord George assured him that 'his great desire...was to see Indian industries developed with Indian capital'. The Secretary of State 'promised to authorize the Government of India to give him all possible help. The promise was faithfully fulfilled. Lord George wrote to India expressing the warmest interest in the project and signifying that any steps the Government of India might take to assist it would receive his ready endorsement. From that time onward Mr. Tata and his successors never had much reason to complain of any lack of official support'. See ibid., pp.155-6.

[21] Lala, *The Creation of Wealth*, p.25.

technical departments of the government in the successful advancement of the project.

How to account for the attitude of the colonial state, keeping in mind the political economy framework within which I have situated myself? Why did the colonial state go out of its way to support an industrial venture in which there was no direct British participation? The question has often been asked but no really satisfactory answer given. The rise of Indian nationalism has often been quoted as one of the factors which influenced the attitude of the government, but in the pre-1917 phase it cannot have been of great significance. A search for more plausible reasons brings to mind firstly a certain amount of strategic foresight on the part of the British rulers of India: having an iron and steel industry could help in the event of war, as it eventually did. There may also have been reasons of a more psychological nature, related to a certain conception of 'fair play'. J.N. Tata was perceived as a risk-taking entrepreneur, conforming to a certain normative ideal, and not subject to the strictures which the British rulers applied to most Indian businessmen, whom they viewed as 'greedy banias'. Helping such a man reinforced the self-image the British had of themselves as fair and liberal; it was also a way of silencing the critics of the raj without endangering any existing British interests.

The Tatas were always very good at getting government support without tarnishing their image as a true 'Swadeshi' firm inspired by an exclusive consideration for the interests of India. J.N. Tata himself, though at heart deeply loyalist, was never a 'toady'; he did not hesitate to criticise the government at several junctures, for instance, over the countervailing excise duty on Indian textiles in 1894.[22] The fact that he was always refused the knighthood he so much desired, and which his services easily deserved (he did not even live to see his son Dorab knighted in 1910), is testimony to a perception by the British that his sympathies were too much on the side of Indian nationalism. His firm reaped the benefit of it when in 1907 the TISCO shares were subscribed in three weeks by the Indian public in the great wave of patriotic enthusiasm generated by the Swadeshi movement in Bengal.[23] The link with Indian nationalist aspirations remained an essential source of strength for the Tatas and the adoption by the Indian Legislature in 1924 of the Steel Protection Bill which saved TISCO from incoming bankruptcy owed as much to the support of the Swaraj Party as to the sympathetic

[22] Harris, *Jamsetji Nusserwanji Tata*, pp.57-8.
[23] Ibid., p.190.

attitude of the government.[24]

Thus the Tatas appear to have had the best of both worlds, enjoying on the one hand the support of the colonial state at different crucial moments in their history, and on the other, benefiting by the growth of Indian economic and political nationalism. A unique position which was threatened when India became independent.

If one relates the Tata story to macroeconomic developments, some disjunctions will become apparent. Thus the firm grew fastest in the 1907-1939 period when overall industrial development in India was fairly sluggish. The great problem here is how to account for the successful development of an iron and steel industry at a time when the railway network had already been completed while there was not yet a mechanical engineering industry in India. Between 1913 and 1939, when TISCO enjoyed a position of quasi-monopoly in steel production in India,[25] the market for steel products did not expand significantly, although the market for some types of steel expanded (steel for constructional engineering) while that for steel rails declined dramatically after 1927-28.[26] The expansion of TISCO occurred almost exclusively on the basis of import-substitution and mainly at the expense of non-British exporters of steel products (Belgium in particular). Tatas were therefore exceptionally well placed to benefit by a policy of protection combined with preference for British products, since their main competitors were non-British producers. The Steel Industry Protection Act of 1924 was the first instance of the introduction in India of differential duties on imports from the UK and from other countries, a policy of 'imperial preference' which was generalised in 1932 with the signing of the Ottawa agreement. Although the impact of protection was not very great in direct terms, the tariffs were instrumental in bringing about a fall in production costs which made TISCO better able to weather

[24] 'Swarajist politicians...proved extremely helpful in prodding the government into granting protection to Tata's steel industry in 1924'; S. Sarkar, *Modern India 1885-1947* (Delhi, 1983), p.232.

[25] Apart from TISCO, only Mysore Iron and Steel produced small quantities of steel from 1936 onwards. W.A. Johnson, *The Steel Industry of India* (Cambridge, Mass., 1966), pp.14-15. The year 1939 saw the launching of the Steel Corporation of Bengal by Martin Burn.

[26] Rail orders received by TISCO from the Indian railways increased regularly between 1923-24 and 1927-28, reaching a maximum of 182,800 tons in the latter year, but afterwards they declined precipitously, falling to a low of 36,500 tons in 1932-33, Indian Tariff Board, *Statutory Enquiry 1933: Steel*, vol.I: *Written evidence given by the Tata Iron and Steel Company Limited* (Delhi, 1934), p.74, quoted in A.K. Bagchi, *Private Investment in India 1900-1939* (Cambridge, 1972), p.315.

foreign competition.[27]

The same trend was noticeable in cotton textiles: the Tata cotton mills, like most Bombay mills, were more threatened by Japanese competition in the lower segments of the market than by Lancashire competition in finer goods, and the Tatas were largely behind the Lees-Mody pact of 1933, an alliance between Bombay and Lancashire millowners against the threat of cheap Japanese textiles flooding the Indian market.[28] The pact led to the conclusion of an Indo-Japanese trade agreement which imposed a ceiling on the sales of Japanese cotton piece-goods to India. The specific 'political economy mix' of the 1917-1947 period, characterised by a limited conjunction of interest between some British and some Indian groups, suited the Tatas particularly well. However it did not survive the Second World War and the coming of independence.

When British rule came to an end, other big Indian firms had a more intimate connection to the Indian state as a result of the support they had given the Congress during the independence struggle. This was particularly true of Birlas and of some of the Ahmedabad textile magnates. As for the Tatas, as I have shown elsewhere,[29] their attitude remained ambiguous at least till 1942; it is only after this date that they can be said to have openly supported Indian national aspirations (although making big profits thanks to government orders during the war). While they had joined hands with other representatives of Indian big business in framing the Bombay Plan, their political influence was never very great in post-1947 India. They did not take very kindly even to the mild form of 'socialism' associated with Nehru, not, I think, mainly because of a strong ideological commitment to economic liberalism, but because, being mostly steel-producers, they were not allowed to expand in an unrestricted manner in that branch, as steel was, par excellence, the kind of basic industry which the state sought to control directly. The extent of their clash with the Indian state should however not be exaggerated: they were allowed an expansion of their Jamshedpur installa-

[27] 'In a way, the credit for a large part of the fall in the cost of production must be given to the successive Tariff Boards appointed by the Government of India: TISCO was compelled to reduce costs because at every staff the tariffs or bounties proposed were just enough to cover the prime costs of production plus given percentages of the replacement value of capital and the working capital the Tariff Board considered necessary'; Bagchi, *Private Investment*, p.319.

[28] B. Chatterji, *Trade, Tariffs and Empire. Lancashire and British policy in India 1919-1939* (Delhi, 1992).

[29] C. Markovits, 'Les hommes d'affaires Indiens et le mouvement nationaliste de 1931 à1947', unpublished doctoral thesis, Paris 1987.

tions, new opportunities opened up in the automobile industry (TELCO) as well as in other branches, and they collaborated with the state in the running of Air India, which developed from Tata Airlines. But their position of dominance in the Indian private sector was gradually eroded in the 1950s and 1960s by the rise of their arch-rivals, the House of Birla.[30] Resentment at alleged government preference for other firms probably explains the role they played in the setting up of the Forum of Free Enterprise, an anti-socialist think-tank, in 1955, and their alleged support to the creation of the Swatantra Party in 1959.[31] Though this support was short-lived and the 1960s saw a rapprochement between big business in general and the government,[32] the Tatas were never as close to the Congress as Birlas. Given the role of the state in the Indian economy and the emergence of the 'licence raj' in the 1960s, it is tempting to relate their relative decline to the influence of political factors. For there was no clear decrease in entrepreneurial ability, no Marshallian generational cycle at work: if the sons of the founder, Dorab and Ratan, mainly completed and consolidated what their father had initiated, the third generation represented by Naval and J.R.D. Tata showed a renewed capacity for initiative, with further diversification moves into such fields as chemicals, automobiles and electronics. They also benefited from the help of exceptional managers such as S. Moolgaokar, for many years the chairman and managing director of TELCO,[33] probably the most successful Tata firm in the post-1947 period.

The Tata paradox is thus also that of one of the few big Indian firms which did not benefit by the coming of independence as much as could have been expected, because it lost the almost unique position, akin to a

[30] In 1965, according to the findings of the Monopolies Inquiry Commission set up by the Government of India, the Tatas were still number one in terms of both assets and sales, but the Birlas' sales were almost as large as the Tatas'. See *Report of the Monopolies Inquiry Commission, 1965*: vols.I and II (New Delhi, 1965). By 1976, the respective turnovers of the two business houses were grossly equal, the Tatas' being still marginally higher than the Birlas'. See N.K. Chandra, 'Monopoly capital, private corporate sector and the Indian economy. A study in relative growth, 1931-76', in *Economic and Political Weekly*, XIV (30-32), August 1979, Table 2, p.1245. The latest estimate I have come across, for 1985, puts the Birlas slightly ahead of the Tatas in terms of turnover, and even more in terms of assets. See Economist Intelligence Unit, *Country Profile India, 1988/89* (London, 1988).

[31] H.L. Erdman, *The Swatantra Party and Indian Conservatism* (Cambridge, 1967).

[32] S.A. Kochanek, *Business and Politics in India* (Berkeley, 1974).

[33] Lala, *The Creation of Wealth*, p.80.

sort of 'niche', it had carved for itself during the colonial period. Having lost their privileged relationship to the state, the Tatas had actually lost their main competitive advantage over their big business rivals and found themselves somewhat at odds with the new logic presiding over the relationship between the state and the private sector. In the new dispensation, the private sector was expected to occupy the interstices left open by the growth of the public sector, an opportunistic model of diversification which perfectly suited operators such as Birla. It was a new kind of 'niche' into which the Tatas found somewhat difficult to insert themselves successfully. With the new liberal policy initiated by the Government of India in 1991, they may again find the right 'niche'. This concept of specific 'niches' occupied by firms in relation to particular configurations in the political economy might be helpful in closing the gap between macro- and micro-levels which is so evident in the existing literature on the history of Indian capitalism and Indian industry.

'Niche' conveys the idea of insulation, of a protected space, of a specific kind of adaptation to an environment. In a political economy perspective it could refer to the capacity for a firm to grow counter-cyclically by exploiting very specific opportunities in very specific markets over a specific period of time, defined by a particular conjunction of political and economic factors. In the case of the Tatas during the interwar period, the crucial political factor was the weakening hold of the British over India which led the colonial rulers to contemplate concessions to Indian interests in order to ensure at least their neutrality; the crucial economic factor was the position of the British steel industry: faced with dwindling markets worldwide, the British steelmakers were content with maintaining more or less their market share in India by squeezing out their major competitors, the European steelmakers, particularly those of Belgium and Luxembourg, and they saw the Tatas as potential allies in that fight. However, it is only because the Tatas had established a close connection with the colonial government that the British steelmakers perceived them in that light. The colonial government was the indispensable broker of the de facto alliance which emerged between the Tatas and the British steelmakers against the more dynamic European producers. Thus, in an ironically paradoxical way, the already eroded imperial relationship between Britain and India nurtured and then protected the most 'national' of all Indian industries, the one which was identified with power and independence. The imperial connection thus acted as a kind of substitute for a thriving industrial environment.

Chapter 11

UNITS OF PRODUCTION IN SOUTH INDIA: AN EXPLANATION OF ARTISANS' CHOICES

Jan Brouwer

Introduction

I propose to explore the extent to which macro-structural possibilities have been utilised by South Indian artisans, given micro-level peculiarities. The macro-structural possibilities may be divided into two: (1) the general macro-economic organisation which offers a wide range of educational, occupational, financial and industrial strategies for the population at large, and (2) those strategies for various categories of small-scale entrepreneurs and artisans which are translated into housing, training, management, credit, technical or infrastructural schemes. On the micro or local level, the artisan manufacturers consist of directly interacting groups which are influenced by communal sentiments, localistic loyalties, kinship and sub-caste. In order to study the artisans' choices of whether to accept or reject the schemes specially designed for them at the level of macro-structural organisation, it is necessary to distinguish the artisans' actual situation from their perceptions and the views of the agents of change.

This contribution then discusses two distinct cases. The first is a specific government scheme which had been offered to carpenters and woodcarvers in two different settings of Karnataka. Rural carpenters successfully made use of the new possibilities, which the urban group of similar artisans had rejected. The two groups have shown a consistent history in their attitudes to government-aided schemes since at least 1915. The second case involves goldsmiths in a single caste but belonging to different sub-castes in small towns of Hassan District of Karnataka who responded differently to opportunities posed by the modern state. Here too, the actual situation is compared with the views of the artisans. An attempt is made to map out the actual situation of artisans to bring to light some of their economic concepts and views on self and society, and to compare the two sets of data. This will lead us to a certain understanding of the impact of macro-economic features on the micro level of household units of production. It is the first outcome of a research project on rural artisans' development needs, their perceptions and social actions in different settings of Karnataka.[1] Three artisanal castes are being compared: carpenters and sculptors of the Gudigara caste; carpenters, sculptors and smiths of the Visvakarma caste; and weavers of the Devanga caste. Visvakarmas and Devangas claim Brahman status, while the Gudigaras claim Kshatriya status. These claims and their indigenous explanation are found in the castes' oral tradition. This includes all kinds of narratives, speech and the caste's 'secret language' (as with the Visvakarmas). From these sources, a group's views on self and society, money, economy and dependence can be deduced.

In the following pages we will first examine the acceptance and rejection of a single government scheme by carpenters and carvers of two different castes. Here, the different status-claims of the two groups will be compared with the artisans' actions in regard to the development scheme. Secondly, we will examines the differential reactions of goldsmiths, belonging to one caste, to programmes offered by the state. This case is preceded by an introduction to the cultural ideology of this caste and its relevance for understanding the artisans' views; it concludes with a discussion of three minor case studies. Finally, the findings on the two cases are placed in the wider context of the impact of ideology and situation on the decision-making process of artisans.

Caste, status claims and development aid

In recent years, the south Indian state of Karnataka has introduced various projects to help both rural and urban artisans. Among them we find the 'Crafts Complexes' and 'Karnataka Industrial Sheds' projects established with the assistance of the Dutch government. These projects are designed for different sectors—handlooms, handicrafts, khadi and village industries, and leather industries, among others. Lately, the central and state governments have placed considerable emphasis on the development of small-scale industries aimed at generating addition-

[1] The project on which the present paper is based was founded by the Indo-Dutch Programme on Alternatives in Development (IDPAD) in collaboration with the Indian Council of Social Science Research (ICSSR), New Delhi, and the Centre for International Research and Advisory Networks (CIRAN), The Hague. IDPAD, however, does not take responsibility for the facts stated, opinions expressed and conclusions reached in this paper. I would like to thank my colleagues Dr. Anand Inbanathan (Institute of Social Sciences, New Delhi) and Dr. N. Jayaram (University of Bangalore) for their collaboration, and the field investigators, D.V. Sreenath, Ashok K. Shetty and V. Narasimhachar for assisting me in data collection.

al employment-opportunities for the local population. In Karnataka, this incentive was provided through the agency of the Karnataka State Small-scale Industries Development Corporation, which for the Sixth Five-year Plan embarked on a massive programme intended almost to double the number of industrial sheds that had been constructed during the last two decades.[2] In addition to the earlier support from government funds and commercial banks, two schemes—the Dutch Assisted Programme and the Small Town Development Programme—will join the construction and implementation effort to produce a total of 2,188 industrial sheds by the end of the Plan period.

Table 1. *Government schemes for artisans in Karnataka in 1981*

Name	Total number of sheds to be constructed	Total cost (lakhs)
1 Dutch-assisted scheme	442	688.40
2 Government funds	762	454.80
3 Industrial scheme	677	917.27
4 Western Ghats Development Programme	188	124.64
5 Small Town Programme	128	92.63
Total	2,188	2,273.47

Source: *Deccan Herald*, 27 August 1981

Artisans' self-perceptions and ideas about these schemes can be deduced from their narratives, speech, and their 'secret language' if they have one. An even more refined picture of their views can be drawn if the names and totems of their lineages are also considered. In this paper I shall restrict myself to the analysis of a few narratives, and, in the case of the Visvakarmas, to a few aspects of their 'secret language'. Like all Hindus, the woodworkers and goldsmiths are aware of the classical theory of *varna* categories which ideally divided society into Brahmans, Kshatriyas, Vaisyas, and Sudras. These categories roughly correspond to priests, warriors, traders, and workers (agriculturists). The classical theory of *varna* does not provide a reference point for manufacturers—blacksmiths, coppersmiths, sculptors, goldsmiths, potters, weavers, carpenters, cane and bamboo craftsmen. The question arises: how do artisans cope with this?

Ethnographic reports are replete with examples of manufacturing castes which claim either Brahman or Kshatriya status. The leather-

[2] S.R. Vijay, 'Exclusively for Karnataka...a unique Shed Construction Programme', *Deccan Herald*, 27 August 1981 (Bangalore).

workers of Lucknow claim Brahman status;[3] the Kaikkolar weavers of Tamil Nadu claim Kshatriya status;[4] Devanga weavers of Karnataka claim to be Brahmans; Gudigara carpenters and sculptors of Karnataka claim to be Kshatriyas; members of the Visvakarma caste of Karnataka, Tamil Nadu and Andhra Pradesh claim to be Brahmans. In other words, in a situation where the classical theory denies them a point of reference, they choose either the Brahman or Kshatriya categories to explain their position in the world. These indigenous status claims are found in the origin stories of the artisans' oral tradition.[5] What matters here is the claim itself. Therefore I shall first attempt to convey an understanding of 'Kshatriya' and 'Brahman' as theoretical concepts.

Two models of respectability

The canonical interpretation of the concept of 'Kshatriya' is 'warrior'. He is a ruler (king) who fights to conquer wealth and to protect his subjects. He rules by maintaining a network, expanding this network and manipulating the elements of which it is made. This requires skill in organisation, co-operation and competition. In other words, the concept covers an inclusive model of maximalised interactions. This model of respectability and mobility emphasises hard work and co-operation in order to attain honourable ends. There is little or no stress on education or ritual and ascetic purity. The Kshatriya is involved in local networks, and is not shy of using force to fight his way up and become an individual at the top of the local hierarchy.

In contrast to the Kshatriya concept, stands the Brahman concept, which is ritual-directed and purity-focused. This means an escape from interdependence, and the emphasis is on education. The Brahman is not merely a priest who, after all, belongs to the world of diverse interests. The ideal Brahman is the renouncer: both the Brahman and the renouncer refer to the same ideal.[6] Thus, the concept covers an exclusive

[3] B.S. Khare, *The Untouchable as Himself: ideology, identity, and pragmatism among the Lucknow Chamars* (Cambridge, 1984), p.25.

[4] M. Mines, *The Warrior Merchants: textiles, trade and territory in South India* (Cambridge, 1984).

[5] All three castes—Gudigara, Visvakarma and Devanga—have a rich oral tradition. The narratives of these traditions (re)formulate basic problems of the caste such as origin, status, difference between claimed and conceded status, settlement and migration, establishment of places of worship, the relationships between the caste's sub-castes, the origin of lineages among others.

[6] J.C. Heesterman, 'Is Indian wisdom at loggerheads with development? Is there an Indian wisdom?', in C.A.O. van Nieuwenhuyze (ed.), *Development Regardless of Culture*? (Leiden, 1984).

model of minimalised transactions. This model does not stress the advantages of mutual dependence, involvement in (local) networks and co-operation, but negates this and 'opts out'.

In projects where local carpenters are among the target groups, the government designed 'crafts complexes'[7] to replace the co-operative societies of an earlier date. In one place—Sagar (Shimoga District)—the crafts complex as well as the earlier co-operative society successfully involved artisans in the modern market economy. In another place, Mysore, both these institutions of governmental aid have failed. One would expect the rural carpenters of Sagar to be less sensitive than the urban carpenters of Mysore city to the larger scale of the money and market economy and to the formally anonymous relationships of governmental-aided institutions (because of their relative remoteness from cosmopolitan centres). The continuous success of the Sagar case and the continuous failure of the Mysore case indicate a structural rather than a functional problem.

In 1915, the Sagar carpenters of the Gudigara caste established a local co-operative society. In 1950 it merged with a similar co-operative of Gudigara carpenters from a neighbouring bloc.[8] This 'Mysore Gudigara Co-operative Society' has always been a successful form of co-operation and a platform for negotiations between artisans and government. In 1980 its function was replaced by the much larger crafts complex, which has been equally successful to the present day. In 1954, the Mysore carpenters of the Visvakarma caste founded the Visvakarma

[7] The Karnataka Industrial Sheds project covers two projects where the target population is dominated by Visvakarmas, namely, Mysore and Shivarapatna (Kolar District), and one project where the majority of beneficiaries are Gudigaras, for example in Sagar (Shimoga District). All projects consist of new residences with workspace for about 100 craftsmen and one common facility centre, and also a few infrastructural facilities related to management, supply and marketing. In Mysore and Sagar the target groups are engaged in woodwork (carpentry, joinery, carving) and sculpture in stone. In Shivarapatna, the target artisans are sculptors in stone and metal. Considering the target population in Mysore and Shivarapatna, a difference has been observed which gains importance with respect to the failure of the Mysore project and the relative success of the Shivarapatna project. In Mysore only 10 per cent of the targeted group are Kulachars, while the remaining 90 per cent are members of various castes (whether scheduled or not). In Shivarapatna the target group—all Sivachars—have accepted that section of the project which provides individual residences with work space, but have rejected the common facilities offered under the project.

[8] K. Balasubramanyam, *Census of India 1961*, vol.XI, *Mysore*, part XII-A. *Handicrafts Survey Monograph: using wood as the chief raw material* (New Delhi, 1965), 16.

Craft and Banking Co-operative Society.[9] This society had many ups and downs, but gradually became defunct. The new crafts complex, designed to take over the functions of the co-operative, as well as those of the local technical institute (the C.T.I.), was not able to involve the carpenters in the same way its equivalent has done in Sagar.

Although both cases deal with carpenters engaged in the same type of work, the two groups have responded differently to the possibilities offered by the modern state. In Sagar, the Gudigara carpenters consistently opted for a collective solution to their problem of dependence, while the Visvakarma carpenters opted out of co-operation, in order to cope with dependence on an individual basis. Could this difference, then, be traced back to a difference in the perception of the problem of dependence?

The Gudigara caste of carpenters explicitly claim Kshatriya status, while the Visvakarma carpenters claim, equally explicitly, to be Brahman. It may be objected that differences arise because the Gudigaras are a relatively small caste, whose members are all engaged in carpentry, whereas the larger Visvakarma caste consists of blacksmiths, carpenters, coppersmiths, sculptors and goldsmiths. The occupations are distributed over four sub-castes, and none of the sub-castes has a monopoly over one craft, except that sometimes the carpenters form a separate sub-caste. None of the Visvakarma craftsmen, whether on an occupational basis or on a sub-caste basis, has chosen a collective solution to their problems.

One would expect the larger urban groups of Mysore city under the development scheme to have an advantage over the rural small-scale Sagar craft complex. However, our expectation has been belied, and the latter has rather successfully expanded in the course of the programme. Neither a difference in the oft-mentioned hazards of bureaucracy, corruption and financial risk, nor a variation in geographical and social proximity between both urban and rural schemes on the one hand, and the project agencies on the other, has played a crucial role in the differential development process in both areas. General infrastructural and politico-economical constraints at the periphery seem to result in a difference in pace.

The Sagar carpenters of the Gudigara caste employ the Kshatriya model for mobility, emphasising hard work and co-operation in order to achieve higher purposes and, ultimately, to improve the well-being of their group. Here the artisans' notion of destiny can be made explicit in terms of their perceptions of their empirical situation, which fundamen-

[9] Ibid., pp.30 and 121.

tally is susceptible to involvement in 'outside' initiatives, aimed at the expansion of local networks and co-operation. Mysore artisans of the Visvakarma caste, by contrast, order their life and destiny according to the Brahman model, emphasising exclusiveness, ritual purity and education. Here the advantage of mutual dependence and co-operation is denied, and the pressure of the government programme results either in retirement into the exclusiveness of their own artisans' group, or even in a transfer to another craft through additional education. Obviously, the lack of affiliation between the Karnataka development scheme and the Mysore carpenter groups goes beyond personal communication, and is located in contrasting perceptions and ideas, impeding co-operation with the government or other artisans' groups.

At the same time, it has become evident that wherever participants' views correspond with those of development agents, such as in the craft complex scheme in Sagar, giving room for co-operation, competition and rivalry, the programme stands a fair prospect of success. Consequently, for integrated development, urban and rural, it is particularly necessary to examine and understand all aspects of the ways in which local perceptions are related to the objectives of the development programme. Intervention, taking local knowledge systems carefully into consideration, is a drastic re-orientation towards the 'soft factors' in the socio-economic development process, in particular towards the different culture-bound views and perceptions of the target population.

The foregoing example shows that to find the rationale behind the artisan's choice to accept or reject a government-aided development scheme, one must consider both his actual situation and his views. Another attempt to explore the extent to which the macro-structural possibilities have been utilised by the artisans and to what degree their decisions have been influenced by micro-level peculiarities, involved goldsmiths' units in two towns of Hassan District in Karnataka. All belong to the Visvakarma caste of artisans. To understand their views, it is necessary briefly to introduce their caste's cultural ideology.

Visvakarmas

The ideal. The Visvakarmas claim Brahmanical status. With the Visvakarma ideal on a par with a Brahmanical order, hence placed outside the world, the *material discourse* considers the crafts in isolation. To mark the crafts' *disconnection* from the world, the participants view the crafts' processes as transcendent acts and have 'ritualised' or 'universalised' the raw materials, tools, workshops, processes of manufacture and finished products. Where the ideal concept of the universe consists of a male and female constituent part, the flaw is here visible in the introduction of the concept of neutrality and the two types of craftsmen: the specialist and the generalist.

In the *social discourse* the ideal caste as a unitary concept leads to the dichotomy of caste in the world. The complementary opposition of two categories of caste in the world is expressed in both spatial and temporal terms. The existence of various and different Visvakarma sub-castes demonstrates a discontinuity between caste and sub-caste, and constitutes a violation of unity. In their oral tradition, the agent who causes the disintegration of the unity and the dispersion of the Visvakarmas (who also co-operate) is the goddess Kali. According to the artisans' ideal order, 'Visvakarma is Gayatri and Gayatri is Visvakarma'; and thus, on this level, the relationship between Visvakarma and *sakti* is explained. On the highest abstract level, there is identification of the Lord and sakti. Each of the five archetypical craftsmen has his own sakti: they are five different manifestations of the single Visvakarma. They were the five Visvakarmas of the Fort, who are all one (completeness). This ideal order is complete, cold and static: the static male part keeps the (potential) dynamic, female part in check.[10]

In the worldly order, the Visvakarmas have a relationship with the goddess through either sacrifice or worship. This situation, in which the unity of the Visvakarmas and the sakti is broken, came into existence through the manipulated interference in the ideal order by the dynamic, violent goddess, who is no longer Gayatri but Kali. Her two faces are clear now: she protects the Visvakarmas, but their unity is ended. Once in the world, a relationship with the goddess is imminent.

The actual situation. The Visvakarmas themselves are aware of the discrepancy between their claimed and conceded status. They explain this and the origin of their present, degenerated condition, in terms of a

[10] In the Fort story, all Visvakarmas, pure and united, lived in a solid, magnetic fort, which could not be destroyed by anything. Secretly at night they manufactured the goods for the five pillars on which society rests. During the day they delivered their products through the fort's only open gate. They were better than Brahmans, for the latter depended on them and they could manufacture without having to cope with violence and dependence. However, the fort was besieged through a conspiracy of the king and the Brahmans. They sent a female figure, resulting in a mixed marriage and the destruction of the fort through fire. As a result, the caste lost its unity, and endogamous sub-castes emerged in the world. For a complete analysis of this story, see J. Brouwer, *The Makers of the World. Caste, craft and mind of South Indian artisans* (Delhi, 1995).

dual classification of the caste. In each region, with its own history and environment, this dual classification has its own shape. The unity and essence of this classification has to be sought in its formal and functional aspects, namely to express a schism (such as the one between Smarta and Vaishnava Visvakarmas in northern Karnataka), a distinction between those who marry widows (elder brothers) and those who do not (younger brothers) in central Karnataka; or an anomaly, such as vegetarian 'children of Siva' versus non-vegetarian 'children of the goddess' in southern Karnataka.[11] .

However, the explanations in either doctrinal or generative terms, do not wholly suffice, for fieldwork revealed a more complicated pattern of four different Visvakarma sub-castes in each region.[12] In southern Karnataka—that is, the region between the Vedavati river in the north, the Tamil border in the south, the ghats in the west and the Telugu border in the east—there are the following Kannada-speaking Visvakarma sub-castes: (1) Sivachars, a vegetarian, multi-craft sub-caste, 'children of the *linga*' (Siva), comprising blacksmiths-cum-carpenters, metal-founders-cum-sculptors and goldsmiths; (2) Kulachars, a non-vegetarian, multi-craft sub-caste ('children of Kali'), comprising specialist blacksmiths, carpenters and goldsmiths; (3) Matachars, a non-vegetarian, single-craft sub-caste ('children of a widow'), of metal-founders;[13] and (4) Uttaradis, a vegetarian, single-craft sub-caste of

[11] Ibid.

[12] On the basis of the Visvakarma marriage and kinship relations, the plains of Karnataka can be divided into three regions. In the northern region the Visvakarmas are divided into Smartas and Vaishnavas. The Smartas are subdivided into Madipattar (only goldsmiths), Konnurpanta (blacksmiths, carpenters, braziers, sculptors, and goldsmiths), and Niligundapanta (blacksmiths, carpenters). Among the Vaishnavas there are blacksmiths, carpenters, and goldsmiths. In the central region, that is between the Tungabhadra and Vedavati rivers, there are Chikkamanes (blacksmiths-cum-carpenters, braziers, founder-cum-sculptors, and goldsmiths); Doddamanes (blacksmiths, carpenters, and goldsmiths); Bayala Akkasaliga (only goldsmiths); and Muddekammara (only blacksmiths). The picture of the caste's composition in the southern region follows in the main text.

[13] In narrative, speech, material culture and 'secret language', the relationships between the sub-castes are explained through divine, social and economic codes. The lay Visvakarma usually knows the code and material expression of a thought, while the scholar Visvakarma (in speech or writing) usually, but not always, knows the code and its interpretation. Relevant information of the social code relates to the aspect of non-vegetarianism. Although both Kulachars and Matachars are non-vegetarians, only the Kulachars sacrifice at temples and during the worship of tools in their workshops and consume the non-vegetarian offerings (*prasad*). In other words, the Kulachars engage themselves collec-

goldsmiths.[14]

Furthermore, there is a relevant traditional economic difference between these sub-castes. From what I have called the 'secret language' of the Visvakarmas I learnt that the Matachars and Kulachars are called '*nityakarma*' and '*ayakarma*' respectively. The former term means 'daily wager' and the latter term 'receiver of *aya*' or payment in kind (from the peasants). In other words, the Matachars were a labour force offering their services against cash payment, while the Kulachars were tied in with the local organisation of the landlords. Neither the Sivachars nor the Uttaradis were linked in that way, but operated in the money and market economy.

Goldsmiths of two towns

The local settings. Between July 1989 and July 1992 fieldwork was carried out among Visvakarma goldsmiths of Hassan District in the southern region of Karnataka. A detailed survey was conducted in Hassan, Arakalagud, Holenarsipur and Channarayapatna. The study focuses on the last two towns.

The oldest is Holenarsipur which was established in the twelfth century. It has a fort and two or more extensions to the north. It is located on one of the present main-road connections from Hassan to Mysore on the river Hemavathi. Channarayapatna, as we know it today, dates back to 1600 when the place (then called Kolatur and consisting only of an *agrahara*) was taken over by the chief of Holenarsipur. It is situated on the south-west bank of the fairly large tank which never dried up. The national highway No.48 passes through the town. Arkalagud, founded about 1560, is the most western town, situated on the present boundary of the cultivated plains and forested hills. If the number of known agricultural labourers is any indication, Arkalagud is the poorest town, and Channarayapatna the richest. Agriculture in Arkalagud mainly depends on rain; in Holenarsipur on river irrigation, and in Channarayapatna on tank irrigation. Of the four towns, Hassan is the best connected with

---

tively and in co-operation in feasts which the Matachars do not do.

[14] Elsewhere I have discussed the history of the Uttaradi sub-caste. The formation of this sub-caste over a period of about 300 years and its disappearance during the past 20 years (through merger with the Chikkamane sub-caste) shows that sub-caste is to be understood as a ongoing process. See J. Brouwer, 'The latecomers. A case study of a caste and sub-caste of goldsmiths in Karnataka, south India', in A.W. Van dan Hoek, D.H.A. Kolff and M.S. Oort (eds.), *Ritual, State and History in South Asia: studies in honour of J.C. Heesterman* (Leiden, 1992).

other major centres, as it is situated on a national highway and connected by rail with both Bangalore and Bombay. It has been the district's headquarters since 1886. In all aspects—agricultural, industrial, financial, economic, social, historical, and ecological—it is the most developed of the towns, followed by Channarayapatna, Holenarsipur, and Arkalagud.

The jewellery market in the towns, as elsewhere in Karnataka, is dominated by Komati Chettis of the Vaishya status, either Kannada or Telugu; by Marwadis of the Jain sect who usually speak Rajasthani; or by Marathi-speaking dealers. In Arkalagud one of the three dominant families is Vaishya, that is, of the trader's caste; in Holenarsipur the four major households are Vaishyas; and in Channarayapatna the dealers consist of two Vaishyas, one Jain and one Marathi.

It seems useful to make a distinction between manufacturers, manufacturer-shopkeepers, shopkeepers, shopkeeper-traders, and trader-dealers. The manufacturers are Visvakarmas of various sub-castes, and mostly have their own workshops (sometimes combined with a residence). Visvakarmas may also be manufacturer-shopkeepers, that is, those who not only run a workshop but also have a retailing unit. Very few among Visvakarmas are only shopkeepers, or have extended their involvement from manufacture into trading. No Visvakarma has been observed acting as trader-dealer. However, licensed and unlicensed pawnbrokers may be found among all the categories, except manufacturers. I shall return to the difference between workshop, shop and trade later, in the context of Visvakarmas who opt out of their craft. The following paragraphs will describe the situation of the goldsmiths of various Visvakarma sub-castes in Holenarsipur and Channarayaptna towns.

The situation of the goldsmiths in Holenarsipur. In 1992 the total number of Visvakarma households in Holenarsipur is found to be 72. They are distributed mainly over two Kannada sub-castes and a few others, as shown in Table 2. Among the Uttaradis 54.5 per cent are craftsmen (all goldsmiths), and 45.5 per cent non-craftsmen. These figures are different for the Kulachars; that is to say, 73.7 per cent are craftsmen (all goldsmiths) and 26.3 per cent are non-craftsmen. Thus, the majority of both the sub-castes are craftsmen, while more Uttaradis than Kulachars have opted out of the craft. A distinction was made also between four income groups (see Table 3). As a sub-caste the Uttaradis are richer than the Kulachars, and none of the Kulachars had entered the highest income group. Forty per cent of both the sub-castes appear as a middle-income group (B and C). Considering the income group in which those members of the two sub-castes appear who had opted out

Table 2. *The Visvakarma population of Holenarsipur by sub-caste*

Uttaradi	40	(54.5% goldsmiths)	Chikkamane	3
Kulachar	26	(73.7% goldsmiths)	Tamil	1
Matachar	1		Malayalam	1
Total				72

Table 3. *Stated income of goldsmiths of two sub-castes in Holenarsipur*

Income Group Sub-caste	A %	B %	C %	D %
Uttaradi	50	22.7	18.2	9.1
Kulachar	52.6	15.8	31.8	–

Key: Stated income per month: A = up to Rs.1,000; B = Rs.1,001 to 1,750; C = Rs.1,751 to 3,000; D = Rs.3,000 or more.

of their craft, those who have entered government service are doing better than those with an occupation in the private sector. All Uttaradis in government service appear in income groups B, C and D, while 85.7 per cent of the Kulachars appear only in the B and C group. Thus, the Uttaradis who have opted out of their craft are doing much better than their counterparts of the Kulachar sub-caste.

The data on stated expenditure of the members of the two sub-castes suggest that, in both the sub-castes, expenditure on the household remains the same irrespective of income group. But there is a significant difference in expenditure on education. The Uttaradis spend more on education than the Kulachars in all income groups. Income spent on big or small donations (mostly to the caste temple) is greater in the higher-income groups (C and D) of both the sub-castes, while the Kulachars of the lower-income groups (A and B) spend more on donations than similar groups among the Uttaradis. The Uttaradis spend more of their income on their craft irrespective of income, while among the Kulachars only those in the higher-income group do so. Irrespective of the level of education, the Kulachars invest more in property (buildings, agricultural land) than the Uttaradis. Notably, more educated Kulachar than Uttaradi non-craftsmen have invested in property. Thus, where stated income and expenditure are concerned, the two sub-castes show a significant difference. The Uttaradis spend their income mainly on their craft, on donations and on *education*, while the Kulachars spent their income mainly on their craft, on donations and on *property*.

The data on goldsmiths of Holenarsipur show that: (a) more Uttaradis than Kulachars have opted out of their craft; (b) non-craftsmen have a higher living standard among Uttaradis than among Kulachars; (c) Uttaradis spend more on education than the Kulachars regardless of income and other expenditure; (d) Kulachars spend more on property than the Uttaradis irrespective of income and other expenditure; and (e) expenditure on the household remains the same whatever the income in both sub-castes.

Table 4. *The Visvakarma population of Channarayapatna by sub-caste*

Uttaradi	13	(10 goldsmiths)	Telugu	16	(15 goldsmiths)
Kulachar	24	(all goldsmiths)	Tamil	5	
Sivachar	23	(all goldsmiths)	Marathi	1	
Matachar	3		Malayalam	1	
Chikkamane	6				
Doddamane	3		Total	95	

Table 5. *Stated income of goldsmiths of four sub-castes in Channarayapatna*

Income Group	A	B	C	D
Sub-caste	%	%	%	%
Uttaradi	12.5	37.5	37.5	12.5
Kulachar	25	25	37.5	12.5
Sivachar	18.6	14.3	28.6	28.6
Telugu	–	–	85.7	14.3

Key: Stated income per month: A = up to Rs.1,000; B = Rs.1,001 to 1,750; C = Rs.1,751 to 3,000; D = Rs.3,000 or more.

The goldsmiths in Channarayapatna. In 1992, the total number of Visvakarma households in Channarayapatna was 95, distributed mainly over three Kannada sub-castes, and also comprising a significant group of Telugu migrant goldsmiths (see Table 4). Among the Uttaradis, 75 per cent are craftsmen (all goldsmiths) and 25 per cent are non-craftsmen, while 12.5 per cent of the Telugus have opted out of their craft. All the other Visvakarmas of this town are goldsmiths. Thus, only among Uttaradis and Telugus do we find Visvakarmas who have opted out. Table 5 gives a picture of the stated income of the three major Kannada sub-castes of the Visvakarmas and that of the largest group of migrants (Telugu goldsmiths) .

As a sub-caste the Sivachars are the richest, followed by the Telugu goldsmiths, the Uttaradis, and lastly the Kulachars. Of the Uttaradis 75 per cent rank as middle-income (B and C); of the Kulachars 60 per cent; of the Sivachars 40 per cent; and of the Telugus 85 per cent. Considering the income group of those who have opted out of their craft (all Uttaradis), all have entered government service and joined higher-income groups B, C or D. Comparing the income groups of the craftsmen in the four sub-castes, we obtain the following: 83.3 per cent of the Telugus are in income groups C and D. In the same income group we find 54.1 per cent of the Sivachars, 50 per cent of the Kulachars, and 30 per cent of the Uttaradis. Apparently, the allochtonous Telugu goldsmiths do better than all other goldsmiths. Among the autochtonous goldsmiths, the Sivachars do better than the Kulachars; they in turn do better than the Uttaradis.

Let us now look at the data on stated expenditure by members of the four sub-castes. In the case of the Kulachars and Telugus, the expenditure on the household remains the same, irrespective of income group. But for both Uttaradis and Sivachars household expenditure is higher in the higher (C and D) than in the lower income groups. In both sub-castes the higher-income groups also spend more on education than the lower-income groups, while the Kulachars and Telugus spend the same amount on education, irrespective of income. The higher-income groups (C and D) among the Uttaradis and the Sivachars give more in donations than the lower-income groups of the same sub-castes. By contrast, the Kulachars devote the same amount to donations irrespective of income. The Telugus (all C or D) donate more than the Kulachars, but not more than the Uttaradis or Sivachars.

The four sub-castes differ from one another in spending on their craft. Such expenditure among the Uttaradis remains the same regardless of income; among the Sivachars and the Kulachars that of the higher-income groups (B, C and D) is greater, but the Kulachars belonging to B, C and D income groups spend a relatively higher percentage of their income than the Sivachars (85.7 per cent against 40 per cent). Over 50 per cent of the Telugus spend more on their craft. The Uttaradis own little property. The higher-educated Sivachars and Telugus own some (mostly buildings), but the Kulachars own more agricultural property than the members of the other sub-castes, again, irrespective of the income group to which they belong. Thus, where stated income and expenditure are concerned, the four sub-castes show the following differences: the Uttaradis invest more in their craft, in education and in donations; the Sivachars in their craft (extended into trade),[15] in education, in property and in donations; and the Kulachars and Telugus invest in their craft, in property and in donations.

Comparing the level of education and occupation reveals that among the Uttaradis, there are more who are highly-educated among non-craftsmen than among craftsmen. Thus, education is non-craft related among the Uttaradis. By contrast, all Sivachars are craftsmen, so that with them education can be said to be craft-related. The latter situation also prevails among the Kulachars, while in this respect the Telugus resemble the Uttaradis.

The foregoing data on goldsmiths of Channarayapatna show that; (a) only Uttaradis have opted out of their crafts; (b) although none of those who have opted out appear in the lowest income group A, they do not have a higher living standard than those who remain with their craft; (c) the Uttaradis and Sivachars spend more on education than the Kulachars and the Telugus; (d) education among the Uttaradis is non-craft-related, while that among the Sivachar is craft-related; (e) Kulachars spend more on property than the Uttaradis irrespective of income and other expenditure; (f) only more educated Sivachars and Telugus own some property; and (g) among Kulachars and Telugus the expenditure on the household remains the same irrespective of income; and (i) household expenditure is higher among the higher-income groups of Uttaradis and Sivachars.

Manufacturers, machines and migrants. In Arkalagud one Kulachar goldsmith opened a shop (jewellery mart) ten years ago. This Kulachar of a goldsmith family learnt his craft from his father and was educated up to the fifth standard. Once he took over from his father, he sold an inherited three acres of land and left for Bangalore. There he made a profit by dealing in jewels. After a few years he returned to Arkalagud and invested his profits in the jewellery mart he now owns. 'Everybody made fun of me, but began to take me seriously when my Vaishya competitor cut the tape to open my shop.'

In Holenarsipur, all Uttaradi goldsmiths claim to work independently; that is, they manufacture jewellery on order for private customers. However, through cross-interviews, I found that all of them supply ready-made articles to one or two of the Vaishyas. In turn, they also receive orders from them. A few Uttaradis have employed workers

[15] Only Sivachars have extended craft into trade, that is, either craft related business such as moneylending and pawnbroking, or a variety of other trades, such as retailing textiles or household utensils. However, no Visvakarma has entered the licensed gold trade, which is the preserve of the Jains and Chettis. But unlicensed gold trade goes on among people of diverse (caste) background.

who are either Uttaradis or Kulachars. No Uttaradi works for a Kulachar goldsmith, or for any other goldsmith for that matter. Two Uttaradi goldsmiths are well-off—one from his previous occupation as an agriculturist, and the other because of his skills. However, neither has a jewellery mart. The single Chikkamane household is interesting. One member of it had left a nearby village as a five-year old boy, to learn his craft from the skilled Uttaradi mentioned above. When old enough, he established his own workshop and later purchased property in the centre of the main bazaar almost opposite the Vaishyas' marts; his craftsmanship and managerial skills have caused jealousy among the Uttaradis. Both his children are engineering students, with no knowledge of their father's craft.

In Channarayapatna too, all Uttaradi goldsmiths claim to work independently. However, only one of them can be called independent. Most of them work for him or through him for one of the four non-Visvakarma dealers. No Uttaradi works for a Kulachar, Sivachar, Chikkamane, Telugu or Malayali goldsmith. The Sivachar goldsmiths only work for other Sivachars. In contrast to both the Uttaradis and the Sivachars, the Kulachars work for any other goldsmith on a daily wages or piece-work basis. They also work directly for the four dealers. All migrants who settled here during the past thirty years work for each other or for the dealers directly.

Among the Sivachars one goldsmith has installed several machines, such as mould-printers and thread-drawers, for hire by any other goldsmith. (No goldsmith in Arkalagud or Holenarsipur has such machines, and anyone wishing to use them has to go to either Hassan or Channarayapatna.) Two Sivachars have so-called jewellery marts in which they also maintain a workshop, where Kulachars are regularly employed. Only one of them also functions as a pawnbroker.

The Telugu goldsmiths arrived at Channarayapatna in two batches. The push-factor of their migration from Andhra Pradesh (then the territory of the Nizam), seems to have been the police action of 1948 which disrupted local Hindu and Muslim networks. From Andhra they first went to Coimbatore in Tamil Nadu, and in 1979 they settled in Channarayapatna. Some of them, however, had an uncle (father's brother) who had settled there in 1939. Gradually some other relatives followed, and the total number of Telugu goldsmith households is now sixteen. They claim that the Kannada goldsmiths of those days were less skilled than they were, so that they could improve their lot by getting many orders from the local dealers. Most of them own their houses and workshops, and one has installed modern goldsmiths' machinery (moulder-printer and thread-drawer), which again is for hire by any other goldsmith.

In sum, the Uttaradis all claim to work independently, but in fact they also work for the dealers; they only have their workshops, and have neither expanded their activities by setting up shops or entering trade, nor improved their workshops with modern fixed assets such as moulding and thread machines. However, if not fully independent, they work only for other Uttaradis. Those Sivachars too who are not fully independent work only for other goldsmiths of their own sub-caste. But, unlike the Uttaradis, they have both expanded their craft activities (in workshop, shops, and by means of trade) and made improvements (by adding modern machines). Moreover, their trade may be linked not only with their work as goldsmiths, but may also involve another trade, such as textiles. In contrast to the Uttaradis and Sivachars, the Kulachars admit to working for goldsmiths of any other sub-caste and to working directly for the dealers. Like the Sivachars they may start a shop, but they do not become traders, let alone diversify their activities. In Hassan, one Kulachar has started a machine hall where the machines are hired out on a piece-work basis regardless of sub-caste.

Workshop, shop and trade. In Holenarsipur, three goldsmiths have a comparable economic and educational status—two Uttaradis and one Kulachar. Both the Uttaradis have a sober life-style and have not set up a mart. By contrast, the Kulachar has made a beginning in establishing a mart and has an ostentatious life-style. In Channarayapatna, three goldsmiths have a comparable economic and educational status. Among them, the Uttaradi (said to be the richest Visvakarma of the town) maintains a simple workshop and a sober life-style. He has not opened a shop or mart and has not entered trade. The other two are Sivachars. One of them has begun an impressive textile trade adjacent to his small goldsmithy where a Kulachar goldsmith is employed. The other has opened a big 'jewellery mart' on the National Highway in a corner of which he maintains a small goldsmithy where two Kulachars are working. None of the Uttaradis is keen to get their children into the craft, and would prefer to invest in their education. Among the Kulachars the emphasis is on craft even when the children are educated to a higher level. Remarkably, none of the Uttaradis of these three towns nor those of Hassan has introduced modern goldsmith's machinery, although some of them could certainly afford to do so. In Hassan, one Kulachar—the cousin of the trader of Arkalagud—had opened such a machine hall. In Channarayapatna, a Sivachar (and a Telugu migrant) has introduced such machines.

In contrast to the Kulachars, the Uttaradis and Sivachars have a similar view on education. But where the Kulachars do not hesitate to work for any goldsmith or trader, the Uttaradis and Sivachars do. But the latter differ in their views on craft and trade. In contrast to the Sivachars, the Uttaradis do not extend their craft into trade, let alone trade in anything other than what the goldsmiths produce. Under the single umbrella of the Visvakarma ideology and apart from the individual variations, there thus seems to be a sub-caste-bound view on such matters as craft, trade and money.

Themes from the narratives of the three sub-castes

At this point it may be useful to have a brief look at some of the narratives in the oral tradition of the three sub-castes. The Uttaradi story of Lakshmi explains why they should not open shops. At the same time, it places their relationship with the goddess through their 'elder brother', that is, the Kulachars. The Lakshmi story was told when I asked the informants why they do not have shops (commonly called a jewellery mart). In this myth, the goddess Lakshmi went to four houses, one Uttaradi, one Vokkaliga, one Brahman, and one Vaishya. All four husbands were alone at home when the goddess called. The Uttaradi refused her entry, because he was alone and did not recognise her. The Brahman refused her, because she was not of his caste. The Vokkaliga said that she was a Visvakarma and asked her to go away. Finally, she came to a Vaishya whose wife had gone to the river to fetch water. He ushered her in, gave her a seat in the puja room, treated her well, and locked the house. When he went out to call his wife, he fell into the river and drowned. So Lakshmi had to stay in his house only.

The Lakshmi story presents the Uttaradi view on money. In their perception, money carries a value contrary to purity: Lakshmi, the goddess of wealth, is refused and the Uttaradis stress their purity by emphasising that they did and do not have wealth (money), and that they refused Lakshmi. The goddess comes between them and money and the market economy. For the Uttaradis money cannot be the means to prosperity and liberation. In contrast, the narrative of the Kulachar tradition places the Kulachars clearly within a local network. Not only in the stories, but even today, the Kulachars all over the southern region are the founders and chief sponsors of the Kali temples.[16]

[16] The Kali temples of southern Karnataka are invariably established by Kulachars. Older temples are run by temple committees in which the Kulachars dominate. Everywhere the Kulachars appear as the chief sponsors of these temples, while the priestly rights are with the Uttaradis.

Situations and views

Situation. First, I shall review the situation of the goldsmiths in the light of their conditions, environment and views. The goldsmiths of the Uttaradi sub-castes in all the towns considered spent significantly more of their income than goldsmiths of all other sub-castes, in their craft and on education, with the aim of opting out of the craft. Their investment in education is clearly directed towards getting non-craft employment, particularly in the public sector. By contrast, the Kulachar goldsmiths of the same towns invest their income not only in the craft, but significantly also in property, such as buildings and agricultural land.

These observations concerning Uttaradi and Kulachar goldsmiths are consistent in both Holenarsipur and Channarayapatna. Since the setting and economy of these two towns are different from one another, and the composition of their Visvakarma populations is different, we have to look for an explanation of the observed consistency not on the empirical level, but on the 'world-view' level.

The situation of the goldsmiths in Holenarsipur leads to the question of what would happen if both Uttaradis and Kulachars had a higher income. The answer can be found in Channarayapatna. The income of both groups of goldsmiths in Channarayapatna is higher than that of their counterparts in Holenarsipur. And in Channarayapatna we see that the Uttaradis spend the difference on education and the household—better food and clothes—while the Kulachars invest it in their craft.

It has been observed that the Uttaradis, if not independent, work only for other Uttaradis, while the Kulachars in the same condition work for any other goldsmith irrespective of sub-caste. As the Kulachars are poorer than the Uttaradis, they have no choice but to work for any goldsmith. However, the number of Uttaradis and Kulachars of Holenarsipur who appear in the lowest income group (A) is almost the same, that is, 50 per cent and 52.6 per cent respectively. Therefore, it seems likely that an explanation for this difference in choice of employers also has to be sought on the level of world-views. As a sub-caste the Uttaradis are vegetarians and not tied in with the organisation of the landlords. The Kulachars as a sub-caste are non-vegetarian and tied in with the local networks. The two sub-castes are thus differently enmeshed in the material and social order. In addition, their respective oral traditions offer different interpretations of the central Visvakarma ideal, so that the Uttaradis appear as an exclusive sub-caste having minimalised interactions and the Kulachar as an inclusive sub-caste with maximalised interactions. The Uttaradis stress the idea of autonomy through education and opting out of their craft. One might say, of course, at the cost of opting out. By contrast, the Kulachars strive after the central ideal in a different, more 'kingly' way by maintaining and expanding a relevant network, through investment in craft and property, particularly land.

The Uttaradis' and Kulachars' investment in their craft supports this explanation. When Uttaradis invest in their craft (irrespective of income), they do not change their workshops or open a jewellery mart. The Kulachars' investment in their craft is visible in their improving or augmenting their workshops, or even in opening jewellery marts. But the Kulachars stop short of becoming traders. A pattern of improvement or expansion of workshops and conspicuous consumption, on the part of the richer Kulachars, stands in sharp contrast to the sober lifestyle of the Uttaradis in all income groups.

In Channarayapatna both the Uttaradis and Sivachars spend more on education than the Kulachars. This is not surprising, for the Sivachars, like the Uttaradis, are exclusive sub-castes. Comparing the situation of the three autochtonous Kannada sub-castes, it may be concluded that the Uttaradis opt out of their craft, the Kulachars opt for jewellery marts, and the Sivachars open shops and extend generally into trade, including diversification.

The question arises why none of the Kulachars of Channarayapatna has abandoned his trade in comparison with the Kulachars of Holenarsipur. Taking note of the income and expenditure variables, it may be that the Kulachars stay in their craft as long as the local economy offers them prospects. It may also be argued that in Channarayapatna the opportunities to opt out have been reduced by the coming of migrants, for 12.5 per cent of the Telugu goldsmiths have abandoned their craft there. In other words, the Kulachars are sensitive to the environmental factor when it comes to a choice.

This brings us to the situation of Telugu goldsmiths. From the life-histories of the early settlers, we know that they had humble beginnings. We can only speculate about the rationale of their relative success. As migrants they are far less tied in with their own sub-caste than the autochtonous goldsmiths. This might have given them more working days and more customers, particularly in a period of rapid economic expansion. The environment worked to their advantage, but they have also recognised it!

Claims and praxis. The situation of the goldsmiths of the three Visvakarma sub-castes in the two towns may now be summarised. The Uttaradis (a) *claim* to be independent of the dealers; (b) if not independent, work only for other Uttaradis; (c) may have workshops but not shops; (d) have not improved their workshops by introducing machines; (e) give priority to spending on education; (f) direct their expenditure towards giving up their craft in favour of mainly public sector employment; and (g) maintain an inconspicuous, sober life-style. The Kulachars (a) admit freely to working directly for dealers; (b) if not independent, work for any other goldsmith, irrespective of sub-caste; (c) may have workshops and/or shops; (d) if possible improve their workshop by adding machines; (e) give priority to spending on property; (f) direct their expenditure towards their craft and immovable property; and (g) maintain a conspicuous, affluent life-style. The Sivachars (a) do not work directly for dealers; (b) if not independent, work only for other Sivachars; (c) may have workshops, shops and be engaged in trade; (d) if possible, do improve their workshop by adding machines; (e) give priority to spending on education; (f) direct their expenditure towards education with the aim of doing better in their craft and/or trade; and (g) maintain a conspicuous, affluent life-style.

Although many differences among the three sub-castes cannot be fully explained, they definitely show the differential use the goldsmiths have made of the macro-economic possibilities of the modern state. I discuss this below. The apparent lack of impact of the immediate environment on the goldsmiths' major decisions may be a result of their common view that the Visvakarmas are autonomous (complete and non-violent, as their cultural ideology has it) and hence like the Brahmans, in the sense that others depend on them.

As we have seen above, the central Visvakarma ideal is expressed by contrasting pairs in each region. Each region, and each sub-caste, provided a different context and the expressions of the ideal vary accordingly. However, the indigenous explanation consistently offers two models, which I have called *exclusive* (Brahman) and *inclusive* (Kshatriya) models, as well as two ways of expressing the ideal of autonomy (comprehensiveness of the sub-caste, or its separation). In the southern region, the exclusive model is evident in the case of the Uttaradis and the Sivachars, while its complementary opposed inclusive model may be seen among the Kulachars and Matachars.

The various narratives suggest first that the Uttaradis should not open shops, for the money and the market economy are perilous and lead to ill-gotten gain; secondly that the Kulachars are invariably enmeshed in local networks, not as yet operating on the market, and found or maintain temples; and thirdly that the Sivachars are already operating in the market and are either autonomous as sculptors or individual landlords at the top of the local hierarchy, or at least are not subordinated to anyone else.

It thus seems that in the Uttaradis' view the best way to prosperity and liberation is through minimalised transactions, which means an exclusiveness even at the cost of opting out of their craft. Their interpretation of the central Visvakarma ideal in the face of actual possibilities seems responsible for their decisions on investment and participation in society. The Kulachars' way is clearly that of a maximalisation of transactions, which means an inclusiveness even, I would almost say, at the cost of relative poverty. Their investment in property, their establishment of temples, their expansive approach to their craft operations, and their affluent life-style, betray a kingly model which stands in sharp contrast to the Brahmanical style of the Uttaradis.

Thus the case of the Uttaradis versus the Kulachars seems clear. The Uttaradis have translated the Visvakarma central ideal of Brahmanical involution, or concentration of all into one point, into investment in themselves (education), with the aim of replacing the inevitable connectiveness of their craft identification by means of opting out of the craft. Those who remain craftsmen and thus need others (the dealers, for example), deny such relations by making them incidental, so that they become valueless. The crux of the incidental transaction lies in its non-comprehensiveness.

In contrast to this Brahmanical line of the Uttaradis, we find the Kulachars involved in a pattern of social comprehensiveness and connections (working for all, owning property, establishing temples, tied in with local networks). Where the Uttaradis negate comprehensiveness or interconnections in order to escape and to reach autonomy, the Kulachars use comprehensiveness and connections by interposing themselves. They do not deny these relationships or make them incidental; they use them in a system of rivalry and co-operation as their means of individualisation in terms of the central Visvakarma ideal.

The Sivachars' decisions can be traced to a double-track: their operations as craftsmen and their investment in education correspond with the actions of the Uttaradis, which reflect their exclusive views. On the other hand, their decisions on improvement and the expansion of their craft and on life-style correspond to similar actions of the Kulachars. Here the inclusive model is visible.

Furthermore, each of the three sub-castes has a unique perception of their situation. The Kulachars who have opened shops, or well-to-do Kulachars (for example, a Kulachar sculptor in Mysore), claim Sivachar status.[17] The Sivachars' occupational expansion into trade and diversification of trade is not seen among the others, and seems a novel interpretation of inclusiveness. The Uttaradis' claim of not working for the dealers is a lie easily checked, and thus seen merely as a denial of relations. When the claims are checked, informants try to present any relationship as incidental—that is, not as a comprehensive connection. The crux of the incidental transaction lies in its non-comprehensiveness, hence an absence of value. The Uttaradis' position is here clearly in the Brahmanical line.

Decision-making between ideology and situation

Views on the crafts complexes. We have examined the views and situation of carpenters and goldsmiths in Karnataka. The case of the carpenters has been described with reference to a specific government scheme designed to improve the living standards and working conditions of the craftsmen. The case of the goldsmiths, by contrast, has been described from the perspective of general macro-structural possibilities.

On the level of macro-economical organisation, India's modern state offers a wide range of educational, occupational, financial and industrial strategies for various categories of small-scale entrepreneurs and artisans. Sometimes these are translated into specific schemes, such as the one called 'Crafts Complexes' under the Karnataka Industrial Sheds programme, which (as said) is a joint venture of the Karnataka and Dutch governments. The project consists of two distinct components, construction and service, while its ultimate objective is to improve the socio-economic situation of project beneficiaries, generating employment, improving product quality, and diversifying the product range. Its

[17] This case of a Visvakarma claiming the status of another sub-caste is not an isolated phenomenon. In the central region of Karnataka, the Muddekammara sub-caste's relationship with the soil has changed since the beginning of this century. About that time, the traditional mode of iron-mining gradually died out, and this opened up possibilities for them to claim a different status, in other words, that of the 'higher' Doddamane sub-caste, a claim which was sanctioned by the guru of the still-higher Chikkamane sub-caste about thirty years ago. It is during the past thirty years that the Chikkamane began to intermarry with the Uttaradis, so that we now see an almost complete merger of the two sub-castes. This and the fact that well-to-do Kulachars claim a different, that is, higher status, for they operate on the money and market economy, may eventually lead to an entirely different set of sub-castes under the Visvakarma umbrella in Karnataka. However, where the impact of the socio-economic environment has changed the elementary pattern, the categorical duality of the caste has not been affected.

target sectors are, among others, handloom weaving, handicrafts, leather work and tanning.

About six years after implementation, one project document discussed various constraints. The most important deficiencies in the artisans' productive activities pertain to communication and interaction with the market place, government support services, and lending channels. Hence the document pleads for high levels of participation by the particular target groups in decision-making and implementation. Such constraints at the level of the beneficiaries are complemented by those at the level of the modern state, such as heavy overheads, long bureaucratic lines of command, complicated management, high transportation costs, difficulties in adapting production to changes in market demand, and unfamiliarity with legal language and with dealing with the authorities. One recommendation is that efforts should be concentrated on the improvement in the capacity of (groups of) households to increase their independence. Overall, the call is for more participation by the beneficiaries themselves.

Where the documents speak about caste-bound versus cosmopolitan occupations, they ignore the cultural dimension of development. In the foregoing case, the views and actions on the macro-structural level do not always correspond to those on the micro-structural level of target groups. More precisely, where success is reported, the views and actions of target groups and agents of change seem to have a high degree of correspondence. Thus, at least in the case of failures, it seems urgent to consider the beneficiaries' views in detail.

Project documents purport to show that the macro-economic organisation works with anonymous *categories* such as 'artisans', 'project beneficiaries' and 'sectors'. Its organisation is an artificial, mechanical construction, the method of which is formal. It functions on the basis of a meticulously-defined system of impersonal laws, rules, regulations and power. Being part of the modern state, its *separate* units are *indirectly* united in a political system. In sum, the macro-structural organisation of the modern state breaks up society into basic, independent units according to grids, which in turn reinforce such units as caste, language, religion, private and public domains, region, village, and town. Projects work with precisely-defined categories which appear as independent, complete units, such as the individual (artisan), the party, the city, the district, and the nation. The system's unity consists in fairly indirect relationships between the units. And finally, people are impersonalised and viewed as mutually interchangeable individuals. Thus, on this level the key concepts are individual, separation, and categories. The modern state's immutable grid of categories does not fully correspond with the diversity of the exclusive and inclusive models operating in society. The two models themselves are the results of a prismatically broken-down central ideal of civilisation. In contrast to the prism of civilisation, the modern society works with a uniform, unified grid.

Goldsmiths under the magnifying glass

Beside specific schemes for selected target groups, the modern state offers general possibilities on the macro-structural level. In contrast to the old dispensation, education is now open to all; there are innumerable new occupations and professions while old ones are no longer group- (caste-)bound. There are various general financial and industrial strategies. The differential reaction to these possibilities has been studied for small-town goldsmith units of production in Karnataka. The study shows that not all decisions taken by the goldsmiths in the field of economic, educational and occupational possibilities can be explained by environmental or socio-economic factors.

Considering the goldsmiths' investment patterns, and the group (sub-caste) to which they belong, it has to be concluded that their investment in education differs from sub-caste to sub-caste irrespective of income and wealth. In other words, the macro-structural category 'goldsmiths' has no substance in actuality. On the other hand, the micro-level group—the sub-caste—in which the goldsmiths have been born, or rather the particular views cultivated and transferred from generation to generation by this group, offers a micro-level structure that provides the basis and direction of economic investment.

The status claimed by the Visvakarma breaks into three categories. (1) The Uttaradis do better in the modern state than the Sivachar and Kulachar, for the Uttaradis' interpretation of the Brahmanical model comes nearest to the original model and its correspondence with that of the modern state. (2) In the case of the Kulachars, the central model breaks down into a Kshatriya realisation which seems to contradict it. Between the general Visvakarma ideal and the actual situation of being tied in with local networks, the Kulachars have their own Brahmanical line, but it is oriented in two different directions. They interpose themselves between two orientations which consolidate one arbitrary process, and the question remains of how the two positions are connected. (3) The Sivachars are relatively successful as contemporary craftsmen whose perceptions are rooted in a double structure in which the Brahmanical and Kshatriya models are played against each other to arrive at a mixture which shows a broad base of correspondence with the concepts of the modern state. On the whole, however, the Visvakarmas who claim Brahman status reject the modern state's concepts of craft and craft-production. They continue as craftsmen in their own style, more or less successfully. Some of them (and this depends on sub-caste views) are successful in the modern state itself, but then they are no longer craftsmen. By contrast, the Gudigaras, who claim Kshatriya status and who are nearly all craftsmen, have been successful craftsmen both in terms of their tradition and in those of the modern state. The inclusive Kshatriya models of Gudigaras and Kulachars are thus essentially different. The two groups were also differentially embedded in their respective environments.

There remain, of course, further questions to be studied. One of the main tests will be the case of the Devanga weavers. Like the Visvakarmas, they claim Brahman status, but their craft is significantly different. They depend on agricultural produce to manufacture products that, unlike the Visvakarma products, are intended to be temporary and to be distributed. How do the Devangas react to specific government schemes for weavers? How did they make use of the macro-economic possibilities of the modern state?

Some project documents predict that, once they have acquired a sufficient degree of self-confidence and self-reliance, the goldsmiths may be able to begin functioning as free mini-entrepreneurs, taking full advantage of market forces or macro-structural possibilities. It seems doubtful. For the writing is already on the wall: those who have opted out of their craft, irrespective of sub-caste, unite themselves in education societies whose interest is opposed to those who have decided to stay in and who have formed craft-based associations often along sub-caste lines. The old dual classification of the caste, I surmise, reappears here in a new form.[18]

[18] Other works used but not cited are: M. Arokiaswamy, *The Kongu Country* (Madras, 1956); J. Bouwer, 'An exploration of the traditional division between the sexes in South Indian crafts', in A.M. Singh and A. Kelles-Viitanan (eds.), *Invisible Hands: women in home-based production* (New Delhi, 1987) and 'Material expression of thought. Aspects of iron-smiths in South India', *Techniques et Culture*, 15 (January-June 1990), pp.105-30; J.C. Heesterman, *The Inner Conflict of Tradition. Essays in Indian ritual, kingship and society* (London, 1985); Nita Kumar, *The Artisans of Benares. Popular culture and identity, 1880-1986* (Princeton, 1988); and W. Zevenbergen, *The Karnataka Industrial Sheds Project: an appraisal* (The Hague, 1986).

Chapter 12

ORDER, ORDER... AGRO-COMMERCIAL MICRO-STRUCTURES AND THE STATE: THE EXPERIENCE OF REGULATION[1]

Barbara Harriss-White

Introduction

It might be considered strange for regulation to be set centrestage here, in the context of a discourse of economic reform dominated by the justification for, and the sequencing of, the deregulation and privatisation of markets. Yet regulation is a major link between the micro-structure of commercial firms, the meso-structure of 'markets' and the macro-structure of the state. Our discussion is divided into five sections. The first explains the necessity for regulation and outlines the concerns and analytical framework of regulation theory. The second examines distinctive features of agro-commercial micro-structure in rural markets in South Asia. The third considers state regulatory practice in such markets. The fourth presents empirical evidence of market regulation in the face of weak state regulatory capacity and considers the implications of such 'auto-regulation' for regulatory policy, which enables a rethinking of the letter and spirit of regulation in the final section.

'The ideology of *laissez-faire* has continued to influence economic analysis and the discussion of economic policy even though the modern political economy has little resemblance to an idealised unregulated competitive world', wrote Shaffer, of industrialised markets in the USA.[2] This observation is even more apposite for the under-developed, agrarian, political economies which form the empirical background here.

[1] I am very grateful to Michael Anderson who discussed this paper at the SOAS conference for his insights; also to participants at Oxford University's Modern Indian History Seminar, to the Food Studies Group's Workshop on Public and Private Sectors in Reformed Food Markets, to the Institute of Development Studies, Sussex, Seminar on Socio-Economics and to the Institute of Social, Studies, The Hague Seminar on Rural Development.

[2] J.D. Shaffer, 'Observations on the political economics of regulation', *American Journal of Agricultural Economics*, 11, 2 (1979).

I. *Why regulate?*

Orthodox economics has no theory of markets and the institution is hardly defined. Attempts to define the market in universalistic terms result in: 'the simultaneous transaction of valued goods and services between two parties (who are) capable of accepting or rejecting the values offered...and (who are) uncoerced...and capable of communication and delivery'.[3] The efficiency and equity outcomes of such a market are axiomatic. Two theoretical attributes of such 'markets' have been subject to widespread criticism for at least three decades. Markets in economic theory have been treated analytically as though (1) they had no institutional structures and conventions (2) they were either allocatively efficient and perfectly competitive, or, if not, could still be evaluated meaningfully in terms of deviations from an operationalised norm of perfect competition. Of late, it has become accepted that if perfect competition were actually to exist, this state would not be viable for long. This is for reasons of uncertainty and bounded rationality. To enter a market (and invest) requires a reliable incentive or an expectation. This in turn involves 'knowledge of a limited competitive supply from other firms'.[4] But the concept of perfect competition places no limit on the crowd of firms expected to compete. Of perfect competition, Joan Robinson commented: 'It is an extravagant abstraction relying excessively on the shaky foundations of timeless equilibrium'. In fact, markets have two economic roles, one allocative, in which efficiency considerations have been paramount and the other extractive, in which analytical attention is focused upon exchange relations and the class, regional and intersectoral terms of trade. In practice, each real market comprises a unique meta-institution replete with constituent institutions with enabling, disciplining and constraining functions and interacting with yet others (legal, social and political; in production, consumption and the state). By means of these constituent institutions, information on production, prices, buying and selling is organised and transfers of ownership effected. We are concerned here with the disciplining aspect of market exchange which affects both the allocative and the redistributive roles of markets.

The regulatory system. In order for markets to develop, certain institutional attributes are necessary: rights to exchange property by

[3]r A. Pandya and N. Dholakia, 'An institutional theory of exchange in marketing', *European Journal of Marketing Research*, 26, 12 (1992), p.24.

[4] G.M. Hodgson, *Economics and Institutions: a manifesto for a modern institutional economics* (London, 1988), pp.188-9.

means of trade, conventions about the scope of economic behaviour, about legitimate tender, mechanisms to establish prices, rules about liability and penalties for delinquency. These are the elements of a regulatory system. In historical fact much variation in the detail of these regulatory parameters has been observed. And not all aspects of these parameters have been equally rigorously or compatibly defined at any given moment. Such conditions of regulatory friction have given rise (along with many other factors) to the institutional evolution of market systems.

But there are also other sources of 'friction' in markets. The 'firms' comprising markets are also structured so as to safeguard themselves from threats to the regulatory system. The principal threats have been theorised by Williamson.[5] The first is the vulnerability that results from the specificity of investments or assets used for marketing. If these are not easily redeployable (and if these act as 'entry barriers') then flexible, competitive behaviour will be constrained by the stabilising behaviour needed to protect such assets. The second is risk and uncertainty. If information can never be complete, and the planning of transactions can never be comprehensive, then contractual regularities may limit the disadvantageous effects of partial ignorance of contingencies. Third there is opportunistic behaviour, what Williamson calls 'self-interest seeking with guile'.[6] Opportunism sets boundaries to the advantages agreed at the outset in a marketing contract and may even lead to their reversal. (This is not to argue that all marketing is opportunistic. Any reading of the literature dealing with trust in markets would put paid to such a generalisation at the outset.[7]

Transaction costs economics therefore takes what neoclassical economics evaluates as 'imperfections' (and what the peasant economy and some of the institutionalist literature identify as aspects of power relations) explaining these institutional features instead as efficient means of safeguarding transactions—as institutions of regulation. This should not be taken to imply that logics other than that of transactions costs are unnecessary to explain existing institutional forms taken by markets. This also does not mean that transactions costs approaches are superior. For a start transactions costs are residuals and/or unmeasurable. Then the risk is run of evaluating institutions as 'efficient given their environment' which is both tautological and ideological. The point

[5] O.E. Willamson, *Economic Oganisations: firms, markets and policy control* (Brighton, 1986), pp.174-91.

[6] Ibid.

[7] D. Gambetta (ed.), *Trust* (London, 1988).

is that transactions costs economics has usefully drawn attention both to the *modus operandi* and to the costs of regulation at the level of the firm.

Markets provide means of allocating resources but markets *sensu stricto* are rather less common than the literature would suggest.[8] There are other objectives to markets than efficiency (co-ordination, and the reduction of uncertainty for example) and there are means other than markets of allocating and distributing resources (hierarchies, political preferences and networks of repeated or relational contracts for example) and regulation is necessary for these to operate too.

The regulation of markets however is commonly understood as being a proper activity for the state. Markets involve legal contracts (or behaviour 'as if' there were legal contracts) and protection through the due process of state law. The legal institutions are important adjuncts to the institution of the market itself.[9] 'The law and economics are inseparable'.[10] Definitions of this sort of state regulation range from: 'the full pattern of government intervention in markets' (including taxes and subsidies); and 'the administrative rules whereby government defines the scope of economic transactions in markets'; to 'the range of statutory and common law defining the operation of a private market economy'.[11] State law is thus not only defined by market economy but is definitive of it. It is in this last sense that regulation will be used here. In practice, the analysis of regulation in underdeveloped agrarian economies has normally been restricted to the theory and practice of state trading. We will hardly consider state trading at all here (but see section 4) so as to emphasise the important point that regulation is a necessary response not only to market failure but to market success.

The evaluation of state regulation has yet to be methodologically systematised but Shaffer has provided a useful taxonomy consisting of the following elements: (1) the enforcement mechanism; (2) the object of regulation (structure, conduct and/or performance); (3) the degree of specification; (4) the type of regulatory incentives; (5) contingencies for implementation; and (6) jurisdiction at the boundaries.[12] This framework permits the examination of the interaction between regulatory

[8] Hodgson, *Economics and Institutions*, p.177.

[9] Ibid., p.176.

[10] J.D. Shaffer, 'Observations'.

[11] D.C. Dahl, 'Regulation analysis as a research focus in agricultural economics', *American Journal of Agricultural Economics*, 11, 1(1979). See also A. Joseph, 'Transactions Governance in Marketing Structures: a study in the Mid-Western hog markets', unpublished PhD thesis, University of Illinois, 1984.

[12] Shaffer, 'Observations on the political economics of regulation', p.725.

practice and civil society in a way which does not exogenise one of the elements or reduce one element (forces implementing the market regulation acts, for example) to the other (forces regulating markets).

II. *Existing markets: agro-commercial micro-structures in India*

'The study of markets cannot be scientific unless carried out in the context of their relevant institutions' wrote David Penny in 1985.[13] It is therefore necessary to determine the relevant institutions of markets. This is a far from finished project. Institutions can be understood in three ways. The first is 'sociological' and set out by Veblen in the early part of the century: any behavioural regularity is an institution, for example the way in which biological sex becomes social gender. The second is micro-economic where institutions are understood in special case terms as organisational and contractual forms. The third which fits here consists of the definition of rights and of economic behaviour and institutions of market regulation. A review of old and new institutional economics and of the political economy literature on markets reveals no consensus on the answer to Penny's implied question. In industrial organisation, commodity systems and transactions costs theories, the key relevant institution is the firm, its international relations and, in the latter school, its internal relations. In political economy relevant institutions comprise class, gender, technology and the state. Sociologists add religion and ethnicity. Here we have economic data to examine the organisation and internal relations of firms; their 'international relations'—contracts and activities and the competitive structure in which they are found; and sociological data to examine, perhaps contentiously, the class structure of markets, the way they are gendered and the role played by caste in structuring market exchange. The content of our sketch of key relevant institutions in Indian agricultural markets has also necessarily to be derived somewhat arbitrarily (and therefore in a way which is falsifiable) from empirical conditions. Rural agricultural markets in India are diverse and complex.

Organisation: firms and their internal relations. In Indian agricultural markets the firm of the institutionalists appears a stylised thing (with owner, manager and workers) to which the firms observed do not closely conform. There are two common organisational forms, though in identifying these patterns we ignore the intense and characteristic diversity. On the one hand there is self-employment under conditions of petty trade with unspecialised individuals as units, optionally with

[13] D. Penny, *Starvation* (Canberra, 1985).

family members. Such firms are not to be supposed to be operating to a capitalist logic due *inter alia* to the absence of wage payments. Astronomically high rates of return to capital may coexist with a lack of capacity to save or invest: wages, profit and dividend are completely indistinguishable, since these families are operating close to subsistence levels and since many such 'firms' are not free agents but tied through credit to others. On the other hand, there are private firms with combinations of joint family firms (property rights to which may be but vaguely specified within a kin group) and partnerships. Family labour may be deployed, but there is also a specialised division of labour with a variety of contracts: ranging from the salariat down to daily casual or piece rate labour or bonded gang labour. Co-existing with these common organisational forms will also be co-operatives with or without wage labour and parastatal institutions whose organisational forms range in turn all the way from a dependent department of government to autonomous joint public-private sector enterprises.

Necessary to the market but organised (and sometimes unionised) quite independently are the gangs of casual labour undertaking some casual work in mills, but in the main used for loading and unloading, and for pulling 'hand' transport.

Organisation—the 'international relations' of firms—contracts. Contracts and price formation may simultaneously take the forms of barter; spot deals; various forms of advanced and futures contracts commonly interlocked with pre-harvest credit for production or consumption; attached, relational, bilateral contracts within caste or kin groups and internalised transfers within vertically integrated firms. These contracts are more often than not verbal. Power is expressed via their type and via delays in payment and degrees of compensation for delayed payment. The object of a contract will be 'a commodity' (see below) but it may also be what Jagannathan has termed 'intangibles' such as loyalty and zeal, an unspecified commitment of labour or the tying of all sales including those in excess of debt repayments.[14]

Activities. The activity vector of traders comprises at the least the following: produce, buy, sell, broker, transport, store, process, finance production and finance trade. Although the possible combinations of such activities numbers 9! (over 130,000), the very robustness of our classifications of traders, as well as that of vernacular classifications, suggests strong clustering and patterning of activities. Disaggregated combinatorial analyses of the activity mixes of private trading firms

[14] V. Jagannathan, *Informal Markets in Developing Countries* (New York, 1988).

reveal on the contrary that both complexity and uniqueness are normal.[15] 'Markets' do not reduce to firms with comparable activities or objectives. So the trading firms comprising markets cannot be compared. Furthermore, the portfolios of trading firms are usually diversified so as both to reduce risk and to enable resources to be extracted out of agriculture through a variety of means simultaneously: through interlocked contracts involving money (or pre-harvest kind) and post-harvest kind repayment, through triadic contractual relations; untied purchase and sale; rent; profits on agro-processing; storage and transport, and lastly through economic crime (fraud on weights and measures, arbitrary deductions, delayed and uncompensated payment, collusive price fixing, misinformation, and so on).[16]

Class and exchange relations. Attempts have been made to model complexity in the terms and conditions of exchange associated with the different kinds of agrarian (and latterly market) structures characteristic of regions of the subcontinent.[17] Bharadwaj has a four class model for a differentiated agrarian structure under owner occupancy where 'market' prices are determined by the terms and conditions of sales of the rich peasantry (which is the only class of truly subsistence producers), where the middle peasantry are price takers and quantity adjusters, and where small and landless peasantry exchange under conditions of lack of choice which she terms 'compulsive involvement in markets'.[18] Sarkar has pursued the implications of Bharadwaj's differentiated exchange for 'multistratum price formation'. Marketing systems comprise multiple layers of transfers of property rights but no attempt has been made yet to model differentiated exchange at other than the point of first transaction.

Bhaduri has refined a model inspired by archetypical conditions in north east India.[19] Normal and forced commerce are distinguished

[15] B. Harriss, 'Markets, society and the state: problems of marketing under conditions of smallholder agriculture in West Bengal' (report to WIDER, Helsinki; Oxford, 1991), and 'Masters of the countryside: a regional political economy of agricultural marketing in an advanced district of south India' (report to ODA, London; Oxford, 1991).

[16] S. Janakarajan, 'Aspects of Market Interrelationships in a Changing Agrarian Economy: a case study from Tamil Nadu', unpublished PhD thesis, University of Madras, 1986.

[17] K. Bharadwaj, *Production Conditions in Indian Agriculture* (London, 1974).

[18] S. Sarkar, 'A theory of multistratum competition for primary agricultural markets of less-developed countries', Proceedings of the International Society of Agricultural Economics Conference (Athens, 1989).

[19] A. Bhaduri, *The Economics of Backward Agriculture* (London, 1983).

under conditions of intense agrarian inequality, share tenure, and the coalescence in a small class of land-renting, moneylending and trade. Marketing by sharecroppers here is lubricated by pre-harvest consumption credit in kind. Marketing is theorised as a superficial economic behaviour masking the deeper compulsion of debt.

The institutional attributes of commodity markets in these models are never specified. In Bharadwaj's formulation, 'the market' is implicitly competitive and in Bhaduri's it has to consist of strategic alliance of landlords, moneylenders and traders (whose internal conflicts of interest are then explored—and have subsequently been criticised).

Competition and class structure within marketing systems. Market structures depend to a certain extent on geographical scale. Villages may have competitive or entirely monopsonistic market structures.[20] Common in the subcontinent are (1) a high degree of economic and locational concentration and specialisation in trade, and (2) the polarised coexistence of oligopolies (competitive or collusive) with petty trade. Gini co-efficients of concentration of output in the Karnatakan paddy trade are 0.62.[21] Nearby in Coimbatore District those for the concentration of control over output varied from 0.63 for groundnut marketing, 0.68 in the paddy-rice trade, through 0.71 for maize and tobacco, to 0.89 in cotton wholesaling.[22] These are higher than summary indices for the concentration of control over land.

Close links between agricultural marketing and grain production in the investment portfolios of mercantile firms take two forms. One is where production is controlled directly through the ownership of land. Though subject to variation, the average landholding of traders is greater than that of the population as a whole and also likelier to be rented out. The other linkage leads to an indirect control over production through pre-harvest credit tied to post-harvest sales. This latter can involve several tiers of more or less tied trading intermediaries who lend onwards at higher (implicit) interest until the post-harvest supplies of financially dependent producers are captured.

The small class of large, accumulating merchants creates diversified investment portfolios. Investment gravitates towards urban property, fi-

[20] W.K. Olsen, 'Distress Sales and Exchange Relations in a Rural Area of Rayalaseema, Andhra Pradesh', unpublished PhD thesis, University of Oxford, 1991.

[21] A. Maheshwari, *Market Regulation of Foodgrains and Oilseeds Markets in Karnataka—a case for the informal sector* (Cochin, 1992).

[22] B. Harriss, 'Agricultural markets and intersectoral resource transfers: cases from the semi-arid tropics of southeast India', in *ICRISAT: Agricultural Markets in the Semi-arid Tropics* (Hyderabad, 1985), p.292.

nance, agro-processing and other kinds of commerce, and rarely to land or to industry proper. Resources then get switched in contingent fashion between the components of such portfolios rendering the calculation of returns to marketing *per se* ever more stylised.

The numerical crowding of intermediaries in markets dominated numerically by petty trade may not signify competition because of (1) incomplete information and (2) tied contracts on money and commodity markets, also for storage, transport and processing binding petty traders to large-scale ones in a parody of vertical integration. Whether such tying of trade is to 'contain opportunism', or whether it arises for want of alternatives in structures of unequal economic or social power, the key feature is the association of crowding with fragmented and differentiated trade. Agricultural seasonality is reflected in the seasonality of market structures and flows.

Gender and caste. Marketing is deeply gendered. Women tend to appear at three points. Women from pauperised households are confined to petty and often seasonal operation, to subsistence orientation and to the 'simple reproduction' of their firms, to particular positions and activities within the system (especially to processing and retailing). Women tend to have local territorial linkages, to trade at small rural periodic market-place sites and to be unlicensed. Secondly, women are used for the caste-based reproduction and expansion of larger firms by means of their dowries on marriage, and through their unwaged provision of that part of the wage to labour in trading firms which takes the form of prepared food. Female casual wage workers form the large substratum of non-unionised and deliberately casualised labour in milling and pre-milling processing.

Although marketing is carried out by a much wider swathe of castes than those with specific trades as a traditional occupation, caste still prevents a large proportion of the population from engaging in wholesale trade. The relatively secure fraction of the wage labour force in mercantile firms tends to be drawn from the same swathe. Few tasks are reserved for traditional castes: accountancy, for example. But untouchable men are barred from even the most menial permanent jobs for example, the nightwatch and the sweeping of trading premises and in the casual labour process where untouchability is not always a complete barrier, untouchable female casual labour is usually forbidden to touch and thereby 'pollute' grain on the drying floor after it has been milled. The substitutability of labour within firms is much constrained by gender and caste.

Though under-theorised, these markets are quite clearly radically different both from the abstractions of existing comparative advantage theory which underpin deregulationist advocacy,[23] or from the stylised institutions the rationales for choices between which are the objectives of theories in institutional economics. Indian markets are best assumed to have an ambivalent developmental role, one requiring specification. Yet, though complex, Indian markets are not disordered, χηαοσ systems. We shall now attempt to show why.

III. *State regulation in South India: policy is what it does*

Market regulation comprises a remarkable set of legislative acts deliberately designed for two purposes: (1) for the first transaction 'as a protective shield to farmers against traders' rapacity',[24] and (2) for the standardisation of management of local market-places which were either privately owned ('zamindari markets') or owned by municipalities or by traders' guilds.[25]

> The Markets Acts provide for fair trading practices, the prohibition of unwanted and excessive deductions on account of market charges and legitimate services rendered by various functionaries. For enforcing discipline among the trading community and other functionaries, the licensing system has been introduced. Further the management of markets is entrusted to market committees which are corporate bodies and on which are represented all the interests viz traders, producers, co-operatives and local bodies. The producers thus have a voice in the management of the markets. The Acts also provide for necessary facilities such as dissemination of market information, temporary storage facilities and various other amenities such as rest houses, drinking water arrangements, lighting etc.[26]

The objective of market regulation is to eliminate unnecessary activities in commerce that are not productive, explicitly :

> to organise the system of sale and purchase in a manner that the grower secures a fair price to protect him from exploitation by middlemen.... The legislation provides a machinery for regulating trade by providing a common place where

[23] A. Gulati, 'Indian agriculture: an agenda for reform', paper presented at conference on India, 'The Future of Economic Reform', Queen Elizabeth House, Oxford, 1993. See also K. Parikh, 'Economic reforms and food and agricultural policy', paper presented at the same conference.

[24] E.A.J. Johnson, *The Organization of Space in Developing Countries* (Harvard, 1970), p.103; Government of India (hereafter GoI), *Interim Report of the High Power Committee on Agricultural Marketing* (Faridabad, 1992).

[25] GoI, *Conference of Ministers on Agricultural Marketing, Resume of Discussions, November 1938* (New Delhi, 1939).

[26] Ministry of Food, Agriculture, Community Development and Co-operation (hereafter MoF), *Regulated Markets in India* (Nagpur, 1968).

facilities would be furnished by way of space, building and storage accommodation, where correct weighment would be ensured and all weights and scales periodically checked...where disputes are settled and where quality standards would be fixed.[27]

In providing physical infrastructure and in standardising the democratic and participative organisation of transactions in rural agricultural markets, the state would enforce the structural and behavioural conditions for an effectively competitive, allocatively efficient, free, private market at minimal cost to itself. That the rule of these laws requires alterations to the structure and performance of marketing systems every bit as radical, if not more so, than land reform legislation requires of the structure of land tenure has gone entirely unappreciated by all save, arguably, certain private traders.

Given these objectives and their obvious relevance to contemporary conditions of economic reform, it is important to examine the historical record. It is possible to do this here for three south Indian states: Andhra Pradesh, Karnataka and Tamil Nadu.

Historical experience. State market regulation has been based on the model colonial acts for cash crops of the 1897 Berar Cotton and Grain Markets Law and the more celebrated 1927 Bombay Cotton Markets Act. The diffusion of market regulation law was slow and serendipitous, however. The inter-war provincial Act comprised little adapted transfers to India of similar but untried legislation from Britain introduced under the aegis of the Viceroy Lord Linlithgow who had himself been instrumental in setting up enquiries into, and legislation for, colourful and squalid, locally managed, English and Welsh agricultural markets in the early twenties.[28] This legislation was imposed on domestic trading systems reeling from the impact of the Depression, not poised to challenge its formulation. It then filtered through provincial and princely state legislatures, was modified and reformulated to suit local conditions and has been implemented in widely differing agrarian structures, agrarian exchange regimes, pre-existing local institutions of market control and taxation and state forms. There are 'wide variations in the provisions and coverage' of all 23 Regulated Markets Acts currently in existence in the states.[29]

[27] Government of Andhra Pradesh (hereafter GoAP), *Statistics of Agricultural Marketing 1967-73* (Hyderabad, 1970), pp.v-vi.

[28] Ministry of Agriculture and Fisheries (UK) (hereafter MAFUK), 'Report on Markets and Fairs in England and Wales', 1 (London, 1927): GoI, *Conference of Ministers.*

[29] GoI, *Interim Report.*

It is useful to start with the colonial law as it developed in what is now Andhra Pradesh where there were big contrasts between the inland Telengana region ruled by the Nizam of Hyderabad on the one hand and coastal Andhra which was part of the Madras Presidency on the other. As early as 1930, Hyderabad passed the 'Hyderabad Agricultural Markets Act'. The Act was unique in a number of respects other than its date. It was a comprehensive piece of law covering all crops and standardising exchange through transactions (legitimating property transfers through licensing and open auction, and banning transactions in other than the regulated market yard), and through contractual stipulations (prompt payment, standardised weights and measures, fees and charges). Physical infrastructure was provided for under the law. Democratically elected committees with four year terms were to represent the interests of producers, traders, commission agents, co-operatives, market labourers and local government officials (though the latter were seconded). The committees had responsibility to organise the markets, provide market information, present accounts and settle disputes. In return for this, they could raise revenue on the market in legally defined ways, through licensing traders and other functionaries and through the levying of *ad valorem* taxes for services rendered. Uniquely early in Indian history, a separate department of government was created to implement the law.[30]

By contrast, coastal Andhra came within the jurisdiction of the Madras Commercial Crops Act of 1933 as did modern Tamil Nadu proper. This act was more modest than it suggests, covering only three commercial crops, using the large and economically arbitrary revenue district as notional catchment areas for local regulated markets. No attempt was made to standardise transactions or fees. Committees were to be larger (up to 18 members) with more direct nomination by the state than was the case under the Hyderabad Act. The government directorate required to operationalise the act was to be financed out of general state funds rather than by revenues from committees. Much to the province's credit, the act was published in the local language, which meant that educated farmers could actually read it, if they ever happened upon a copy.

With the formation of the new state of Andhra Pradesh in 1956 the Hyderabad model was adopted for the complete territory, with a new department, funded from revenue remitted from markets, up and running by 1966.

Karnataka meanwhile had been partitioned in the colonial period

[30] GoAP, *Annual Report of the Marketing Department* (Hyderabad, 1977).

under five different marketing laws. It was not until 1968 that these five different laws were replaced by one act similar in scope to that of Hyderabad and covering all crops. Karnataka, where the state was prescient in its anticipation of enforcement difficulties, established not only a department to implement the act but also a Board, early on, charged with promotional activity involving information and market extension, planning and investment.[31]

Thereafter all three states embarked upon paths of expansion, amendment and reformulation to their agricultural marketing law. Karnataka expanded the spatial and crop coverage of its department and Board in a methodical way aided by IDA funding. Now one third of Karnataka's 1352 agricultural markets are regulated under the act.[32] Andhra Pradesh went in for two crash programmes, the first in 1969 to bring regulated markets in what had been Madras up to the same spatial density as those of what had been Hyderabad. The second crash programme in 1976 involved the legal recognition of a rash of sub-yards, without which the parastatal Cotton Corporation of India (which had been punished for scandals involving collusion between its officials and private commission agents) would have been legally unentitled to carry out its own purchase operations. The latter were frequently at prices above those of local markets because of delays in price decisions.[33] By 1992 74 per cent of Andhra Pradesh's 1,107 markets were included in the scope of the act.[34]

Tamil Nadu's experience illustrates themes common elsewhere in the country: (1) a diffident diffusion from regions of export agriculture and cash crops to regions of subsistence agriculture, staple grains and latterly even to cover the sale of livestock. This diffusion is accompanied by a rhetorical reinterpretation of the late nineteenth-century objectives of regulation which stressed efficiency in the supply response of export crops for the colonial metropolis towards populist expressions of social justice to small farmers. By 1992, however, only 28 per cent of Tamil Nadu's 977 market-places were regulated. (2) A Marketing Board needed to be established and, pressurised to accelerate the implementation of the act by parastatal institutions (particularly the Cotton Corporation of India for the reasons explained above) partho-

[31] Institute of Development Studies (hereafter IDS), *Agricultural Produce Markets: pre-investment surveys*, 1 (Mysore, 1976).

[32] GoI, *Interim Report*, Annexure IV.

[33] Committee on Public Undertakings (hereafter CoPU), *Cotton Corporation of India*, 68th Report (New Delhi, 1975).

[34] GoI, *Interim Report*, Annexure IV.

generated a Department of Agricultural Marketing, on a par with that of Agriculture proper, to negotiate authoritatively with other parastatal institutions. (3) During the Emergency, problems with tighter levels of regulatory enforcement led to the supercession (apparently indefinitely) of the elected Committees by Special Officers appointed by the State (but not to be assumed politically neutral).[35] (4) More recent developments have included (a) increased financial assistance from Central Government, at its least controversial where confined to the new market-places envisaged on irrigation projects and to other project-based components of the so-called anti-poverty policy and (b) applications for international funding for market development.

Latterly the hands have turned an incoherent full circle in the course of the political ferment surrounding the deregulation of industry and international trade and the RM Act in Tamil Nadu and elsewhere is justified as necessary to standardise the quality of the new generation of export crops. At the same time the law is clearly stated to have as objective 'the regulation of trade practices' so as to 'eliminate' the 'malady...of superfluous intermediaries'.[36]

Impact. The impact of this process of state regulation can be assessed in various ways. First let us consider its fiscal impact. Justified as a cost minimising form of intervention, market regulation is actually a revenue-raising activity. With respect to government revenue, the intervention has had unambiguous success wherever it has been implemented. The fee levied for services rendered (frequently, though not universally, one per cent, *ad valorem*) has taxed trade, even in common instances where actual revenue raised is far less than potential due to evasion. In Tamil Nadu, for instance, by 1980 less than 3 per cent of production had fees levied upon it.[37] Yet expenditure, even including development investment, was exceeded by revenue so that 25 to 35 per cent of fees raised have regularly entered the general revenues of the states concerned [38]

Secondly we can examine the impact of regulation on market behaviour. We proceed with the greatest caution because of black box problems in theorising the attribution of the result. Using price data for the first decade of consolidation under the modern acts we can test two hypotheses: (1) that market regulation should improve the integration

[35] GoI, *Interim Report.*

[36] Ibid., p.1.2; 2.1; Annexure IV.

[37] B. Harriss, *State and Market* (New Delhi, 1984), p.79.

[38] B. Harriss, 'Coarse grains, coarse interventions', *UNRISD*, Food Systems and Society Working Paper (Geneva, 1980), pp.32-8.

of prices, leading to a reduced price dispersion over space at any given time, and (2) that crops most extensively regulated should be better integrated than those which have been comparatively neglected. Data from Season and Crop Reports have been used to calculate co-efficients of price variation (Tables 1 and 2) for four basic staples for two states: Karnataka over the period when 35 per cent of its regulated markets were brought under the legislation, and Andhra Pradesh for the period when 77 per cent of its markets were regulated.

Neither hypothesis derives much encouragement from the results. There is no uniform trend towards a secular decline in the coefficients

Table 1. *Coefficients of price variation, Karnataka State*

Crop:	Paddy	Kharif sorghum	Rabi sorghum	Toovar dal
No. of markets	18	13	9	13
1968-69	6.5	8.0	4.5	25
1969-70	12.7	10.0	7.3	16
1970-71	8.6	14.2	6.1	13.6
1971-72	6.8	11.7	7.4	17.1
1972-73	14.8	11.5	11.4	15.4
1973-74	14.4	14.8	12.7	17.8
1974-75	12.1	19.3	6.9	n.d.
Average 1968-75	7.8	9.9	7.0	8.7

Source: Annual Season and Crop Report Data (unpublished).

Table 2: *Coefficients of price variation, Andhra Pradesh*

Crop	Rice	Sorghum	Millet	Toovar dal
No. of markets	21	18	17	17
1965-66	13.7	8.5	11.7	15.9
1966-67	14.7	8.8	12.5	14.3
1967-68	15.1	5.4	10.2	13.3
1969-70	10.9	10.7	10.0	10.2
1970-71	9.2	13.9	10.4	5.9
1971-72	7.6	12.5	8.8	7.3
1972-73	9.3	10.9	9.1	8.2
1973-74	10.9	11.1	10.7	4.4
1974-75	12.2	10.1	n.d.	4.9
1975-76	12.2	11.6	11.1	17.4
Average 1965-76	6.6	10.7	5.4	9.7

Source: Annual Season and Crop Report Data.

of variation which summarise price dispersions. Regulated markets at best slowed the rate of deterioration in the pricing integration of themost important grains (rice and sorghum). And the lower co-efficients for paddy are not statistically significant. A similar inconclusive result was obtained for 24 crops over a longer time period for Tamil Nadu State.[39] Regulated markets did not prove capable of controlling the behaviour of wholesale prices in the direction of greater spatial stability over a crucial period of implementation of the law.

With regard to exchange relations, the reservations expressed in the light of the older act and in advance of the new one by the Law Commission of Andhra Pradesh have enduring relevance:

> The legislation does not enable the cultivator to free himself from the clutches of the commission agent.... His indebtedness to the commission agent...is not regulated. The object with which the legislation for regulating markets was initiated is not only to see that the producer gets a fair price for his produce but also to free him if possible from the clutches of the middlemen. As there is no provision in the proposed bill or in similar legislation in other States to solve this difficulty, we must observe that this is a serious lacuna which requires to be remedied. The (debt) problem is not easy to tackle.... [40]

Indeed it has proved most recalcitrant.[41]

The third way in which state regulation may be evaluated is via the study of its practice. What follows here is based on a comprehensive review of experience over the first 15 years of the modern legislation.[42] While it summarises the insertion of a new layer of law into the local political economy, it cannot pretend, however, to be rigorous.

Despite rapid commercialisation and the consolidation of interregional trade in the contemporary period, regulated markets were and are not created from a *tabula rasa* but represent state bureaucratic modifications to the pre-colonial marketing systems regulated in a more piecemeal manner previously. As the modern legislation was and is formulated to curb the monopoly power of merchants, we may expect this intervention to be an arena of conflict between those curbing and those curbed. The outcome of such conflict will depend upon the power of those competing groups and might involve a protracted series of conflicts.

The first feature to note is that local regulations are allowed to vary.

[39] Harriss, *State and Market*, pp.45-53.

[40] Law Commission of Andhra Pradesh, 'Laws Relating to the Establishment and Regulation of Markets for the Sale and Purchase of Agricultural Produce, etc.', 14th Report (Hyderabad, 1962), pp.16-17.

[41] Harriss, *State and Market*, pp.72-116.

[42] Harriss, 'Coarse grains', pp.21-32.

Licence fees vary by a factor of 20 between districts. Spatial regulation and crop notification do not proceed hand-in-hand. There is a continual tension in the law itself between the desire to maximise revenue (making for large-sized notified regions surrounding market towns) on the one hand and the reduction of state supervision costs requiring *inter alia* the minimisation of the franchise area for the committee on the other. In practice the administrative boundaries of the notified area around a town proved easy for producers and traders to ignore.[43]

Next, implementation has been a lengthy process. By the late 1970s, of the 115 regulated markets created in Andhra Pradesh, one third had no functioning committees and in Karnataka of the 97 regulated, 54 had no physical yards. The creation of regulated market places inevitably meant the development of sites peripheral to established market places, often at some distance from them. There have been long delays in granting this land, and resistance not only by traders (even when sweetened by subsidised loans to them for the construction of private storage capacity) but also by local government.[44]

Most transactions in regulated markets take place in dispersed fashion in villages and in the historical bazaar site with its economies of agglomeration. These locations increased the supervision costs, and reduced the revenue, for the State. They also increased the scope for opportunistic behaviour by private traders. Powerful collective action on the part of traders resisting the peripheral resiting of their shops and stores has led to the courts and the police implementing judgments against the RM law but in favour of merchants.[45]

Other regulations may be ignored by merchants and prove unenforceable by the state. Commonly reported examples which disadvantage producers include (1) price and contract formation by mutual agreement rather than by open auction; (2) use of specialised commission agents; (3) refusal to follow practices of 'scientific grading' (which means that goods are graded, sometimes very finely, using customary systems of quality assessment); (4) refusal to use independent weighers and measurers (such labour being attached to firms rather than 'properly' to market places) and refusal to allow the independent audit of weights and measures; (5) uncompensated delays in payment to

[43] F. Pesneaud, V.T. Raju and M. von Oppen, 'Markets for *ICRISAT* crops in Andhra Pradesh' (Hyderabad, 1976).

[44] GoAP, *Report on the Marketing of Howar in Andhra Pradesh* (Hyderabad, 1977); IDS, *Agricultural Produce Markets* (1978); Govt. of Tamil Nadu, *Report of the Department of Agricultural Marketing* (Madras, 1979).

[45] Harriss, *State and Market*, pp.108-12.

producers; and (6) arbitrary deductions and unauthorised charges exacted from producers. The committees have been emasculated by means of (1) evasion of licence fees, (2) evasion or overdue payment of *ad valorem* fees, and (3) refusal to submit both accounts and stock statements for scrutiny by the Committee.

During the Emergency in Tamil Nadu, merchants were still able to resist the centralisation of transactions, and sufficiently empowered to have 'over-scrupulous' market officials transferred elsewhere. Merchants have moulded their operations pre-emptively, switching from permanent licensing (with voting rights on committees but with the obligation to show accounts) to casual licensing (with neither these rights nor, more to the point, these obligations). In Karnataka over the first decade of modern regulation there was a 40 per cent decline in the numbers of traders regulated. In Andhra Pradesh it was 47 per cent!

The RM committees have been in conflict with other state institutions which have hitherto benefited from the revenue now raised under RM legislation. This is commonly the case with Municipal Administrations (such as the procrastinating Leigh Bazaar in Salem city of Tamil Nadu) which lose revenue either directly (from the loss of markets they administered) or indirectly, (from the loss of markets whose management was auctioned off annually). Leigh Bazaar responded to market regulation by ignoring it and continuing to levy its usual taxes upon traders. The imposition elsewhere of RM fees on top of those levied by Commercial Taxes, Public Works, or Revenue Departments may actually repel and decentralise trade—the opposite of what is intended under the law.[46] Contradictory custom and/or law may mess up these juridical interfaces. Recent research in Karnataka shows that market regulation has led to an enforcement of neither a reduction nor a standardisation of fees. Furthermore, small and middle peasants pay higher ad valorem commissions than do large-scale sellers, on a scale not justified by legitimately higher transactions costs on smaller consignments.[47]

Market administration has failed to reconcile unequal and conflicting interests within consensual committees and has under represented intended beneficiaries. Many farmer members have been merchants in thin disguise. The committee is the site of additional conflicts between the private and public interests represented by individual members and, further, between the committee in all its private and public complexity

[46] Harriss, 'Coarse grains', pp.21-32.

[47] IDS, *The Changing Structure of Agricultural Marketing and Credit in Karnataka* (Mysore, 1988).

as a political arena and the Marketing Department supplying to this committee its executives and secretaries, officials with grand titles but low pay and status:

It has been found that in every market the Committee Officials (from the Marketing Dept) owe their allegiance to the individual members of the market committee rather than to the market as an institution. The Secretary or Assistant Secretary has little or no powers to take action against the Committee staff for their misdemeanours, omissions or commissions. Further the Committee officials are not transferable from one market to another market with the result that they have become ingrained in their offices and are immune to corrective action contemplated by the Secretary or Assistant Secretary. The powers of the Secretary in the matter of disciplinary action…are recommendatory and the Committee may reject it. This has resulted in laxity of discipline among the officials who may act hand in glove with the committee members... The Secretary can either get himself involved with them or is transferred on the recommendation of the Committee…. This has spelt indiscipline, insubordination and in many cases sheltering of undesirable elements.[48]

On the other hand in the higher echelons of the Marketing Department, in Headquarters and at the Divisional and Market Secretary level, the reverse may occur and dysfunctionally high levels of turnover have been reported.[49] Those with greatest discretionary power are forever panting up the steepest part of the learning curve. There is also a tension between the standardisation of conduct and the improvement of enforcement capacity (which require national coverage), the maximsation of local revenues (which needs large sized administrative territories) and the reduction of supervision costs by the state (which needs small spatial territories).

A recent in-house review of the impact of the laws alleged that 'farmers' power' had increased, but could point only to the rationalisation of charges as supporting evidence. Otherwise, on site sales and open auction were 'exceptional' and 'rare'. Brokers persisted. Traders avoided the yards. And, significantly, manual labour was paid by traders and not by the market committee. Information was ineffective.[50] Of the estimated 37,000 primary market-places, only 6,640 had been regulated by 1992, even in this highly contested fashion.[51]

This brief review of the experience of modern regulation shows that

[48] IDS, *Agricultural Produce Markets* (1976), pp.72 and 116.

[49] GoAP, *Annual Report of the Marketing Department* (1976), pp.48-54; Government of Karnataka (hereafter GoK), *Annual Report of the Marketing Department*, 1973-74 (Bangalore, 1974).

[50] GoI, *Proceedings of the Second National Workshop on Regulation and Management of Agricultural Produce Markets* (Rajasthan, 1984), pp.22-5.

[51] GoI, *Interim Report*, p.25.

the state administration of rural and agricultural markets has been riven with unanticipated outcomes and is an arena of conflict which has been enhanced rather than mitigated by regulatory law. The acts are partial, completely ignoring and not regulating agro-commercial credit, (often borrowed in turn from 'formal' financial institutions) which ties contracts to locations, times and certain forms. Contracts actually made inside RM yards are therefore often not the first transaction for which the acts are intended to be relevant. RMs also do not cover the conditions of first transaction to state marketing institutions which are assumed, by default, to take exemplary forms! Incentives for compliance are weakly developed, and take a negative rather than positive form. The acts regulate conduct in an extremely highly specified way, presumed to have a direct impact on performance or structure. Actually the capacity of the committee to alter market structures and behaviour in the direction of 'efficiency' is very weak. Faced with a parastatal such as the Food Corporation of India or a large private commercial or industrial house such as the cotton mill at Gokak in Karnataka, the committee has no power at all. The *modus operandi* of market management enshrined in the act has placed participation higher than authoritative control. Local control was also given greater weight than was the need for interregional standardisation in contractual conditions. Committees have been vulnerable to opportunistic co-option by private interests (as with the case of commission agents in Tirupur, Tamil Nadu) or to supercession by more or less specialised and competent officials. In its most primitive form, regulated market legislation is merely a tax on private trade. Committee officials paid through general revenue or through fees revenues have responsibilities out of all commensurability to their power. The regulated market supervisor is like a medieval knight in armour equipped with an unwieldy lance and ordered to catch a cloud of nimble butterflies. Later developments have responded to the recognition of unanticipated outcomes (particularly to the administrative disadvantages of decentralisation) but without tackling the need for countervailing power. They have tended to increase the centralisation of management and investment decisions without increasing the capacity of this bureaucratic system for vigilance and enforcement.

It seems that the law works effectively only (1) when there are already fairly competitive and efficient markets in existence; (2) when agro-industrial produce requiring transformation is sold to absentee traders under unindebted conditions as is often the case with groundnuts and other oil seeds for reasons of risk and lack of information; (3) in the rare conditions when cash repayment is accepted by commodity traders in return for pre-harvest loans in cash or kind, which has been encountered for instance in the advanced district of Coimbatore;[52] and (4) where state trading institutions use the RM sites to procure at prices equal to or above open market ones (as appears to be the case for wheat and rice in Punjab).[53]

Market exchange, embedded in production relations, resists regulation based on a technocracy. State regulated markets are therefore not sufficient for competitive and efficient private trade, but are they necessary? Market failure has provided reasons for forms of state regulation but state failure does not imply lack of market regulation. If state regulatory legislation is not necessary, then what is necessary in order for private trade to be regulated in India under conditions of highly unequal assets distributions in production and trade? It is to such questions that we can now turn.

IV. *State regulation by other means and endogenous regulation: the case of West Bengal in North India*

The markets of West Bengal are useful for our argument because, although the state has tardily enacted a Regulated Markets Act, these are operating according neither to the letter nor the spirit of the law. Only 13 per cent of market-places came under the Act, compared with 44 per cent in the states of Karnataka Andhra Pradesh and Tamil Nadu examined earlier. Fees are levied not *ad valorem* but *ad hoc.* Price information is sometimes collected but rarely published. There are no elections to governing committees, no inspections of weights and measures, no competitive bidding and open auction, no regulated payments to seller by traders and no dispute resolution by RM Committees. Central government financial assistance for market-place infrastructure in West Bengal (at Rs.88 lakhs in 1992) is under one third of that disbursed on average to the three southern states.[54]

Under conditions such as these, why do agricultural markets not descend into states of chaos? There are three kinds of reasons for market order (which is certainly not to argue that West Bengal's agricultural markets epitomise orderliness). We will examine each in turn with respect to three staple commodities: potato, rice and oil from field

[52] Harriss, 'Masters of the countryside'.

[53] D.S. Sidhu, 'Some aspects of agricultural marketing and pricing policies in India', Presidential Address, *Indian Joural of Agricultural Economics*, XLV, 4 (1990), pp.443-7.

[54] GoI, *Interim Report*, Annexures IV and VI.

experience in 1990 in Burdwan district.[55]

The state regulatory agenda. Though the regulated markets acts do not operate, agricultural wholesale markets in West Bengal are quite extensively regulated in terms of a large mass of procedure and law, some with long histories, which covers not only the first transaction but also the post-harvest system of multiple product forms and transfers of property rights.

With respect to potatoes, regulation focuses on the key technology of cold storage at which point control over potatoes (if not ownership of them) is at its most concentrated. The West Bengal Cold Storage (Licensing and Regulation) Act and Rules enacted in 1966-67 stipulate regulation by licensing, technical standards, limits to the reservation of cold-store space by various categories of landowners. Rents are fixed by law, as is the timing of the cold storage season. There are limits on the transfer of ownership rights from producers to cold-store owners, and on the latters' finance of producers. There are official restrictions on store owners' trading on their own account. Potato wholesalers are regulated through licensing.

Oil and rice mills are regulated through licensing and security deposits, through the specification of technical standards and through storage restrictions. Both oil and rice trading are subject to inspection by the Commercial Taxes Department. Rice milling is heavily circumscribed by law. Under the Rice Control and Levy Order of 1960, a prescribed proportion of traded rice (currently 50 per cent) has to be sold to a state trading corporation at administered prices always below those of the open market. Paddy agents are regulated by licence and are attached to specific rice mills. Rice wholesalers are regulated by licence and have protected access to the unprocured output of rice mills. Rice retailers are regulated, under the Food Control Order of 1967, by licence and by restrictions on volumes of operation and storage quantities. Small-scale husking mills, operating on a custom basis and rarely on own account are regulated by licence conditional upon technology and power supply.

We see that the mass of laws and enforcement mechanisms involve a number of different government departments (Revenue, Co-operation, Agriculture, Social Welfare and Local Government).

The allocative practice of state regulation. Let us first consider the legally regulated sub-system. With respect to the regulation of potato marketing, certain aspects of the regulatory canon are performed. Dates of closing and opening of cold-stores are observed and checked, as are

[55] Harriss, 'Markets, society and the state'.

inventory, temperatures and the conditions of the potatoes. Other aspects are creatively interpreted 'beyond the point of recognition'.[56] State administered cold-store rents evolve into a fluctuating market. State-administered labour laws fixing minimum wages can be flouted using non-local labour on contract. Official rules about the allocation of cold-store space to various categories of farmers, traders and owners, change regularly. These undergo further transformation through the development of active markets in space and through the neglect of the rules stipulating minimum consignments. Two regulatory loopholes enable cold-stores owners to trade. First, though cold-store owners are constrained on own account trading, other members of joint families are not. The bond recording the type and quantity of potatoes stored is transferable and farmers are allowed to sell while potatoes are in store. Bank credit is also allowed on stored potatoes using receipts as collateral. Transfer of ownership to cold-stores owners financed by formal sector credit is therefore common practice. Second, cold-stores owners are legally required to remove rotting potatoes within 48 hours of notification to owners, and their sales are subsequently to be remitted. Rotting is widely alleged to be maximised at times of maximum intra-seasonal prices. Remittances are lagged and often at current prices if lower than those at which potatoes were actually sold.

Until the last decade rice mills have operated under a state protected monopoly in order for the state to externalise and to offload onto the private sector the transactions costs involved in bulking marketed surplus to supply the state trading system. It has therefore been necessary and possible to inflate residual open market prices by sums compensating the mills for their actual losses on rice sold to the state. Recent competition from an exploding sub-system of petty trade, exempt from procurement because unlicensed and illegal, has meant that this hoist has been constrained. The state trading agency has made an appropriate response but one not allowed in law. Proportional levies to state trading institutions have been comminuted to a fixed quota negotiated idiosyncratically with each mill on the basis of a verbal contract. In this way supervision costs and transactions costs to both private millers and the regulating state have been reduced. But this arrangement intensifies the incentive for rice mills to purchase stock immediately post-harvest at the lowest prices so as to minimise the uncompensated losses on procurement. Other state-imposed quantitative and time-based restrictions on stock holding are now widely flouted, and without penalty.

[56] S. Kaviraj, 'On state, society and discourse in India', *Bulletin of the Institute of Development Studies*, 21, 3, pp.10-15.

The legal monopoly of paddy traders and their stipulated attachment to specific named mills have both broken down, although the law has not been changed to reflect this. Paddy agents have accumulated sufficient capital to trade on their own account. Rice mills can no longer enforce attachment. A certain pre-emptive structuring can be observed. The existence of movement restrictions and of commercial taxes checkposts on district borders prevents paddy trade across those borders where more is forfeited in bribes than is gained from interregional price differences, which in practice are serious performance distortions.[57] This mostly effective, regulatory barrier encourages the local transformation of paddy into rice. It is thus not only the response of petty-scale accumulation resulting from the Left Front government's tenurial reforms and from technical change in production that leads to the mass entry into markets of petty traders. It is also in response to (1) the state-protected wide distributive margins formerly maintained by the large-scale licensed sub-system of rice marketing and processing, and (2) state-administered constraints on regional trade flows provoked by the system of taxation that petty-scale commercial activity has caused to proliferate over the last decade.

This sub-system is illegal. Small-scale rice processors are unlicensed, and rent licensed and unlicensed husking mills in order to process the paddy they have parboiled and dried using domestic labour. There are two consequences to this illegality. One is that the sub-system is turned over to the coercive wing of the state, thereby perpetuating an institutionalised bribery and harassment. The other is that the sub-system is ineligible for state subsidised credit which turns it over to 'informal' credit markets often operating under monopoly conditions (and not seasonally either) at interest exceeding 10 per cent per month.

Much the same relations characterise petty rice traders (who may actually wholesale, retail or act as commission agents). In one rice market, only one wholesale licence had been issued. Groups of traders formed around licences which rotated among members as necessary for confronting forces of vigilance.

Power supply to husking mills is regulated by enforcing a minimum spacing of two kilometres. This penalty to late entrants is evaded by the use of diesel engines as prime movers and by the poaching of electricity supplied for a less stringently regulated purpose (for example, flour or spice milling). Husking mill licences are also conditional upon the

[57] T. Palaskas and B. Harriss, 'Testing market integration: a new methodology and an institutional application with reference to domestic commodity markets in India', *Journal of Development Studies*, 30, 1 (1993).

adoption of the sheller technology inappropriate for local factor endowments and for the material culture of rice.[58] With the legally enforceable technology comes a scale of operation requiring a wage labour force. Thus the law would, intentionally or otherwise, be a mechanism whereby the micro-structures of markets would be transformed in the direction of a capitalist labour process. The use of sheller technology for husking mills is unenforceable. The illegal nature of the huller technology and of petty commodity social relations, which are 'cost effective' given the 'factor endowment', stem from a tension in regulation between the local state and central governments. While agriculture is a state responsibility, post-harvest processing is labelled as 'food', the administration of which is a central government responsibility.

The local state government has responded to this impossible regulatory situation by the expedient of turning a blind eye, refusing to attempt to levy commercial taxes on the operations of huller mills, for instance. Yet this has, as with the other unregulated elements in the markets for rice, resulted in institutionalised bribery and harassment.

Oil mills are quite regularly scrutinised by the state because of the private incentive to adulterate. The Food Department checks inventory and controls supplies of substitutes to mustard—the preferred oil. Oil millers themselves have an interest in informing the Health Department if they find adulterated supplies in local markets. This they do. There is a High Court Order requiring the technological upgrading of their mills. This they do not do.

State regulation by means other than the Regulated Markets Acts fails systematically to regulate private trade in this region of India. The practice of marketing is radically different from that regulated by law. The law as written is interpreted idiosyncratically by local administrations in series of rules and regulations which may not be binding in law. Law may be ignored. It may be flouted or reinterpreted by powerful trading elites and used in oppressive forms on weaker traders. The practice of marketing is capable of being moulded to some extent and sometimes pre-emptively by these *ad hoc* rules (and by threats of sanction), but frequently flouts even these. As Fitzpatrick observes in a deconstruction of legal plurality and underdevelopment; while state law is the object of capture, 'even when it appears that state law is operating in a straightforward way, it can be the case that it is being utterly subordinated to strategies and purposes located in pre-capitalist (we would

[58] B. Harriss and C. Kelly, 'Food processing: policy for rice and oil technology in South Asia', *Bulletin of the Institute of Development Studies*, 13, 2 (1982), pp.32-44.

here say 'social') relations'.[59] In defence of the manifest failure of legally determined development, it is sometimes argued that laws may have important symbolic functions indicating desirable directions for social change.[60] But at present these laws are the basis of a diffused appropriation of bureaucratic rent.

Actually existing regulation. The rural agricultural markets of West Bengal are not completely disorganised systems however, and trading behaviour displays elements of order. Table 3 shows the meso-level, institutional means whereby the performance of the potato, rice and oil markets comes to be ordered. First it can be seen that the prevalent 'customary' regulation is underdeveloped. Norms for marketing are not standardised—both weights and measures and contractual forms cannot be assured. Conditions for marketing are not very secure—either in terms of property rights or in terms or moral hazard and of crime. Crime detection rarely involves the police but is carried out instead by a variety of institutions of civil society which are endowed—socially and haphazardly if not legally—with coercive power to penalise. Secondly, the state is seen to play a negligible role in actual market regulation, confined to the Health Department which regulates the adulteration of oil, local government which severely rations licences and political institutions of local government which are drawn in upon occasion to adjudicate in disputes. Disputes about quantity, quality, price and payment are common; in fact disputes are an inherent aspect of the process of bargaining. The institution of 'mutual agreement' may mask a coercive solution accepted strategically by the loser. Where no bilateral solution is possible, a choice of non-state arbitration is available comprising kin, bazaar committees, brokers, business associations and political institutions. The state machinery is used as a last resort.

For the rest it can be seen that a multitude of institutions (organised on the basis of neighbourhood proximity, occupation, caste and religion, technology and scale) are involved. Apart from those of the state, regulation is either privately organised where costly environmental externalities can be internalised (as with security, hygiene and crime detection) or institutionalised in spontaneous collective action (for security and contract adherence, for example).

Collective institutions of civil society are evolving rapidly. These meso-level organisations have been brought into being for three main

[59] P. Fitzpatrick, 'Law, plurality and underdevelopment', in D. Sugarman (ed.), *Legality, Ideology and the State* (London, 1983), pp.171-2.

[60] V. Dhagamwar, 'The law and the disadvantaged', in B. Harriss, S. Guhan and R. Cassen (eds.), *Poverty in India* (Bombay, 1992).

Table 3. *Regulation in West Bengal*

	Cold Stores	Potato Warehouse	Oil mills	Rice mills	Husking mills	P/R-R/R trades
Licence	Local govt.	Market architecture	Local govt.	Local govt./FCI	Local govt. but rationed, many unlicenced	Local govt. but rationed; group membership or
Security	Physical fortification & private force	Various[1]	Own private force local collective action	Own private force	Local collective action	Market architect-ture; local collective action
Public hygiene	Privately paid sweepers	Mkt. landlord; *ad hoc*, occasional	Privately paid sweepers	Privately paid sweepers	Private sweepers; farmers & traders	None
Weights & measures	Kgs. but sack-weight varies (50–60 kgs.)	Calibrated by largest trader in local syndicate	—	Maunds & seers still used by some farmers	—	If at all by bazaar committee
Contract adherence; dispute resolution	Political institutions of BDO or syndicate	BDO; bazaar committee; regulated market officers; trade association; agreement	Bazaar management committee; brokers; mutual agreement; trade association	Largest trader in association; mutual agreement	Mutual agreement	Bazaar committee; town business association
Common crime	Credit embezzlement	Credit default; pilferage in transit	Adulteration; repayment	Credit & repayment	Theft of stored rice	Default on payment
Detection; punishment	Private agents	Trade association	Collective action; bazaar committee (?); Health Dept.	Private agents	—	Trade association

Note: [1] Various = market architecture; organised by landlord; own private force; local collective action. *Source*: Field Survey.

reasons: (1) to curb opportunistic behaviour; (2) to respond institutionally to organised labour—here the party political process involving competitive unionisation has had a multiplier effect on other social classes—; and (3) to relate to institutions inside the state either for purposes of defence against regulation (for example, rate fixing, negotiations with enforcement agencies) or to compensate for inadequacies of regulation (for example, physical security and the public health environment).

The scope of these groups has rapidly expanded and now includes:

(1) Ownership or renting of sites as group property.

(2) Reaping scale economies (as with the collective organisation by subscription of security and of the cleaning, sweeping and waste disposal that comes under 'public hygiene'). Political scale economies are reaped by groups over a certain size threshold in representations to the state (about regulation as above; about policy change and in order to institutionalise rents).

(3) Collusive activity such as price and rate fixing.

(4) Entry restriction, permitting competitive oligopolies.

(5) Risk spreading (as in cases of interest free group credit and group insurance by subscription for accident, calamity, loss, fraud and legal expenses).

(6) Reduction in transactions costs. This is an important function of these collectives and takes a number of forms. Information (about price but also about production, big deals, the *dramatis personae*, fraud and delinquency) is diffused within the group. Some regulation of transactions emerges (for example, calibration of weights and measures). Property rights are clarified and mechanisms for disputes over contract collectively enforced, with sanctions imposed on deviance. Groups are evolving mechanisms of protection against moral hazard, free riding and adverse selection (the most obvious of which are restrictive of entry using attributes about which information is of low cost (such as being licensed) as criteria. There is, however, some experimentation with mechanisms of protection for a number of objectives. Uncertainty on related markets is being reduced by collective negotiation of advantageous set rates (maxima for labour and transport, minima for processing) where relevant with other collective institutions. Conflicts of interest are also being institutionalised. Such new relations replace old norms, based often upon caste and 'faith', by new ones based on contract.

(7) Social expressions of solidarity. In defining themselves these institutions of collective action also define the excluded. This boundary

creation is not manifested only in economic regulation and political representation but also in philanthropy, relief and other expressions of piety and social celebration.

Collective institutions which have failed have done so for reasons of adverse selection (as when the costs of incorporating illegal husking mills have destroyed associations) or for reasons of opportunistic behaviour and covariate risk (which destroyed the traders' credit association).

Thus we found a variety of institutions of collective action embedded in markets hitherto characterised as epicentres of individualistic competition and moulded in subtle ways around selectively implemented regulatory law. These groups are not all lawful. Neither are their norms always those allowed in law. The groups overlap inconsistently and are also spatially and socially patchy. Sometimes these groups are organised on a neighbourhood basis, sometimes they are the expression of restrictive oligopolies, sometime the response of subordinated traders. Simultaneously, they restrict entry to markets and may facilitate collusive behaviour. But in the absence of strong enforceable state regulation these groups are necessary to the development of markets.

The state has to reckon with the existence of such groups when implementing future reform to regulatory policy. There is no evidence that these issues are being seriously considered anywhere undergoing structural adjustment.

'Standard operating practice': non-market marketing. In considering the regulatory conduct of the firm at the micro-level using experience from West Bengal, 'the market' is revealed as replete with non-market institutions.

> Firms develop standard operating procedures and an ideology which influences their responses to specific regulations on the ground.... They will attempt to influence both the design and the implementation of the regulations. They will anticipate regulations and their response to the expected regulations may have significant consequences.[61]

The firm itself has been identified as a non-market institution. In its interior there is found to be a division of labour but no internal exchange of commodities: instead, labour is structured by relations of authority. Within the firm it is not possible to monitor and cost performance or continually to renegotiate contracts. Hence the basic component of markets is not a market institution. The explanations for the ex-

[61] Shaffer, 'Observations on the political economics of regulation', p.729.

istence of firms are controversial: (1) firms are an institutional means of reducing the transactions costs of market exchange; (2) since transactions costs cannot be measured, firms actually supersede the calculus of costs and provide unpriceable intangibles (such as protection from the lack of social relations in 'true' markets); and (3) firms are mechanisms to reduce uncertainty via norms and conventions.[62]

Two types of power relation exist within this stylised firm. One is the authority of the manager or owner, with power to dismiss subordinates. The second is the capacity for opportunistic action by employees based on knowledge concealed from the manager or owner (or, *mutatis mutandis*, by managers against owners). Mercantile firms regulate their internal conduct in a variety of ways, depending mainly on the size of firm and type of labour process within it. In the petty firm, the roles of principal and agent are combined and the operator has continual access to performance indicators. 'Contracts', if the concept has relevance for the working relationships of close kin, are general, unspecified but not renegotiable. By contrast, consider the joint-family firm within which property rights may be but vaguely specified, and family labour deployed alongside wage labour with a variety of contractual terms and conditions. Here the conduct of the labour force can be regulated by bonding desirable individual workers by means of debt and perks, by the restriction of work to caste-specific occupations and by the reference of honour to caste reputation, and by the supervision of unskilled labour by maistries paid by performance. The conduct of family members is regulated by strong codes of loyalty.

Such institutional structuring applies equally to the regulation of external conduct and transactions. Caste and locality are means of screening. Brokers who activate networks based on kin and locality are employed for the establishment of long distance contacts. Information leading to price formation is strongly socially and spatially structured (in one influential instance through a formalised syndicate). Information about people, and about production is as important to trade as that, so beloved of economists, about prices. Turning to negotiation and bargaining, spot contracts and open auction are exceedingly rare. A range of advance contracts and bilateral relational contracts are common. Power is expressed explicitly via the degree of attachment of intermediaries and via price formation and implicitly via uncompensated lags in payment for the transaction, and through fraud and cheating. Contracts are verbal and policing and enforcement is carried out proximately through kin, or in cases of failure, via the institutions of associa-

[62] Hodgson, *Economics and Institutions*, ch.9.

tion described above and only in the last instance via the slow and socially and economically costly institutions of the state. Such markets are still far from being a continual flux of prices and impersonal contacts based on a system of individual (rather than social) rights.

These markets perform poorly by established standards. 'Prices' (expressed for regulators in the form of a weekly stylisation) appear to move discretely by convention rather than continuously. Spatial price differences on the average greatly exceed transport costs per unit. Analysis of weekly price behaviour over a recent period of three years reveal striking short-term inefficiency co-existing with long-term integration.[63]

Endogenous regulation takes place through an intense filigree of institutions. Standard operating practice, norms and conventions are a complex set of social relations of trade, requiring a long apprenticeship in order for a trader to understand and operate them.

V. *Conclusions: so what?*

In the rural marketing systems analysed here, there are at least three layers of transactions and supervision costs, the objective of which is regulation: one at the level of the firm, the second, diffusely, at the level of associational institutions and the third, also diffusely, at the level of the state which is the legitimator of last resort. We have seen that, although opportunism is not a universal motivation in marketing, none of these levels can contain opportunistic behaviour. Marketing institutions at these three levels not only regulate behaviour, they also express economic power. Custom and law are in neither case fixed. How transactions are construed as legitimate has varied historically. While a regulatory pluralism has elsewhere been argued to be the results of the imposition by the modern (post) colonial state-law on to precapitalist legal orders,[64] here we can see how the modern capitalist social order develops the conditions of legal plurality in a great variety of ways so as to reinforce its interests and resist challenge to them.

Law and economics have proved inseparable in undreamt ways. The Indian state has declared itself obliged to organise fair and efficient private marketing. But the law is defined through social interaction. Due to the inability of state-law to enforce the conditions of the first transaction, we see that the rights of producers and of market labour are still quite imperfectly met in many regions of India. Since there is little

[63] Palaskas and Harriss, 'Testing market integration'.
[64] Fitzpatrick, 'Law, plurality and underdevelopment'.

Table 4. *Taxonomy of agricultural market regulation*

	Reg. Mkts. Acts	Regulated mkts.[1]	Other state reg.	Other state reg.[1]	Non-state regulation
Enforcement	Committees; Courts; Directorates of Marketing	Directorates → boards → central govt. crash programmes; foreign funds; unanticipated governing structures	Various institutions of local, state, and central govt.	Unsystemic; threat is important regulator; enforcement → pre-emptive development	Diffuse multitude of institutions; individualised, state marginalised; used as threat
Objects: (s) structure (c) conduct (p) performance	(s) Centralisation; licencing (c) Standardisation[2] (p) Information	(s) Weak; reasonable (c) Variable (p) Weak	(s) Licensing technology (c) Highly specified (p) Physical (movement restrictions)	(s) Pre-empted (c) Variable: evasion + abuse (p) Variable	By convention, loosely
Specification	Very high	Variable and flexible	Very high	Idiosyncratic verbally negotiated	High
Incentives (–) negative (+) positive	(–) For regulated weak; (+) For regulators	(–) Weak	(–)	(+) Bureaucratic rent (+) Evasion, excess profits; coercion	(+)[3]
Contingencies for implementation	No contingencies except first	Civil society proves contingent	Few contingencies most transactions	Highly contingent, increasingly fewer transactions covered	Highly contingent according to caste, gender, location
Jurisdiction at boundaries	Weakly unspecified	RM subordinated to diffuse jurisdiction[4]	Weakly specified	As with RM law	Boundaries transparent but jurisdiction is unsystematic

Notes: [1] As implemented; [2] fees, contract, grading, weights, measures, payment; [3] to lower transactions costs; collude over price; resist entry; penalise non-completion of contract; reap scale economics; reduce risk; express social solidarity; [4] collective commercial associations; municipalities; parastatals; other departments of government.

Source: Field survey.

organised activity to claim such rights, the law is poorly operationalised in their interests and used in the interests of others. It is implemented as foreseen only under restrictive conditions described earlier. While order and fairness cannot be obtained by legislation, nor behaviour be changed by legal fiat alone, the law can be interpreted, manipulated and subverted to reinforce the power of certain commercial classes.

Table 4, which summarises our analysis with respect to the taxonomy of regulation set out by Shaffer,[65] gives clear indications of the purely technical, 'regulatory' reasons for the weakness of regulatory law. There are other reasons for its incapacity to control and standardise exchange grounded in non-egalitarian agrarian and agro-commercial structures:

(1) Specification. The regulatory law focuses upon conduct at one restricted part of the post-harvest system of exchange. Market structure, which is conditional upon entry and upon assets distributions in trade, is far less easy to include within the scope of regulatory legislation. Where misconduct is prevalent, this focus on conduct is appropriate and desirable. Transactions costs economics cautions us, however, against the evaluation of all deviations from the state of perfect competition as 'misconduct'. Yet as a result of this latter type of highly ideological evaluation, conduct has been excessively specified in relation to the state's capacity to enforce. In fact there is a legally fixed notion of the efficient contractual arrangement. Given the state's lack of capacity with regard to enforcement or otherwise to create competitive markets, transactional forms other than those specified might be entirely appropriate and 'institutionally efficient'. And spot contracts through open auction may not be the cost effective form of transaction. If enforcement capacity and other 'environmental' aspects of the marketing system such as informational opacity and assets specificity cannot (or should not) be changed, then, instead of a tight definition of one legal contractual form, it might be more progressive to define what is *un*acceptable, thereby leaving contractual forms more legal space to vary.

(2) Enforcement. This was vested in democratically elected committees intended to represent different economic interests in a systematic way. This was a mistaken institutional transfer from the colonial metropolis where it was never properly implemented anyway, and a disastrous response to local inegalitarian agrarian and commercial structures. Not only was the committee endowed with power completely incommensurate with its heavy responsibilities, but also it was an internal arena of conflict. Moreover, local control was not conducive to the

[65] Shaffer, 'Observations on the political economics of regulation'.

standardisation of transactions necessary for the development of long distance trade. Supportive enforcement by civil society institutions of producers and consumers has always been weak. The cause of romantic free market populism has been ill served by the experience of these committees. Of late 'participation' has been institutionally superseded by centralisation and professionalisation of administration. By itself, however, this does not empower or increase enforcement capacity. The latter has to be addressed directly.

If the larger mass of Indian regulatory law is considered as a body, institutions of enforcement are extremely diffuse. Since the enforcement of state-law is also the major mechanism by which bureaucratic rent is extracted from traders, issues such as the degree of pervasiveness desired of such rents, or the degree of autonomy of enforcing institutions and the severity with which enforcers are themselves policed and regulated need placing on the policy agenda. All that has been considered officially so far is the empowerment of the Directorate of Agricultural Marketing to exact penal provisions from the committees for misappropriation of funds, losses and waste![66]

(3) Incentives. Associated with poor enforcement capacity has been the deployment of negative incentives. It is an open question whether positive incentives may be used for market regulation by the state. The experience of collective action suggests that positive incentives (to reduce private transactions costs, reap scale economies, reduce risk and express social solidarity) may result in more effective regulation than do negative incentives. But it has to be recognised that not all collective action by traders may be socially desirable (for example institutions may construct positive incentives to collude over price fixing, to resist entry into trade, to resist claims by labour and state regulation and to impose excessively coercive punishment on non-members for default etc). It does not seem prudent from the perspective of the interests of the mass of Indian society for regulation to be left to these meso-level institutions of civil society.

(4) Contingency. Regulatory law tends to minimise contingency in implementation. It is intended to be implemented everywhere. There is a case to be made from India's experience for contingency deliberately to be allowed for so that regulatory law is implemented only where and when it is necessary, but with adequate enforcement.

(5) Jurisdiction at boundaries. The RM Act restricts consideration of the interfaces to those between Regulated Market Committees and Mar-

[66] GoI, *Report of the Working Group on Drawing up a Model Agricultural Produce Act* (Faridabad, 1984).

keting Departments, Boards and Directorates involved in implementation of the Act.[67] The problem of order at the legal boundary is well recognised and RM committees are encouraged to improve co-ordination with co-operatives and with state trading and warehousing corporations. Yet, the relationships between regulatory laws and other market institutions and functions (for example, procurement and taxation) have been exposed here as inadequately specified. Local, provincial and central state regulatory roles need reassessment. Legal priorities at the interface between RM laws and those governing municipalities and parastatals were particularly relevant here. In some regions the legal rights of associational institutions of regulation vis-à-vis those of regulated markets may need definition and disentangling. There is a tension between revenue raising and enforcement functions. Agricultural markets used to be 'nice little earners' for local government. It may be more appropriate to administer regulations conducive to long-distance trade via a centrally organised administration, along with a fiscal redistribution to localities, if necessary.

Instead, strides in the opposite direction are being taken. Attempts are being made to make delinquent states (such as the Himalayan and oceanic mini-states, Jammu and Kashmir and Kerala) accept a standard model agricultural products marketing law more highly specified than hitherto.[68]

Official advocacy also favours the development of a 'coherent law' covering the entire pre-and post-production system of transactions involving trader-moneylenders: a 'stupendous task needing the business operation of a public utility'.[69] This would of necessity cover specialised and terminal markets as well as the estimated 30,000 periodic markets. Of the latter it has been said that they operate in a 'complete regulatory vacuum' infested with commission agents, trading with unstandardised weights and measures, the sites of unauthorised credit relations, lacking information.[70]

The re-democratisation of committees is actively canvassed and (in the light of their inability to carry out current responsibilities) massive new responsibilities are to be placed upon them: (1) administration of road construction grants; (2) management of fertiliser and pesticide

[67] Ibid.

[68] GoI, *Report of the Task Force on Agricultural Marketing and Trade set up by the Working Group on Agricultural Price Policy, Trade and Marketing for the 8th Five-year Plan, 1990-95* (Faridabad, 1989); *Interim Report*, pp.2-3.

[69] GoI, *Proceedings of the Second National Workshop*, p.30.

[70] Ibid., p.35.

stocks; (3) the recovery of co-operative loans and 'vigorous enforcement' by means unspecified; (4) introduction and operation of the mechanisation of the handling and drying of post-harvest gluts; (5) increased control over storage and transport provided there is no duplication with other public sector enterprises; and (6) expanded extension with producers to render them 'market-wise'.[71]

Much stronger central government control over development finance for training and infrastructure has been called for. It is argued that there are two problems. One is that existing financial institutions (National Board of Agricultural Refinance and Development (NABARD) and the nationalised banks) prioritise investments in market infrastructure very low on their agendas. Such projects amounted to 0.7 per cent of NABARD loans in the period 1989-91. Funds were disbursed at a rate which would require 200 years to cover the modernisation of market-place infrastructure of the subset of markets currently regulated under the Act.[72] Hence a separate financial institution—a National Agricultural Marketing Board—is proposed. This would deal with the second problem—that of traders' persistent pre-harvest finance of producers. A system of 'pledge loans' administered by the bank would 'break the bonds of credit linkages established by the commission agents with the producer-sellers'[73]

Two interpretations of these recommendations are possible. First, this is an eloquent testimony to the faith in the rule of law, in legal determinism and in institutional engineering on which this current barrage of recommendations is based. It seems that existing law is thought to fail because of its confinement to the first transaction. The scope of the recommendations, however, reflects an admission of the contumaceous response to existing law. Second, the distinguished teams of administrators and scholars place their signatures under this expanded interventionism as a last ditch witness to their faith in the state and in its capacity to plan rationally, as the whirlwind of deregulation howls outside their offices.

That the existing 'model' law is very far from a model will be seized on by deregulators as justification for neglect or dismantling of the regulated market administration. This has been the response to evidence of low rates of income transfer to poor households via the Fair Price Shop and Public Distribution System.[74] But we have shown here that

[71] Ibid.; GoI, *Report of the Task Force.*
[72] GoI, *Interim Report*, p.4.2.
[73] Ibid., p.4.4.
[74] K. Parikh, 'Economic reforms and food and agricultural policy'.

no state regulation at all will be likely to have an adverse social impact. That inappropriate law cannot be imposed does not mean that there should be no law at all to regulate part of the agrarian economy—marketing under conditions of rapid commercialisation—which is as important as that of land tenure.

Neither utopian legal determinism, cynical or committed interventionism nor gung-ho *laissez faire* will result in the engineering of institutions of socially fair and economically cost effective private marketing without which the gains to domestic economic reforms will not reach back to the mass of producers. As Schaffer wrote:

> There is no lack of political will, but a scatter and conflict of wills, inconvenient for some, not for others.... But reform is not just a question of removing impediments once they have been listed by a 'methodologist'. Reform means indicating just where the interests are grounded, where the lines of opposition are drawn, the pain and guilt felt and hidden.[75]

It is hoped that perhaps a first attempt has been made here.[76]

[75] B.B. Schaffer, 'Towards responsibility: public policy in concept and practice', in E.H. Clay and B.B. Schaffer (eds.), *Room for Manoeuvre* (London, 1984), p.182.

[76] In additon to the references cited above, see also B. Crow, *Partial Markets: agrarian exchange in Bangladesh; development policy and practice* (Milton Keynes, 1992); B. Harriss, 'Order and efficiency in private agricultural markets: a summary for DSE of the experience of regulation in four Indian states', in L. Camman (ed.), *Traditional Marketing Systems* (Feldafing, 1992), pp.156-64; and B. Harriss and C. Kelly, 'Food processing: policy for rice and oil technology in South Asia', *Bulletin of the Institute of Development Studies*, 13, 2 (1982).

APPENDIX: *Collective Action in Markets, West Bengal*

POTATO

1. *Mamari Potato Syndicate* (1988, about 50 members)
   Active officers: 6
   Function: price-setting; contract adherence and dispute resolution
2. *West Bengal Cold Stores Owners' Association* (275 members)
   Function: negotiate rents with government; collude over and negotiate trade policy; lobby MLAs and ministers on reservations for categories of producers on export policy

OIL

3. *Katwa Oil Millers' Association* (35 members)
   Function: set minimum crushing rate; 'regulate' prices; lobby state for electricity power supply, better conditions for maintenance of machines, and against sales tax
4. *Gulsi Oil Mills Association* (1984, 20 members)
   Function: fix rates
5. *Burdwan District Oil Millers' Association* (1972)
   Function: defence of oil price increases; fix wages of labour

RICE

6. *Mamari Rice Retailers' Association* (*Chal Bazaar Samiti*) (1973, about 50 members, 5-6 officers)
   Function: restrict entry; fix commissions; calibrate weights and measures; rotate guarding; resolve disputes; recompense for losses/accidents/calamities among members via subscriptions; mutual credit; resistance to state regulation
7. *Mamari Husking Mill Association* (defunct)
   No longer able to fix rates; unable to bear costs of litigation and campaigning to protect unlicensed members
8. *Katwa Husking Mill Association* (1986, defunct)
   Same reason as Mamari (no.6, above)
9. *Katwa Association of Rice Retail Traders* (1983, 32 members, serving over 100 because of 'group membership' of licences)
   Function: dispute resolution/curbing of anti-social behaviour; fix minimum commissions; fix rates for weighing and measuring; organise security on subscription; mutual interest free credit; compensation on defaulted payments by subscription; management of relations with labour gang; accommodation of police; resistance to state regulation, sales taxes, licence fees, lobby against storage rules
10. *Gulsi Paddy Agents' Association* (1990, 130 members)
    Function: dispute resolution
    prevention of competition from unlicensed agents; resistance to regulation and fees from the state
11. *Burdwan District Rice Mill Owners' Association* (1972, 170 members, 6 active officers)
    Function: negotiations with organised labour about rates and working

conditions; representations to government on quotas and transport rates; lobbying State Food Ministers, District Food Controller, District Magistrate; relief and philanthropy; 'fixing open market paddy price when necessary'

12. *Burdwan District Husking Mill Association* (1982)
    Function: resistance to state on closure of unlicensed mills; collective protest and campaigning (for example, collective default on electricity bills if charges rise); defence of victims of arbitrary action by state through subscriptions of money for income and court expenses
13. *Solvent Oil Extractors' Association* (1965, representing industrialists and government)
    Function: meets in Bombay to develop industry; regulation of international export of bran oil cake

NEIGHBOURHOOD

14. *Bazaar Street Committee* (m) (1974, 45 members, 2 active officials, variety of trades)
    Function: resolution of dispute and 'abuse by strangers'; security via monthly subscriptions
15. *Bazaar Committee* (k) (1976, 250 members, 12 active officials)
    Function: security organised by subscription
16. *Vegetable Market Committee* (40 members)
    Function: constitutive group for Businessmen's Association (see below); dispute resolution; security (by subscription); resistance to 'spying by Municipality'

LOCALITY

17. *Mamari Chamber of Commerce*
18. *Mamari Credit Samiti* (defunct, membership of small paddy/rice traders)
    Function: collective supply of production to farmers (failed because implicit tying of credit contract with grain supplies was not adhered to by farmers)
19. *Gulsi Coolies' Association* (100 members)
    Function: fix minimum rates and perks with traders
20. *Katwa Truck Owners' Association* (100 members)
    Function: fix minimum rates
21. *Katwa Rickshaw Pullers' Association*
    Function: fix minimum rates
22. *Gulsi Traders' Committee* (1987, 300 members)
    Function: dispute resolution; restrictions on entry; lobby state for credit
23. *Katwa Town Businessmen's Association* (*Mahakumar Byabasayee Samiti*) (1983, 500 members, representing 1,500 because of group membership on licences)
    Function: intermediation with state information diffusion about a wide range of commodity markets; organisation of protest (trade bandhs); religious—subscription for *pujas*
24. *Katwa Marvari Association* (about 50 members)
    Function: caste solidarity
25. *Burdwan Agricultural Co-operative Society* (offices dominated by large

private merchants)
Function: credit and marketing

STATE
26. *Bengal Chamber of Commerce*
27. *Association of Small-scale Industrialists*